THE INDUSTRIAL ARCHAEOLOGY

of

SHROPSHIRE

*Daniel's Mill, Eardington (SO 718917), viewed through
the viaduct of the Severn Valley Railway.*

THE INDUSTRIAL
ARCHAEOLOGY
of
SHROPSHIRE

Barrie Trinder

Phillimore

1996

Published by
PHILLIMORE & CO. LTD.
Shopwyke Manor Barn, Chichester, West Sussex

ISBN 0 85033 989 8

Printed and bound in Great Britain by
BUTLER & TANNER LTD.
Frome, Somerset

CONTENTS

◆　◆　◆

LIST OF ILLUSTRATIONS

◆   ◆   ◆

Frontispiece: Daniel's Mill, Eardington

ACKNOWLEDGEMENTS

◆　◆　◆

This book springs from nearly three decades of teaching and fieldwork in Shropshire, and has been influenced by conversations with countless students and colleagues, to all of whom I express my thanks. Barbara and Helen Trinder have participated in numerous expeditions to sites considered here, and I acknowledge with pleasure their patience and forbearance. Janet Markland and Carol Sampson of the Ironbridge Institute have done much to assist with the production of the book. David Houlston has provided immaculate photographic prints, and Shelley White has produced excellent plans. I am particularly grateful to those who have commented on the text, Michael Stratton of the University of York, John Powell of the Ironbridge Gorge Museum, Peter Wakelin of Cadw, James Lawson of Shrewsbury School and David Lloyd of Ludlow.

BARRIE TRINDER

Nene College, February 1996

x

1

INTRODUCTION

◆　◆　◆

Shropshire was one of the birthplaces of Industrial Archaeology. The county
featured in Michael Rix's first article on the subject in Britain in 1955 and
hosted the first international conference on the discipline in 1973. The
Ironbridge Gorge is a UNESCO World Heritage Site and its industrial monuments
are much visited. Postgraduate teaching of Industrial Archaeology began at the
Ironbridge Institute in 1982. Conservation of the Ellesmere Canal, the monuments
of the Ironbridge Gorge, and the Severn Valley Railway set standards which have
attracted attention from all over the world. Yet this is the first book concerned
solely with industrial archaeology in the county.

It is pertinent to enquire what, in the current state of development of the
discipline, should be the objectives of a regional survey of Industrial Archaeology.
A topographically-based inventory of sites which might be welcomed in some little-
studied areas is not an urgent necessity in Shropshire. The county's principal industries,
ironmaking, coalmining and ceramics in the Coalbrookdale Coalfield, the lead-
mines of the Stiperstones region, are the subjects of substantial histories, and the
Iron Bridge and the Ditherington Flax Mill have been exhaustively analysed. The
county's water mills, canals and railways have been well-documented, and some of
its products, Coalport and Caughley china, Jackfield tiles and Sentinel steam wagons,
are assiduously collected. The objective of this survey is to integrate such specialised
work with the less heroic elements in the Shropshire's industrial history; to perceive
the first iron-framed building within a wider pattern of textile manufacturing, to see
the Ironbridge Gorge, not as 'the cradle of the Industrial Revolution' but as one
of several parts of the county with distinctive coalfield landscapes, to attempt to
discern the broad patterns of manufacturing in both town and country.

One purpose of this book is thus to show what understanding has been gained
in recent decades from the disciplined archaeological study of Shropshire's industrial
past, to bring together different kinds of research, and use them to create broader
pictures of the roles of mines and manufactures within different landscape contexts.
It is hoped that by examining one county some broader insights will emerge into
the changing role of industry within British society during recent centuries. A
further objective is to provide for the student of the particular watermill, foundry
or copper mine, a context which enables the object of his or her study to be

evaluated, showing whether it was an early or late example, or an exceptionally large or merely modest concern of its kind. A final concern is with methodology. It can be argued that industrial archaeologists have been insufficiently concerned with theoretical approaches to their discipline. This book is, consciously, an exercise assessing the potential of one particular approach to the industrial past—the analysis of contrasting landscapes.

Some justification is required for setting this kind of study in a county context. Shropshire is not an homogeneous region. It is the largest inland county, extending from the fringes of Wolverhampton to the Cheshire plain, from the edges of the Potteries to the wild uplands of Clun Forest. Geologists regard its landscapes as some of the most varied in Britain, with ten of the 12 characteristic rock types being found within the county. Much of Shropshire is rural, with few manufactures.

This variety can be a justification for analysing the industrial past in a county setting. This study is based primarily on landscapes, and much of the book considers the role of industry in contrasting settings, in the countryside, in market towns, in coalfields, in the uplands and along transport corridors. A county context ensures diversity of subject matter, five coalfields, sixteen market towns, and a diverse range of countryside. These are arbitrary classifications. Some characteristic market town activities like malting and tanning also took place in the countryside. Concentrations of water mills were as important in towns and in coalfields as they were in

1 *The bleak uplands: the White Grit engine house (SO 319979) in its landscape context. There are several disused shafts in the disturbed ground to the left of the picture. The Old Grit mines lie just over the hill.*

rural settings. In some parts of Shropshire coalmining was a small part of an economy which was primarily agricultural. Nevertheless a landscape approach is inherently more illuminating than one based on technology, which is beset by contradictions which are more inhibiting. Should a beam engine be regarded as a prime mover or is it part of a water supply system? Is a bridge part of a transport system or the product of a foundry? A landscape approach provides a ready means of comparing sites, and avoids treating some forms of manufacture as marginal. It is a more fitting context for testing hypotheses than a technological approach, for which a national or international setting may be more appropriate. This approach dictates that some subjects are considered in different sections of the book—most ironworks which flourished before 1750 in the context of rural manufactures, but those of the Industrial Revolution as one of the principal industries of the coalfields. Brickmaking was important in the countryside, on the fringes of market towns, and in the coalfields.

Some subjects are best approached from different angles. Non-ferrous metals were mined in several parts of Shropshire, but only in one did mining activities dominate the landscape. To examine the industry as a whole, including the processing sector, seems preferable. Textile manufacturing was primarily an urban industry in Shropshire, but the need to examine the origins of large-scale manufactures, and to explain the persistence of domestic production, make it preferable to view it as a whole.

2 *The prosperous lowlands: Beanstone Mill, the first mill in Shropshire on the River Tern, upstream from Market Drayton (SJ 725390), architecturally one of the most distinguished mills in the county. The wheel remains in the bay to the left.*

3 *Industrial complexity: an aerial view of the Upper Works, Coalbrookdale, probably in the 1920s. To the left (north) is the complex of buildings covering the Old Furnaces (SJ 667048), ranges of sheds, long demolished alongside the railway viaduct, the Long Warehouse (which now houses the Ironbridge Gorge Museum Library and the Ironbridge Institute) with north-lit sheds to the east and a range of other buildings now demolished to the west. In the centre is the Great Warehouse (now housing the Museum of Iron) with the bridge linking it to the office block on the other side of the road. In shadow, to the right, is the Engineering Building of 1879. Carpenters' Row is just left of centre, while the terrace next to the ex-Wesleyan chapel is Chapel Row.*

Likewise long–distance transport systems, the River Severn, turnpike roads, main line railways and some canals cut across different landscapes and merit separate treatment. Some features of the Great Western Railway were the same in an urban setting at Shrewsbury, in the heart of the Coalbrookdale Coalfield at Hollinswood, or in the countryside at Hodnet. Short distance transport systems, tub boat canals, mineral railways, or brickworks tramways are treated in their appropriate landscape settings.

The Shropshire which is the subject of this study is the modern county as it has existed since 1895, except that Dowles, in Worcestershire since that year, is included. Halesowen, taken back into Worcestershire in 1844, is not part of the study, but Farlow in Herefordshire until that year is included. Changes to the county's boundaries since 1895 have been insignificant.

This survey does not have precise chronological limits. Its focus is on mining and manufacturing since 1660, but evidence from earlier periods is used where appropriate. No attempt has been made to evaluate industrial buildings constructed in the new town of Telford since the 1960s, nor to consider other factories or transport structures of the past three decades elsewhere in the county.

This study places particular stress on quantification, in the belief that analysis of one site or artefact makes sense only if there is some awareness of its typicality. There is a concern throughout to show how many manufacturing sites of particular kinds there were in Shropshire, and how they related to others of the same types further afield.

The book is also concerned to make comparisons, in the belief that by examining what is common and what is different in market towns as diverse as Shrewsbury and Clun, or coalfield communities as unalike as St George's and Horsebridge, our understanding of both extremes will be increased.

A particular range of documentary sources has consciously been used as the foundation for this study. Fieldwork has been based on current 2° inch Pathfinder maps published by the Ordnance Survey. The two inch survey of 1827, the first edition 25 inch maps and those by Baugh and Greenwood have been analysed for all parts of the county, supplemented where appropriate by later editions, and by the 1:500 map for Shrewsbury. Census enumerators' returns have been employed to locate and in part to quantify manufacturing and mining activities. Much use has also been made of trade directories, particularly those published by Bagshaw in 1851 and by Casey in 1871. The collections of probate inventories which have been transcribed in the county are used in the discussion of many early industries.

Like any historical study which attempts to provide an overview, this book depends heavily on the work of others, particularly on the work of staff and students

4 *A passage through Shropshire: a narrow boat converted to residential use passes the warehouses at St. Martin's Moor (SJ 324356) on the Ellesmere Canal.*

at the Ironbridge Institute, and at adult education research classes, and on numerous local historical writings which are not primarily concerned with industrial archaeology. The full range of sources is listed in the bibliography. A gazetteer in this kind of publication is inevitably repetitious and none has been provided, since a comprehensive index of places and liberal use of map references should enable any particular place to be located with ease, both in the text and on the ground.

The justification for this survey is that Industrial Archaeology is a living and thriving discipline in Shropshire. Our understanding of the county's industrial past is expanding, through the work of the Ironbridge Institute, and that of numerous scholars who are amateurs in the best sense, molinologists, the restorers of steam wagons, canal 'navvies', mining historians and enthusiasts for stage-coaching. This study offers a context in which such work can be placed, something which does rather more than reveal to the many a range of sites known to a few, or elucidate the mysteries of processes known only to the initiated. The justification for a survey of this kind must be that it uses archaeological evidence in a disciplined manner to enhance understanding of the past, to set up models, to pose questions, to accumulate data about the artefacts, images, structures, sites and landscapes which form the subject matter of Industrial Archaeology, to analyse it and reach conclusions about it which enhance our understanding of the past. Its purpose is not merely to summarise nor to ossify but to stimulate, not to bring comfort and congratulation but to provoke, to consider not just questions of local history but the place of mining and manufactures in man's past. If, within a few years, the hypotheses which follow are disproved and the models discarded for something better, the book will have achieved its purpose.

◆   ◆   ◆

2

RURAL INDUSTRIES

◆   ◆   ◆

'Industry' in the countryside is a paradoxical concept. The dominant economic activity in the Shropshire countryside has always been agriculture, yet manufacturing has remained a persistent feature of the rural economy. Water power, space, minerals, the produce of farms and forests and the availability of labour have over many centuries sustained manufactures in the countryside, and rural entrepreneurs have shown a remarkable ability in the late 20th century for adapting old sites to new uses.

RURAL COMMUNITIES

The development of mining and manufactures is shaped by the nature of communities, which in turn is determined by patterns of landholding. Industrial as well as agricultural communities can be classed as 'open' or 'closed', according to the extent to which they were controlled by landowners. Ironically, 'industry' could be most highly developed at either extreme. In an open community settlement was easy, incomers and new generations could readily be accommodated. Space could be found for new enterprises and there might be access to a range of practical skills. In an estate village there might be facilities to meet the needs of the thousands of acres dependent on a great house, a brick and tile works, a saw mill, a quarry which could be opened up when there was a need for building stone. A great house might utilise new technologies. There were gasworks at The Quinta, Apley Park and Eyton Hall, and early electric lighting systems at Henley Hall, Yeaton Peverey and Acton Reynald.

Ruling class observers saw open communities as resorts of idleness rather than industry. Sir Richard Hill (1732-1808) considered that those who lived on the waste of Prees Heath could scarcely raise enough to support themselves, and that their children consequently sank through idleness into vice and profanity. John Bishton in 1794 maintained that the miserable huts erected by the poor on open commons, and the small plots which they had enclosed round about them, could not sustain a family, and that they encouraged a false sense of independence.[1]

Nevertheless analysis of squatter settlements shows that they stimulated rural manufactures. The remnants of squatter communities, crudely built cottages, whose alignments are disrespectful of roads laid out as parts of enclosures, can be observed in all kinds of terrain, along the boggy margins of the Long Lane which leads from Wrockwardine to the Weald Moors, in the peaty depths of Whixall Moss, on parish boundaries at Vernolds Common, on sandy heathlands like Myddle Wood, or in the folds of hills as at Cockshutford or Llanymynech.

Some squatter settlements served as reservoirs of labour for industry, particularly for mines. Cockshutford, on the edge of the extensive upland waste in Clee St Margaret, housed the colliers who worked in the coal mines on Brown Clee. Among the residents on Myddle Common in the 17th century were masons, carpenters, shoemakers, coopers, blacksmiths and weavers. Even in the mid-19th century, long after the common had been enclosed, the community included a butcher, stone masons, a saddler, a ropemaker, a washerwoman, a market woman, a dressmaker, a wheelwright, a carpenter, a clockmaker and a weaver. Richard Gough recorded the encroachment of land in Newton Field by Morgan Clarke, a weaver, the son of a squatter from Hadley who had settled on Harmer Hill.[2] Cockshutford's residents in the 1840s and '50s included shoemakers, charwomen, carpenters, a tea dealer, a weaver, a laundress, a carrier, blacksmiths, a schoolmaster, tailors and a dressmaker. The independent status of those who lived on commons is revealed by such census entries as that for Evan Watkin of Stretton Heath in Westbury whose occupation was described in 1861 as 'Cooper and holding 8 acres of land'. In 1861 the cottagers at Cockshutford included Edward Howells, 'Stone Mason and Landowner of 2 acres 2 roods', 'William Edwards, Shoemaker and Landowner of 1 acre 2 roods' and Edward Woodhouse, 'Lime Maker and Land-owner of 1 acre'. A cottage in an isolated part of Selattyn, occupied in 1871 by a miner with seven acres of land, was called the 'Queen's Palace'.

On Vennington Common in Westbury, where a settlement of ten dwellings had been established by 1677, and where cottage building reached a peak in the last two decades of the 18th century, residents in 1851 included William Bradwick, a 54-year-old 'Tinman', probably a repairer of domestic hardware, born in the parish of St George, Hanover Square, London, with four sons aged between 29 and 16, all following the same occupation. His wife, an Oxfordshire woman, was a basket maker, as were her 78-year-old father, and her daughter-in-law, who shared the same cottage. Not far away, two nailers, father and son, lodged with an aged labourer.

Clock cleaners were amongst the most skilled dwellers in open communities. There were two on Wattlesborough Heath in 1861, and in 1851 on the side of the Moelyd Hill in Trefonen township in Oswestry, lived Elex Hughes, a 49-year-old bachelor, of whom the enumerator recorded:

> A country clock cleaner and maker who has spent a deal of his time in trying to complete perpetual motion and I believe he is now at the point of completing it.

Many cottages in open communities within the county were built of turf or similar ephemeral materials and no longer remain to be studied, although some sites would repay excavation. Stone cottages often have large, clumsily-built gable chimney stacks. They stand in irregularly shaped enclosures, bounded by banks, the latter topped by hedges of crab apple, hazel, holly and laburnum.

CORN MILLS

Water power was the most significant factor in the development of rural manufactures. Shropshire's principal river, the Severn, is a turbulent stream whose levels are variable, and it powered only five waterwheels. Most of Shropshire's water-power sites were located on small streams, only a few on the lower reaches of the Tern, the Teme and the Worfe having mills of substantial size. The most intensive rural concentrations of mills were eight in 3.75km. on the River Morda, and five in 1.5km. on the Morlas Brook.

The commonest application of water power was to the grinding of grain, to make flour and animal feedstuffs. Flour milling was ubiquitous in Shropshire, scarcely a settlement of consequence being located more than two or three miles from a mill.

Some 396 sites at which water power has been used in the period since 1660 have been identified in Shropshire, of which 319 have been used for at least some time in grinding grain. Water remained the principal source of power for corn milling as long as grain was ground locally. No more than 30 windmills operated in Shropshire in the 18th and 19th centuries. Less than twenty Shropshire corn mills were totally dependent on steam power, and only those at West Felton, Queen's

5   *The imposing water cornmill at Penyllan (SJ 278281) on the River Morda in Oswestry parish. Steam power was never employed at the mill and the chimney, erected in the mid-19th century, was never put to use.*

Head, Whixall, Hadnall, Lower Hordley and Chinnel (Whitchurch) were rural mills. Between 20 and 30 water corn mills employed supplementary steam power, including those at Cruckmeole, Eyton on the Weald Moors, Wollerton and Hanwood, where a steam engine driver lived next to the mill. The ancient mill at Vennington which had been operated in conjunction with a windmill acquired a third source of power in the form of a steam engine during the 1880s. A steam engine was installed before 1829 at the Hem Mill in Shifnal. After its removal, and the abandonment of water power *c.*1930, an oil engine and then an electric motor provided power for grinding. The mill retains its extensive pool.

The researches of molinologists and of the Victoria County History suggest that many water mills closed during the 18th century. In the area south of Shrewsbury, Leebotwood corn mill had passed out of use by 1796, Cressage Mill was destroyed by fire in 1774 and never rebuilt, Pitchford Mill was demolished by 1795, and the last records of the mills at Langley and Stapleton are respectively in 1694 and 1678.[3] About 200 corn mills were working in Shropshire in the mid-19th century. The subsequent decline of rural milling was rapid.

Table 2.1:	**Watermills in Shropshire** (Source: sundry directories)
1885: 178
1891: 169
1900: 148
1905: 131
1909: 104
1913: 98
1922: 73
1926: 71
1934: 49
1937: 47

Few Shropshire mills adopted roller milling technology in the late 19th century, Henry Deakin's mill at Walcot being the only known rural example, and the closure of many water corn mills from the 1880s is unsurprising. Only four mills, those at Maesbury Hall, Market Drayton, Donnington Wood and Mytton, were grinding flour in 1935. The remainder were sustained by modest local demands for cattle feed.

Many water corn mill buildings remain in a recognisable condition, and over 40 waterwheels survive in situ. Where mill machinery can be identified it is usually the product of local founders or millwrights of the 19th century. In the south of the county there are examples of the work of Turtons of Kidderminster at Wrickton and Ditton. The iron wheel at Cleobury North Mill was made by John Hazledine of Bridgnorth, while the oak gearing at Broadstone Mill, probably follows the plan of William Hazledine, who installed new machinery at a cost of £350 in 1794, in a manner commended by Thomas Telford in his treatise *On Mills*.[4]

Daniels Mill, Eardington (SO 718917) is one of the least conventional of Shropshire's water corn mills. Its source of water is the stream less than a mile long flowing from the Potseething Spring to the Severn. There was a mill on the site by the 15th century, but the present structure dates from a rebuilding in 1854-55. The 11.7m. (38ft.) wheel, with cast iron hub and wrought iron buckets, is on the same axle as an external pit wheel, which through a wallower drives a horizontal shaft powering three sets of French burr stones. Full-time operation of the mill was no longer viable by the 1890s, although it was worked on a part-time basis until 1957. It has been lovingly restored by its present owners.[5]

The mill at Bouldon (SO 547850), a three-storey, three-bay structure of the late 18th century in grey sandstone, was of more conventional layout, and in the late 1960s was a perfect time capsule, although it ceased work in 1934. Its external cast iron pitch-back waterwheel, 4.3m. x 1m. (14ft. x 3ft. 3in.), drove the machinery through an internal cast iron pit wheel, operating a timber upright shaft through a wallower. A spur wheel worked two stone nuts operating hopper-fed tuns, while a crown wheel on the first floor worked a sack hoist on the second. Conversion to a residence has altered the character of the building, and some machinery has been removed.

The best preserved water mill on a substantial river is at Ashford Carbonel (SO 511711). It ground cattle feed until 1953. The building is of stone, and water is diverted to it by a horseshoe weir. The undershot wheel, approximately 4.3m. in diameter, has a cast iron rim and centre with wooden paddles and spokes. The iron pit wheel was cast in two halves. The milling machinery follows a conventional layout, with much of the gearing in pear, apple, ash and hornbeam having been renewed since commercial operation ceased. A turbine drove sawmilling machinery, an electric generator from which current was conveyed to Ashford Court on poles about 1.3m. high following the river bank, and pumps which supplied water to the same house.

Wrickton Mill (SO 642858) in Stottesdon parish on the Cleobury Brook is a stone building of the early 19th century, probably an extended version of an earlier brick building. The external overshot waterwheel, 2.85m. x 1.77m. (9ft. 3in. x 5ft. 9in.) retains its original iron rings probably cast by Turtons of Kidderminster in the 1830s. An iron pit wheel meshes with a wallower on an iron upright shaft, from which a spur wheel, in iron but with wooden cogs, drives two stone nuts. Most of this equipment appears to date from the 1830s, but machinery to operate a third pair of stones was added by Richard Wyer, a millwright from Cleobury Mortimer in 1863. Wrickton Mill worked until about 1950, and has been under restoration since 1979.[6]

Rindleford Mill (SJ 738955) on the River Worfe is a distinguished four-storey brick structure, with a front elevation of four bays, with an adjacent malthouse. The mill accommodated five pairs of French stones in the mid-19th century. The internal machinery has been removed but the undershot wheel, 4.6m. in diameter and 2.2m. wide, remains in the outshot wheelhouse, together with a cast iron pit wheel.

6 *The water wheel at Daniel's Mill, Eardington (SO 718917), showing the cast iron hub and wrought iron buckets, the external pit wheel, and, at the bottom, centre, the wallower through which power is transmitted to a horizontal shaft which drives three sets of stones.*

An oil mill and a fulling mill once occupied the site. Cattle feed was ground at the mill until 1950.[7]

Chadwell Mill (SJ 638208), on the Lynn Brook on the upper reaches of the Meese, was one of the last Shropshire watermills to be reconditioned for commercial use. It was substantially rebuilt in 1922 and used for grinding cattle feed until 1950. The building, in Lilleshall Company brick, dates from 1881. An overshot wheel, 7m. in diameter, provides a conventional drive to two sets of stones through a pit wheel, a wallower and a crown wheel, all in cast iron. The wheel also powered an endless rope system working barn machinery some 300m. distant.[8]

Clun Mill (SO 304813), now a Youth Hostel, is the best example in Shropshire of a mill converted to turbine operation. The mill is large, approximately 15.4m. x 9.2m. A Whitelaw turbine made in Glasgow was installed *c*.1854 in a pit in the middle of the building, and drives three sets of French burr stones, which remain as a feature of a dormitory. Maps from the 1840s show substantial fish ponds on the upstream side of the mill. They are now dry.[9]

IRON AND GLASS

Ironmaking, after corn milling was the principal use for water power in Shropshire. The indirect process for the production of iron, the smelting of iron ore in a blast furnace to produce pig iron, and the subsequent reduction of the pig iron to wrought iron in a finery and chafery forge, was introduced to the county in the mid-16th century, when furnaces were constructed at the Hurst in Aldenham Park, Morville (SO 672960), at Manor Mill, Shifnal (SJ 742067), at Willey (SO 672980), at Kenley (SO 564985) and Cleobury Park (SO 711764). A blast furnace of this period was a masonry stack, supported on at least two sides by arches, one accommodating the tuyere pipe, through which air was conveyed from water-powered bellows to the interior, the other the forehearth, from which were tapped molten iron and molten slag, the waste product of the process. Furnaces were usually built into banks or were approached by earthen ramps to facilitate the charging of iron ore, limestone, used as a flux, and the fuel, at this stage charcoal. Other components of a furnace complex might include barns for the storage of ore and charcoal, and reservoirs where water could be stored to enable the bellows to work throughout a campaign of up to eight months' duration. Slag would be piled up around a furnace site, and might be utilised locally as road metal. Furnaces needed to be within convenient distance of iron ore, which in Shropshire came from seams in the coalfields. Charcoal was burned from cordwood, grown as a crop, and might be drawn from an extensive hinterland.

Of the Shropshire furnaces with 16th-century origins, only Willey and possibly Kenley were still working in 1660, but seven furnaces of 17th-century foundation were probably operating in that year: those at Abdon, Bouldon, Coalbrookdale, Ifton Rhyn, Leighton, Tilsop and Wombridge. By the second decade of the 18th century, Abdon, Ifton Rhyn, Tilsop and Wombridge had ceased to work, but new furnaces had been erected at Charlcott and Kemberton. The use of coke as a fuel for smelting iron, introduced by Abraham Darby at Coalbrookdale in 1709, ultimately destroyed the ironworks of the Shropshire countryside, but the expansion of coke iron smelting only began in the 1750s, and some furnaces worked for much of the 18th century, Charlcott probably continuing until the 1780s, although working intermittently from the 1750s, and Bouldon into the 1790s.

There are archaeological remains at most of the rural sites in Shropshire which operated after 1660. At Kenley and Kemberton (SJ 744045) there are only scatterings of slag about the surrounding fields and along the banks of leats and streams. At Abdon (SO 567867) foundations of the furnace remains together with a weir and a pool, and traces of slag along the bottom of a wooded dingle. There is a complex pattern of leats at Bouldon as well as much slag, many lumps containing unconsumed charcoal. Tilsop furnace (SO 516725) was built alongside the Corn Brook. The site is surrounded by slag, and an iron casting in the church of St Peter, Coreley commemorates Elinor, wife of Edward Hussey 'of Tilsop furnace', who died in 1684.[10]

Charlcott (SO 637861) is the best preserved of Shropshire's rural blast furnaces. The red sandstone stack, 6.2m. x 6.2m. (20ft. x 20ft.) is complete, and is approached by an earthen ramp. The print of a hand appears in the iron lintel above the forehearth. There are remains of the water power system which served the furnace and the adjacent paper mill, but the mode of operation of the furnace water wheel is no longer evident, its pit having been filled in, and the course of the tail race can no longer be traced. The site is ringed with slag tips.[11]

The remains of the blast furnace structure at Leighton (SJ 610055) are less complete but the landscape evidence is more comprehensive. Only the tuyere arch

7   *The tuyere arch of the 18th-century blast furnace at Charlcott (SO 637861).*

of the furnace remains, having been incorporated in 1762 into a corn mill, whose wheel and machinery survive, which in turn was rebuilt as a public house in the third quarter of the 19th century. On the opposite side of the B4380 the outline of the lowest pool of the water power system can be recognised, while Myfanwy Eaves and Sharon Hall have suggested that a steam pumping engine, noted on the site by Reinhold Angenstein in 1753 and Charles Wood in 1754, was located on the site of the modern 'Mill House', west of the inn, where there are large quantities of slag and cinder. The record of Leighton furnace is completed by two artefacts, a pair of 17th-century cast iron memorials on the floor of the church of St Mary.[12]

The reduction of pig iron to wrought iron took place in a forge. Until the second half of the 18th century a forge contained at least two hearths, a finery and a chafery, and a hammer for shaping the wrought iron. From the 1770s the stamping and potting process, and from the 1780s the puddling process were used in some rural as well as in coalfield forges. The iron produced at forges was slit at slitting mills into rods which could be used by nailers.

There were 11 finery and chafery forges working in Shropshire in the first decade of the 18th century. As many as seven others may have been operating in 1660 but had ceased working by 1700. A further nine were established in the 18th century. Three slitting mills operated during this period.

There were concentrations of forges along the Tern and its tributaries in north Shropshire, and on the Rea in the south of the county. Most were modest concerns, some producing less than 150 tons of iron a year. Forges could be operated throughout the year, so that output could have been as little as three tons of iron rods per week, being reduced from no more than twice that quantity of pig iron. In 1766 Richard Whitworth estimated that Sambrook Forge consumed no more than three tons of pig iron, two tons of coal and three tons of charcoal per week.

Only at Eardington, a works of the late 18th century, do significant structures remain of a forge in a rural setting. Every other site retains at most the traces of a water power system, and lumps of slag.

There is some documentary evidence of the characteristic components of rural forges. Most employed relatively few workers; the workforce of 40 forgemen who signed a loyalty declaration at Upton Forge in 1793 must have been one of the largest in the county. Workers' cottages formed part of the 17th-century forge at Hubbals Mill and dwellings which remain at the present farm at Upton Forge could well have been some of the 12 on the site in 1794. In 1794 there were six houses at the Uffington slitting mill complex and six at Moreton Corbet forge. A terrace at the Upper Forge, Cleobury Mortimer, remained until the 1960s, nine tenements for workmen and a house for the superintendent having formed part of the complex in 1811. At Eardington forgemen were accommodated in terraces which still survive.[14]

Warehouses, for raw materials or for finished iron, were found at most forges. There were three at Uffington slitting mill and one at Upton Forge in 1794, and a charcoal barn and a coke house at the Lower Forge, Cleobury Mortimer in 1811. All forges had smiths' shops for reworking tools.[15]

Table 2.2: **Rural forges in Shropshire** (Sources: Various [13])

Name	Parish	Grid ref.	First known date	Last Known date
Bromley's Forge	Montford	SJ 439167	pre 1623	c. 1660
Caynton/Kaynton	Edgmond	SJ 694230	pre 1694	c. 1820
Cleobury Mortimer Lower Forge	Cleobury Mortimer	SO 688747	1571	c. 1810
Cleobury Mortimer Upper Forge	Cleobury Mortimer	SO 787757	pre 1598	c. 1810
Dorrington	Dorrington	SJ 487020	1606	c. 1680
Eardington Lower Forge	Quatford	SO 733895	1777-78	1889
Eardington Upper Forge	Quatford	SO 725897	1782-89	c. 1830
Fernhill	Whittington	SJ 318333	1627	c. 1660
Grindle	Ryton	SJ 753034	pre 1609	1670
Hampton Loade	Quatt	SO 748864	1796	1866
Hardwick/Rotherham	Stottesdon	SO 660818	pre 1757	c. 1794
Harley	Harley	SO 588001	pre 1607	1664
Hubbals Mill	Morville	SO 691915	c. 1631	c. 1674
Lizard	Tong	SJ 784082	1564	c. 1800
Longnor	Longnor	SJ 486014	1605	1800
Maesbury	Oswestry	SJ 304259	1627	c. 1660
Moreton Corbet	Moreton Corbet	SJ 574228	1601	c. 1794
Norton in Hales	Norton	SJ 704379	pre 1685	c. 1794
Pendlestone/Bridgnorth	Worfield	SO 724944	1760	1795
Pitchford/Eaton Mascott	Pitchford	SJ 534054	1715	c. 1800
Prescott	Stottesdon	SO 668820	c. 1708	c. 1794
Ryton Slitting Mill	Ryton	SJ 759028	1683	1714
Sambrook	Cheswardine	SJ 714248	pre 1690	c. 1830
Sheinton	Sheinton	SJ 607041	pre 1637	1790
Sutton	Sutton	SJ 497608	c. 1720	c. 1790
Tern	Atcham	SJ 552098	1710	1757
Tibberton Slitting Mill	Edgmond	SJ 681203	pre 1653	1804
Uffington Slitting Mill	Uffington	SJ 527138	c. 1790	pre 1828
Upton	Upton Magna	SJ 560112	1653	c. 1830
Wytheford	Shawbury	SJ 569188	pre 1642	c. 1796

The most innovative of the Shropshire forges was at Tern, in Attingham Park, established in 1710 by a Bristol partnership for whom the first Abraham Darby acted as agent.[16] It was described as 'the first Joint Work of this kind in England', indicating that it was used for fabricating both iron and brass. Components included a finery and chafery forge, a steel furnace, rolling mills for brass and for hoop iron, a slitting mill and a wire mill. Brass working ceased after the death of Francis Pinnell, the expert in brass rolling, and the range of work contracted. In 1717 output at Tern, at 300 tons a year, was the highest at any Shropshire forge, but by the early 1750s production was no more than 150 tons a year. The works passed in 1725 to William and Richard Wood, and in 1733 to Joshua Gee, who was still able to claim that the closure of the works, demanded by the landowner's agent, would 'put a stop to one of the biggest works in the county [and] turn fourscore people a starving'. The forge closed in 1756 to be replaced by corn mills, which themselves were demolished in 1787-89. A causeway across the river 100m. east of the house at Attingham is a relic of the dam, in which were accommodated the many waterwheels of Tern Forge. Apart from a thin scatter of slag, it is all that remains of the ironworks.

The outstanding feature of the forge complex at Eardington is the canal which conveys water between the Upper (SO 726897) and Lower (SO 734895) Forges, and which was also used for transport between the two works. A deed of 1782 refers to a 'subterraneous navigable cut' some 750 yards long. The canal was explored in the 1960s, and is approximately 3 m. wide and 2 m. high, sufficient to allow a small boat to be legged through, although there are remains of a winch at the upstream end. The Upper Forge pool is silted, but its curved stone weir survives, and the outline of the forge building 21.5m. x 12m. can be traced. At the Lower Forge is a 33m.-high chimney, built into a fissure in the sandstone, together with flue chambers, and tail races from the water power system. The upper forge was built in 1777-78 and the lower forge in the mid-1780s. The complex continued to use charcoal to make wrought iron until its closure in 1889.[17]

The operation of the charcoal iron trade involved the carriage of iron over long distances. At Wytheford in the 1680s, for example, pig iron from the Forest of Dean and from Willey was used. Iron in transit was stored at warehouses, the sites of three of which have been identified, at Montford Bridge (SJ 432152) and at Pimley (SJ 520142) on the Severn, and at Roundthorn (SO 554788) east of Ludlow, but nothing remains on any of these sites.[18]

There were several rural glassworks in Shropshire before the patent of 1615 which prohibited the use of wood as fuel in glassmaking. The workers at the celebrated early 17th-century glasshouse in the Bishop's Wood on the county's eastern border, which was excavated in the 1930s, regarded themselves as parishioners of Cheswardine, where 15 events relating to glassworkers were recorded in the registers between 1600 and 1613, although the works itself (SJ 759313) was in Staffordshire. In 1967 remnants of glassmaking were uncovered in fields called Glasshouse Bank at Ruyton-XI-Towns (SJ 396229). Excavation revealed fragments of drinking glasses and crucibles of the early 17th century. Neither these works, nor one which may have operated in Market Drayton, is likely to have been working in 1660, and glassmaking in Shropshire, as elsewhere, was thereafter a coalfield industry.[19]

THE VARIED USES OF WATER POWER

Paper was made in Shropshire for three centuries. The paper mill at Cound, working in 1616, is the first of which there is any record. As many as five mills may have been operating in 1660, and several more by 1700. The Gloucester Port Books indicate the dispatch of considerable quantities of paper from the Severn ports of Shrewsbury, Bridgnorth and Broseley in the first decade of the 18th century. Around fifteen mills were operating during the second half of the 18th century, a total which increased slightly between 1800 and 1830. As paper manufacturers elsewhere in Britain adopted Fourdrinier machines, production in Shropshire declined. Only six mills were working in 1851, and only that at Tibberton survived into the 20th century.[20]

Most Shropshire paper mill sites were used at other times for different manufactures. Except perhaps at Ludford, no significant buildings survive, most sites retaining only the overgrown remnants of their water-power systems, or buildings which relate to subsequent uses.

Paper was made from rags pulped by water-powered machinery. A 'vatman' would dip into the pulp a wire sieve called a mould, shake off surplus liquid, and turn out what remained on to a felt. Felts and paper were stacked by the 'coucher' and put beneath a screw press. The resulting sheets were then dried. Pure water was essential, and an advertisement for the Ludford mill in 1816 drew attention both to the constant supply of water for power afforded by the River Teme, and to the never failing spring which provided water for processes.[21] The probate inventory of Richard Fosbrook of Alveley taken in 1730 lists best rags worth £5, second quality rags worth four guineas and cordage, that is old ropes, to the value of £12. William Fosbrook of Claverley[22] whose possessions were listed in 1731 had 18 cwt of rags worth £11 14s.0d. 'Ragg-men' were among those who worked at the Bolas mill in the 1660s. Richard Fosbrook had moulds worth £1 2s. 6d., and felts worth 15s, while there were eight pairs of moulds and five posts of felts at Weston Rhyn in 1788, and double crown and foolscap lay boards at Longnor in 1825.[23] Most Shropshire mills produced brown wrapping paper, trade in which was said to be 'lucrative' when the Sturts and Bradley mill at Neen Sollars was offered for sale in 1831. Writing paper was made at Hopton Wafers, glazed boards at Longnor, paper for book printing at Ludford, blue sugar paper at Ludford and Tibberton, and filter and blotting paper at Lloyds Mill, Neen Savage. At the Claverley Mill in 1731 were several grades of cap paper, one of which was used for printing, and two grades of pot paper. Paper from the mill had been delivered to customers in Stafford, Worcester, Birmingham and Dublin.

The last mill to operate in Shropshire was the two vat mill constructed on the site of the former slitting mill on the River Meese at Tibberton in 1804 by William Palmer, Thomas Brindley and George Brindley.[24] The main building, square in plan, spanned the leat which provided it with power. The complex was enlarged by Martin Billing, a Birmingham printer, who took it over about 1860. Papermaking

Table 2.3: Paper Mills in Shropshire
Sources: L.C.Lloyd, 'Paper-making in Shropshire', TSAS, vol.44 (1937–38) and other sources.

Name	Parish	Grid ref.	Earliest Date	Latest Date
Alveley	Alveley	SO 765856	*c.* 1705	1817
Besford	Lee Brockhurst	SJ 553258	pre 1640	pre 1750
Bouldon	Holgate	SO 547850	*c.* 1790	*c.* 1845
Charlcott	Aston Botterell	SO 637861	*c.* 1725	*c.* 1825
Chesterton	Worfield	SJ 792978	*c.* 1690	*c.* 1750
Claverley/Hopstone	Claverley	SJ 789945	*c.* 1725	*c.* 1805
Cound	Cound	SJ 553050	1616	1841
Ellerton	Cheswardine	SJ 714260	*c.* 1730	1789
Great Bolas	Bolas	SJ 648208	*c.* 1660	*c.* 1760
Grindle	Ryton	SJ 753034	*c.* 1650	*c.* 1715
Hopton Wafers	Hopton Wafers			
Upper Mill		SO 638769	*c.* 1730	1826
Middle Mill		SO 639766	*c.* 1730	1840
Lower Mill		SO 638762	*c.* 1730	1840
Kemberton	Kemberton	SJ 744044	*c.* 1790	*c.* 1840
Longnor	Longnor	SJ 685013	*c.* 1802	*c.* 1825
Ludford	Ludford	SO 519743	*c.* 1715	*c.* 1870
Market Drayton	Market Drayton			
Old Mill		SJ 656331	*c.* 1750	*c.* 1846
Walk Mill		SJ 671334	*c.* 1750	*c.* 1846
Tyrley Mill		SJ 679337	*c.* 1830	*c.* 1846
Morda	Oswestry	SJ 289281	*c.* 1710	*c.* 1875
Neen Savage	Neen Savage			
Walfords Mill		SO 675767	*c.* 1827	*c.* 1885
Lloyds Mill/Cleobury Mill		SO 677763	*c.* 1827	*c.* 1885
Neen Sollars	Neen Sollars			
Langley Mill		SO 653730	*c.* 1660	*c.* 1880
Sturts/Bradley Mill		SO 654712	pre 1830	*c.* 1850
Shifnal	Shifnal	SJ 741058	*c.* 1810	*c.* 1840
Tibberton	Edgmond	SJ 681203	1804	1912
Weston Rhyn	St Martin's		*c.* 1745	*c.* 1875
Old Mill		SJ 273344		
Wern Mill		SJ 275345		

NOTE: *Mills of which there is only place-name or hearsay evidence, uncorroborated from other sources, are omitted.*

machinery was worked by a steam engine, supplied with steam from a boiler house with a 47.5m. chimney constructed in 1874. The mill had 11employees in 1861 and 21 in 1891, the largest total recorded at any Shropshire mill. The maximum elsewhere was at Morda where there were nine employees in 1851.

At Hopton Wafers three single vat mills were situated alongside a short section of the Hopton Brook. One was operating as early as 1736. In 1798 the Hopton estate was bought by the ironmaster Thomas Botfield, who, with his brothers, operated the three until 1824. Others worked them until 1840, and the mills were vainly offered for sale two years later. They had been demolished by 1858 and only traces of the water-power systems provide evidence of their existence.[25]

There were at least four oil mills in Shropshire. At Caynton (SJ 692214) a mill on the Meese was operating by 1766 and continued until the bankruptcy of its operator William Briscoe in the late 1820s.[26] Rindleford Mill (SJ 738955) on the Worfe was adapted for crushing linseed, probably in the second quarter of the 18th century, and continued as an oil mill until c.1820.[27] The 23.5m.-diameter waterwheel at Swinney Mill, Coalport (SJ 706017) was utilised for oil manufacture, probably for colourings for the chinaworks.[28] The contents of an oil mill at Sandford, in Prees (SJ 581341), are listed in the inventory of Thomas Sandford taken in 1726.[29] The mill was processing both linseed and rape, and had a stock of 427 gallons 1 pint of linseed oil valued at £53 7s.6d., that is 2s. 6d. per gallon. Debts for oil supplied to customers amounted to £100. The largest item of movable equipment was a lead cistern. Oil was strained, leaving linseed dust as a waste produce, while linseed cakes, probably for animal feed, were made from the seed husks. Oil was delivered to customers in staved casks. The mill building at Sandford is a rectangular structure, approximately 16m. x 6m., in soft red brick, located on a dam which encloses a large pool. A waterwheel, with a cast iron hub and wooden outer parts, remains in situ at the south end. While the building was used as a corn mill in the 19th century, it could not have accommodated milling machinery of conventional layout. The wheel would have been better placed to operate seed-crushing machinery, and the building could well be that described in the inventory of 1726.

Water power has served other functions in Shropshire. Several fulling mills operated in the county after 1660, and water power has been used at other stages of textile manufacture at Coleham (Shrewsbury), Knighton and Ludlow. Leather dressers employed water power at Allscott, Hungerford, Widnall and Pontesford. Six water mills were adapted to crush barytes, and water power has been used in saw mills at Bromfield, Ashford Carbonel, Moreton Corbet and elsewhere. The Lower Mill at Cleobury Mortimer crushed cider apples. In the late 19th century small waterwheels like those at Badger Hall, Stableford Hall and Faintree were installed to pump water to mansions and farmhouses. The mills at Woolstaston and Ashford Carbonel are among those which have been used to generate electricity.

WIND POWER

Shropshire has never enjoyed the abundance of wind power generated in areas like the Fylde or Lincolnshire. Only illustrative evidence remains of post mills, like that on Shrewsbury Racecourse at Bicton, portrayed by W. Pearson in 1808 in a picture in the Old House, Dogpole, Shrewsbury. There is conclusive evidence for some 30 tower mills which have worked since 1660.[30] Most of the 16 surviving windmill towers are of modest dimensions, when complete were of no more than three storeys, and were built for grinding grain in the late 18th century or early 19th century. Lyth Hill Mill was used for preparing hemp for ropemaking, while those at Chetwynd, Hadley Park and Uffington pumped water in addition to grinding grain. The mills at Asterley, Coton Wood, Vennington and Shackerley have been converted to dwellings, while those at Hadnall, Much Wenlock and Hadley Park have been given the appearance of follies. The remainder are derelict or serve as stores. The largest tower mills in Shropshire were in urban locations. Most rural windmills closed in the last two decades of the 19th century, although the towers remain of some which ceased work much earlier.

Table 2.4: **Windmills in Shropshire of which the towers remain**
Source: W A Seaby & A C Smith, Windmills in Shropshire, Hereford and Worcester: a contemporary survey, Stevenage: Stevenage Museum, 1984.

Name	Parish	Grid ref.	Earliest known date	Last date of operation
Asterley	Pontesbury	SJ 372075	1809	c. 1890
Chetwynd/Sambrook	Chetwynd	SJ 695235	1845	—
Cluddley	Wrockwardine	SJ 630104	pre 1752	c. 1890
Coton Wood	Wem	SJ 542351	1813	c. 1900
Ditton Priors	Ditton Priors	SO 593877	c. 1845	c. 1880
Hadley Park	Hadley	SJ 657115	c. 1787	c. 1835
Hadnall	Hadnall	SJ 523210	1787	c. 1800
Hawkstone	Weston under Redcastle	SJ 566297	pre 1808	—
Lyth Hill	Condover	SJ 469067	c. 1835	c. 1890
Madeley Court	Madeley	SJ 695053	pre 1827	c. 1840
Much Wenlock	Much Wenlock	SJ 624008	pre 1750	c. 1890
Rodington	Rodington	SJ 590144	pre 1830	c. 1890
Rowton	Alberbury	SJ 365129	1774	c. 1800
Shackerley	Albrighton	SJ 802039	1768	c. 1895
Upton	Shifnal	SJ 756067	pre 1797	c. 1890
Vennington	Westbury	SJ 337096	pre 1800	c. 1912

BUILDING MATERIALS

Building stone was quarried for local use in most parts of Shropshire. In Ditton Priors and in several squatter communities the dhustone, the dolerite from the summits of the Clee Hills was employed in cottages, although it causes dampness. Tolerably good local stones were employed in several distinct regions. The brecchia outcrop provided materials for buildings on the Loton Park and Rowton estates from the late 18th century, the last of them Wattlesborough School erected in 1904. The Chatwall Sandstone, characteristically banded in purple, brown and green, was widely used around Church Stretton and as far south as Cheney Longville. Rubble limestone is unsurprisingly found in the walls of older buildings in Much Wenlock and Ludlow.[31]

Ann Scard has observed that many quarries were exploited intermittently whenever there was a need for quality building materials, as when a school or a bridge was being constructed, or a mansion or church extended.[32] On the Sweeney Estate carboniferous sandstone was employed in the walls of Sweeney Hall, but inferior sandstones from the lower beds in the same quarries were used for farm buildings. Quarries in the Silurian limestone in Moor Park were opened up for the construction of Richard Norman Shaw's church of All Saints, Richards Castle (SJ 494707) in 1891-92, while a quarry called Rock Hollow was the source of stone for Benjamin Ferrey's church of St Luke, Sambrook (SJ 714245) in 1846. Former quarries of this type which are accessible, because they are protected for their ecological value, include Quarry Wood, Hinstock (SJ 685272) where the Bunter Sandstone was exploited until the 1880s, Tasker Quarry, Linley (SO 326956) where the Stapeley Volcanic rock was extracted, and Hope Mill Quarry (SJ 355021) in the Silurian limestone.

Some building stone quarries were worked regularly over long periods, and provided stone for buildings of consequence, at a distance. The sandstone quarries in Alveley and Highley remain impressive. Severn barges enabled quarrymasters to sell stone to customers as far away as Gloucester. Grinshill stone commanded wider markets. It was used in Shrewsbury's two 18th-century bridges, the Salopian Infirmary and other buildings in the county town, and in buildings in Birmingham, Liverpool and Aberystwyth. By the late 19th century powered machines, including two steam cranes, were employed in the quarries, and stone was despatched from a siding at Yorton station. Several former quarries are accessible from Corbet Wood (SJ 526237). One of the archaeological features is a series of stone setts put down in 1839-40 to enable wagons to carry away stone for John Carline's rebuilding of All Saints, Grinshill (SJ 520234).[33] The Nesscliffe sandstone was regularly worked in the 19th century but probably not for distant markets.

Quarries were and are exploited for roadstone. The extraction of road metals on Pontesbury Hill (SJ 390046) began about the time of its enclosure in 1848. At first only one or two men were involved, but the number increased to a dozen during the 1880s, when Quarry Terrace was built to accommodate some of their number. Callow Hill Quarry (SJ 385050) was opened in 1926, and leased in 1931 to the county council, who bought it in 1956, after hauling some of its produce along the Snailbeach District Railway with a farm tractor.[34] Other roadstone quarries are in the limestone of Wenlock Edge, around Llanymynech Hill and on Sharpstones Hill. Those in the dolerite on the summits of the Clee Hills are considered elsewhere.

Stones for abrasive purposes were produced in quarries in Highley and Alveley. Most, given the nature of the sandstones, must have been for grinding, but in 1821 a quarryman was killed when trying to move what was described as a millstone from workings in Alveley. At the entrance to one quarry (SO 754825) about 1km. down river from Highley station there remain five large circular grinding stones, the largest 1.75m. in diameter.[35]

Sand was a further quarry product. In the early 20th century moulding sand for foundries was extracted from quarries alongside the Wellington-Wolverhampton railway at Ruckley (SJ 773060). At Queen's Head (SJ 341267) on the Ellesmere Canal the face remains of a quarry from which, in the early 20th century, sand was conveyed to canal boats by a railway which passed under the road in a tunnel.[36]

Bricks were made in almost every part of Shropshire in the 18th and 19th centuries. The Coalbrookdale Coalfield supplied regional if not national markets, but until the end of the 19th century most parts of Shropshire appear to have been self-sufficient, although bricks for prestigious buildings were purchased elsewhere.[37]

When bricks were required in rural areas in the the 18th century it was common practice to dig local clay, mould it with a minimum of preparation, and fire the bricks in a clamp, or temporary kiln, for which coal would be brought from the nearest colliery. When the parish vestry at Prees decided to build a workhouse in 1773, one Thomas Roberts agreed to make a kiln to fire 40,000 bricks. When the architect John Hiram Haycock made a contract to build Apley Castle, Wellington, in 1791, it was agreed that bricks should be made on the estate. Temporary clamps and modest clay pits leave scarcely any trace on undisturbed ground.

In the 19th century, with the improvement of roads, and the ready availability of pug mills and other equipment, rural brickworks proliferated. By the 1880s there were about fifty in rural Shropshire, mostly with permanent kilns, and some with

8 *The typical form of a brickworks drying shed at Bourton (SO 601957).*

substantial buildings housing clay preparation and moulding machinery. Many made roofing tiles and field drainage pipes, while a few produced terracotta, glazed pipes and earthenware.

Evidence remains in the landscape of most of the brickworks of this period. Some sites have continued in industrial use. The Chinnel brickworks outside Whitchurch became a creamery, while one of the two at Kinnersley became the locomotive depot of the Shropshire & Montgomeryshire Railway. The site of the Osbaston works is now the Brookside Kennels. Many more remain as rough ground, often with pools, and covered by trees.

Structures remain on some sites. A brickworks at Bourton (SO 606956), operated in the 1880s and '90s by a local farmer, which probably closed c.1904, was surveyed in 1991. Its principal building is a single storey rectangular structure, a little over 25m. long and about 7m. wide, with the bricks spaced to give perforated walls. It was doubtless a drying shed but it may also have accommodated clay preparation. The Scotch downdraught kiln, measuring approximately 10m. x 13m., had 16 fireholes. The clay pits could still be recognised, and a small square pit was probably the site of the pug mill.[38]

The brickworks at Long Wood (SJ 591067) had been established by the 1830s, and in 1881 provided employment for five men and two boys. It had closed by 1928. The drying shed has been demolished, but a downdraught kiln, approximately 9.5m. x 5.5m., remains, probably in the form in which it was rebuilt in 1894, the date on the works chimney.

Table 2.5: **Rural Brickworks in Shropshire** (excluding those in the coalfields and major towns) shown on the Ordnance Survey First Edition 25 inch maps of the early 1880s.

Site	Grid ref.	Parish	Indications on map
Adeney	SJ 710185	Edgmond	Brick & tile works, kiln
Astley Abbots	SO 713957	Astley Abbots	Pool
Aston Eyre	SO 640941	Aston Eyre	Square kiln
Barkers Green	SJ 527282	Wem	Brick & tile works
The Bold	SO 642848	Aston Botterell	Kiln, pools
Bourton (i)	SO 602957	Much Wenlock	
Bourton (ii)	SO 606956	Much Wenlock	Brick & pipe works, kiln
Brownhills	SJ 685361	Norton in Hales	Rectangular building, square kiln
Cantlop	SJ 508054	Berrington	Pools
Cherrington	SJ 668195	Edgmond	Brickfield
Cheswardine Park Farm	SJ 714313	Cheswardine	
Chinnel	SJ 553432	Whitchurch	Kiln
Dernhill	SO 716794	Kinlet	Rectangular building, pool

Table 2.5 *continued*

Dorrington	SJ 727407	Woore	3 kilns, rectangular building
Dowles	SO 782761	Dowles	3 long rectangular kilns
Eaton	SO 378889	Lydbury North	Brickfield
Echoes Hill	SO 737994	Stockton	Brick and pipe works
Ensdon	SJ 405178	Montford	Brick & tile works, 2 round kilns, H-plan building
Frodesley	SJ 512017	Frodesley	
Hadnall	SJ 525196	Myddle	Kiln
Hargrove	SO 497922	Rushbury	
Hesterworth	SO 393828	Hopesay	Kiln
Highfields	SJ 509256	Wem	Rectangular building
Hughley	SJ 571975	Hughley	Brick & tile works
Kinnerley	SJ 336198	Kinnerley	Pool
Kinnerley	SJ 346200	Kinnerley	
Lack Sarn	SO 267940	Churchstoke (Shropshire)	Pool
Lane Green	SO 786864	Alveley	Pool
Lightwood	SO 808937	Claverley	Kilns
Long Lane	SJ 635155	Wrockwardine	Brick & Pipe works
Long Wood	SJ 591067	Eaton Constantine	Kiln
Lower Fenemere	SJ 447215	Myddle	Rectangular building
Marshbrook	SO 638907	Church Stretton	Rectangular building, 2 round kilns, tramway
Marton	SJ 443241	Myddle	Round kiln
Millenheath	SJ 587356	Ightfield	Brickfield
Ollerton	SJ 652243	Stoke on Term	Kiln
Oldwood	SJ 455203	Baschurch	Round kiln, rectangular kiln
Osbaston	SJ 595203	High Ercall	Kilns
Oswestry Waterworks	SJ 273304	Oswestry	Kilns
Painsmore	SO 778766	Dowles	Kilns
Prees Heath	SJ 551376	Prees	Clay pits
Ratlinghope	SO 404967	Ratlinghope	Kiln
Ruyton	SJ 386221	Ruyton-XI-Towns	Kiln, rectangular building
Tasley	SO 694947	Tasley	Square kiln
Ticklerton	SO 491917	Eaton under Heywood	
Westbury	SJ 346110	Westbury	Brick & tile works, tramway
Weston Common	SJ 426263	Baschurch	Brick & tile works, 2 round kilns
Wheathill	SO 602823	Wheathill	Brick & tile works
Wistanstow	SO 431857	Wistanstow	Brick & tile works
Yorton	SJ 505236	Broughton	

Concrete products have been manufactured as an adjunct to limestone workings on Wenlock Edge in recent decades, but the most significant rural concrete works in the county was established c.1915 by Hamish Cross of the Abdon Clee Stone Quarry Co. at Ditton Priors (SO 612886). The houses around the hydro-electric power station at Dolgarrog in North Wales, which were erected in 1927 after earlier buildings had been destroyed by a flood, were made at Ditton Priors, as were extensive estates in Neasden (London) and Wolverhampton, and some houses in Ditton Priors (SO 612893).[39]

LIME AND LIMESTONE

In every part of Shropshire where there was limestone it was quarried or mined. Some was used for building, and a few quarries provided stone for blast furnaces, but most was burned in kilns to produce lime (i.e. calcium oxide, CaO) for builders or farmers. Limestone is more easily transported than quicklime, and many kilns were located at the nodes of local transport systems, where they could readily be supplied with limestone and coal and from which lime could conveniently be distributed to customers.

To the south west of the Coalbrookdale Coalfield the Silurian limestone extends from Benthall Edge along Wenlock Edge and south of Craven Arms to the Aymestrey limestones of Herefordshire. The archaeology of the quarries has been systematically surveyed by Williams and by Holmes.[40] Documentary and field research has revealed the existence of some 183 kilns between Lincoln Hill, Ironbridge, and Easthope, of which there are substantial remains of at least eighty. The peak of quarrying activity was in the 19th century when limestone was taken by rail to the blast furnaces of the Shropshire coalfield and South Staffordshire along the railway west of Much Wenlock, opened in 1867. The despatch of fluxing stone to blast furnaces in the Black Country continued until the 1930s, when there were concrete works in several quarries. Lime burning in the area ceased in 1965. Present-day quarries mainly produce aggregates.

North of Much Wenlock the Farley and Bradley quarries (SJ 637024-639024) were being worked in the early 18th century, but for much of the 19th century were operated by ironworking companies. In the early 20th century A. Boulton & Co. employed there up to 60 men, using tramways to feed their kilns, and despatching lime from railway sidings. Photographic evidence suggests that there were three bottle-shaped kilns, and a Hoffman kiln. The quarry became an RAF fuel depot in 1939, and there are no significant remains of limeworking structures.

The New Works or Wenlock Edge and Smokeyhole quarries (SJ 609002-611003) were leased in 1801 by Thomas Telford and various partners who had interests in the colliery at Lower Long Wood, and in Cressage Bridge, the transport link between the two undertakings. An inclined plane was constructed to link the quarries with three lime kilns adjacent to the Red House on the Shrewsbury-Wenlock Road. Coal from Lower Long Wood was carried to the kilns, and the same wagons took a return freight of limestone to be burned in kilns at the colliery. Foundations of kilns remain in this area in Smokey Hole quarry (SJ 611003),

Trowes and Stokes Barn quarries (SJ 614999) and Meakins quarry (SJ 610996), while a pair of kilns survives in good condition in Ballstone quarry (SJ 613997).[41]

The Stretton Westwood Quarry (SO 595984) occupies land allocated for stone production by the Enclosure Commission in 1808. From the 1860s it was worked by George Lloyd who constructed standard gauge rail sidings and a network of 3 ft.-gauge tramways. Quarrying continued until 1954, since when the site has been used for other industrial purposes. A massive pair of conventional kilns built against the quarry face still survives.

The Lilleshall Quarry (SO 575968), one of the largest on Wenlock Edge, takes its name from the Lilleshall Company who from 1862 extracted from it limestone for their blast furnaces as well as carrying on a lime burning business. Tramways linked quarry faces with kilns and sidings on a mineral railway which joined the Great Western near Presthope station. Production reached 1,000 tons a week in 1900 but activities were subsequently run down and the rails were lifted in 1917. The mineral railway can still be traced but modern workings have destroyed ten former kilns and all evidence of the tramways.

Elsewhere on Wenlock Edge several kilns and a tramway embankment remain at the Old Knowle quarry at Presthope (SO 585977), together with four kilns alongside the former GWR line at the Plough quarry (SO 583974). A small kiln remains in the Edge Wood nature reserve (SO 479876).

At the southern end of Wenlock Edge there were two lime enterprises along the Craven Arms—Pedlars Rest turnpike, the Dinchope Works, where there were kilns at the roadside at SO 454828, and others within the quarries workings stretching north into Halford Wood (SO 452836), and the Shawbank Lime Works (SO 463832). There were further kilns at Whettleton Bank (SO 445805) near the Shrewsbury—Ludlow main road. The substantial View Edge Lime Works at SO 426807 in Aldon township, which was active by the early 1770s, must always have been difficult of access. All these sites have the untidy characteristics of former quarries.

The beds of limestone around the Clee Hills also sustained lime-burning businesses, and until the end of the 18th century supplied some fluxing stone for blast furnaces. The Ditton Lime Works (SO 601877) served a local market inaccessible to other suppliers. Two surviving kilns at the Studley Lime Works (SO 603745) must be amongst the smallest and crudest remaining in Shropshire. The workings at Oreton in Stottesdon parish (SO 650805) were on a larger scale. Six individuals were operating lime businesses at Oreton in the 1870s. On the southern border of the county there were limestone mines at The Knowle, where there were 14 kilns producing 7,000 bushels of lime per week in 1814, Gorstley Rough (SO 593747) and the Novers (SO 596736) where an adit remains, with a bank of four limekilns. Cast iron plate rails have been found on the site. Working ceased in 1912, having been on a small scale for some years previously.[42]

The Alberbury Breccia ridge was a source of lime before 1660. Small quarries line the north-eastern edge of Loton Deer Park (SJ 360140), and the road from Rowton to Cardington. There were 28 kilns on the Loton Park estate in 1834, and some 5,000 tons of rock were being burnt annually between 1828 and 1842.[43]

In north-west Shropshire the chief source of limestone was Llanymynech Hill, described by Pennant in 1773 as 'the magazine of limestone for a vast tract of country'. Output increased with the development of the turnpike road system, but was still seasonable, carriage being possible only between March and October. Aikin in 1797 recorded that limestone was sent as far into Wales as Llanidloes, that it was sold at the kilns for 7d a bushel, and that a wagon load was reckoned to be 30-36 bushels.[44] Lime was still being burnt on the hill in the 1930s. In the mid-19th century limestone was being despatched by canal to blast furnaces in the Coalbrookdale Coalfield and the Black Country. Evidence of the cutting of deeper levels in the top quarry on the hill suggests that owners remained optimistic about its prospects around 1900. Quarry workers in Llanymynech were universally called 'rockmen'. Their number declined from 45 to 33 between 1861 and 1871, with a further decline to 21 ten years later. In the neighbouring hamlet of Pant the number fell from 43 to 11 during the 1870s.

Four tramway systems brought stone from the quarries on the hill to the main road, the canal and the railway at its foot. One was operating at least as early as 1809, and in 1820 a man was killed at the 'Old Rail Road'. This was probably the line which ran to the Ellesmere Canal along what is still a distinctive narrow plot in which stands Rock Cottage (SJ 266214). This line had fallen out of use by 1838. To the east is a system which in its final form linked the topmost quarries on the hill by means of three inclined planes, one through a tunnel, probably not driven

9 *A stone with grooves worn by the action of the winding rope on the most southerly of the inclined planes on Llanymynech Hill (SJ 264125).*

until the 20th century, with wharves on the canal. Foundations remain of the winding houses of all three inclines, on the slopes of which stones bearing the marks of winding ropes, and some wooden sleepers can still be seen.

To the north a tramway, in operation by 1838, ran on the level past Pant Methodist Church, across the turnpike road, and descended by an inclined plane to kilns alongside the Ellesmere Canal (SJ 275217). The winding drum on the inclined plane (SJ 273218) was restored by local enterprise in the 1970s, but the slope of the incline was subsequently destroyed by the construction of a house in the early 1980s. The most northerly tramway, constructed between 1838 and 1882, ran from a wharf near Pant Station (SJ 276223), through its own arch in the bridge carrying a lane over the canal, along what is now a footpath, past a pair of large limekilns west of the Oswestry—Welshpool main road (SJ 277236), to ascend to the Llynclys portion of the hill by a long inclined plane, at the top of which remains a stable, presumably for horses moving wagons to and from the quarries.

The two southerly tramway systems ran into the canal basin at Llanymynech which had been constructed by 1838. Much stone was loaded directly into narrow boats to be shipped away, but considerable quantities were burned to make lime. Two large conventional lime kilns remain, one with a lining which appears to have been almost new when production was abandoned. The rolled steel joists protruding from the kilns suggest that their present form is of 20th-century date. The most prominent feature of the site is a Hoffman kiln, built after 1900, perhaps as an attempt to develop the market for lime as that for fluxing stone declined.

North of Llanymynech Hill is a further range of limestone quarries, partly in Llanyblodwell and partly in the township of Treflach in Oswestry, and incorporating workings at Porthywaen, Whitehaven and Nant Mawr. These also reached a peak of production in the mid-19th century. In 1841 there were no more than 27 ‘rockmen’ living in Oswestry parish, but this total had risen to 98 by 1861, and reached a peak of 118 ten years later before declining to 66 in 1881. The quarries were served by the Porthywaen branch of the Cambrian Railways, opened in 1861, by the Nant Mawr extension of the Potteries, Shrewsbury and North Wales Railway, opened in 1866, and by the Tanat Valley Light Railway, utilising part of the track of the former, and opened in 1904. These quarries became one of the principal sources of ballast for the Great Western Railway, and many ballast wagons bore the legend ‘Return empty to Llynclys’. Dolgoch Quarry (SJ 276244) is accessible as a nature reserve.

The scale of workings in the area is revealed by a sale notice of 1841 for a set of lime kilns at Porthywaen, three were 25 ft. deep and held 14 wagon loads of lime each, three were 16ft. deep and held six wagon loads of lime each. Stone was obtained from a breast of rock 180 yards wide behind the kilns. Equipment included 115 yards of railway plates and sleepers, railway stone carriages, eight iron crowbars, six stone hammers, five pick mattocks, four iron and eight wood wheelbarrows, eight lime shovels and an iron-bound lime measure.[45]

To the north a scatter of small quarries serving local markets extended towards the Ceiriog. There was a limerock west of Trefonen Hall (SJ 245263), and kilns, in the quarries south of Wernddu (SJ 233261). The landscape around Craig-llwyn

(SJ 237276) is scarred with remnants of quarries, and there were kilns and a quarry at Cynynion (SJ 2433030). None employed more than two or three workers.

At Llawnt (SJ 249309) on the turnpike road from Oswestry to Llansilin quarries line the eastern bank of the infant River Morda. In the late 19th century there were two banks of kilns. Further quarries line the turnpike road from Oswestry to Glyn Ceiriog at Craignant (SJ 252349) near the Victorian tower which marks the course of Offa's Dyke. Some kilns remain alongside the lane north of the road.

On Shropshire's north-west frontier stand the celebrated limekilns of Bronygarth, on the south side of the River Ceiriog, across which a bridge gave access to the Chirk-Glyn Ceiriog turnpike road. In the late 19th century the bridge carried a siding from the Glyn Valley Tramway. Customers to the east were supplied along the turnpike road of 1771 from Wem. A quarry remains in the angle between the road and Offa's Dyke, and the road is lined with a bank of four kilns, round in plan, behind a retaining wall over 10m. high, from the mortar joints of which sprout hazel saplings, Hart's Tongue ferns and wild strawberries.

MALTING AND TANNING

In the 18th and 19th centuries much of the barley used for brewing beer in Shropshire was malted in small malthouses which formed parts of farmsteads or inns. The maltings at Barrow Farm, Barrow was probably converted from a barn when the surviving malt kiln was built around 1830. The *Hare and Hounds* at Cruckton (SJ 432107) is one of many inns which had malthouses.[46] A few malthouses were of the same order of size as their urban equivalents. At Diddlebury (SO 518851) is a three-storey malthouse in neatly coursed sandstone with a clay tile roof, L-shaped in plan, with five bays on the main elevation, and taking-in doors on each floor. At Minsterley (SJ 372050) is a bow-ended, three-storey malthouse of eight bays, in rubble stone, with a lucam on the top storey, and the remains of a taking-in door on the first floor. Malting became an urban trade during the 19th century.

The processing of leather similarly progressed towards the towns. In the 18th century there were tanners at Myddle, Worthen, Wollerton (Hodnet), Pontesford, Whittington, Hungerford Mill in Munslow, Gadlis in Ellesmere and Cheney Longville, of which only the last three appear to have been working in 1851.

WOODWORKING

Wood is the other principal natural resource of the Shropshire countryside. Until the late 18th century charcoal for smelting iron ore was was most important product of the county's woodlands. Most blast furnaces and forges drew charcoal from distinct hinterlands. Trevor Rowley has shown that charcoal the costs of charcoal at Bouldon blast furnace increased from '£1 16s.0d. a douzon' in 1736 to £2 16s.0d. in 1775, and the owners of Charlcott furnace after 1750 obtained supplies from up to 16km. away, as far as Nash, Acton Scott and Spoonhill Wood.[47] An early 19th-century writer, acknowledging the diminished consumption of charcoal caused by the use of coke in blast furnaces, noted that there were still many thousand acres of coppice wood in the county, which were valued at seven shillings an acre.[48] In some areas a modest level of charcoal production continued through the 19th century—there was a wood collier in Leighton for example until the 1890s, and coppices continued to produce poles for pit props.

The largest extent of woodland in Shropshire is the Wyre Forest on the Worcestershire border in the parishes of Kinlet and Dowles. Seven woodcutters were living in Kinlet in 1871. Disciplined study of the forest is revealing changing patterns of past management reflected in the distribution of species, in different patterns of coppicing, and in the effects on ground flora of charcoal burning.[49]

Shropshire oak was used in shipbuilding, both within the county and at ports on the lower Severn. Sale notices for timber trees in the early 19th century usually detail the means of access from the point of sale to the Severn. Sawmills powered by water and steam proliferated in the county in the 19th century, especially on great estates. The buildings of the mills at Uppington (SJ 602097), built for the Duke of Cleveland (now part of Lord Barnard's estate), remain little-altered. The reciprocating saw from the Bromfield mill, made by John Pickles & Son of Hebden Bridge *c*.1890, together with a Fielding & Platt oil engine of *c*.1914 which once powered it, is preserved at the Blists Hill Open Air Museum. Overhead cranes were installed at many rural railway stations to aid the loading of timber. On the Shrewsbury & Hereford line there were such cranes at Bromfield, Marshbrook, Ludlow and Woofferton. Several trackside sawmills in the county still flourish, amongst them those at Bucknell (SO 355736), Elson (SJ 313360) and Woofferton (SO 514680), although they no longer use the railway.

Shropshire's woodlands were the source of other products than cordwood and timber. Bark used in tanning was a by-product of timber production whether in the forest or at the saw mill. An early 20th-century photograph of the Bucknell sawmill shows huge piles of bark awaiting despatch by rail. A sale of the produce of coppices in the Cressage area in 1868 included crate heads, crate rods, and stales for shovels and hammers.[50] Alders were sought by itinerant cloggers. In 1861 the census revealed the presence of five cloggers from Lancashire at the *Raven Inn*, Ludlow. William Dudley of Welshhampton made his living as a clogwood dealer in the 1870s, and the practice continued at Wistanstow in the early 20th century when alder wood was taken away by lorry. Basket making was a significant manufacture at Montford and Welshhampton. Besoms were made from twigs, usually by the itinerant besom makers revealed by census returns in lodging houses and barns all over the county, but two resident tradesmen in Button Oak were thus occupied in the late 1870s. Some rural timber firms developed complex ranges of products, often from the nucleus of a sawmill or a railway siding. J. C. Edge of Craven Arms, John Upton of Church Aston and Richard Kay of Prees all made bendware. During the 1870s a 'Steam Chair Manufactory' was established at Whittington, employing skilled workers who originated in High Wycombe.

ARTIFICIAL MANURE

There were artificial manure works in the late 19th century at Allscott, Maesbury, Rednal, Ruckley, the Calcutts and Quatford. The best evidence of the technology employed comes from the Calcutts in the Ironbridge Gorge. In 1871 the premises

10   *The former artificial manure works on the banks of the Ellesmere Canal behind the* Navigation Inn *at Maesbury (SJ 315250), established in the 1860s by Edward Richard on the site of a former lead smelter.*

comprised a manufactory, divided into a mill room, oil room, acid room and rectifying room, with power provided by a 7h.p. steam engine, two warehouses, 18.5m. x 5.2m., and 12.3m. x 4.6m. respectively, and a dwelling house. Equipment include a bone mill, wrought iron cisterns glass retorts, Woulfe's Jars and about one hundred carboys, together with stocks of acetic acid, sodium acetate, sulphur, hydrochloric acid, palm nuts and cotton seed.[51]

The largest of the Shropshire manure works was established by John Austin alongside the railway at Allscott (SJ 614126) in 1858. Austin, born at Longdon-on-Tern, was a wealthy farmer, who began to manufacture manure in Wellington in 1854, and was working 1,170 acres and employing 24 men in 1871. His chief chemist was Edward Smith, a Liverpudlian, who, like Austin, lived in Allscott village. The works operated until 1958 and, after various changes of ownership, remains a fertiliser depot.[52]

Technical expertise from Merseyside also supported superphosphate works in North Shropshire. A factory at Maesbury on the site of the former lead smelter was established in the 1860s by Edward Richards, a native of Meifod, Monts., who had lived in Liverpool, where his sons, David, an analytical chemist, and Robert, who also worked in the business, were born in 1853 and 1858. The building remains alongside the Ellesmere Canal behind the *Navigation Inn* at Maesbury (SJ 315251), a two-storey brick structure, rectangular in plan and sparsely fenestrated, with a tiled roof, with a round chimney. A larger chimney, 46m. high and 7.6m. in diameter, was demolished in 1892 after the company had moved to a former warehouse at

Rednal Canal Wharf (SJ 350280), where manufacturing continued until the early 1950s. Only concrete floors and some fragments of walls survive.[53]

Nothing remains of the bone works at the Calcutts, and Bonehill Bridge over the Wolverhampton—Shrewsbury railway (SJ 770064) is almost the only evidence on the ground of what seems to have been the first manure works in Shropshire, established at Ruckley by William Bradburn before 1851. A few mounds remain on the site of the water-powered mill at Dudmaston (SO 737896), which was operated by George Fisher between *c.*1860 and 1880.[54]

THE FOOD INDUSTRIES

Much cheese was being produced in Shropshire for national markets by 1700. Shropshire formed the southern part of what agrarian historians have defined as the Cheshire Cheese Region, and cheese was the principal cash product of many of the farms between the Cheshire border and the fringes of the Coalbrookdale Coalfield. Cheese-making was particularly important at Adderley, a closed parish of large farms. Richard Furber who died in 1660 had a dairy herd of 134 beasts, and cheese worth £168, probably about eight tons, stored in his house. William Tankard who died in 1695 had 80 cwt of cheese, valued at £80.[55] Cheese from Shropshire ports passed down the River Severn through Gloucester. During 1713 the *Prosperity* of Shrewsbury carried 230 tons in the course of 17 voyages down the river. In 1722 the *Thomas and Mary* of Broseley made 11 voyages, carrying in all 140 tons of cheese.[56]

11 *The first cheese factory in Shropshire, opened by Thomas Pugh Johnson at Tern Hill (SJ 635321) c.1878.*

The scale of the cheese trade in the early 19th century is shown by the county's cheese markets, particularly the three in Shrewsbury, but cheesemaking remained a farmhouse activity. The first cheese factory in England was established at Longford, Derbyshire, in 1870, utilising American technology.[57] The first in Shropshire came a little later. By 1879 Thomas Pugh Johnston was operating a 'milk and cheese factory' at Tern Hill (SJ 635321), probably opened in 1878, the date on the adjacent cottages.[58] The factory subsequently passed into other hands and was still used for dairying in the 1930s, but has since been adapted for other purposes. Creameries multiplied in Shropshire from the 1880s until the 1930s, both in adapted premises and in purpose-built structures. Most balanced the production of cheese and butter with the supply of liquid milk for distribution to households. In more recent times chilled products, cottage cheese, yoghurt and fromage frais have been made in the county.

At the Chinnel, Mile End, Whitchurch (SJ 552430) Thomas William Horner was making butter and dealing in cheese by the early 1890s, on a site which had formerly been a brickyard. The creamery alongside the North Staffordshire Railway at Pipe Gate, Woore (SJ 737408) was established before 1909 by Henry Edwards & Son, of Market Drayton, and continued until after the Second World War. The buildings are now occupied by a rubber manufacturer. The most prominent is a three-storey polychrome brick tower, with a north elevation of four bays and an east elevation of five bays, with an extension to the south. It is flanked on each side by pairs of high, single-storey brick sheds in the same combination of red and buff brick, with circular lights in the gable ends.

12 *A postcard of the 1930s showing the creamery alongside the North Staffordshire Railway at Pipe Gate (SJ 737408). The line of the road has been altered, leaving the cottages on the right on a service road.*

Minsterley Creamery (SJ 375051) originated in 1909 when the barytes mill south of the village was adapted by Wathes Bros., of Birmingham, as a collecting depot for liquid milk. After the First World War the company purchased a military forage depot, which itself had been adapted from a sawmill, and established a model creamery. Products in the 1930s included cheese, butter, fresh and tinned cream and evaporated milk. A herd of 300 pigs was kept to consume by-products. Pork and bacon were processed in an adjacent factory, which still operates as a meat cannery under different ownership. The buildings at Minsterley have been constantly adapted to new uses, and few structures now remain from before the Second World War, although the cottages on the opposite side of the A488 bear the initials of the owners of the sawmill.[59]

During the First World War a farmers' co-operative established the creamery at Ruyton-XI-Towns (SJ 391223), which, until its closure in 1992 was celebrated for its cheese, made in varied buildings, some brick sheds which probably dated from the time the factory was founded, and some modern structures, like the evaporator tower, which produced whey powder. The factory had subsidiary plants at Whittington (SJ 323310), which was closed in 1990 and demolished in 1992, and Baschurch (SJ 423216), a three-storey structure clad in corrugated iron, which ceased to be used as a dairy in the late 1940s and was subsequently used for packing frozen peas.[60]

The creamery adjacent to Dorrington station (SJ 480032) on the Shrewsbury & Hereford Railway, established in 1921, also supplied milk to London. From 1936 until the late 1960s about half a dozen 3,000-gallon, six-wheel, glass-lined tanks

13 *The one-time creamery at Baschurch (SJ 423216), a subsidiary plant of the factory at Ruyton-XI-Towns. The building was used for packing frozen peas in the 1950s.*

Russell Mulford Collection

14 *The Dorrington-Marylebone milk train in 1954, approaching Shrewsbury along the Shrewsbury & Hereford Railway. The five glass-lined, 3,000-gallon tankers are hauled by locomotive 6976,* Graithwaite Hall, *from Banbury depot, which shared the working with Coleham shed in Shrewsbury.*

were despatched each afternoon to Abbey Foregate sidings, Shrewsbury, and thence to Marylebone, with a dedicated brake van inscribed 'Marylebone and Dorrington Milk Train'. The train travelled through Birmingham, Snow Hill to Banbury, where the locomotive which had brought the train from Shrewsbury was replaced by one from Neasden depot, London.

Apart from the meat-packing plant next to Minsterley creamery, Shropshire's principal cannery in the inter-war period was at Walford, Baschurch (SJ 442203), established in 1933 by Col. C.R. Morris-Eyton, initially to can locally-grown peas. After harvesting the peas were taken to a viner which extracted them from their pods. At the factory they were blanched and graded, before being placed in cans and placed in an exhauster. They were marketed as *Golden Mere* and *Silver Mere* peas. Strawberries, raspberries, gooseberries, plums, bilberries and damson were canned later in the summer season. At its peak the factory employed about 200 girls on a seasonal basis. It closed soon after the outbreak of the Second World War.[61]

A wholly new industry arrived in Shropshire in 1927 with the construction by the Shropshire Beet Sugar Co. Ltd. of the factory at Allscott (actually in Walcot, SJ 605125). The works used German technology, and the menus at the dinner on 10 November 1927 celebrating its completion were bilingual. The factory was one of the first building projects in the county to employ concrete construction on a large scale.[62]

THE ESSENCE OF RURAL MANUFACTURES

Varied manufacturing enterprises now flourish in the Shropshire countryside, most of them in places whose industrial use is historically determined, the sites of water mills, railway stations and brickworks. The most significant influence on industrial location has been the availability of space on military bases constructed during the Second World War. The ex-RAF bases at Atcham, Stanmore, Rednal, Prees Heath and Condover, and parts of the army bases at Park Hall, Leaton, Rosehill, Nesscliffe, St Martin's and Wem, and the Royal Navy munitions depot at Ditton Priors have all become industrial estates.

PMC (Shrewsbury) Ltd. were one of the first companies to become involved in the redevelopment of military bases, acquiring part of the Condover airfield (SO 503037) in 1964.[63] A hangar, some personnel buildings and a tower used for training bomb aimers were taken over, and used largely by metal-working concerns. In the early 1970s the same company converted to industrial uses the NAAFI, the dining block, the sergeants' mess and numerous personnel buildings of the Rosehill base (SJ 660301), which had housed servicemen from the Ternhill flying field. In 1969 PMC bought the ex-RASC base at Leaton (SJ 473186), where there had been a butchery and bakery. Nissen huts and precast concrete buildings were adapted for industrial uses, principally motor car body workshops and plating concerns.

Two industrial estates utilising buildings of Second World War vintage remain on the edges of the runway at Rednal. On Site A (SJ 370286) a timber company and a piling concern occupy wartime buildings now surrounded by plantations of conifers.

15 *Some of the military buildings adapted to industrial uses at the bakery and butchery depot established during the Second World War at Leaton (SJ 473186).*

At Site B (SJ 368277) scarcely-altered accommodation blocks house a road haulage depot, and firms making fencing, paint and upholstery, while a multi-storey concrete structure is utilised by a farmer.

The Ditton Priors naval base was constructed for the storage of ammunition, and the industrial units are 'magazines', substantial buildings protected by earth banks, which extend for some 2km. south east of the entrance (SO 613893). Present-day users include engineering works, motor body workshops and a fireworks factory.

The 'problem' in understanding 'industry' in the countryside is largely linguistic. The use of the word 'industry' as an abstract noun and stereotyped impressions of the 'Industrial Revolution' and its landscapes of multi-storied mills and smoking chimneys, make it difficult to link the term with activities in the Corvedale or Whixall Moss. The landscape of rural Shropshire nevertheless reflects a long history of manufactures, centred around sources of water power, raw materials or labour, or simply where land happened to be available. Such manufactures have changed over time, but their nature remains much the same. A milk tanker heading for Minsterley, a truck of sugar beet en route for Allscott, a load of limestone hardcore from Wenlock Edge, form part of a continuous process of utilising the resources of the countryside, just as the enterprises which flourish in former military camps, in what were once railway goods depots or on the sites of old brickworks, are continuing a tradition, which has its origins in the squatter settlements of the 17th and 18th centuries, of making use of available space and labour, which is the essence of rural manufactures.

◆ ◆ ◆

3

MARKET TOWN INDUSTRIES

◆ ◆ ◆

George Eliot described her fictional St Ogg's as 'one of those old, old towns which impress one as a continuation and outgrowth of nature, a town which carries the traces of its long growth and history like a millennial tree'.[1] Towns in the 18th and 19th centuries were meeting places, for trade, recreation, religion, culture or the services of professional men. They were also centres for various long-established manufactures, some of which demanded the provision of large and specialised buildings. This chapter explores the hypothesis that a market town was as much a cluster of maltsters, millers, brickmakers and tanners, and later of iron founders, as it was a concentration of bankers, attorneys and linen drapers.

THE SHROPSHIRE TOWNS

Sixteen communities in Shropshire can reasonably be regarded as market towns between 1660 and 1960. Shrewsbury was by far the largest; with a population in 1801 of nearly 15,000, it remained at that date amongst the thirty largest towns in England, slightly smaller than Leicester, Exeter and Coventry, and rather larger than Derby, Oxford, Preston or Reading, a regional capital whose influence extended to the Welsh coast. Shrewsbury had grown rapidly in the second half of the 18th century, but its growth was not sustained. It actually lost population in the 1830s, and in the course of the 19th century the number of its inhabitants only doubled. Wellington, the market town for the agricultural region to the north and for the Coalbrookdale Coalfield, came next in order of size. Bridgnorth, one of the principal ports on the Severn, and Ludlow, which had prospered on the business brought by the Council in the Marches and Wales, both had pretensions to being resorts as well as market towns. Oswestry, market centre for the Welsh uplands to the west, prospered in the early 19th century, and from the 1860s became a railway town, a miniature Ashford or Swindon. The five market towns of north Shropshire, Whitchurch, Market Drayton, Newport, Ellesmere and Wem, all owed some of their 19th-century prosperity to canals. Wem was the smallest Shropshire town to have a full range of manufactures. The remaining six, all with populations below 2,000 in 1841, were little more than local retailing centres, although all had maltsters, and most had tanners.

16   *Market towns in Shropshire.*

Table 3.1 **Shropshire Market Towns in 1841**, in order of size by population: Source: 1841 census.

	Population	Number of houses
Shrewsbury	18,285	4,092
Wellington	6,084	1,300
Bridgnorth	5,770	1,204
Ludlow	5,064	1,086
Oswestry	4,566	987
Whitchurch	3,403	668
Market Drayton	3,161	713
Newport	2,497	553
Ellesmere	2,326	446
Wem	1,932	–
Shifnal	1,872	412
Much Wenlock	1,627	504
Bishop's Castle	1,510	373
Cleobury Mortimer	1,122	211
Clun	913	191
Church Stretton	860	183

NOTE: For towns which were parts of large parishes, like Wellington, Clun or Shifnal, figures given are for the township or townships which comprised the urban areas.

DISTRIBUTION AND EXCHANGE

Towns were places of distribution and exchange for which purposes some had buildings which were already venerable in 1660, amongst them Walter Hancock's Market Hall of 1596 in Shrewsbury, used for buying cloth by the Drapers' Company, as a corn market, and as the focus of the Saturday produce market, or Much Wenlock's Guildhall of 1577. William Baker's Butter Cross of 1743-44 at Ludlow was the most distinguished market building constructed in the county in the 18th century. Market buildings proliferated in the 19th century. In Shrewsbury by the 1840s three establishments competed for the wholesale trade in butter and cheese: Henry Newton's Circus market near the Welsh Bridge, a Doric market hall of 1844 by Edward Haycock on Pride Hill, and the Butter Market in Howard Street, designed by the Birmingham architects Fallows & Hart, and opened at the terminus of the Shrewsbury Canal in 1836.[2] In Oswestry the Powis Market and the Cross Market opened in 1849. The Butter Market in Market Drayton, a shelter for sellers of dairy produce, supported by Tuscan columns, dates from 1826.

After 1850 the tendency was towards larger multi-purpose buildings, which were usually given a measure of civic recognition, even if built by private companies. One of the first, and the least successful, was the New Market Hall in Bridgnorth, built in 1855, an exercise in red, white and blue Italianate by John Smallman of Quatford, which failed, after much legal contention, to attract the town's market traders, who remain in the open air in the High Street.[3]   Shrewsbury's general market, designed by Robert Griffith, and completed in 1869, accommodated the corn exchange, the wholesale market for dairy produce, and the retail markets for fish, meat, fruit and vegetables.[4]   Ludlow's combination of town hall and market hall was completed in 1887. In Much Wenlock the Corn Exchange was opened in 1852 and the Market Hall in 1878, both designed by Samuel Pountney Smith.

Facilities for selling cattle were improved in most Shropshire towns during the 19th century. The pattern was set in Shrewsbury where the ambitious project, completed in 1850, to drain and drive a road across riverside land upstream of the Welsh Bridge included the construction of a new cattle market on a site which it subsequently occupied for over a century.[5]   At Ellesmere cattle selling moved to a new Smithfield alongside the railway station shortly after the opening of the Cambrian line. Two markets on the fringe of the town centre, one close to the station, were opened in Ludlow.

Warehouses for wool and grain were natural appendages of markets, and their existence is confirmed in many documentary sources. Most survivors are of relatively late date like the wool warehouse by the Welsh Bridge in Shrewsbury now occupied by an auction room, a three-storey brick structure of 1888, with a mansard roof, designed by A. B. Deakin for the merchant Isaac Eakin,[6] and the Corn House, a four-storey polychrome brick structure on the corner of Wyle Cop and St Julian Friars, built about 1880 for the grain merchant T. E. Matthews.

Shops are also part of the essence of a market town. The late medieval frontages in Butcher Row, Shrewsbury, were still hung with meat by traders in the 19th century. In Ludlow small shop fronts of the late 18th century and early 19th century remain at Nos. 9/11 Bell Lane (SO 511743). Typical retailing properties of the 18th and 19th centuries, with spacious accommodation for traders on the upper floors, remain in most towns. An outstanding early 20th-century shopfront was installed at No 40 High Street, Whitchurch (SJ 541415) by Birchalls, agricultural implement dealers, when they took over the premises in 1904. William Webb of Bargates designed for the building a nine-bay, three-storey, arcaded cast iron frontage, with semi-circular headed arches, and tracery springing from cylindrical columns. On the top floor it follows the Decorated style with trefoils. The castings were supplied by McFarlanes of Glasgow.[7] Early chain stores secured only a modest presence in Shropshire but some premises can readily be recognised. A mosaic doorstep and a panel in decorative tiles at 15 King Street, Ludlow (SO 512745), show that a Maypole Dairy once occupied this ancient timber-framed building, and in Pride Hill, Shrewsbury, the Boots store (SJ 492125), of 1907 and 1920, is in the characteristic Elizabethan style of that company's architect, A.N. Bromley. Most co-operative stores were located in pre-existing buildings. The one-time department store in Castle Street, Shrewsbury, a three-storey, seven-bay building with three gables and a corner turret, combining star-panelled cosmetic timber-framing with precisely-laid Ruabon bricks and stone dressings, opened in 1923, is the outstanding exception.

Until the second half of the 19th century most consumer goods, footwear, furniture, clothing and some kinds of metal ware were made in the towns where they were purchased. The larger the town the more specialised were the trades. Every town had shoemakers, tailors, blacksmiths and cabinet makers. Ludlow in the mid-19th century could boast gunmakers, trunkmakers and four straw hat makers. Shrewsbury had a sword cutler in the 1690s, and in 1851 numbered amongst its tradesmen five clog and patten makers, a cork cutter, three soda water manufacturers and a stained glass maker. The premises in which such craftsmen worked were rarely distinctive, and most master craftsmen employed no more than two or three workers. Thomas Bowen, upholsterer in the Bullring, Ludlow, in 1871 employed six men and two apprentices, but there is nothing to distinguish his premises. An outstanding record of a craft workshop is a picture taken *c.*1870 of the Old Cooperage in Whitchurch, where, in a timber-framed building whose oldest parts date from the 16th century, a cooper displays barrels and dolly pegs on an open counter.[8] Customers in market towns often chose to deal with traders who shared their political and religious opinions, and some craftsmen sought markets elsewhere which were not subject to such pressures. The outstanding example in Shropshire is the Whitchurch clockmaker J. B. Joyce, who, as a result of his successes with church, turret and spring clocks, moved in 1904 from a conventional shop at No 40 High Street to a factory on Station Road (SJ 546414). The company supplied clocks for buildings all over the world including the Refuge Assurance Building in Manchester,

17   *The factory of the clockmaker, J.B. Joyce, in Station Road, Whitchurch (SJ 546414), constructed in 1904.*

the government buildings in Sydney, the Dilkusha Palace in Kabul, the Shanghai Custom House and the Chamberlain Tower of the University of Birmingham, and provided 1,500 clocks for stations on the London & North Western Railway. The bakers of gingerbread in Market Drayton pursued a similar if more modest course. The firms of Billingtons, established in 1817, and Chesters, founded in 1850, exported gingerbread in small quantities to Australia, India, China and the Americas. A Cheswardine baker continues to employ the traditional recipe.

TOWN MILLS

Every prosperous market town had access to water power. The citizens of Shrewsbury were able to utilise the seven mills along the 4 km. course of the Rea Brook between Meole Brace and its confluence with the Severn. Ludlovians enjoyed the services of a mill on the Corve and of six on the River Teme. The infant River Tern powered seven mills as it passed through Market Drayton. The ancient link between urban status and water power is shown by the inclusion of Walcot, with its powerful mill on the Tern, in the parish of Wellington, whose church is some 6 km. distance, and by the Town Mills of Bridgnorth at Pendlestone in Worfield parish, given to the corporation by Henry III in 1227. Urban mills were used for purposes other than grinding grain. An iron forge flourished in the 18th century at Sutton, Shrewsbury, while paper mills operated at Market Drayton and Cleobury Mortimer. The Ludlow mills were used by a foundry, by makers of woollen cloth and paper, and for silk throwing. Pendlestone Mill had five pairs of stones in 1817 and, in addition to the corn mill, its waters powered an iron forge between 1760 and the 1790s, and wool-spinning machines in the 19th century.

Townspeople found other forms of power for grinding grain. There were windmills in Shrewsbury, Wellington, Bishop's Castle, Wem, Ellesmere, Much Wenlock and Newport. The latter, built by Marsh Trustees in 1796 at a cost of £2000, was the outstanding windmill in the county, 16.76m. high, 8.23m. in diameter at the base, with five storeys, oak stocks 16.76m. long, and two pairs of stones, one 1.52m. and 1.73m. in diameter, and designed by Joseph Jackson, of Lane End, Staffs. The mill was not a commercial success and was sold in 1802 for less than half the cost of erection. All trace of it has now disappeared.[9] In Shrewsbury the Kingsland windmill, built by the poor law authorities, also began operation in 1796.

The earliest surviving steam mill building in Shropshire is the four-storey, five-bay structure of 1826 at the canal terminus at Whitchurch (SJ 541414). The Castle Mills in Shrewsbury (SJ 496132) on the western bank of the canal, north of the New Park Road bridge, formed the largest steam milling complex in the county. They were adapted for milling from canal carriers' warehouses by Richard and William Blakeway about 1850. In the 1870s two beam engines, one of 40 h.p. and one of 30 h.p., were driving nine pairs of French burr stones.[10] The steam mill alongside the Wesley Brook in Shifnal (SJ 747078) was built around 1870 and operated until about the turn of the century, when it was converted to a brewery and has since served as a provision warehouse, military stables and a garden centre. The stub of its chimney remains. The ancient water mill on the River Roden at Wem (SJ 512285), already supplemented by a windmill on the mill dam by 1800,

18 *The steam mill in Shifnal (SJ 747078).*

19 *The mill on the River Roden at Wem (SJ 512285), where power was also obtained by 1800 from a windmill, from a steam engine by 1819, and subsequently from a gas engine and from electric motors.*

20   *The buildings of the mill at Ludford (SO 518742), used for paper making until the 1870s, and from the early 1880s as one of Shropshire's few roller flour mills.*

21   *The roller flour mill of W. Rogers & Son at Market Drayton   (SJ 673344), constructed in the 1890s.*

was enlarged in 1819 when the miller John Boughey installed a steam engine, and in the 1890s when a gas engine was added.[11]

The introduction of roller milling which transformed the flour milling trade from the early 1880s made little impact in Shropshire. In Ludlow the substantial buildings of the Ludford Paper Mill (S) 518742) were adapted to accommodate roller milling equipment in the early 1880s. At Market Drayton a purpose-built, three-storey, steam-powered roller mill was constructed by W. Rogers & Sons in Station Road, (SJ 673344) shortly before 1900. The building has cast iron columns supporting massive timber beams, and retains some line shafting. It was used for milling cattle feed until the early 1990s.

MALTING

Malting was the most characteristic of market town manufactures yet it was only in the second half of the 19th century that it became predominantly an urban trade. Probate inventories suggest that in the early 18th century many people were involved in malting but that few relied upon it for their livings.[12] One of the few specialist maltsters was William Podmore of Newport, who died in 1744, with 500 strikes of malt worth £60 in his malthouse. By the 1850s there were about 250 malting businesses in Shropshire, of which only about 150 were in the market towns.

Table 3.2: **Maltsters in Shropshire market towns in 1851** Source: S Bagshaw, *History, Gazetteer and Directory of Shropshire* (1851).	
Shrewsbury	29
Wellington	12
Bridgnorth	20
Ludlow	12
Oswestry	17
Whitchurch	8
Market Drayton	6
Newport	9
Ellesmere	10
Wem	7
Shifnal	10
Much Wenlock	4
Bishop's Castle	2
Cleobury Mortimer	2
Clun	2
Church Stretton	2
Total:	**147**

In the second half of the 19th century the number of malting enterprises contracted and the trade became essentially urban. There were 139 maltsters in the
county in 1879, 90 in 1885, 81 in 1900, 68 in 1906, 39 in 1913, and only 13 by
1934. In some towns the trade disappeared early. The malthouses in Watergate,
reckoned to be the economic mainstay of Ellesmere, ceased to be profitable in the
1860s and all have been demolished.[13]

In Much Wenlock there were 11 malting businesses in 1808 but only four by
1851. Three substantial buildings remain, one on the Bourton Road (SO 620996)
which was operating by the late 1790s, now converted to apartments, one in the
High Street, now a café (SO 621997), and a third at the rear of the *Talbot Hotel* (SO
623997), a three-storey, three-bay structure, with a west elevation of brick and an
eastern elevation in local limestone, which has been adapted as the residential wing
of the hotel. The buildings of two substantial malting complexes remain off Park
Street, Wellington. In Wem a characteristic maltings building, with low ceilings,
and the recognisable remnants of a kiln, remains in Noble Street (SJ 511289), and
is now used by a printer, but the extensive maltings near the station which formed
part of the town's brewery have been demolished. Two malting complexes remain
in Low Town in Bridgnorth. One, next to the Crown Meadow football ground
(SO 719932), consists of two parallel two-storey, 11-bay malthouses, with iron-
barred windows, and three-brick segmental lintels over the ground floor windows.
They abut against a three-storey building at the east end of the plot, while the kiln
remains at the western end. The other, on the premises of Messrs. Ridley at No 48
Mill Street (SO 720931), consists of two three-storey buildings, one of six and one

22   *The maltings complex behind No.139a Corve Street, Ludlow (SO 512749).*

23   *The maltings complex converted from the town theatre in Willow Street, Oswestry (SJ 288297). The building to the left is the* White Lion Inn.

of 12 bays, in brick with a clay tile pitched roof, and a kiln at the eastern end, extending eastwards from a three-storey, three-bay house of 1700.

The largest malthouse in Ludlow behind Nos 23/24 Corve Street (SO 511749), built about 1800, was valued, with the adjacent residential property, at £2,000 in 1827. After use as a brewery and a laundry it was demolished to make way for a garage. Ludlow's best-preserved maltings is at 139a Corve Street (SO 512749), the premises in 1870s of the maltster Joseph Hand. Fronting Corve Street is a three-storey, four bay early Georgian house, behind which are several outbuildings, a cottage and an eight-bay, three-storey building, which was originally sparsely fenestrated, and appears to have been built for malting, although part has been used as cottages. Behind this building is a six-bay, three-storey, purpose-built malthouse. At its end is a pyramid-topped kiln, with three blind semi-circular arches on the north side, with slits for dampers. The tiled floor of the kiln remains.

Malthouse buildings are frequently associated with adaptive re-use, a celebrated example being the Snape Maltings in Suffolk, converted to a concert hall at the instigation of Benjamin Britten. In Oswestry a maltings was converted in the 1850s *from* the town's theatre, which had opened in 1819 in Willow Street, next to the *White Lion Inn* (SJ 288297).[14] The main building, of red brick, stands on a stone plinth, and has a stone cornice below the pediment on the three-storey, three-bay Willow Street elevation. The north elevation is of five bays with taking-in doors on all three floors in the bay nearest the street. The windows are shallow and

24   *The west elevation of the maltings complex at the Glen, Frankwell, Shrewsbury (SJ 489127).*

barred. The southern wall is of rubble stone and the western elevation is ashlar. Malting was still reckoned to be one of Oswestry's principal trades in the 1870s, although only one other malthouse seems to survive, a much-altered, seven-bay, two-storey building at the east end of Coney Green (SJ 293296).

Malting was especially important in Shrewsbury, and several maltings buildings can be still be identified in the central area. One stands within a tangled pattern of old buildings behind No 53 Mardol (SJ 490126), a four-storey brick structure, retaining a lucam, and some characteristically low windows. Construction of maltings of relatively modest size continued in the late 19th century. The building on the corner of Roushill and Phoenix Place (SJ 491127) , a two-storey structure in Ruabon brick with blue brick string courses, 18.2m. x 11m., with a taking in door at first floor level in the wide central bay of the nine-bay Roushill elevation, was designed for Edward Mullard by the architect A. B. Deakin in 1888.[15]

The largest malting complex before the 1880s was probably The Glen, Frankwell (SJ 489127), which was operated by John Hughes between 1836 and 1855. The premises comprised a three-storey, twelve-bay double malthouse, in red brick with a clay tile roof, with a wetting floor 24m. x 11m., capable of wetting 160 bushels every four days, with two adjacent kilns, another three-storey, eight-bay malthouse alongside, with a 22m. x 5m. floor, capable of wetting 80 bushels every four days, and a kiln, together with a large house and three cottages.[16] As in other maltings complexes, the windows are barred. The buildings remain substantially intact, in the occupation of various tenants, although the house is in ruins. The capacity of the Glen was 240 bushels, yet a malthouse in Park Street, Wellington (SJ 651120), offered for sale in 1847, with a capacity of only 130 bushels, was described as 'gigantic'.

In the late 19th century the Shropshire malting trade was dominated by the company established by William Jones in 1869. Jones had emigrated to Pennsylvania in 1857 with the intention of settling in a Welsh-speaking colony, but returned to Britain during the Civil War. His first maltings in Shrewsbury was probably that which remains at No 17a Hills Lane, a building in soft red brick with a clay tile roof, rectangular in plan, measuring approximately 17m. x 6m. He acquired numerous malthouses in Shrewsbury, including The Glen, which his company was operating by 1900 and occupied until *c.*1930, and businesses at Oswestry, Gobowen, Whittington, Ackleton and Pontesford.[17] In Shrewsbury he developed three large new complexes. A purpose-built maltings, which also housed the company offices, was built in Bynner Street, Belle Vue (SJ 497128), in 1888. It was converted into offices in the early 1990s. In March 1897 Jones acquired the former flax mill at Ditherington (SJ 498137), which was converted into a maltings, with a pyramid-topped kiln at the northern end of the main building. Subsequently Jones acquired Castle Foregate corn mills (SJ 496132), where a malthouse had been built at the western end. Under his direction the whole site was converted into a malting concern. Much of the complex has now been demolished but two two-storey malthouses which probably pre-date Jones's acquisition of the site remain.

BREWING

Shropshire was always more celebrated for its malting than for its brewing. The county was largely self-sufficient in beer until the late 19th century, although Guinness and some Burton bottled beers were advertised from the 1830s. Most beer was brewed in public houses or private homes. The brewing trade was modest in size, and few of the Shropshire breweries despatched beer beyond the hinterlands of their tied houses. The Wem Brewery (SJ 513290) was the last in the county to operate on an industrial scale. Since closure in the early 1980s it buildings have been adapted as industrial units.

The most important survival in Shropshire is the brewery attached to the *Three Tuns*, Bishop's Castle (SO 324889). It is more than a mere brewhouse attached to an inn, rather a

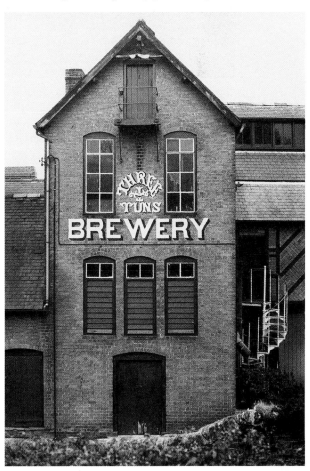

25 *The brewery at the* Three Tuns, *Bishop's Castle (SO 324889).*

small-scale Victorian tower brewery of a kind which would often have supplied a string of public houses.

A brewery stood on the site of The Gateway in Chester Street, Shrewsbury (492131), for at least 150 years. It was established before 1820 by Thomas Hawley of Caus Castle. Its first brewhouse was topped by a lead reservoir, and housed a 120-bushel mash tun and two large coppers. There were six oak vats, the largest with a capacity of 260 barrels, and the output was calculated at 5,000 barrels per year. By 1868 a steam engine had been installed, and a well of spring water was regarded as one of the merits of the site.[18] It was later acquired by Thomas Southam who was responsible for a major rebuilding in 1889, commemorated in the foundation stone, the only relic of the concern. Southam's main building, an eight-bay structure with three storeys and a basement, of brick, with bold string courses, presented a forbidding elevation to the river.

The Circus Brewery (SJ 488126) by the Welsh Bridge was established by Henry Newton within a complex which was also used as a market for dairy products and a venue for public performances. Among its components in the 1890s, when it was being worked by Richards & Hearn, were the original 'circus' building, a high, two-storey rectangular structure, with six bays of blind arcading on its western elevation, a high narrow brewhouse on its southern side, and a steam engine which had recently replaced a 10 h.p. engine operating in the 1860s. The company later amalgamated with the Wem Brewery and the site was cleared in the 1920s.[19]

The most complete surviving brewery complex in Shropshire is that in Coleham, Shrewsbury (SJ 492119), established in 1806-07, purchased in 1830 by William Hazledine for use as a timber depot, and sold in 1846 to Thomas and Thomas William Trouncer, whose family operated it until 1955. In 1828 the brewery was estimated to produce 120 barrels per day. It had eight vats holding 17,000 barrels, and a nearly new 6 h.p. steam engine. Most of the buildings remain, having been occupied since 1959 by a greengrocery wholesaler. The brewhouse is of four storeys, and stands alongside a three storey engine house and a tall, square-section chimney, the adjacent boiler house having been demolished. The two-storey cooling house is of three arcaded bays, and formerly housed the condensing vessel on the first floor with a racking room and cellars beneath. The

26 *The Crown Brewery, Market Drayton (SJ 372345), designed by T. Tindal of Longton and completed in 1899.*

vat house was a single-storey structure of eight arcaded bays, now partially demolished to provide space for a modern building.[20] A four-storey malt store remains, now used by an egg packer, but the malthouse has been replaced by the apartments known as *Pengrove*.

The Crown Brewery, Market Drayton, (SJ 673345) is architecturally the most distinguished of Shropshire's surviving brewery buildings. It comprises a steel-framed, six-storey, three-bay brick tower flanked to the south by a two-storey, four-bay block through which a wagon arch gives access to a yard behind. It was constructed in 1899 to the design of T. Tindal of Longton. Power was provided by a 35 h.p. steam engine. The building is now occupied by a tyre company and a removals concern.[21]

THE LEATHER TRADES

A tannery in 1800 was one of the symbols of a market town. Around twenty were operating in the 1850s, but numbers steady declined. There were four in Market Drayton in 1837 but only one in 1849. By 1905 there were only seven tanning concerns in Shropshire. Only five, in Ludlow, Shrewsbury, Oswestry, Bridgnorth and Wem, remained in 1913, and only two, in Shrewsbury and Oswestry, by 1926. The last, Cock's Tannery in Shrewsbury, closed in the early 1960s.

Most tanneries remained in the same locations over long periods, in Corve Street in Ludlow, below the church at Market Drayton, by the English and Welsh bridges in Shrewsbury. Characteristic components are detailed in the sale in 1891 of the tannery in Much Wenlock (SJ 623003), which was subsequently converted to a brewery. It included a 'lofty bark barn', 6m. x 18m., capable of holding 100 tons of bark, a scoring room and shed, a large three-storey building, 8.8m. x 8.8m. with drying rooms and warehousing facilities, a building 27.5m. x 6m. accommodating a drying room and an office with 31 pits beneath it, a bark mill room with store room above, an inner yard with 22 large and 20 small pits and an outer yard with 11 pits.[22]

The only significant survival of the trade in Shrewsbury is No 131-33 Longden Coleham (SJ 495121), a three-storey, eight-bay structure called Terrace Buildings, used as a brush factory from the 1890s. Charles Hulbert recalled that it had been built in the early 19th century as part of a tannery. The piered construction and shallow depth, of only 7m., suggests that it was the drying house.[23]

The tannery at the northern end of Oak Street in Oswestry (SJ 288299) was built before 1841 by the Revd. Foulk Parry, a Calvinistic Methodist minister.[24] Map evidence suggests that it grew substantially after 1850. Most of the buildings remain, including the appropriately named Tannery Cottage. A two-storey block in Ruabon brick houses a gymnasium, while an older two-storey structure is a taxi base. A three-storey building, converted to apartments might have been a drying house, but the largest structure, in the north-eastern corner of the site, has been replaced by houses.

The tanhouse at the southern end of Church Street in Bishop's Castle (SO 624884) retained a large drying shed with wooden, louvered sides until *c*.1990. It was a tannery site at least as early as 1750, and was occupied until 1831 by William Beddoes, who was succeeded by John Norton, who combined tanning with farming, malting and running a butcher's business.[25]

27 *The drying sheds of the tannery at the south end of Church Street, Bishop's Castle (SO 324884), photographed in the mid-1980s.*

Curriers, who prepared leather for shoemakers, glovers and saddlers, occupied less distinctive premises, but at Much Wenlock the top floor of St Milburga Row in Barrow Street (SO 623998) retains hooks, rails, hoists, which are relics of its use as a currier's workshop. The glove trade in Ludlow enjoyed a boom during the Napoleonic Wars, when it was recalled, perhaps none too accurately, that a thousand people were employed. Certainly it declined in the post-war period, and had disappeared by 1840.[26]

WOODWORKERS

All the Shropshire market towns had sawmills which cut locally-grown and imported timber, and many made smaller items. There were 17 basket and sievemakers in the county in 1879, almost all in the towns. The timber yard in the appropriately named Wood Street (SJ 494135) in Shrewsbury was opened in the 1890s by Treasures the builders as a complement to their brickworks at Buttington.[27] An account in 1897 of Henry Farmer of Wyle Cop, who produced mouldings and joinery, referred to the 'phenomenal activity of the building trade in and near Shrewsbury'. Some firms served wider markets. A business in Oswestry in 1827 worked lime and sycamore for curriers' and shoemakers' cutting boards. Isherwoods of Wem, who occupied an extensive site alongside the railway (SJ 516289) until the 1980s, specialised in the 1930s in making butchers' blocks. Henry Addison, who established the Waterloo Works in Wellington (SJ 642117) in 1881, manufactured seating and interior woodwork, including the reredos panels at St Lawrence Church, Little Wenlock.

Perhaps the widest range of products was made by Grooms of Wellington. Richard Groom (1818-92) began basket making in New Street about 1841, then developed a timber business, subsequently expanding into sawmilling and the making of turned and bendware. In the late 19th century his range included washing dollies, wood bowls in sycamore or willow, butter boards and butter workers in sycamore, butchers' skewers in maple, bakers' peels in ash, oval tubs in oak, children's hoops, toy spades and heavy engineering timbers. Many products were stamped 'R.G.S.& Co..' By 1882 the company occupied the Shropshire Works, the former railway engineering works, to the south of the railway and west of Bridge Road (SJ 647116) which had extensive railway sidings.[28]

The best preserved woodworking site in the county is the Smithfield Road works (SJ 492129) in Shrewsbury, established by John Metcalf in the early 19th century, taken over by Barker Brothers during the 1870s, and now used for selling garden furniture.[29] In the late 19th century, when the company specialised in making bendware, the site included saw mills, drying sheds and workshops with steam-powered machines. The outstanding surviving feature is a sawmill, at least a century old, whose massive four-bay timber frame appears to have supported a primitive overhead crane.

48   THE IRONMONGER DIARY.

DOMESTIC AND DAIRY WOODWARE.

ILLUSTRATED PRICE LIST ON APPLICATION.

R. GROOM, SONS & CO., LIMITED,
WELLINGTON, SALOP.

Ironbridge Gorge Museum Trust

28   *A page from an early 20th-century catalogue of Richard Groom & Sons of Wellington.*

COACHBUILDERS

There were coach-building concerns in eight of the larger Shropshire market towns in the 1850s, and a new workshop was built in Bishop's Castle as late as 1904-05. The most venerable works was the County Carriage Works in Dogpole, Shrewsbury (SJ 493124), which was opened by Thomas Mountford in 1819. Like other coachbuilders Mountford combined the construction of vehicles with a hiring and funeral business. He was proud in 1864 that his omnibuses were built by a craftsman who had once worked for Silk & Co. in London. There were 18 employees in 1888. The firm was taken over by Charles Hughes in 1894 and by 1914 had become part of the Shrewsbury Motor Garage whose principal premises were in Coton Hill. The building in Dogpole is now used as offices by the borough council.[30]

The carriage works in St Julian Friars, Shrewsbury (SJ 494123), was established by David Davies in the late 1830s. In 1854 he was offering dog carts at £21, Whitechapels at £14 and £18, and Phaetons between £20 and £40. He went bankrupt in 1892 after some years when the business had been chiefly repair work. The premises are now used as motor car showrooms.[31]

The Tan Bank coachworks in Wellington (SJ 651113), examined before demolition in the late 1960s, had a broad staircase with flaps fixed to the banisters which could be let down to enable carriages to be pushed up to or lowered from workshops on the first floor. The site was in use as a coachworks in the 1850s, and was subsequently the Excelsior Carriage Works of Clift & Son.[32]

The carriage works behind the *Six Bells*, No 1 Church Street, Bishop's Castle (SO 323884), was built by Charles Jones, the inn's landlord, in 1904-05, and closed when he died in 1922, by which time the premises were also used as a motor garage. The principal range of buildings, measuring 26.6m x 5.6m., is built into a bank at the western end, while the western end projects over the yard on cast iron columns. There is a blacksmith's hearth on the ground floor. The building materials suggest that the building was constructed cheaply. The walls are a mixture of rubble limestone and bricks, while the timbers are of irregular size and may have been re-used.[33]

29   *The carriage works behind the* Six Bells, *Bishop's Castle, built in 1904-05.*

FOUNDRIES: THE FIRST GENERATION

To have a foundry in the 1850s was as much as sign of a town's virility as to have a market hall, a railway station or a member of parliament. Shropshire's most celebrated foundries were, of course, in the Coalbrookale Coalfield, but the spread to every town of consequence in England of the basic techniques of mechanical engineering, the ability to make castings and forgings, to machine them to fine tolerances, and to assemble components into machines, were among the most significant developments of the Industrial Revolution. Most such works developed from millwrights', ironmongers' or blacksmiths' businesses.[34]

In the 18th century machines were assembled by their users, often with the assistance of a consultant who might prepare drawings and supervise erection. The best known example of such practice is the system by which Boulton & Watt provided steam engines for their customers. During the 1790s a new pattern of engineering works emerged, which undertook the complete manufacture of machines or structures. The best documented example is the Soho Foundry of Boulton & Watt, opened in 1796, but Matthew Murray's Round Foundry in Leeds began operation the previous year. Foundries in the Shropshire coalfield were beginning to produce bridges or complete steam engines at much the same time. Two new market town foundries in Shropshire also opened in the 1790s and were pioneers of the species.[35]

The four brothers Hazledine, John (1760-1810), William (1763-1840), Robert (1768-1837) and Thomas (1771-1842), sons of a millwright, grew up in the Shropshire iron trade. By 1795 John and the two younger brothers had established a foundry between Mill Street and the River Severn in Bridgnorth (SO 719932). The company began by making millwrights' castings, but by 1804 it was associated with Richard Trevithick, the pioneer of high pressure steam engines. John Hazledine died in 1810, when his principal partner was Joel Shuttleworth, but between July 1811 and February 1812 the engineer John Urpeth Rastrick became managing partner, and the company was known as Hazledine, Rastrick & Co.. Rastrick withdrew from the company around 1816. Operations ceased in the early 1820s, but had resumed by the end of 1827, when a cannon cast at the foundry burst when fired, killing one bystander, and severely wounding another. By 1838 the foundry was the subject of a suit in Chancery, and the land and machinery were sold. Subsequently William Pope, who had worked as a smith under Hazledine, operated a foundry of only local significance from No 53 Mill Street.[36]

The two-acre site of Hazledine's foundry now comprises several different properties, and none of its buildings remain, although a plaque commemorates its existence. In 1834 the components of the works included the iron foundry building, a steam engine, air furnaces, stoves, carpenters' and smiths' shops, turning and boring mills, three dwelling houses, two offices and fitting up rooms. J.U. Rastrick recalled that pig iron melted at Bridgnorth came from the Lightmoor, Coalbrookdale and Old Park companies.

The products of the Bridgnorth foundry confirm that it was indeed a pioneering engineering works. Many Trevithick engines were manufactured. Some were used locally, at a tannery and a corn mill in Bridgnorth, at the ironworks at Billingsley,

30   *A Trevithick engine built by Hazledine's foundry at Bridgnorth. Nothing is known of its working life before it was rescued from a scrapyard at Hereford and presented to the Science Museum, London, by the railway engineer Francis William Webb in the 1880s.*

and at a farm at Stableford in Worfield parish. The company were among the first manufacturers of threshing machines, seven of which were offered for sale in 1812. Machinery ordered by Richard Trevithick was exported to South America, one consignment in 1814 being worth £16,152. The company built two substantial iron bridges, the second bridge at Stourport, erected after the destruction of the first in the flood of February 1795, and the bridge over the Wye at Chepstow (ST 536944). A steam engine numbered 14 was rescued from scrapping at Hereford by Francis William Webb (1836-1906) in the 1880s, and is now in the Science Museum, London. The engine, Chepstow Bridge, the waterwheel at Cleobury North Mill (SO 626872) and possibly some grave slabs in St Mary's churchyard (SO 716928), Bridgnorth, are the only products of the foundry known to survive.

William Hazledine, the second of the four brothers, established an engineering concern in Shrewsbury at about the same time as his brothers began their works in Bridgnorth. It was the first of many enterprises but, even when he had become the owner of blast furnaces, coal mines, lime quarries and of much of Shrewsbury, Hazledine was known to the leading engineers of his day as *the great ironfounder*. Hazledine is commemorated by a bust by Sir Francis Chantry in St Chad's Church, Shrewsbury.[37]

By 1789 William Hazledine was working as a millwright and forge carpenter from premises on Wyle Cop, Shrewsbury, and subsequently established a foundry in Cole Hall, between Claremont Street and Barker Street, which he moved about 1796 to a site in Longden Coleham (SJ 493120). By the time of his death in 1840 the foundry had a street frontage of 93m., the exact distance from the eastern end of the *Crown Inn* to the western end of Terrace Buildings, and occupied a space of 4350 sq m. between Longden Coleham and the Severn. The centrepiece of the works was a clock tower bearing the date 1805. A steam engine provided power for lathes, cranes and other machinery, and the labour force totalled over 400 workers. The works subsequently declined under the management of William Stuttle, formerly Hazledine's clerk, and only some of the buildings were in use in 1856. Operations ceased completely during the 1870s but in 1878 it was taken over by Lowcock and Barr, and by Arthur Lowcock alone the following year. The main components were then a foundry building, 30m. x 15m., a fitting shop, 21m. x 12m., a turning shop, a smiths' shop, an engine house and a showroom, 30m. x 16m. next to the river. Lowcock used only about two thirds of the premises, the remainder, to the east of the approach to Greyfriars Bridge, which was opened in 1882, remaining in the ownership of the Hazledine family. Lowcock's business continued in Coleham until the mid-1920s, after which most of the buildings were demolished and replaced by shops and houses. The only remaining building is that now numbered 116-117 Longden Coleham, a three-storey, 10-bay structure, in soft red brick, whose dimensions, approximately 24m. x 12m., suggest that it was a fitting shop. A photograph taken when the premises were complete suggests that two buildings on the riverside with ventilators on their roofs housed the cupolas.

Hazledine supplied the ironwork for many of Thomas Telford's bridges and canal installations, but he operated three foundries and it is not possible to credit particular structures to Coleham, except for the roof of a bonded warehouse in

Shropshire Records & Research

31   *An early 20th-century view of the river frontage of the Coleham Foundry, Shrewsbury (SJ 493120).*

Dublin, cast for John Rennie in 1821, and gates for the docks at Newport, Mon., each pair of which weighed 120 tons, made in 1840. Several iron chimney pots on houses in the Coleham area which once belonged to Hazledine are also likely to be products of the foundry. In the late 19th century the foundry was noted for the production of Lowcock's economiser, a device which used waste heat from a boiler to pre-heat feedwater, developed in 1882-83.

VICTORIAN FOUNDRIES

There were several other foundries in Shrewsbury. The Eagle Foundry, established by 1834 and active in the 1880s, stood north of Roushill (SJ 491127) at the bottom of the Seventy Steps. Its equipment in 1847 included a 10 h.p. steam engine and a cupola furnace. Nearby, immediately south-west of the cattle market, stood the Smithfield Foundry, which in 1879 had a 10 h.p. horizontal engine, and three 3 h.p. vertical engines. No traces remain of either foundry, nor are there any records of their products, which were mostly agricultural implements.[38]

Several foundries were situated near to the canal wharf in Castle Foregate. In the 1830s the Phoenix Foundry was being worked by William Picken. It was from the Salopian Ironworks, in this vicinity, that Lowcock & Barr moved in 1878-79 to the foundry in Coleham. Nevertheless the best known foundry in the area was the Perseverance Ironworks of Thomas Corbett.[39]

Thomas Corbett (1843-1917) was a self-made and self-congratulating entrepreneur. His obituarist recalled that

> It was Mr Corbett's privilege to have conversed with half a dozen crowned heads and to receive from them warm congratulations on the services he had rendered to civilisation by his inventions.

He travelled as far afield as Australia and South Africa selling his machines. The son of Samuel Corbett (1820-1865), a Wellington ironmonger and foundryman, Corbett began at the age of 20 to act as agent in Shropshire for reaping machines made by Bernhard Samuelson of Banbury, selling 377 within five years. In 1867 he began to manufacture the Eclipse Winnower in a workshop in Chester Street, and was soon employing nearly forty men. In 1868-69 he purchased a yard in Castle Foregate (SJ 495133) from Treasures the builders, which was the nucleus of a factory which by 1900 had a street frontage of 76m. and occupied 0.6 ha. From 1872 until 1881 he worked in partnership with Arthur J. Peele (1838-1905).[40]

The buildings were designed by Corbett's kinsman, A. B. Deakin, and were crowned by a 20m.-high clock tower which incorporated a water tank. Components in 1876 include a 26m. x 8m. erecting shop, a 24m. x 9m. smith's shop with 10 hearths, an 18m. x 6m. packing room, a 15m. x 7m. machine and implement store equipped with a crane and a 16m. x 12m. moulding shop with two cupolas. Machine tools were powered by a 10 h.p. steam engine, and the sawmill complex by a 12 h.p. engine by Marshall of Gainsborough.

The Perseverance Ironworks was gutted by fire in 1905. It was subsequently rebuilt, although the clock tower was never fully restored. Thomas Corbett died in 1917. His executors maintained the business through the 1920s but in 1929 it was closed and the premises were adapted as an oil blending works. The façade on Castle Foregate reflects five phases in the growth of Corbett's enterprise. The oldest and most altered portion is a four-bay, two-storey structure, with a wide arched entrance, now blocked, bearing the date 1871, and a still readable inscription 'Speed the Plough' on an entablature above the wagon arch. On the western side are two two-storey buildings flanking the four-storey clock tower, each in red brick with blue and yellow brick dressings, each of ten bays in pairs divided by pilasters, and each with a blocked wagon arch in the central bays. The northerly building is dated 1873, while the clock tower and the southerly building are inscribed 1876. North of the 1871 building is a two storey structure in red brick with blue brick dressings, of five wide bays divided by pilasters with elliptical arcading above the first-floor windows. The ground floor windows are rectangular and divided by miniature cast iron columns inscribed 'Corbett'. On the western side of Castle Foregate is a two-storey building in red brick with blue brick dressings, of ten bays in pairs divided by plain pilasters, dated 1884.

Corbett's products are preserved in several agricultural museums. One 'Eclipse' winnower is displayed in the museum at Welshpool, while another ornaments a shopping mall not far from the *Queen Mary* at Long Beach, California.

Three foundries were making agricultural implements in Market Drayton from the mid-19th century. The Eagle (or Raven) Foundry in Cheshire Street (SJ 674343) was established in 1849 by the ironmongers William and John Rodenhurst. The buildings have been demolished, but the name is preserved in the shopping centre, Rodenhurst Court. The Britannia Foundry in Stafford Street (SJ 677343), one of many to be so named, was operated from 1841 by A.W. Gower. Several small buildings remain, and some old cast iron columns have been incorporated into a more recent structure. Only advertisements for elevators provide evidence of the products of the foundry worked by John Bruckshaw in Tinker's Lane (SJ 676342) in the 1860s and 1870s.[41]

In Ludlow a foundry in the Castle Mill (SO 507754) by Chaplin Hodges, a millwright, was employing 20 people by 1851. Later, William Roberts's Phoenix Foundry occupied the premises of the town's first gasworks in Upper Galdeford (SO 514750), and specialised in casting jaws for stone breaking machines. W. Clay was operating the Bridgewater Foundry on the canal wharf in Ellesmere (SJ 397345) by the mid-1850s. After 1920 its site was occupied by a creamery. W. H. Smith had established a foundry in Dodington, Whitchurch (SJ 542411) by 1856, with the intention of supplying 'anything his neighbour might want'. The frontage building of the site remains, a two-storey, three-bay structure now occupied by a garage. Smith moved to a site near the station (SJ 549415) in 1879 where the company continued until the 1970s. The foundry's specialisms included cheese presses, but the company was best known for its structural steelwork, particularly its Dutch barns.[42]

One of the leading British suppliers of valves evolved from the ironmonger's shop of William Underhill of Newport. In 1869 he extended his business by erecting a foundry near to the town's gasworks (SJ 748190), and was making steam engines in the 1870s. In 1906 the foundry was taken over by the Audly Engineering Co. who made valves on which was cast the inscription AUDCO which subsequently became the name of the company. It continued to operate in Newport until the early 1980s.[43]

The best preserved foundry complex in Shropshire is the Victoria Works (SJ 290291) in Oswestry, built by J Ellis & Son in 1870, and now used as a garage. The four main buildings form a quadrangle. The front range, in red brick, is a two-storey, 12-bay building, with the two middle bays projecting under a pediment above a wagon-arch. Each of the two single-storey side ranges to east and west is formed of 12 irregular bays, and has three wide elliptical arches on the courtyard elevations. The rear wing is also a single-storey building with two elliptical arched entrances and possibly another now obscured by a modern entrance on its courtyard elevation. The whole range has semi-circular headed iron-framed windows. Products included portable steam engines, grinding mills and threshing machines.

RAILWAY ENGINEERING

The first railway engineering concern in the county was the Shropshire Works, a 3.2ha. site, immediately west of Wellington station (SJ 647116), established by John Dickson, the railway contractor, in 1852. Its products ranged from keys for fixing rails to chairs to passenger carriages for the Great Western Railway. The business had a short life, and the site was taken over by Richard Groom the woodworker.[44]

The construction of the locomotive and carriage works at Oswestry (SJ 296300) was authorised by the Oswestry & Newtown Railway in 1864, and the works was in use by May 1866. The main components were an erecting shop, a foundry, a tender shop, a boiler shop, a locomotive machine shop, a brass foundry, a smithy, a carriage machine shop, a carriage-building shop, a wagon shop and a paint shop. All were accommodated within a single 247m. x 64m. factory designed by John Robinson of Manchester. The main front is the north elevation which looks across the tracks leading to Whittington. In the centre of the elevation is a three-storey block, with two bays of arcading on the ground floor and a cupola above, which is flanked on each side by five-bay structures, with semi-circular arcade headings and windows and circular lights in the gables. A seven-bay building at the northern end provides the only non-symmetrical element.[45]

The establishment of the works stimulated the growth of Oswestry, whose population increased from 5414 in 1861 to 7306 in 1871. Nevertheless the works employed only 137 people in 1893. Its main concern was the construction of passenger carriages and freight wagons, and the repair of the Cambrian Railways' locomotives, most of which were built by outside contractors, although two express locomotives, the 4-4-0s 11 and 19 of 1904, were built at Oswestry. The works was retained by the Great Western Railway after the grouping in 1923, and by British Railways. Steam locomotives were overhauled at Oswestry until the works closed at the end of 1966. It has subsequently been tenemented, although its exterior appearance has been little altered. A Cambrian Railways carriage is under restoration at the Welsh Industrial and Maritime Museum.

The Midland Railway Carriage & Wagon Co. of Saltley, Birmingham, established its Abbey Works (SJ 498122) in Shrewsbury, between the Shrewsbury & Hereford Railway viaduct and the line running into Abbey Foregate Station in the early 1870s. Eleven sidings ran into the main building, fanning out from a turntable at the southern end of the site, two lines ran to an engine shed in the north-eastern corner of the premises, and another to five short sidings between Abbey Pool and the Shrewsbury & Hereford viaduct. The only connection to the national rail network in 1882 was by a siding connection to the Potteries, Shrewsbury & North Wales Railway, but after its closure a link with the Shrewsbury & Hereford was established near to Coleham locomotive depot. The company was operating in 1910 but during the Second World War its site was used as a prisoner-of-war camp, and production was never resumed. The company claimed to produce all kinds of railway vehicles, but specialised in refurbishing secondhand coal, coke, ironstone and ballast wagons. The construction of a supermarket and a new road in the early 1990s has destroyed the last traces of the works.[46]

20TH-CENTURY ENGINEERING

The Sentinel Waggon Works (SJ 505146) was also concerned with railway engineering, although its principal products were road vehicles.[47] The company had its origins in Shropshire around the turn of the century when Daniel Simpson experimented with a steam-powered road vehicle at his uncle's engineering works at Horsehay. Development was taken over in 1903 by Alley & MacLellen and transferred to Polmadie, Glasgow. By 1914 the Polmadie works was short of space. George Woodvine, an apprentice from Horsehay who had become works manager, was instructed to seek a location for a factory. He chose a 20 ha. site on the Whitchurch Road in Shrewsbury, where construction began in March 1915. A new company, the Sentinel Wagonworks Co. Ltd, was formed in 1917, and from 1919 a model estate, Sentinel Gardens, was built on the opposite side of the Whitchurch Road.

32   *A product of the Sentinel Wagonworks, an S4 steam lorry, built in May 1937. It worked for the Buckley Firebrick Co., Flintshire, until 1957, and then for Early Transport of Wareham, Dorset. It is now in private ownership in Shropshire.*

By 1920 the Sentinel Works was employing 500 men and producing up to 32 vehicles a week. The principal product in the 1920s was the Super Sentinel steam wagon. A new model, the DG or double-geared wagon, was produced in 1927, and a new range of shaft-driven vehicles, the S6 and S8, in 1933. Variants included tipper waggons used in quarries and on civil engineering contracts like the Mersey Tunnel, the first British ready-mixed concrete vehicle supplied in 1930 to the British Steel Piling Co., tar sprayers and logging tractors. By the 1930s competition from oil-engined commercial vehicles was increasing. Losses were sustained in 1933 and 1934, and the company was liquidated in 1935. A new concern, the 'Sentinel

Wagonworks (1936) Ltd' was formed the following year. During the Second World War products included turret lathes and Bren gun carriers, and kitchen and bathroom units for prefabricated houses were made between 1946 and 1949. The last steam wagons, a hundred ordered for a coal-mining project in Argentina, were completed in 1949-50. The principal products of the 1950s were more than 140 buses and coaches, and over 1200 oil-engined lorries. In 1956 the company was taken over by Rolls Royce who, three years later, launched a range of diesel hydraulic shunting locomotives, 292 of which were built by 1971, along with a range of oil engines. After the collapse of the Rolls Royce company in 1971, the Shrewsbury works became part of Rolls Royce Motors, and was sold to Perkins plc in 1985. A new factory has been completed on the western side of the railway. Vickers Precision Components use part of the original factory together with the office block, but much of the site is occupied by a supermarket.

The Sentinel works was celebrated for its locomotives and steam railcars, carriage work for which was supplied by outside contractors. The first Sentinel locomotive was completed in 1923, and over six hundred had been built by 1958, many of the latter products being converted to diesel operation. Traction equipment was supplied for 292 railcars, more than two thirds of which were completed before 1930. The principal customer in Britain was the LNER which acquired 81 railcars and 58 steam shunting locomotives. More than 20 locomotives are preserved. Over 130 Sentinel steam waggons are preserved, together with nine motor coaches and more than thirty diesel lorries. Documents relating to production are held by the archives section of the Sentinel Trust.

Muller & Co., makers of watch screws, established a factory at Cleobury Mortimer (SO 670756) in 1940 as a consequence of the Second World War. Joseph Muller and Jacob Schweizer of Soleure, Switzerland, opened a branch in London in 1932. Such was its importance in manufacturing armaments that it was moved to a district unlikely to be affected by bombing, one factor in the choice of Cleobury Mortimer being the parish church's crooked spire, similar to that at Soleure. By 1945 the firm employed 350 people, and the labour force totalled 500 in the 1950s. The growing sophistication of machinery has necessitated two generations of new buildings, in the 1950s and in the late 1980s. The houses in Curdale Close were provided by the company for their employees, together with a canteen and a sports field.[48]

ELECTRICAL ENGINEERING

One Shropshire company was for a time in the forefront of electrical engineering. It sprang from the ironmongery trade, from Alltrees, of 43 Castle Street, Shrewsbury, in which James Aran Lea became a partner on 1 January 1867, when a speciality was the hiring-out of lighting for balls and bazaars. Between 1880 and 1886 the company acquired premises at 8 Chester Street (SJ 493130), where Lea's son, Francis James Lea (1866-1940), began to manufacture electrical equipment, which came to public notice when he installed a 16,000 candle power electric beacon on Titterstone Clee during Queen Victoria's Golden Jubilee in 1887. By 1893 he was operating independently of the ironmongery business, supplying bells, lightning conductors and telecommunications equipment, but his speciality was high quality light fittings, electroliers and lamps in wrought iron, brass and copper. Fittings were installed locally at Yeaton Pevery, Acton Reynald and at the Victoria Hotel, Wolverhampton, but the most notable contracts were at Sandringham in 1903, at McGill University, Montreal, and in 1894 at Cragside, Northumberland, the mansion built by Richard Norman Shaw for Lord Armstrong, where Lea's lamps and electroliers are proudly displayed by the National Trust. After the Sandringham contract the company became a merely local electrical contracting concern. The Chester Street workshop, demolished in the 1960s, was a three-storey, two-bay structure, with a broad bow window at first-floor level in the easterly bay, and two scalloped gables topped by pediments and spheres, above which was a sign in cut-out lettering.[49]

BUILDING MATERIALS

Landscape evidence from most Shropshire towns accords well with the hypothesis that until late in the 19th century materials for most urban dwellings were obtained locally. In Much Wenlock rubble limestone was used for many dwellings, and there are stone cottages which appear to be of 18th-century date in Shrewsbury, Ludlow and Bridgnorth, but brick was the predominant building material in the county. Only in Bridgnorth, where most 19th-century building was in the characteristic buff-coloured bricks manufactured in the Ironbridge Gorge, does there appear to have been significant use of bricks from elsewhere. There were many brickyards in the county's coalfields and in the countryside which are considered in chapters 2 and 4. The urban or suburban brickyard was a distinct species. It could be extensive. Substantial structures other than kilns were rare until the third quarter of the 19th century, and the nature of many bricks in earlier buildings suggests that clay preparation was minimal. Most yards operated seasonally and were worked by no more than three or four brickmakers.

In Shrewsbury a tract of waste land and an oddly-shaped recreation ground alongside the former canal mark the site of the brickfields of Castle Foregate. Examples of the products can be seen in the adjacent Primrose Terrace (SJ 496134), 32 houses, built in eight stages between 1886 and 1907 by the brickmakers, Thomas and William Thomas Williams. For much of the 19th century 1880s seem to have been made in the area in open clamps but in the 1880s a substantial clay preparation plant fed by two short tramways was built behind Primrose Terrace, together with a trio of round kilns. Production had ceased by the mid-1920s.[50]

The Shrewsbury suburb of Kingsland illustrates several aspects of the supply of building materials in the 19th century. The suburb was built on leasehold plots made available from the early 1880s by the borough corporation as part of a process which included the closure of the Old Shrewsbury Show from 1878, the re-location of Shrewsbury School which opened on its new site in 1882, and the construction of the Kingsland toll bridge, completed in the same year. Common bricks were delivered along a tramway constructed by the builders, Treasure & Son, and authorised in 1879.[51] It began at brickfields (SJ 477126) near Copthorne Road, whose site, formerly covered in hummocks, was developed for housing in 1993, and continued along the line of Porthill Drive which remains a narrow thoroughfare, continuing along the eastern side of Porthill Road, and the northern side of the lane whose course became the Shrewsbury by-pass in the 1930s, before cutting across the fields towards the School (SJ 485120). Many of Kingsland's houses were roofed with tiles made by J. Pearson Smith, the builder of Nos 13/15 Kennedy Road. Facing bricks came from further afield. In the White House, built in 1881, the Shrewsbury architect A.H. Taylor combined white-faced bricks, which were certainly not of local origin, with stone dressings and red brick string courses. Lloyd Oswell, architect of Nos 13/15 Kennedy Road, used bricks supplied by the Lilleshall Company, whilst the house of the tanner, James Cock, now the Junior High School, was constructed of bricks and terracotta provided by J.C. Edwards of Ruabon.

The same change, from locally-produced bricks to those obtained from a distance, is revealed in the contemporary but humbler suburb of Greenfields. Eighty lots off the Ellesmere Road, potentially 'one of the most attractive suburbs in the town', were offered for sale in 1880, but found few buyers. Nevertheless the streets had been laid out by May 1881, and the first houses, nos 25 Falstaff Street (SJ 493138) and 34/35 Hotspur Street, were completed by the end of the year. No 30 Hotspur Street was built in 1882, but most of the plots were not developed until the end of the decade; at least six houses date from 1888, 17 from 1889, four from 1890, 12 from 1891 and eight from 1892. Most the latter buildings are fronted with hard, shiny red bricks which might have come from Ruabon or the Lilleshall Company, but the earliest houses of 1881-82 are of the soft, buff-coloured brick, typical of many Shrewsbury dwellings up to that time. Many of the houses in Greenfields were constructed by Thomas Pace (1855-1933), a self-made builder, Liberal and Congregationalist, who migrated to Shrewsbury from Brierley Hill, and worked as foreman for Treasure & Son before setting up his own company in 1888. His political opinions may be reflected in the names of Hawarden Cottage and Gladstone Terrace, although Cecil Cottages and Primrose Cottages indicate that some builders held contrary views.[52]

There were brickyards in all Shrewsbury's suburbs in the 19th century. The availability of brick clay was one of the supposed merits of nine building plots along Wenlock Road and Sutton Road (SJ 506116) advertised in 1831, while 'an almost inexhaustible bed of superior clay' was available on a building site opposite Trinity Church in Belle Vue (SJ 496119) offered for sale in 1865.[53] Near the Column, the present Preston Street was called Brickyard Lane and an irregularly-shaped enclosure, Brickyard Field, bordered its northern side. It appears to have been a working brickyard in the 1840s. Seven enclosures south-east of Belvidere Road, known as Brick Kiln Fields in the 1840s, were occupied by Portland Nurseries before being covered by houses in the 1960s.

The change from local to regional sources for bricks was marked by the opening in 1896 of the brickworks at Buttington, Monts. (SJ 263097), constructed by Treasure & Son with the specific purpose of supplying Shrewsbury with 'a good, hard-burnt, sound, red common pressed brick'.[54]

Most other Shropshire towns drew their building materials from local brickyards which flourished until about 1900. In Ludlow the high quarry face of the clay pit

33   *Houses constructed with concrete blocks just before First World War, Nos. 14/16 Lime Street, off Longden Coleham, Shrewsbury (SJ 493118).*

used by brickworks north of the town and immediately east of the railway remains a feature of the landscape, and vitrified bricks, used for stopping the entrances of kilns, can be seen in garden walls along New Road (SO 513753). In Market Drayton there were clay pits in the 1880s just north of the railway (SJ 667345), and at Cleobury Mortimer there were two brickworks in the 1880s alongside the road to Ludlow (SO 667757, SO 669757).

About a hundred suburban houses in Shrewsbury were built with concrete blocks in the years before the First World War. The principal concentration is in Copthorne (SJ 498127), where there are 37, including dated examples of 1909 and 1911 on Copthorne Road and nine in Copthorne Drive. Others are in Longden Road, Armoury Gardens, Ditherington and Cherry Orchard. Four houses in Copthorne Drive, 11 in Porthill Drive, and six in Oakley Street are of brick with concrete block dressings, as if utilising concrete blocks remaining on the site when building resumed after the First World War. Most of the blocks are of 'Cyclops' concrete stone, supplied by G. & W. Edwards from their works next to the *Quarry Inn* by the Welsh Bridge (SJ 487126).[55]

MARKET TOWN HOUSING

The Shropshire market towns provide evidence of various patterns of housing development, and of several types of housing agency. In most towns by 1800 plots were lined with cottages, often of an insanitary nature. Picken's Court, later Britannia

Place (SJ 494131), on Castle Foregate was lined by 27 dwellings and two work-shops and a block of 16 privies. Only the entrance arch remains. Similar entrances to courts survive in Longden Coleham, and in Frankwell where a visitor in 1912 described

> many tortuous passages, shiny with the grease of generations, that lead to the holes there where men and women live and little children are dragged up....The courts and alleys lead nowhere; their entrances are difficult to find; their inhabitants are uninviting; the odours an abomination'.[56]

In Shrewsbury the cottages which lined such plots have long since disappeared. Many remain in Ludlow, Bishop's Castle and Bridgnorth.

Most Shropshire towns began to expand beyond their medieval limits only in the closing years of the 18th century. The first buildings to colonise the fields were often terraces, whether of four-storey dwellings for the middle class, like Holywell Terrace (SJ 501125) in Shrewsbury, built about 1830 by the bricklayer Thomas Groves, or the two ranges each of artisans' cottages, now numbered 26-48 and 50-76 Copthorne Road (SJ 483128), built by the Whitehurst family of The Mount House at about the same date.[57] Charlotte Row in Ellesmere (SJ 398350), which appears to be of the same period, is a terrace of 20 catslide outshot cottages, built in four phases, characterised by roofs of exceptionally thick slates.

In Shrewsbury houses for different social classes were developed in the 1850s on the corner of Belle Vue Road and Trinity Street by the architect Daniel Climie in the 1850s. On the main road he built the *Masonic Arms* public house (SJ 496117), and Honiton Terrace, consisting of three identical four-storey dwellings in blue and yellow brick, and a larger double-fronted house, with schoolroom attached, where Climie himself lived. Round the corner in Trinity Street was a row of 15 simple two-storey cottages in red brick. Climie used a similar system of colour-coding on the railway between Shrewsbury and Crewe, where he built the first-class stations, Wem, Whitchurch and Nantwich in blue brick, and the lesser stations in red brick.[58] On the opposite corner of Trinity Street was a development of the early 1860s, comprising a corner provision shop with living accommodation, next to which were four dwelling houses, which were adjoined by 12 smaller cottages which together now form the north side of Besford Square (SJ 495116), which had been built by the spring of 1866, when the 10 houses on the other side of the Square, which differ in detail, were standing half-completed. The first houses built in Oswestry as the town's growth was stimulated by the opening of the railway works were terraces of similar dimensions, of which Llwyn Place of 1863 (SJ 293298) is a surviving example.

Archaeological analysis of the speculator housing of the last quarter of the 19th century reveals something of the slumps and booms of the period, and of the small scale of individual developments. A peak of building activity in Shrewsbury seems to have been reached in 1882, when Edward Burley, an incomer

34 *The builder's plaque on Walnut Cottage, Gittins Street, Oswestry (SJ 294301).*

from Birmingham, constructed many houses in Tankerville Street and Cleveland Street (SJ 502127), Cherry Orchard.[59] The polychrome style of the latter was popular throughout the town at the time.

The best impression of the rhythms and fashions of the late 19th-century building industry is found in Oswestry, particularly in York Street (SJ 288299-290302), Albert Road (SJ 289301-292299) and their offshoots, where it is possible to sense the nature of a summer's work by a developer, and the waxing and waning of fashions like polychromatism. In Gittins Street (SJ 294301), Walnut Cottage (No 3) was built in 1881 by R Jones and Stanley Villas (Nos 7/9/11) by S Price. In Albert Road there are houses of 1880, 1884, 1885, 1886, 1889 and 1895. It is is possible to observe the supplanting of soft, locally-produced bricks by hard Ruabon-type bricks during the 1880s, and the introduction of pressed ornamental bricks in the later buildings.

The Shrewsbury Freehold Land Society was formed after the originator of such schemes, James Taylor of Birmingham, lectured in the town in October 1851.[60] Within fifteen months 278 shares had been taken out, and plots on an area of garden ground behind the prison (SJ 496130) were almost ready for distribution. By 1861 Albert Street, Victoria Street, the south side of Severn Street, Benyon Street and part of North Street had been built up by society members. In 1866 a further phase in Castlefields was developed across the Dorsetts Barn estate incorporating the remainder of North Street, Queen Street, Burton Street and Severn Bank.

The Society was less successful in Monkmoor where it acquired the five-acre property on which John Beck the banker had built the dwelling now called Orchard House (SJ 503130) in 1819. By 1855 plots had been laid out along a new

thoroughfare, then called Union Street, now Bradford Street, with several along Underdale Road. All the plots in the latter (Nos 26-46) were occupied by houses in 1875, but only five dwellings had been erected in Union Street.[61]

In 1860 the Society laid out the Oakley Cottage estate (SJ 493113) in Belle Vue, consisting of Oak Street, the eastern end of Oakley Street and Drawwell Street, originally Cemetery Road.

Castlefields and Drawwell Street illustrate well the characteristic pattern of Freehold Land Society development. Houses are built singly or in short terraces, rarely of more than four dwellings, with differences of building materials, roof lines and fenestration. It is likely that in

35 *The water tower of the Sentinel Gardens factory village, Albert Road, Shrewsbury (SJ 507148).*

36   *Houses in Harlescott Crescent, Shrewsbury (SJ 505160), built for the Chatwood Security Co. to the design of William Green in 1926.*

Shrewsbury, as elsewhere, the Freehold Land Society provided a vehicle for the small-scale speculator gradually acquiring a portfolio of residential property, rather than a means by which significant numbers of the working class could become property-holders. Societies in other Shropshire towns were insignificant. A society in Bridgnorth built a pair of cottages in Oldbury, while the Ludlow society in 1853 gave the name Constitution Hill to a property on Sheet Road but probably never developed it.[62]

There are two company villages in the suburbs of Shrewsbury. The Sentinel Wagonworks Co. began construction of Sentinel Gardens, opposite their factory, in 1919. The houses were of a high standard, modelled on Garden City principles, some arranged in cul-de-sacs, resembling those at New Earswick, York. A district heating system was installed, but corrosion in the pipe system led to its abandonment in the late 1920s. Its water tower remains in Albert Road (SJ 507148).[63]

In the mid-1920s an ambitious 'new town' was planned at Harlescott. The only part of the plan to be realised was the relocation of the factory of the Chatwood Security Co. (now Stadco Ltd) from Bolton to Little Harlescott Lane, on part of a 150ha. estate which purchased by the parent company, Hall Engineering. On the opposite side of the Lane was built a 'garden village' of 44 dwellings (SJ 505160), gabled semi-detached pairs of dwellings, with brickwork and woodwork of exceptional quality, grouped around a tennis court. The architect was William Green of Birmingham, who designed a similar estate for Hall Engineering at Burton Manor, Stafford. For three decades Harlescott Crescent stood isolated in the fields alongside the factory, but it was engulfed in a tide of suburban expansion from the late 1950s. The houses are well-preserved and the estate has been designated a Conservation Area.[64]

37   *Steel 'prefabs' off Crowmere Road, Shrewsbury (SJ 505126), constructed in 1945-6.*

There are suburban houses of the 1920s and '30s in most Shropshire towns. The construction by local authorities of 'homes fit for heroes to live in' began soon after the conclusion of the First World War. Shrewsbury Borough Council in 1919 hoped to range its houses on Longden Green (SJ 489114) around a village institute on a village green but such refinements were abandoned, and by the end of the decade councillors were regretting the poor quality of the houses they had constructed in Sultan Road (SJ 500137).[65] Some good examples of the prefabricated houses built by local authorities after the Second World War remain, particularly in Shrewsbury where there are many steel 'prefabs' in the Crowmere Road area (SJ 505126) and on the east side of Ludlow where there are concrete 'Airey houses' in Ridding Road (SO 520750) and Clee View.

The outstanding private developer was Fletcher Homes Ltd, a Blackpool company, who in 1934 acquired the former Royal Flying Corps road transport depot alongside Whitchurch Road in Harlescott (SJ 506152). Some of the depot's concrete buildings were offered for rent to industrial tenants, but most were demolished and replaced by housing, typical semi-detached pairs of the 1930s, with characteristic steel-framed windows, which could be acquired in 1935 for as little as £430. Some of the R.F.C. buildings in Harlescott remain in industrial use. Fletchers also built estates at Whitchurch and Wellington in the 1930s.[66]

On the other side of the River Severn in Monkmoor (SJ 514136) another First World War base was converted to industrial and residential use. A flying field intended for training was designed towards the end of 1917 but closed before the end of 1918, although the site was occupied by a non-flying maintenance unit from 1940 until 1945. Two Belfast-truss hangars remain in commercial use, while several huts from both World Wars are used by small firms, and some barrack blocks and offices of the First World War have been converted to private residences.[67]

Several Shropshire towns had 'rough suburbs' resembling Mixen Lane in Hardy's Casterbridge:

> .. the hiding place of those who were in distress and in debt and trouble of every kind. Farm labourers and other peasants who combined a little poaching with their farming, and a little brawling and bibbing with their poaching...The lane and its surrounding thicket of thatched cottages stretched out like a spit into the moist and misty lowland.[68]

In Shrewsbury such characteristics were to be found in the courts on the burgage plots of the medieval suburbs of Frankwell, Longden Coleham and Castle Foregate. In Much Wenlock, The Bank (SO 615996) on the road to Church Stretton was a collection of crudely-built limestone cottages housing 396 residents in 1851, most of them farm labourers and limeburners. On the edge of Bridgnorth, Bernard's Hill (SO 723927), one of whose thoroughfares was The Mall, was a similar extra-mural suburb. Market Drayton's western suburb, Little Drayton Common (SJ 663336), was less disreputable, even if the cottages were small, ill-ventilated and of miserable appearance. By 1837 there were 27 encroachments on the 36ha. common, which was enclosed in 1852. Subsequently population grew rapidly, 37 new houses having been erected by 1861, most of them occupied by migrants from neighbouring parishes. Like many such suburbs it had a small Baptist chapel, but it lacked the traditional beerhouse.[69] Ludlow's Rock Lane (SO 521749), a thoroughfare with some 'island' houses in the middle of the road, was an archetypal rough suburb, with an alehouse, the *Mousetrap*, a tiny Baptist chapel, and a changing population of agricultural labourers, brickmakers, knife grinders and washerwomen. A visitor in the 1870s commented on 'the squalid appearance of the poor cottagers'.[70]

PUBLIC UTILITIES

The relatively early provision of public utilities is one of the factors which distinguishes towns from the countryside. The most venerable of Shropshire's public water supply systems was that installed in Shrewsbury in the late 16th century, a line of lead pipes from springs at Mousecroft Lane (SJ 472112) to a cistern on Pride Hill. A second system was installed in the county town in the early 18th century. A waterwheel in one of the arches of the English Bridge, of the adjustable pattern designed by John Hadley for London Bridge, operated pumps which lifted water to a cistern in the town centre. The latter was replaced *c.*1830 by a waterworks in Chester Street (SJ 493131), where a steam pumping engine was employed. Many Salopians nevertheless drew their water from contaminated wells and from the Severn for decades afterwards. The Chester Street works was subsequently enlarged, and its last generation of buildings remains in use as a working men's club. It was superseded in 1934 by the waterworks at Shelton (SJ 464133).

Bridgnorth too had a Hadley-system waterwheel alongside the bridge, pumping to a tank on the Castle Walk. Wellington had a conduit system leading water along the Town Brook to a point of public supply on Tan Bank in the late 17th century. A water company, established in 1851, had built the Ercall Pool reservoir by 1859. In Ludlow in the early 19th century the corporation was responsible for pumps which raised water from the river to a reservoir at the top of the Butter Market from which pipes led to various parts of the town. Whitchurch gained its public supply from the waterworks at Fenns Bank in 1882. Wem's supply, pumped from Preston Brockhurst, was completed two years later. By 1900 most towns had healthy supplies. Some 19th-century reservoirs and small pumping installations remain, and there is a modest public display at the Conduit Head, source of Shrewsbury's 16th-century supply, from which some water is still extracted.

The process of draining towns in the county took a similar course. Lord Brownlow was instrumental in draining Ellesmere in 1869, after the formation of a Local Board of Health a decade earlier. Wellington's sewage flowed into the Bratton Brook until 1898 when a disposal works was built at Dothill. In Shrewsbury a system of ancient sewers, decanting their contents into the Severn at 'mudholes' near the two bridges, remained in use until the 1890s. The pumping station in Longden Coleham (SJ 496122) began to pump sewage to a treatment works at Monkmoor (SJ 520137) on 1 January 1901. The two Woolf compound beam engines, by W.R. Renshaw & Co. of Stoke-on-Trent, are now cared for by the County of Salop Steam Engine Society.[71]

The first gas lighting installations in Shropshire were at the Ditherington and Castlefields flax mills in Shrewsbury, drawings for which were prepared in April 1811. Gas lighting was demonstrated at the theatre in Oswestry in 1819. The first public supply, in Shrewsbury, began in 1820. Gasworks were built soon afterwards in Wellington and Oswestry, and by the 1880s every town except Clun was supplied. There were some gasworks outside the market towns, in the Coalbrookdale Coalfield, and in the large villages of Albrighton and Craven Arms. The gasworks for the Worcestershire towns of Tenbury Wells and Bewdley were also in Shropshire.

Some of the small companies amalgamated, the industry was nationalised in 1949, and during the 1960s coal gas production was abandoned, to be replaced by natural gas. There are few significant monuments of the industry, although several former gasworks sites retain equipment used in the distribution network. The stone perimeter walls of the first gasworks in Ludlow, abandoned in 1840, remain in Upper Galdeford (SO 514747). The site was occupied by the Phoenix Foundry in the late 19th century and now houses an agricultural engineering business. A muted expression of the industry's importance is provided by the truncated remains of the Shrewsbury Gas Light Co.'s offices in Castle Foregate (SJ 495133), a flamboyant structure of 1884 in polychrome brick and terracotta, originally of three storeys.

The benefits of electricity supply were demonstrated in Shrewsbury through the 1880s by J. A. Lea, who was supposedly closely concerned with the establishment of the town's power station in Roushill (SJ 492127) in 1893. It was initially steam-powered but diesel engines were used up to the time of closure in the mid-1950s.

A power station in Oswestry also opened in 1893, and subsequently local supplies were provided in Church Stretton in 1904, Ludlow in 1906 and Bishop's Castle in 1914. It was not until the early 1930s that other towns obtained public supplies. Power was brought to Whitchurch in 1931 by the North Wales Power Co., and the completion of the Ironbridge Power Station in 1932 enabled the West Midlands Joint Electricity Authority to supply Newport, Shifnal, Wellington and Much Wenlock.

The sites of several power stations are occupied by sub-stations including those at Roushill in Shrewsbury, and Corporation Street in Bishop's Castle (SO 322888). Fragments of buildings remain at Station Road in Bishop's Castle (SO 324886), at Crossways, Church Stretton (SO 458935), Portcullis Lane, Ludlow (SO 513749) and Coney Green, Oswestry (SJ 292296).[72]

Less is recorded of the development of telecommunications in Shropshire. The first telephone installation appears to have been the network established by the Western & South Wales Telephone Co. in Shrewsbury in August 1887 with a switchboard in Dogpole Court (SJ 673124), and subsequently in the *Clarendon Hotel*. From 1912 when the General Post Office took over telephone services the exchange was part of the post office in St Mary's Street, where it remained until the exchange on Town Walls was commissioned in the late 1950s. Early exchanges

38 *One of the largest buildings of the Second-World-War RAF base at Stanmore, Bridgnorth (SO 742929), of a type usually used as workshops in maintenance units. It is now converted to industrial use.*

were in shops or private houses like No 11 The Wharfage, Ironbridge (SJ 670035) where the National Telephone Co. opened for business in 1905, remaining until the late 1940s.[73]

CONCLUSIONS

Shropshire's 16 market towns all shared certain characteristic manufactures, the range and importance of which rose according to the size of the town—the larger the town the greater the number of maltings, and the more likely it was to have a tannery and a foundry. The larger towns, Shrewsbury, Wellington, Bridgnorth, Ludlow, Oswestry, Market Drayton and Whitchurch were also concerned with textiles, but none was primarily a manufacturing town. Many Salopians in the late 19th century expressed regret at the loss of manufacturing capacity, and a local newspaper published a list of enterprises which had closed. Twentieth-century industry in Shrewsbury has flourished largely on land which became available for manufacturing during the First World War, and on that envisaged as the site of the visionary new town of the 1920s. Military bases of the Second World War have influenced the industrial development of Oswestry, Bridgnorth and Wem.

The traditional market town manufactures have disappeared. Shropshire's last tannery, by the Welsh Bridge in Shrewsbury, closed in the 1960s. Wem Brewery, the last industrial scale brewing enterprise in the county, Wem Mill, the last to grind grain on a traditional urban water-power site, and Albrew Malsters in Shrewsbury, all ceased to operate during the 1980s. Coachmaking has been absorbed in the motor trade, and the links between modern engineering concerns and the forges and foundries from which some of them emerged are now distant. The Atlas Foundry (SJ 488127) in Shrewsbury was probably the last market town foundry to produce castings in the 1970s. Nevertheless the historic identities of Shropshire towns have been shaped in part by their manufactures. Over many centuries each was a concentration of corn milling, malting, brewing and tanning. Each had a range of craft occupations, all provided their own building materials, most had foundries and most developed public utilities. When reminiscing about Wem around 1850, General Sir Charles Warren recalled not only 'the sound of lowing cattle and squealing pigs and the rumble of carts and vans along the streets', but also 'the smell of tanyards and breweries'. Manufactures were part of the very essence of the traditional market town.

◆ ◆ ◆

4
COALFIELD LANDSCAPES

◆　◆　◆

Coalfields are unmistakably different from other landscapes, even when they have long ceased to be productive. Clay mounts topped with gangly birches, fringes of prickly grass at the bases of clay-faced cliffs, soot-grubby red brick terraces, underfoot layers of shale, clinker, crushed bricks or blast furnace slag, tracks apparently without purpose leading across ill-drained fields, wrought iron rattle chain used in fences, are the visible signs of past social and economic patterns which differ radically from those of towns or of the agricultural countryside.

The five Shropshire coalfields are all small by comparison with those of Northumberland and Durham, South Wales, Nottinghamshire or south Yorkshire, and less than a dozen substantial mines have operated in the 20th century. This study is designed to use archaeological evidence to draw out the economic and social significance of each, in the belief that coalfields comprise distinct landscapes, that they are made up of distinct types of community, and that our understanding of them is increased by comparative study.

THE SHREWSBURY COALFIELD

The Shrewsbury coalfield extends 20 km. westwards from the banks of the Severn at Uffington and Eaton Constantine to the slopes of the Breiddens and the Welsh border at Bragginton, and 15 km. southwards from the county town to Leebotwood.[1] The mines were all in the Upper Coal Measures, and were widely dispersed. Most were small, shallow and isolated, with the most productive pits in the area bounded by Hanwood, Exfords Green, Pontesford and Westbury. The deepest workings extended from the 128m. shaft of Hanwood Colliery.

The discovery of coal in the vicinity of Shrewsbury in the 16th century was greeted with enthusiasm, but it is doubtful whether local supplies ever satisfied the needs of the county town. In the 1840s locally mined coal in Shrewsbury ranged in price from 10s to 15s a ton, while that from the Coalbrookdale Coalfield cost between 12s and 17s, but large quantities of the latter were consumed nevertheless.[2] The peak of activity in the Shrewsbury Coalfield appears to have been reached in the 1850s and 1860s when over 300 miners were employed. The majority lived in Pontesbury parish, particularly at Hanwood, Longden Common, Asterley and on Pontesbury Hill. Most miners and colliery proprietors were locally born, although

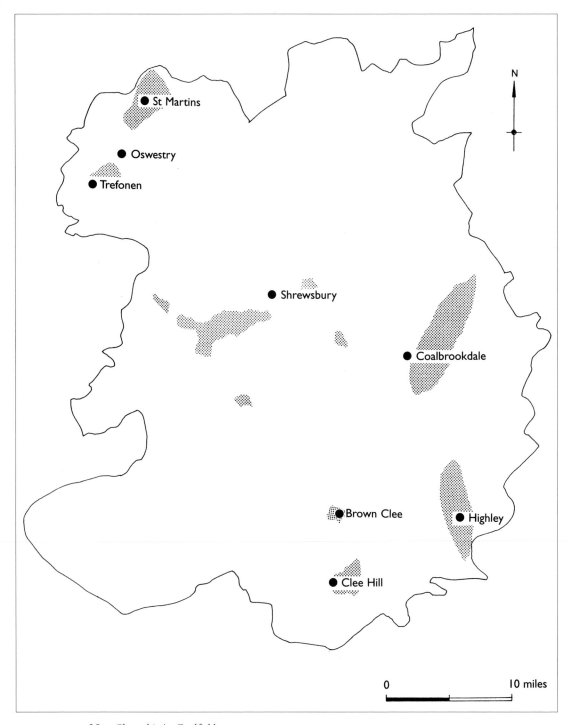

39 *Shropshire's Coalfields.*

Thomas Proctor who worked the Arscott pits in the 1870s was from Whaley Bridge, Derbyshire, and several qualified mining engineers from the Lancashire coalfield were working in the Hanwood area in the 1880s and 1890s.

The economic significance of a coalfield can be determined by its markets and the best archaeological indicators of markets are the remains of transport systems. Few of the pits in the Shrewsbury Coalfield were linked with regional and still fewer with national networks. Most coal was consumed in the immediate vicinity of the pitheads, or was distributed by road over short distances. In the 1840s coal from the mines at Uffington (SJ 533126), in what Murchison called 'the little patch of coal measures occupying the low ground between Haughmond Hill and the Severn', was conveyed along the Shrewsbury Canal to the Golden Ball basin (SJ 499138) near the Ditherington Flax Mill, which is now a housing estate.[3] In 1812 Richard Boothby built a railway from the colliery north of Moat Hall (SJ 450090) to a landsale wharf at Annscroft (SJ 455081) on the Shrewsbury-Longden turnpike road, which was extended in 1886 and remained in use until the closure of the colliery in 1934, being worked in its last years by a single horse called *Curley*. This was the only primitive railway in the area, except for short tramways at Bragginton and Pontesford. Most coal was conveyed to customers by road. In 1800 and in 1831 buyers were urged to collect coal direct from the pits at Welbatch (SJ 458087) alongside the Shrewsbury-Longden turnpike. In 1868 coal from Asterley was being sold at a wharf in Minsterley, to which it could only have been conveyed by road.[4]

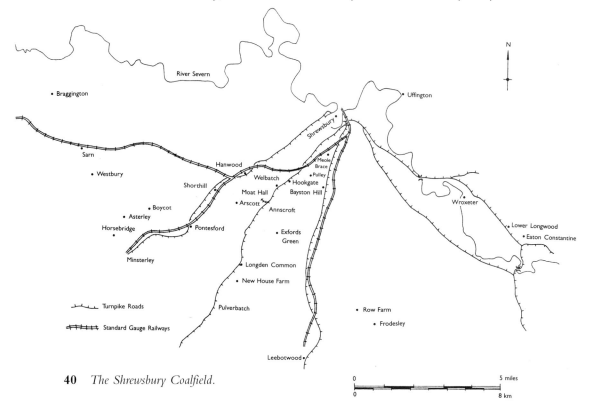

40 *The Shrewsbury Coalfield.*

The only pits with standard gauge railway sidings were at Shorthill and Hanwood, alongside the Minsterley line, and pits near Moat Hall (SJ 444081) served by the only mineral railway in the coalfield which ran two km. in a south-easterly direction from a junction west of Hanwood (SJ 434093).

Almost all the coal produced in the Shrewsbury Coalfield was for landsale (i.e. sale to customers in the locality who collected it by road), for lime burning, or for brickmaking. The only ceramics works which catered for distant markets was the Sarn Terracotta Works (later the Sarn Brick & Tile Works) near Westbury Station (SJ 347110), established in the 1860s by Thomas Kough and later worked by Edward and Thomas Greenwood, which probably employed most of the 18 brickworkers living in Westbury parish in 1871.[5] Bricks marked *Sarn* are commonplace in late 19th-century middle-class houses in Shrewsbury. Clay was delivered until the 1960s by a 2ft.-gauge railway from pits 400m. to the north laid in 1886.

The only other significant use for coal in the area was in smelting lead, for which the Nag's Head colliery at Pontesford and the Boycott mine near Malehurst were the chief suppliers.[6]

Some steam engines were used in the coalfield, the first of them a Boulton & Watt pumping engine erected at Westbury Colliery (SJ 366087) in 1781. An 18 h.p. engine was offered for sale at Meole Brace colliery in 1843, and a 12 h.p. machine at Homley Pit, Hookagate, in 1857. There were 14 colliery steam engine drivers living in Pontesbury in 1861. The only surviving engine house in the coalfield housed a beam pumping engine at Pontesford (SJ 410065), and was probably constructed by Samuel or William Heighway before 1800. The first documentary reference to the engine dates from 1817. It was out of use by 1828 and had been adapted as a dwelling by 1842, which purpose it still serves. The pump shaft lies about two meters from the bob wall. Insufficient evidence remains to determine whether it housed a Newcomen or a Boulton & Watt engine.[7]

Pits were small and widely dispersed. A mine was being worked near Row Farm in Frodesley (SJ 505019) in the 1740s. In the late 1830s only 200 tons p.a. of coal were being produced and only two min-

41   *The north elevation of the late 18th-century coal mine pumping engine house at Pontesford (SJ 410065).*

ers were living in the parish in 1841. The workings closed soon afterwards but traces of the shafts remain. Coal was mined in Pulverbatch as early as 1717. In the 19th century the centre of operations was New House Farm (SJ 436036), the home of George Fenn, a native of Shifnal, who combined farming 250 acres with mining. He employed 10 miners in 1851 and 28, including the driver of an engine in 1871, when his colliery manager was living close to the pits at Castle Place (SJ 446039). Fenn's son was employing 28 miners ten years later. The pits at Lower Long Wood (SJ 588062), between Wroxeter and Eaton Constantine, were sunk in the late 1790s and were worked in conjunction with a limeworks at Harley, and with a nearby brickworks. Working appears to have ceased in the 1820s.[8] There were workings at Bragginton (SJ 331135) in Alberbury parish in the 18th century, but about 1830 a considerable investment was made in the colliery, where a railway system, using both wrought iron and cast iron rails was established. Llanymynech limestone was burned there, and the proprietors offered to deliver the resultant lime to customers in Shrewsbury by Severn barge. Murchison observed that the thinness of the seams, extensive faulting and the remoteness of the mine from markets led to its closure in the late 1830s, although some activity continued into the 1850s.[9]

The most southerly workings in the Shrewsbury Coalfield, on the borders of Leebotwood and Longnor, were established in 1784 and operated until the 1870s, extending over 2.8 ha in 1796, 7.7 ha in 1807 and 16.6 ha in 1832-33, when annual output was 3,664 tons. The main colliery lay close to the turnpike road (SO 482999) where waste tips can still be seen. A steam engine had been installed by 1815. Much of the coal was used in limekilns and at two brickworks, one near the Shrewsbury & Hereford Railway (SO 475997), and the other east of the colliery (SO 482000), and there were lime kilns within the complex in 1810.[10]

The area immediately south west of Shrewsbury bears many traces of coal mining, although little remains of the pits which once operated at Meole Brace and Pulley Common, other than the occasional old cottage amongst the suburban sprawl of Bayston Hill. On the turnpike road to Longden, the settlements of Hookagate and Annscroft retain traces of their squatter origins. Around twenty coal miners were living in Hookagate throughout the second half of the 19th century. To the north of the Longden turnpike waste tips, some covered with woodland, mark the sites of Moat Hall (SJ 450802), Arscott (SJ 436081) and Asterton (SJ 375075) collieries. Along the Minsterley turnpike the surface workings of the Hanwood (SJ 436093) and Shorthill (SJ 430092) pits have been adapted for residential purposes. The Hanwood shaft was sunk in the 1870s, and in 1921 as many as 248 miners were employed at the pit, although only 50 were working there at the time of closure in 1942.[11]

The best surviving mining landscape in the coalfield is between Westbury, Minsterley and Pontesbury. The Westbury Colliery (SJ 366087) had four shafts in the 1820s, and closed in 1862, after which the Old Engine and the weighing machine (SJ 361087) continued in use as dwellings. [12] The number of coal miners in Westbury parish reached a peak of 55 in 1861, but only one remained 30 years later. There were six coal pits in the mid-19th century within a short distance of the centre of Asterley in Pontesbury parish (SJ 374071), celebrated as the birthplace of Richard Weaver, the Victorian evangelist who was known as the 'converted collier'. Waste tips remain at the Windmill Pit (SJ 373075) and the Farley Mine (SJ 382076), and extensive mounts extend along the road east of the lancet-windowed mission church of 1869, which is now a dwelling. North of the road a ruin remains on the site of the Big Engine (SJ 375075), adjacent to which was a brickworks. Many of the miners' houses in Asterley have been replaced or altered, but the ex-Primitive Chapel of 1834 remains open. Horsebridge (SJ 368061) in Westbury parish, 1 km. south of Asterley, typifies the small mining settlements of the region, consisting of about a dozen small brick cottages in short terraces, all with long garden plots.

THE WYRE FOREST COALFIELD

The luxuriantly wooded valleys through which the Borle Brook and the Mor Brook flow to the Severn form one of the most idyllic landscapes in England but beneath the surface lies the Brooch seam in the Upper Coal Measures, over 1 m. thick, and the countryside retains many traces of past mining activity.[13] The Wyre Forest Coalfield occupies much of the western bank of the Severn between Eardington, below Bridgnorth, and Bewdley. Most of the coalfield lies within Shropshire, although there were important workings around Mamble in Worcestershire. The coalfield experienced two principal periods of activity, one during the

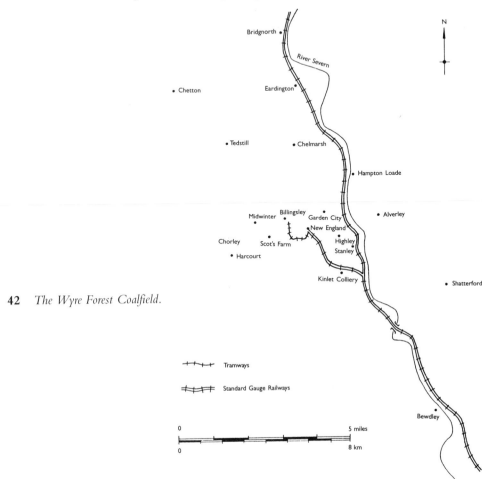

42   *The Wyre Forest Coalfield.*

Napoleonic Wars, the other in the last quarter of the 19th century, and the opening years of the 20th century, when coal masters realised that the Brooch seam could be mined, and took advantage of markets opened up by the Severn Valley Railway.

Spoil tips provide evidence of small-scale mining activity. A small 220m.-deep colliery with a steam winding engine, was operating near Eardington Mill (SO 715903) by 1847, but only three colliers and an 'engine tender' were living in the 'enclosure about the coal pits' in 1851. On the western side of Chelmarsh (SO 720872) are the remains of a small colliery, employing about a dozen miners in the 1850s, and about twenty in the 1880s and '90s, which provided fuel for William Partridge, a native of Broseley, who was operating a nearby brickworks in 1871. Mining on a modest scale took place for much of the 19th century around Chorley and Harcourt in Stottesdon parish. The coal from the shallow pits at Lower Harcourt (SO 693827) was prized in the 1830s for its low sulphur content. In 1881 nine miners and an engine driver were employed in the area and, in 1891, 17 miners lived in cottages scattered between Chorley, Harcourt, Midwinter (SO 702841) and Scots Farm (SO 707835). Mining at Harcourt ceased in 1924 but some workings at Chorley continued until 1933. Tips of coal waste are encountered during ploughing in the area. Waste tips around old shafts at Tedstill in Chetton parish (SO 693884) indicate the sites of coal and iron ore mines offered for sale in 1827. A steam engine was employed in 1851, when an adjacent brick and tile works was being worked by Thomas Evans. Only ten miners lived in Chetton in 1851, indicating the small scale of the operation.

Stanley Colliery (SO 749828) in Highley on the west bank of the Severn was developed in the first decade of the 19th century. A 20 h.p. pumping engine was installed together with two 7 h.p. engines which wound coal up the 100-yard shaft. Some 900 yards of plateway track conveyed coal to the Severn where it was loaded into the partners' two 60-ton barges, the *Sarah Mytton* and the *Bridget*. Coal appears to have been supplied to the forges at Hampton Loade, to limeworks at Shatterford and to a brickworks near Stourport. The colliery closed in the early 1820s and has left no significant remains.[14] Highley was certainly not a mining community in the mid-19th century. In 1851 only four miners were working in the parish, three of them in the employ of a John Davies, coal master, who lived at Netherton. There were only two miners in the parish in 1861 and just one in 1871.

The other substantial venture of the Industrial Revolution period in the Wyre Forest coalfield was at Billingsley, based on a 1,000-acre estate leased from William Pulteney. The parish clerk noted in his register in 1796 that a mine was being sunk by miners 'from the North of England', chief amongst whom was George Johnson of Byker, who was buried at Billingsley four years later. Two blast furnaces were constructed by his successor, George Stokes, the first completed by 1800. They were blown by a steam engine, which cost more than £4,000, and had a 52-in. cylinder, and a cast iron beam, still noteworthy at that date. Adjacent to the furnace were coke hearths and calcining kilns. The mine appears to have been drained by a 38-in. pumping engine, and minerals were wound up the shafts by two Trevithick steam engines and several horse gins. The workings were linked with the River Severn by a 4-km. plateway, with cast iron rails and a mixture of cast iron and

Shropshire Records & Research

43   *An early 20th-century photograph of the colliery at Billingsley (SO 715844).*

wooden sleepers, which descended into the valley of the Borle Brook by an inclined plane at the head of which (SO 716842) was a 2 h.p. steam engine. The trackbed at the bottom of the incline cutting is about 2m. wide. About fifty wagons were used on the line. The ironworks was taken over after Johnson's death by a new partnership which went bankrupt in 1812. It was offered for sale between 1814 and 1817, but it appears that no buyer was found and the buildings were demolished.[15]

The colliery at Billingsley (SO 715844) was revived in the 1870s after William Birchley discovered the Brooch seam beneath the sulphur-rich seams. A man was killed during the sinking of a new 200-yard shaft in 1876. By 1881 a steam engine was employed, driven by Issacher Jones, then aged 27, who lived next door to the *Cape of Good Hope* public house. Much of the coal was doubtless used by Thomas Davies, a brickmaker employing eight, who lived at Brickhill House. Coal was taken by road about 800m. to a wharf on the mineral railway serving Kinlet Colliery along which it was conveyed about 5km. to the Severn Valley Railway. In 1908 the colliery was acquired by the Powell Duffryn company from South Wales, but it was closed in 1921 with the loss of 200 jobs. The site is marked by waste tips and by several red brick colliery buildings.[16]

The shafts of Kinlet Colliery (SO 738818) were sunk from 1892 and the substantial engine house of 1896 remains as a ruin. It stood close to a brickworks, whose clay pit (SO 373819) is now a pool, and was linked with the Severn Valley Railway (SO 752815) by a mineral line along the south bank of the Borle Brook. The mine closed in the early 1930s.

The Highley Mining Co. located the Brooch seam in 1879 and began producing coal soon afterwards. The company had links with the North Staffordshire coalfield. William Viggars, the principal contractor and engineer, and Jabez Lawton, company secretary, were both born at Silverdale. By contrast, most of the 71 miners living in the parish in 1891 were from Shropshire, either from other mining parishes in the Wyre Forest or from the Coalbrookale or Clee Hill coalfields. Coal was despatched from the colliery (SO 745830) by a rope-worked inclined plane to a siding off the Severn Valley Railway at the south end of Highley station (SO 748830), which is still a well-known feature of the Severn Valley Railway. Some coal was used at an associated brickworks (SO 742829). The workings extended under the Severn and in the 1930s the mining company sank a new shaft 345m. deep on the east bank at Alveley (SO 752842). Its concrete headstock began winding in 1935 and it became the main production shaft for the mine, although the Highley shafts were retained for ventilation and access. The new facilities were linked with the Severn Valley Railway by a cable-worked inclined plane crossing the Severn on a concrete bridge, and subsequently by an aerial ropeway. In the 1950s the mine employed 1,250 men and was producing up to 30,000 tons of coal a year. It was closed in 1969.[17]

The sites of the Alveley and Highley mines now form part of the Severn Valley Country Park. At the Highley Mine (SO 745830) only what appears to have been an administrative building remains at the entrance to what is now the car park for the country park. The bridge (SO 753839) which carried coal over the river now forms part of the footpath network, leading to the Alveley site, where there is a visitor centre (SO 753839) giving panoramic views over the valley. The remainder of the mine complex is an industrial estate. The weighbridge house remains at the entrance, while the pithead baths (SO 753842) are now occupied by a building products firm, and some workshops have also been adapted to new uses.

Highley is an archetypal mining village, which is reminiscent of settlements in the South Wales valleys, the Yorkshire coalfield or Co. Durham. Its character is determined as much by the history of the parish as by its coal deposits. Highley was from medieval times an open parish, and in 1841 its 1,527 acres were shared by 39 landowners. As new pits were sunk in the late 19th century their owners sought to accommodate the workers not in closed parishes like Billingsley or Kinlet, but in Highley, whose population grew from 293 in 1871 to 1,985 in 1921, during which that of Kinlet rose from 432 to 501, and that of Billingsley from 119 to 148. Highley is characterised by its long brick terraces. Silverdale Terrace (previously Providence Terrace), a row of 25 dwellings (SO 741835) built during the 1880s, recalls Highley's links with North Staffordshire. The longest row, Clee View (SO 783843), consists of 35 two-storey tunnel-back houses, in soft red brick, and appears to have been built in the 1890s. In Church Street are six pairs of villas with terracotta ornamentation, mostly built in 1911-12, which were probably intended for supervisory staff at the mine. The Co-operative Store, built in 1905 and extended in 1912, which retains its beehive emblem, is remembered as the principal shop in Highley, supportive of the miners during strikes, and the centre for organising charabanc outings, sporting occasions and children's parties. Near to the Co-op is the Methodist chapel of 1913, in fiery red brick with a Decorated window at the ecclesiastical west end, which is similarly remembered as one of the centres of social life in Highley. The choir sang in the village on summer Sunday evenings, while the local brass band and representatives from other Midlands collieries attended the

44 *Clee View (SO 783843), the longest terrace in Highley, consisting of 35 two-storey tunnel-back dwellings, probably constructed in the 1890s.*

annual miners' service, when the names of miners who had died during the year were recited with respect.[18]

The most interesting housing is in 'Garden Village' a triangular area including Oak Street, Ash Street and Beech Street, extending south from an apex (SO 733847) at the north end of Highley, more than a mile from the colliery. Construction began before the First World War, and it appears that the housing was originally intended for miners from Billingsley. Nearly a hundred houses in what was then called the 'Garden City' were standing empty in 1919. The houses were built in 'blocks', whose numbers, on blue enamel plaques, remain on 13 Oak Street (Block 25), 13 Ash Street (Block 19) and 1 Woodhill Road (Block 1). The houses are constructed of bright red, Ruabon-type bricks, with some rough cast, and some timber framing. There are floral devices in some gables, and the doors have stained glass panels. The inclusion of bathrooms in pre-First World War houses in the countryside was considered a luxury.[19]

THE OSWESTRY COALFIELD

The mines in the parishes of Oswestry and St Martin's form the southern part of the North Wales Coalfield. The productive seams were in the Middle Coal Measures.[20] There were mines in most parts of St Martin's parish, except on the limestone slopes along its western border. In Oswestry most pits were in the upper

45 *Nos. 1/3 Woodhill Road, Highley (SO 733844), part of the Garden Village, built in the second decade of the 20th century.*

(Inset) The plaque on No. 1 Woodhill Road, Highley, identifying it as Block 1 of the Garden Village.

reaches of the Morda Valley around Coed-y-go and Trefonen. Some miners lived in Selattyn and by 1891 there were nearly forty were living in Whittington. Mining was was established by the late 18th century and was stimulated by the new markets opened up by the Ellesmere Canal during the Napoleonic Wars.

The mines in the southern part of the Oswestry Coalfield lay in the townships of Trefonen, Sweeney and Trefarclawdd, within an area less than 4 km. from north to south and extending less than 4 km. west from the Oswestry—Welshpool turnpike road, between the River Morda and Sweeney. At least 200 colliers were working in the area by the 1790s. The Croxon family, bankers of Oswestry, were working at least ten pits in the area in the early 19th century. The main outlet to the Ellesmere Canal was a tramway from the Gronwen pits to Redwith. In 1863 a standard gauge rail link was constructed south from Gronwen (SJ 277264) to a junction with the Porthywaen branch of the Cambrian Railway, on which an 0-4-0 saddle tank locomotive, *Tiny*, conveyed about twenty wagons a day. The northern part of the route is now a footpath, west of Sweeney Mountain. The railway closed when the colliery ceased operation in 1881.[21]

There were 140 miners in Oswestry in 1841, doubtless a decline from the period of the Napoleonic Wars. The total slumped to 113 in 1851, and to 99 in 1861, but there was a slight revival to 127 in 1871, probably linked to the increased

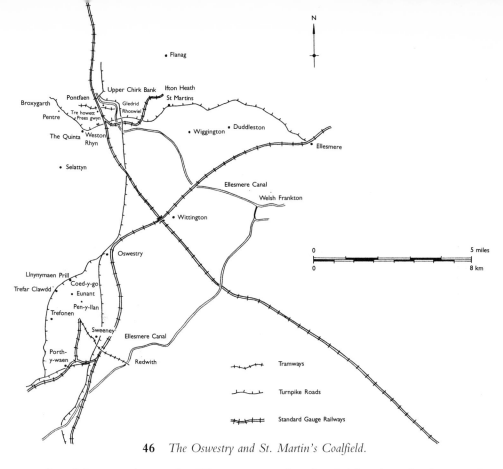

Map labels:

N

Flanag

Upper Chirk Bank   Ifton Heath
Pontfaen   St Martins
Broxygarth   Gledrid
                    Rhoswiel
Tre howett
Pentre   Prees gwyn
                                Wiggington   Duddleston
The Quinta Weston
            Rhyn   Ellesmere

Selattyn

Ellesmere Canal
Welsh Frankton

Wittington

0   5 miles
0   8 km

Oswestry

Llnynymaen Prill
              Coed-y-go
Trefar Clawdd
              Eunant
              Pen-y-llan
Trefonen

Sweeney   Ellesmere Canal

Porth-
y-waen   Redwith

Tramways

Turnpike Roads

Standard Gauge Railways

46   *The Oswestry and St. Martin's Coalfield.*

use of coal in ceramics works. There were only nine brickmakers in the area in 1861, but the number increased to 34 by 1871. Subsequently both brickmaking and mining declined. Only seven brickmakers lived in the coalfield in 1881, while the number of miners fell to 39 in 1881 and remained at that level in 1891. Coalmining had ceased at Trefonen by 1900 and large-scale brickmaking by 1905.

The monuments of this part of the coalfield are unspectacular. West of the village of Morda the former coal wharf of the Drill Colliery (SO 286277) is now a depot for minibuses, bordered by waste tips. Adjacent to it are six pairs of two-storey tunnel-back houses. Along the road towards Trefonen the sites of two further pits are by waste tips (SJ 282277, SJ 279278) as is that of the Pen-y-llan colliery (SJ 278282) on the north bank of the Morda. The British Colliery, opened by the Croxons in the 1830s, leased in 1860 by the railway contractor Thomas Savin and closed three years later, was at Coed-y-go (SJ 276277). The terrace called Eunant (SJ 272276), consisting of double-fronted, two-storey cottages of rubble sandstone, bears the date 1859. It formerly incorporated the company shop of the British Colliery. To the west is a terrace of six two-storey cottages (SJ 271275) dating from 1860.[22]

The turnpike road from Oswestry to Trefonen south of Llwyn-y-Maen (SJ 272283) was lined with coalworkings in the early 19th century, most of them closing in the 1830s. Some tips of waste coal remain near Pottery Cottages (SJ 262274) which were adapted from the drying sheds of the associated ceramics works.[23] Trefonen, where mine workings were scattered around Offa's Dyke, is a

47 *The waste tip is all that remains of the Penyllan Colliery (SJ 278282), which worked in the mid-19th century.*

48 Eunant, *a terrace adjacent to the site of the British Colliery at Coed-y-go (SJ 272276). The terrace was built in 1859 and accommodated the company store, a butcher's shop and a beerhouse. The cross-wing dates from 1875.*
(Inset) The inscription on the Eunant *terrace.*

squatter settlement, where in 1881 two groups of cottages bore the grandiose names of Piccadilly Row and Babylon. To the east of the turnpike road a waste tip has been adapted as a children's playground (SJ 262270) and what appears to be a former weighbridge house is now a hairdressing saloon (SJ 261269). From 1870 the Trefonen Colliery was worked by the railway promoter Richard S. France in association with the limestone quarries at Nantmawr. France re-ordered the workings, closing the Old Trefonen Pit and in 1880 opening the New Trefonen mine, which had two shafts, 44m. and 50m. deep, working the 6-ft. seam of coal and a 4-ft. bed of fireclay, with an intended output of 24,000 tons of coal a year. Surface components included a 15 h.p. winding engine, workers' cabins, a blacksmiths' shop and a weighing machine. The colliery continued to work after France's bankruptcy in 1881, and the census of 1891 recorded 25 miners at Trefonen, but it closed later in the same year.

Limeburning and ceramics manufactures were the only coal-using industries of the Oswestry portion of the coalfield. At a works opposite the rectory at Trefonen in 1851 John Howell was making tiles and firebricks, and a steam engine was employed at the works by 1871. By 1891 the Trefonen works had closed and a brickyard at Sweeney, managed by Philip Kent, a native of Silverdale, Staffs., employing eight men appears to have been the principal works in the region. Characteristic bricks were of a yellowish hue, and can be seen in 19th-century houses in the coalfield itself, and in middle-class dwellings in the town of Oswestry. The neo-Romanesque terracotta ornamentation of the west front of Thomas Penson's church of St Agatha, Llanymynech (SJ 268308) may have come from Trefonen, as may the bright yellow firebricks used in the astonishing Decorated Gothic facade of the Congregationalist Chapel in New Street, Welshpool.[24]

Mining flourished in the St Martin's portion of the coalfield during the Napoleonic Wars, particularly in the Chirk Bank area. Activity probably declined thereafter and the number of mineworkers in the parish fell from 128 in 1841 to 97 in 1851, but, with the stimulus of the Shrewsbury & Chester Railway, numbers subsequently increased steadily, to 215 in 1861, 261 in 1871, 299 in 1881 and 405 in 1891. The scale of investment is indicated by the increase in the number of colliery enginemen—four in 1851, 10 in 1861 and 16 in 1871. Initially the focus of growth was at Rhoswiel, where the turnpike road to Bron-y-garth crosses the canal and the railway.

A cosmopolitan mining community developed in the area. The principal investor in the Ifton colliery complex was Thomas Barnes, the Lancashire cotton manufacturer and railway director, and eminent Congregationalist who lived at The Quinta. Colliery managers in 1871 included men from Tynemouth (Northumberland), Kearsley (Lancashire) and Easington (Co. Durham). Most miners however were born in north Shropshire or adjoining parts of Wales. In the 1860s terraces constructed at The Lodge, and principally occupied by miners, were named after Prince Albert, Guiseppe Garibaldi and Abraham Lincoln. By 1881 there was a British Workman, a temperance public house, at Pentre.

The landscape around Weston Rhyn illustrates two centuries of coalmining history. In the early 19th century the principal mines were at Chirk Bank between

49 *Upper Chirk Bank—the footpath, following the line of the Glyn Valley Tramway, constructed in 1873, cuts through the early 19th-century waste tip of Upper Chirk Bank Colliery (SJ 292368).*

the Holyhead Road and the Ellesmere Canal. At Upper Chirk Bank the line of the Glyn Valley Tramway, opened in 1873, cuts through pit mounts of the early 19th century, providing a perfect example of archaeological phasing (SJ 292367). Two terraces are evidence of different periods of mining, Quinta Terrace (SJ 291366), a row of six two-storey cottages in soft yellow brick, probably dating from the third quarter of the 19th century, and, on the opposite side of the road, a terrace now largely rendered, originally of six very small houses, and of much earlier date. Pitmounts east of the main line railway (SJ 291363) mark the site of other early 19th-century workings. Further north are a few traces of Trehowell Colliery (SJ 290365) which was active in the 1880s. Only stunted mounds survive of the extensive surface buildings and adjacent brickworks of the Quinta Colliery (SJ 286367) which closed in 1880. East of the canal a range of coke ovens had been built at Gledrid (SJ 297365), part of the site of which by the 1880s was occupied by a brickworks, from which a short tramway led to the canal bank opposite the Glyn Valley Tramway's Gledrid Wharf. The brickyard was derelict by 1900 and subsequently replaced by a sawmill which still flourishes.

East of the Shrewsbury & Chester Railway John McKiernin's brickworks, operating in the 1840s, was displaced by Preesgwyn Colliery (SJ 293363), whose components in the 1880s included a headstock above a 152m.-deep shaft, a tall chimney, a powder magazine, a smithy, screens and railway sidings. By 1900 the colliery had closed but its site in 1921 became the terminus of the 3.2-km. mineral railway from St Martin's (or Ifton Heath) Colliery.[25] While mining ceased in Weston Rhyn, miners were taken to St Martin's along the mineral line in a train of three ex-GWR six-wheel carriages, and the mining community continued to grow.

50   *The pithead baths at Ifton Colliery, St Martin's (SJ 323363).*

Garden City style cottages in the village were commended by the Council for the Preservation of Rural England in the late 1920s, and Salop County Council constructed a large new school there in the early 1930s.

Mining in the eastern townships of St Martin's was on a small scale in the mid-19th century. In 1851 the Flanag pit (SJ 323397) was being worked by a spinster, Magalene (sic) Evans, who employed 12 men and five boys. Much of the coal was used in the manufacture at Duddleston of bricks, tiles, and black and brown earthenware. Ten years later it was operated by Evan Davies, a local preacher as well as a miner, who employed 13 men and four boys. The Wigginton colliery in 1857 was worked by four partners, all of whom were illiterate.[26] From circa 1880 the area around the parish church became the chief focus of mining in the parish. The number of miners in Wigginton and Ifton grew from 101 in 1881 to 181 in 1991. A new shaft was sunk by W.T. Craig & Son in 1912 at Ifton Heath. Production at the new pit began in 1921 and in 1923 it was linked underground with the earlier Brynkinalt pit, and the two were developed jointly into the largest mine ever to operate in Shropshire, which employed 1,357 men by 1928. It continued working until 1968.

The new pit stimulated growth in the old village of St Martin's, although many miners lived at Weston Rhyn, which became a dormitory satellite. A mass of small fields around the pit suggests that the northern part of the village had squatter origins, and the irregular pattern of older housing in this area appears to predate the modern roads. St Martin's grew in the 20th century, and has no long terraces.

Houses like *Garden Village* (SJ 321367), a T-plan cul-de-sac, of semi-detached pairs, with Ruabon brick on the ground floors and rough-cast first floors, with low-pitched slate roofs and integral porches, give the village its character. A Methodist Church, in Tudor Revival style, has rough-cast walls rising from a stone plinth. The Miners Welfare Institute, with its Baroque lozenge windows, is still at the centre of the village. The site of the pit is easily recognised. Part is used by road transport contractors, while the elegantly Cubist pithead baths has been converted to small industrial units.

THE CLEE HILL COALFIELD

The mines on the Clee Hills, between Bridgnorth and Ludlow, the highest points in Shropshire, form a coalfield, unusual for its situation, its longevity, and for the variety of its products. Almost all of it lies above the 1,000-ft. contour, and workings are recorded from the 13th century until the 1920s. The coal mines on Brown Clee, Titterstone Clee and around the village of Clee Hill are situated below and around the dolerite or dhustone, which was penetrated by shafts from the late 18th century. Since the 1860s the landscape has been totally reshaped by the quarrying of the dhustone itself.[27]

Brown Clee is the highest point in Shropshire. It has two principal summits, Clee Burf and Abdon Burf, the height of which has been reduced from 1,806ft. to just under 1,800ft. by 20th-century quarrying. Until the 18th century much of the summit was common pasture for surrounding parishes, and large parts remain unenclosed. A third but lower summit, Nordy Bank, provides shelter for the squatter community of Cockshutford on the north side of the hill.

The most obvious industrial monuments on Brown Clee are those of dhustone quarrying. A 2.4-km. inclined plane railway lifted wagons 244m. from Ditton Priors station yard (SO 610882) to the summit of the hill (SO 596866) from 1908 until 1936. The substantial foundations of the winding drum remain, together with traces of the railway tracks where wagons were shunted by four standard gauge steam locomotives and two 2ft. gauge petrol locomotives. The operation of the railway system has been described in detail by Smith and Beddoes.[28] Around the rim of the flooded quarry on the summit are ruins of crushing plants. A concrete tarmac plant of the 1930s remains at Cockshutford (SO 580850).

The mines on Brown Clee were probably of more economic significance for iron ore than for coal, which occurs only in thin seams. Ironstone was being extracted in the mid-17th century and the early 18th century, and in the 1830s Sir Roderick Murchison noted that vast heaps of high quality ore were lying on the hill. [29] The route by which ore was conveyed down the track from Monkeys' Fold through Cockshutford and Clee St Margaret to the blast furnace at Bouldon can still be followed on tracks and lanes. Bell pits on Abdon Burf in the area south of the inclined plane below the 1,600-ft. contour SO 597871) form an early industrial landscape of outstanding interest. The shale-like quality of much of the spoil suggests that they were iron ore mines.

Some mines on the summit of Abdon Burf were up to 64m. deep but all traces of them have been destroyed by quarrying. The sites of 19th-century shafts are still evident on Clee Burf (SO 592844). Murchison noted in 1830 that these mines were between 12 and 73m. deep, all were wound by common windlasses, and that funnels, of canvas fixed to wooden frames, were erected at pitheads to reduce the turbulence in ventilation systems caused by high winds on the exposed summit.[30] Nine miners were living in the hillside area of Ditton Priors in 1851, and 13 in Cockshutford and adjacent parts of Abdon, a number which fell to 10 in 1861, three in 1871 and two in 1881. Ten years later just one man and a 14-year-old boy were extracting coal. The lack of turnpike roads in the vicinity of the hill restricted markets, but some coal was used to burn the sandy limestone which underlies the Coal Measures, in the kilns between Cockshutford and Ditton Priors.

Coal workings around Clee Hill village to the south of Titterstone Clee extended from the Angel and Knowbury some 7 km. east to Hopton Brook and the edge of Catherton Common. At no point does the coalfield extend more than three km. from north to south. It includes parts of the parishes of Caynham, Bitterley, Coreley and Hopton Wafers. The early history of mining on the hill was analysed by the late Keith Goodman, who showed that extraction on a considerable scale had begun by the 1660s.[31] Much of the area has never been enclosed and many cottages were erected by squatters in the 18th century. Between 1745 and 1778 the number of cottages on the wastes of Snitton in Caynham parish increased from 49 to 68. The Knight family of Downton were mining iron ore for the blast furnaces at Charlcott and Bringewood (SO 452750) in the early 18th century. It would have been transported by packhorse, but the construction of the turnpike road from Ludlow to Cleobury Mortimer in the 1750s opened up new markets for coal, and the passage of Mr Botfield's cumbersome coal wagons down Angel Bank was regarded as one of the characteristic features of the region in the early 19th century. Output from the principal groups of mines, those of the Earl of Craven, was estimated to be about 9,000 tons in the 1780s. By the 1830s coal was being carried to Radnorshire and other parts of mid-Wales.[32]

Manufactures using coal were established on Clee Hill in the late 17th century. The lime kilns at Oreton and around the Novers provided a market for small coal until the early 20th century. Bricks were being made at Hints (SO 611252) in the 1660s, and tobacco pipes from white clay deposits near Hopton Bank (SO 620768) in the 1670s.[33] The name of the settlement of Glass House (SO 626773) suggests that glass may have been made on the hill, but this has yet to be confirmed from other sources. Pottery was manufactured on several parts of the hill and by the 1690s *Clee Hill ware*, distinguishable from *Boslom ware* from North Staffordshire, was on sale in Ludlow.[34] Wares and sherds have yet to be identified and analysed, but pottery manufacture certainly continued into the 19th century. One potbank working in the 1820s was on Angel Bank (SO 582758). Eight potters were living on the hill in 1851, but only one in 1881, and he was out of employment.

The Industrial Revolution brought changes to the coalfield in the latter part of the 18th century, not least because the Botfield family, ironmasters of Dawley, were from the 1780s working pits on the land of the Earls of Craven in the parish of Coreley. Steam engines appear not to have been used on the hill in the 18th century, doubtless because there were few drainage problems on a high plateau from which streams flowed through ravines. A navigable level serving the mines in Snitton was proposed in 1778.[35] The principal change of the Industrial Revolution period was the construction of two substantial ironworks. Each was sometimes known as the *Clee Hill Furnace* but they are better distinguished as the ironworks at Cornbrook and Knowbury.

The Cornbrook Furnace (SO 604754) was constructed in 1783-84 by Thomas Botfield, who considered at some length whether it should be fired with coke or charcoal, and whether its bellows should be worked by a steam engine or by water power.[36] It appears that coke was used rather than charcoal, and the bellows were powered by the waters of the Corn Brook, at least at the time the furnace was blown in. In 1786 the furnace produced 822 tons of pig iron but the output in 1796 was only 482 tons. The furnace was out of blast in 1804 and produced only 292 tons in 1805. In the 1780s the pig iron seems to have been refined into wrought iron at Botfield's Cleobury Dale forge. By 1810 the furnace appears to have been blown out, and it is doubtful whether it was ever commercially successful.

The shaft of the furnace is no longer visible, but may be covered by trees. The high level charging area can readily be recognised, and there are still traces of a leat from the bubbling Corn Brook, which was later utilised to generate electricity. A tip of hard, brittle, blue-black, glass-like slag remains on the site, intermingled with strata of a hardened, whitish material, rather like a coarse cement.

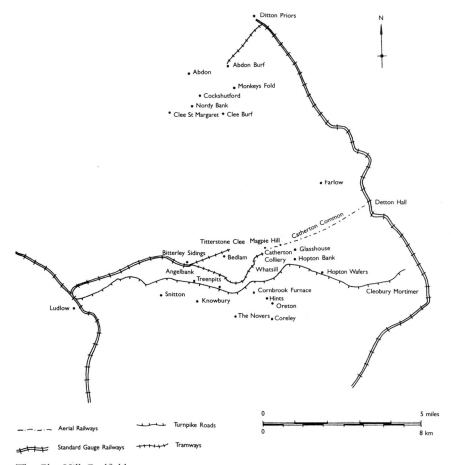

51 *The Clee Hill Coalfield.*

The ironworks at Knowbury (SO 580752) lasted rather longer, yet remained unrecorded in national listings. The blast furnace was built *c*.1804 by James George (d. 1816), who worked the ancient charcoal-fired furnace and forge at Bringewood. It produced 303 tons of iron in 1805. In 1825 it was reported to be out of blast but appears to have resumed operation, and a forge with puddling furnaces was built alongside. In 1845 and again in 1851 the furnace and forge, capable of producing 40 tons of wrought iron a week, were offered for sale. The furnace was blown by a 34h.p. steam engine, while an engine with a 28-inch cylinder operated the rolling mill, and a smaller high pressure engine worked the forge hammer. A range of 18 coke ovens stood alongside the furnace. Transport within the site was provided by plateways, and railways with wrought iron edge rails. The works was again offered for sale in 1853, together with associated coal workings and brickyards, the whole enterprise employing 13 steam engines.[37] Ironmaking ceased but the manufacture of bricks and tiles continued until the early 20th century. A house, probably adapted from an engine house, remains on the site, alongside a slag tip. James George Lewis, the last operator of the ironworks, arrived in New Zealand on the ship *Stately* on 22 February 1854. He pioneered the development of coal mining in Otago province, and died in Otago at the age of 88 in 1887, at the house which he had named *Knowbury Villa*.[38]

There were three principal coalmining enterprises on Clee Hill in the early 19th century: the Cleehill Colliery in Hopton Wafers worked by the Botfields, the Treen Pits in Bitterley north of Cleehill village, and the collieries along the Corn Brook in Coreley, worked by J. & W. Pearson. Peter Hewitt has shown that the Botfield mines reached a peak annual output of 20,983 tons in 1845. Output remained consistently just below 10,000 tons during the 1860s. Much of the coal mined in the 1850s was used for the manufacture of bricks and tiles which flourished between 1841 when there were only two brickmakers on the hill, and 1861 when there were 40, eight of them migrants from Broseley. Ten years later the trade had declined and only eight brickmakers lived in the area.[39]

There were 193 coal miners living on the hill in 1841, 273 in 1851, 186 in 1861, and 194 in 1871, but only 99 in 1881. Thereafter mining declined. Catherton Colliery ceased work in 1889, and its site was to be destroyed by quarrying. Watsill closed in 1912, and Cutley in 1922, while the last workings in Knowbury were abandoned in 1908. The Barn Pit was employing 27 miners when it closed in 1927. A short-lived mine with a wooden headstock above a 73m. shaft began operation in Coreley in 1935.[40]

From the 1860s the quarrying of dhustone replaced the mining of coal as the principal industry of the Clee Hills. The economy of quarrying depended critically on railways. When the Ludlow & Clee Hill Railway was projected in 1861 it was acknowledged that the market for Clee Hill coal in Ludlow had been destroyed by coal delivered by the Shrewsbury & Hereford Railway. It was anticipated that the railway to Clee Hill would stimulate ironmaking and ceramics manufacture.[41] Ironmaking was beyond revival, and brickmaking enjoyed only a brief spell of prosperity, but quarrying prospered. The Clee Hill Dhu Stone Co. under the direction of William Clark began quarrying in 1863. Most stone was shaped into setts in sheds around the quarries. By 1881, 194 quarrymen were living on the hill, 75 of whom were sett makers. More than half were migrants from other counties, chiefly from the Mountsorrell district of Leicestershire. By 1891 the output of stone from the Clee Hill quarries totalled 90,000 tons.[42]

The Ludlow & Clee Hill Railway extended 8 km. from its junction with the Shrewsbury & Hereford Railway north of Ludlow station to Bitterley Sidings (SO 574768), at the foot of a 2 km.-long self-acting inclined plane which raised wagons to sidings which ran along the south side of the Dhustone quarries. A system of 3 ft.-gauge railways extended through the quarries. The railway was operated jointly by the GWR and the L&NWR (later the LMSR), the usual practice being for a Great Western locomotive to work between Ludlow and Bitterley, and for the North Western to keep a shunting locomotive in the sidings at the head of the incline. A concrete-framed locomotive shed was built to house it in the 20th century. At the end of the sidings (SO 599761) was a warehouse where goods for shops in Clee Hill village were received, and from where a standard gauge mineral line (opened around New Year's Day 1867) continued across the bleak, boulder-strewn common, past the Stooping Stone (SO 604771) to Catherton Colliery (SO 611774).[43]

In 1881 another company, formed by William Field and John Mackay, leased land on Titterstone Clee and established quarries. A 3 ft.-gauge railway system, which extended down a long inclined plane to Bitterley Sidings, opened in May 1881, where stone was transferred to standard gauge wagons.[44]

In 1909 large scale quarrying was commenced on Magpie Hill (SO 313774) to the east of Clee Hill by Thomas Roberts of Ludlow. Stone was conveyed to Detton Ford (SO 663795) station on the Cleobury Mortimer & Ditton Priors Light Railway, by an aerial ropeway, 5.6 km. long, installed by J. M. Henderson of Aberdeen.[45] The development of quarrying brought patterns of terraced housing, new to the Clee Hills, like that at Bedlam (SO 582773) below the Titterstone quarries.

Field & Mackay began to manufacture tarmac on Titterstone Hill in 1911, and the quarries increasingly provided materials for roads designed for motor traffic. Quarrying reached the peak of its prosperity in the Edwardian period. Population of the area reached a maximum of 3,587 in 1901, then fell slightly to 3,290 in 1911 and 3,033 in 1921, before falling sharply to 1,856 ten years later. The demand for setts, the most labour intensive quarry product, was declining, although it continued on a small scale until the late 1950s. The Magpie Hill quarries closed, and the Detton Hall ropeway ceased operation by 1928.[46] The narrow gauge incline to Titterstone Clee survived the Second World War but ceased operation soon afterwards, and the incline to Clee Hill was closed in 1960, to be followed by the railway from Ludlow to Bitterley in 1962. The Clee Hill quarries continue to produce roadstone which is distributed by road.

The Clee Hills retain one of the most interesting industrial landscapes in Britain. On Catherton Common is an extensive area of bellpits, where the nature of 18th-century and earlier mining can readily be sensed. Two blast furnace sites are evidence of the ambitions of entrepreneurs during the Industrial Revolution. Above all, the cottages, crudely built in dhustone, and extended into terraces to accommodate succeeding generations, their plots delineated by low ramparts topped by hedges of holly, damson, crabapple and hazel, show the importance of open settlement, a key element in the industrialisation of other regions where the physical evidence has been destroyed by subsequent urban growth.

The Coalbrookdale Coalfield

The Coalbrookdale Coalfield is celebrated as the scene of innovations in ironmaking in the 18th century, as a region whose rapid growth after 1750 characterised the 'industrial revolution', and, above all, as the place where the Iron Bridge was built. More recently the museum which takes its name from the bridge has set internationally-acknowledged standards for the conservation and interpretation of industrial monuments. Nevertheless it is enlightening, initially, to examine the region in the context of the other Shropshire coalfields.

The Coalbrookdale Coalfield is compact in area but rich in mineral deposits. It extends no more than 16 km. north to south, from Lilleshall to Linley, and is nowhere more than 6 km. from east to west. Twenty-one seams of coal in the Lower and Middle Coal Measures bear specific names, indicating that they have been worked in the past. Several seams of iron ore, of fire clay and brick clay have also been worked. Carboniferous limestone occurs at Lilleshall and around Little Wenlock, while the Silurian or Wenlock limestone forms Benthall Edge and the eastern side of Coalbrookdale. Brine and natural bitumen are also found in the coalfield. The Ironbridge Gorge, where the River Severn cuts through the Silurian limestone and the Coal Measures, was cut by the overflow of a glacial lake, and proved to be the principal outlet for the mineral wealth of the area.[47] The natural resources of the coalfield were thus infinitely greater than those of others in Shropshire, and the means of transporting them much more convenient.

The economy of the Coalbrookdale Coalfield expanded in the late 16th century and through the 17th century. Malcolm Wanklyn has shown that the population of Broseley grew from less than 150 in 1570 to around 2,000 in 1700, while that of Benthall rose from less than 80 to over 500. This prosperity was based on the export of coal, on the application of new technology to coal mining, and on a proliferation of new coal-based manufactures.[48] In the 18th century the industrial uses of coal increased further, and in particular it came to be used in ironmaking. In the 1750s nine blast furnaces were built in the coalfield, transforming its economy, which was to be dominated for more than a century by large concerns which leased mines from landowners, extracted coal, iron ore, clay and limestone, smelted iron ore in blast furnaces, refined pig iron in forges, made iron castings, fabricated machines in engineering shops, and sold wide ranges of products, coal, limestone, lime, bricks, pig iron, wrought iron, and iron products. The population of the coalfield grew from around 20,000 in 1760 to 34,000 in 1801, and to over 50,000 by 1851. The closing years of the 18th century were a time of intellectual ferment, when the first steam railway locomotive was constructed, and an integrated alkali works and an oil engine were contemplated. The iron industry suffered severely during the recession following the Napoleonic Wars, but recovered in the 1820s, when new ironworks were constructed along the eastern edge of the coalfield.

The region lost its zeal for innovation, but in some areas remained in the vanguard of industrial progress. The Coalbrookdale Company was one of the principal manufacturers of decorative castings. The New Yard of the Lilleshall Company, built in the late 1850s, was one of Britain's leading engineering works. The decorative tile works built by Maw & Co. and Craven Dunnill & Co. in Jackfield were rivalled in size by only one other works in Britain. From the 1870s the ironworks began to close, the integrated companies were broken up, the economy of the coalfield went into rapid decline, and population declined as many sought employment elsewhere. A few companies, notably GKN Sankey at Hadley, prospered during the first half of the 20th century, and low labour costs and the availability of cheap, low quality accommodation, combined with the removal of the Woolwich Arsenal to Donnington, created a veneer of economic well-being after the Second World War. Nevertheless traditional industries—mining, ceramics, ironworking, railways—were continuing to decline, and the underlying situation in 1960 was not essentially different from that of three decades earlier, when Ramsay Macdonald described the Wrekin area as 'a summary of the nation's problems'.

Since the 1960s the coalfield has been transformed by the creation of the new town of Telford, which has brought to the region many new manufactures, and transformed its housing and landscape. Traditional industries have continued to decline. The last blast furnace ceased operation in 1959, the last coal mine 20 years later, and one brickworks is all that remains of the coalfield's ceramics manufactures. Much has been conserved, particularly in the Ironbridge Gorge, but much archaeological evidence has been lost. Many houses were recorded, if inadequately, and those parts of the canal system which disappeared were reasonably well documented and photographed. The opportunity presented by open-cast coal and clay workings to learn more about 17th-century, 18th-century and 19th-century mining technology has been lost. Some old workings have been photographed, with their pit props and slack-filled gobs, where coal had been removed by longwall methods, and some tools, rails and pipes have been retrieved, but demands for coherent programmes of recording have been consistently resisted.

THE COALBROOKDALE COALFIELD: SETTLEMENTS

The growth of mining and manufactures was not due simply to natural resources and to the will of entrepreneurs to exploit them. It depended crucially on the availability of labour, and of settlements where workers could live. It is evident that in some parts of the coalfield were areas of open settlement, either common land on which newcomers could erect squatter cottages, or land on which landowners readily permitted the construction or extension of dwellings. The Ironbridge Gorge is the prime area of such settlement, but it also occurred in Broseley Wood, at Ketley Bank, at Wrockwardine Wood, and in several smaller pockets. Such patterns of settlement had begun by 1600, but the earliest buildings of which there is archaeological evidence in the form of surviving buildings or photographs date from the late 17th century, and it is clear that they were constructed by specialist builders.[49] Evidence from wills shows that many small houses were extended into terraces to accommodate succeeding generations of families, and several examples remain in the Ironbridge Gorge.

LOST HOUSING IN THE COALBROOKDALE COALFIELD

52 *The rear elevation of No.24 Forge Row, Old Park (SJ 697093), a four-bedroom cottage constructed in the 1790s by the Botfields, one of the most spacious workers' dwellings in the coalfield.*
53 *The Long Row or Top Row at Dark Lane (SJ 703087) built by the Botfields c.1830. The terrace was 168m. long and contained 30 interlocking dwellings.*

The building of more formal terraced housing accompanied the growing scale of industrial enterprises in the mid-18th century. Tea Kettle Row (SJ 666049), the first terrace in Coalbrookdale, was built in three phases between 1735 and 1742 by Richard Ford, manager of the ironworks, as a private speculation, each dwelling having two rooms and a pantry. [50] When the Coalbrookdale Company set up the ironworks at Horsehay in the 1750s, a terrace of 27 four-room cottages, the Old Row (SJ 673072), was built in three stages, and well into the 19th century continued to accommodate the more skilled workers. The company built a row of 28 back-to-back houses at their ironworking settlement at Newdale (SJ 674095) *c.*1760. A succession of rows of interlocking cottages with characteristic L-plans was built in Coalbrookdale in the 1780s and 1790s, of which Carpenters' Row (SJ 668046) and Engine Row (SJ 669048) still remain. Further rows were built in the Horsehay area in the 1830s, the New Row (SJ 672073) alongside the furnace pool, with ceramic devices over the doors and drip moulds over the windows, 'for the principal workmen', and Sandy Bank Row (SJ 679066) which is now demolished and Frame Lane Row (SJ 677068), plainer houses for brickmakers. The Old Park Company built over 50 houses in the 1790s. Some, like Forge Row (SJ 673093), were spacious and were doubtless designed to attract skilled workers at a time of labour shortage. All were demolished in the 1970s, as were the less spacious dwellings built by the company in the 1820s, the interlocking cottages at Dark Lane (SJ 703087), and the back-to-back row which formed part of the settlement of Hinkshay (SJ 696074). Terraces were also constructed by the Lightmoor Company, by the Madeley Wood Company at Blists Hill (SJ 696036), by William Reynolds at Coalport, and by James Foster, who built the settlement at The Aqueduct (SJ 694058) to accommodate ironworkers moving from Wombridge to Madeley Court in the 1840s. In the north of the coalfield the long terraces of single storey dwellings, known as *barrack houses*, appear to have been built in the 18th century, not by entrepreneurs, nor by landlords nor by occupiers, but by speculators. A few isolated examples remain, and the barracks at Lilleshall (SJ 732164) were surveyed, but there are few records other than maps of the long rows at Donnington Barracks or Waxhill Barracks.[51]

While the ironworking companies built rows, the tradition of squatter building continued. In 1772 there were six cottages in Holywell Lane (SJ 677058) in Little Dawley, but 20 more had been constructed by 1825, untidily crammed together on what had been garden plots, with the bedrooms of some dwellings extending over the ground floor rooms of others. The cottage from nearby Burroughs Bank (SJ 675056), which was removed to the Blists Hill Open Air Museum in 1978, was not built until the 1840s. It is a crude structure in Coal Measure sandstone, 6m. x 3.6m., with a roof of uncut timbers, which in 1861 was accommodating a family of nine. The same tradition of building continued at Ketley, Bank where it was probably curtailed when James Loch became agent on the Marquess of Stafford's estate in 1812, and elsewhere, but it had probably ceased throughout the Coalfield by 1850.[52]

St George's, which grew up in the 1850s and 1860s to accommodate workers at the Lilleshall Company's Priorslee ironworks and New Yard engineering works, and was formally named at a public meeting on 19 December 1859, was the most urban part of the coalfield. While many of its communal facilities were provided by the Lilleshall Company and the Dukes of Sutherland, its terraced housing appears to have been constructed by small-scale speculators. The two southern corners of the crossroads at St George's retain an essentially urban Victorian quality.[53]

The coalfield failed to develop a single commercial, administrative and cultural centre. Only at Ironbridge are there shops and public buildings consciously designed as part of an urban landscape. The settlement at the northern end of the bridge was developed, probably by the bridge proprietors acting in other capacities, in the last 20 years of the 18th century. Most of the buildings which overlook The Square have a distinct urban quality, but the shops on its fringes are domestic in scale. There was further concern with buildings of distinction in the early 1860s when the Severn Valley Railway was opened. The *Station Inn* on the south bank of the river, the police station and St Luke's School were all built in the blue facing bricks which were being produced by the Coalbrookdale Company at that time.[54]

Archaeological study of other retailing centres, Dawley, Madeley and Oakengates, shows that almost all the shops, public houses and even the branch banks were built in the mid-19th century, and were domestic in scale, probably replacing the first generations of buildings on the sites concerned. Few are more than three bays wide, or more than two storeys in height. Most look like converted houses even if they were built as shops, and the few imposing facades appear to be relatively late additions. Competition between centres, between Broseley, Ironbridge and Madeley in the south of the coalfield, and between Wellington, Oakengates, St George's and Dawley in the centre, prevented the emergence of any one of them as the acknowledged urban centre of the region.[55]

THE COALBROOKDALE COALFIELD: MARKETS AND TRANSPORT

One difference between the Coalbrookdale Coalfield and others is expressed in two archaic expressions, *landsale* of coal, which occurred in all the Shropshire coalfields, and *Severn sale*, the despatch of coal along the river, which took place only in the Ironbridge Gorge. There was some landsale in the Coalbrookdale coalfield; a railway in the 1740s took coal from the Horse Pasture workings in Wombridge to a wharf on Watling Street, somewhere on the site of the main street of Oakengates (SJ 697109), coal from Little Wenlock was conveyed to a wharf at the Old Hall (SJ 656110), also on Watling Street, and the Donnington Wood Canal, dug in the 1760s, terminated at a landsale wharf on the Newport—Wolverhampton road at Pave Lane (SJ 760115).[56] Nevertheless it was the trade in coal on the Severn from the wharves in the Ironbridge Gorge which was the basis of the Coalfield's prosperity from the late 16th century until after 1850. In the 1660s it was claimed that the coal trade supported 2,500 families, and that as much as 100,000 tons of coal per year were sent down the Severn from the Gorge. By 1800 around 50,000 tons p.a. were being despatched from Coalport alone, a total which reached a peak of nearly 80,000 tons in 1830. Navigation on the Severn was always unpredictable, but the river remained until the third quarter of the 19th century the chief outlet not just for coal, but for all the varied products of the Coalbrookdale Coalfield.

The role of the river was emphasised by primitive railway systems, most of which terminated at wharves on the bank of the Severn. The first to be recorded ran from the Birch Leasows near Broseley parish church (SJ 678014) to the River Severn near the Calcutts (SJ 686030), and was the subject of a dispute in the court of Star Chamber in 1608.[57] When in 1634 John Weld wrote his memorandum on the future of the Willey estate, he mentioned railways in ways which show that they were an accepted and unremarkable part of the landscape of the district, and at least five lines ran to the Severn by 1700. Most primitive railways had few cuttings, embankments or bridges of note, and have left few traces, even in plough soil. A flanged wheel, found at Caughley early in the 20th century and now in the custody of the Ironbridge Gorge Museum, is one of the few surviving artefacts of early railways. It is shaped from a single block of elm, and is 25cm. in diameter over the flange, and 20cm. over the tread, the latter being 9.5cm. wide. The only wooden railway track found in the district was uncovered near Bedlam Furnaces in 1986. Both rails and sleepers were of oak, the gauge was 1.14m., and furnace slag had been used as ballast.[58]

Iron wheels for railway vehicles were cast at Coalbrookdale in 1729, probably for Richard Hartshorne's line from Little Wenlock to the wharf at Strethill (SJ 658041). By the 1750s a system of two-level wooden rails known as the *double way* was in use, and in 1767 iron rails, 6ft. long, 3˜in. wide and 1˜in. thick were used by Richard Reynolds to replace the top layers of wood. In the late 1780s at the instigation of the Sheffield coal viewer John Curr, L-section iron *plate rails* known in Shropshire as *jinny* or *jenny* rails were introduced, necessitating the replacement of flanged wheels by smooth-rimmed wheels on railway vehicles. The new system had many advantages over previous forms of railway, and wooden rails and iron edge rails appear to have been replaced quickly.

Plate rails, in wrought iron or cast iron, are some of the most frequently found archaeological artefacts in the coalfield. Sleepers were mostly of cast iron, but some wrought iron examples have been found, together with some stone blocks, and documentary sources show that wooden sleepers were used on some lines. Archaeo-logical investigations have demonstrated a contrast between plateways laid very simply, for such purposes as carrying waste to tips, and some which were con-structed with great care, with sleepers at the joints and mid-points of rails, brick trotting paths between the rails, hammered clay over the sleepers at joints, and wooden longitudinal sleepers beneath the rails. Railways of at least six different gauges were used in the area, and the Coalbrookdale Co. had dual gauge plateways, a section of which remains in situ at Rose Cottage, Coalbrookdale (SJ 668041). The characteristic form of Shropshire railway vehicles, small, with low sides, so that minerals had to be affixed by wrought iron hoops, was unaffected by the introduc-tion of plateways. A few specialist vehicles were used. A box wagon with a sloping top is shown in an early 19th-century picture. A tank wagon appears in a photo-graph of the 1860s, and a similar vehicle, once used for carrying waste tar at Horsehay, is preserved at Blists Hill, together with chassis of conventional wagons from the Coalbrookdale and Madeley Wood companies. The Ironbridge Gorge Museum holds a collection of rails, sleepers, and wagon wheels, together with stone

54   *Plateway track uncovered during building work at Ketley (SJ 676105) in 1969. The rails are of cast iron, the sleepers of wrought iron with the inner faces of the shoes secured by rivets. On the left is a cast iron railing plate used to guide wheels of vehicles raised up pit shafts on to the rails.*

blocks from the Yard Rails at Donnington Wood (SJ 706124). The longest plateway route extended 9 km. from Oakengates to Sutton Wharf (SJ 709015), built in 1797, and closed, by agreement with the rival Shropshire Canal Co., in 1814. Excavations on its course through Halesfield in the late 1960s revealed that its trotting path was made up of puddling furnace slag. The density of the mid-19th-century network of plateways in the coalfield is illustrated on Greenwood's map of 1827. Plateways remained in use as feeders of standard gauge railways, which crossed them on bridges, which allowed a much narrower track for the plateway than that for a road, examples of which survive at Lightmoor (SJ 677050) and Trench 683126). Plateways remained in use on a small scale until the 1960s.[59]

The most impressive civil engineering monument of an 18th-century railway in the coalfield is a two-arch masonry bridge over the Ketley Brook at Newdale (SJ 675095), probably of *c.*1760. The high-level latticework bridge across Lee Dingle (SJ 694035) built in the 1880s is evidence of the continuing use of plateways in the late 19th century. Several primitive railways descended the slopes of the Ironbridge Gorge on inclined planes, the first of which were operating by 1750. The best traces of such inclines are at Bagley's Wind (SJ 693036) west of Blists Hill, on Benthall Edge rising from the limekilns by the Severn Valley Railway (SJ 666034), and the Old Wind above Coalbrookale (SJ 670051), but there were others which cannot easily be traced, like Jigger's Bank, north of Coalbrookdale, and the incline which took traffic from the Old Wind to the riverside at Dale End. There were several small inclines within ironworks complexes like that behind the south engine house at Blists Hill. The outstanding innovation in mechanical railway engineering was the construction at Coalbrookdale by Richard Trevithick in 1802 of the world's first steam railway locomotive. There is no evidence that it was set to work, and the death of William Reynolds the following year may have brought the experiment to a halt, but the locomotive was drawn, and a working replica is now displayed in the Ironbridge Gorge Museum.[60]

Innovation in railway technology ceased in Shropshire after 1802 and the developments which produced the main line railway in 1830 took place in the North of England. Archaeological evidence has revealed just one intermediate phase in the Coalbrookdale Coalfield, the construction by James Foster of a network of narrow gauge lines laid with Birkinshaw rails, wrought iron, T–section edge rails, set in cast iron sleepers, when he developed the Madeley Court collieries and ironworks from 1843. Samples are held in the Ironbridge Gorge Museum.

The first main line railways in the coalfield, from Shrewsbury to Wellington and thence to Stafford and Wolverhampton, opened in 1849. Lines which ultimately belonged to the Great Western Railway extended from Wellington and from a junction near Shifnal to Lightmoor and Coalbrookdale, crossing the Severn by the Coalbrookdale Company's Albert Edward Bridge, opened in 1862, to join the Severn Valley Railway which ran through the Ironbridge Gorge. The London &

55 *The easterly arch of the railway bridge at Newdale (SJ 676095) which probably dates from c.1760.*

Ironbridge Gorge Museum Archaeology Unit

56   *A dome-shaped crossing keeper's shelter recorded by the Ironbridge Gorge Museum Archaeology Unit in 1986, on part of the Lilleshall Company's mineral railway system (SJ 703136) near Donnington, which was closed by 1887.*

North Western Railway converted much of the Shropshire Canal into its branch line from Wellington to Coalport.

Many of the principal industrial concerns in the coalfield built their own links to the main line railways. The most extensive system was that of the Lilleshall Company, built in 1851-55, which joined the L&NWR at Donnington (SJ 705141) and the Great Western at Hollinswood (SJ 706091). At its maximum extent during the First World War the system totalled 42 track km., had 200 main line and 250 internal wagons, and was worked by five locomotives.[61] The main locomotive depot adjoined the New Yard engineering works (SJ 704116). During a century of operation, 22 locomotives were used, six of them built by the company. Crossing keepers' shelters, domed-shaped and constructed of brick were an unusual feature of the line. One example, recorded in 1986, was 2.85m. high and 2.5m. in diameter. The closure of the system in 1959 was marked by a rail tour by company staff in open wagons headed by the locomotive *Constance*.

No Lilleshall Company locomotives survive but one of the six saddle tanks built by the Coalbrookdale Company when standard gauge tracks reached Coalbrookdale in 1863 is preserved by the Ironbridge Gorge Museum Trust. Other companies who retained locomotives for working sidings were the brickworks of William Exley at Jackfield, connected to the Severn Valley Railway where traffic ceased in

1956, the Hadley Castle Works of GKN Sankey, rail-served until 1972, C. & W. Walker's works at Donnington where three saddle tanks worked until 1952, and the Old Park Ironworks, which closed well before the end of the 19th century.[62] In the 20th century connections were laid to the Ordnance Depot at Donnington, where traffic ceased in 1991, and to the Ironbridge Power Station, which is still rail-served. In the 1920s and '30s several companies replaced or supplemented plateway systems with narrow gauge 'Jubilee' edge rails of the type used on the Western Front during the First World War.

The construction of the first tub boat canal in the coalfield was foreseen in the agreement of 1764 by which the Lilleshall Company (not then so named) was established, and within a few years a canal linked the mines at Donnington Wood (SJ 705125) with a landsale wharf at Pave Lane (SJ 760165) and with quarries at Lilleshall, the latter line eventually terminating in three distinct branches. A tunnel-and-shaft system, replaced in 1796 by an inclined plane, achieved a change of level of 13m. at the junction of the Lilleshall and Pave Lane lines at Hugh's Bridge (SJ 740151), and seven locks took boats 10.6m. down to the level of the canal at Lilleshall. In 1798 the canal was principally worked by rectangular boats measuring 20ft. x 6ft. 4in. (6m. x 1.9m.), 70 carrying eight and 20 carrying five tons, but 19 boats were of approximately twice that size. In 1787 the ironmaster William Reynolds built the 2.8km.-long Wombridge Canal from a junction with the southern end of the Donnington Wood Canal to mines near Wombridge Church. Its only engineering feature was a seemingly inexplicable tunnel near to the church (SJ 691115) which was visible for a time during roadworks in the 1960s. In the same year Reynolds built a canal serving his ironworks at Ketley, which was approached by an inclined plane (SJ 679108), a pair of parallel railway tracks on which boats were conveyed in cradles, 22m. to and from a level serving the works. A short tunnel (SJ 683110) nearby is blocked but probably intact on private land.[63]

In 1788 an Act of Parliament was obtained for the Shropshire Canal by which the ironmasters of the coalfield hoped to convey their produce to the Severn. The canal ran from Donnington Wood through Oakengates, where it was joined by the Ketley Canal, to Southall Bank, from where one branch, probably opened in 1793, led to the eastern end of the Ironbridge Gorge, to the settlement which was to gain the name of Coalport by 1794, while the other, operating by 1791, followed a circuitous course which was intended to terminate by the Severn, but came to an end at Brierly Hill (SJ 670051) above Coalbrookdale, whence a tunnel-and-shaft system conveyed cargoes to plateway wagons which took them to the river. Three inclined

57 *The curious tunnel near the western terminus of the Wombridge Canal (SJ 690115), when it was revealed by roadworks in the late 1960s.*

planes were built, at Wrockwardine Wood (SJ 702123), Windmill Farm (SJ 693064) and The Hay (SJ 695028). They were to a standard design by Henry Williams and John Loudon, which utilised docks at the summit instead of the locks used on Reynold's Ketley incline. A steam engine provided water from reservoirs at Hinkshay (SJ 695070). A stone aqueduct crossing the turnpike road on the borders of Dawley and Madeley (SJ 694058) gave the name 'Aqueduct' to the adjoining settlement. The canal company paid substantial dividends, but by the mid-19th century its fabric had been severely damaged by subsidence. As part of the Shropshire Union Railway & Canal Co., it was acquired by the London & North Western Railway, and closed apart from the section between Tweedale Basin (SJ 701050) and Coalport. Much of the canal bed was used for the railway from Hadley Junction to Coalport opened in 1861. From the last time that the Hay Incline was used, in the 1880s or early 1890s, the working section was restricted to the 1.5km.-stretch between Tweedale and Blists Hill.[64]

Many remaining features of the tub boat canal system were recorded by industrial archaeologists in the 1960s, notably by the late W.H. Williams and by Roger Tonkinson, who provided a definitive record of the inclined planes.[65] Relatively little now remains. The section of canal through the Blists Hill Museum is in water, a curving section cut off by the railway remains in the Hinkshay Nature Study Area (SJ 695071), and several stretches near Lilleshall can be followed on footpaths. The Trench incline on the Shrewsbury Canal (SJ 688121) has been entirely destroyed by a new main road. The foot of the Wrockwardine Wood incline was destroyed when bungalows were built in the 1960s, and the section immediately above by a new road in the early 1980s, although the remainder survives as a track. All traces of Windmill Farm were obliterated by the construction of the Brookside Estate. The slope of the Ketley incline disappeared under a housing estate in the early 1970s. Hugh's Bridge remains in rural seclusion, the lines of both the upper and lower canals survive, together with the embanked slope of the incline, and the portal of the tunnel and shaft system which preceded it. The Hay Incline, as part of the Blists Hill Open Air Museum, is one of the most visited industrial monuments in Britain, although excavation still has much to reveal of its history. The basin at the Brierly Hill terminus above Coalbrookdale remains, together with the cutting of the plateway incline which replaced the tunnel-and-shaft system after 1794. The suggestion that earthworks to the east of the basin represent an incline used after the tunnels were abandoned and before the cutting was completed cannot be sustained. Levels of traffic in 1794 were low, suggesting that customers could easily have managed for a time without using the canal, and the railway which the intermediate incline is supposed to have joined was not built until the 1820s.[66]

The movable effects of the Shropshire Canal were sold in 1861, and included the engines from the Wrockwardine Wood and Windmill Farm inclines, of 20 and 22 h.p., the beam pumping engine from Hinkshay Pool, three oak incline carriages with cast iron wheels, the materials which had made up a ticket office, and 26 iron and 20 wooden tub boats.[67] It is evident that many tub boats were made of wrought iron plates, and fortunate that one, which served as a water tank on a farm near Newport, has been preserved at the Ironbridge Gorge Museum since 1973. An unsuccessful attempt was made to preserve a wooden boat from Tweedale, but sufficient was learned to enable the construction of a replica. The remains of another wooden boat are in the bed of the Lubstree Arm of the Shrewsbury Canal (SJ 686163).

THE COALBROOKDALE COALFIELD: COAL-MINING

The Coalbrookdale Coalfield was the birthplace of the longwall method of mining coal. Malcolm Wanklyn has shown that in the mid-17th century there were drift mines up to 1,000 yards long in Madeley Wood, where the method was possibly pioneered.[68] The earliest archaeological evidence of mining is not of such large-scale operations, but of humble bell pits, which are impossible to date, although likely to be of early rather than later date. Landscapes of bell pits remain at the Deer Leap (SJ 668015) in Broseley and in the woods near Caughley (SJ 695001).[69] Many of the mines in the Ironbridge Gorge before the 19th century were adits, which are illustrated on several 17th-century maps. One, from which the Crawstone iron ore was extracted, remains in Ironbridge (SJ 670035) in good condition.[70] Roadways give access to the face from which the ore was being extracted by longwall methods. The last adit mines in the Gorge, clay workings on the south bank of the river (SJ 670032) near the Iron Bridge, ceased work in 1953. They remained recognisable as mines in the 1960s, but slumping has reduced them to mere depressions amongst the trees.

The first steam engine used to drain a mine in the coalfield was probably set to work in 1719 in Madeley. Within a few years the Coalbrookdale Company was casting iron cylinders for such engines and several more were installed in the following decades. At the Lloyds (SJ 688031) in the Ironbridge Gorge is a pumping shaft in which the pump rod of the last engine still remains, alongside the foundations of the last engine house. It is possible that this is the site of one of the earliest engines in the coalfield, erected by the 1720s. There were probably between 20 and 30 pumping engines in local mines by 1800. The first colliery winding engine in the coalfield was probably installed at Wombridge in 1787. Such engines quickly became one of the dominant features of the landscape. A miner born in 1779 recalled in his old age the time when 'there was not a single steam engine in the district to draw up...the coals'. There were probably more than a hundred steam winding engines in operation by 1800, and many more were built in the 19th century.[71] The foundations of many engines have been revealed during the construction of Telford new town, but few survive to be examined. Within the Blists Hill Museum (SJ 694034) are the substantial foundations of a Heslop engine, built in the 1790s, and, with amazement, observed working by a visitor from New York in 1912.[72] The nearby horizontal winding engine was removed from the Milburgh Tileries, Jackfield (SJ 684026), and occupies the site of a somewhat larger engine. The winding engine house of Muxton Bridge Colliery (SJ 722133), which dates from c.1884 and housed a pair of horizontal engines which worked until 1912, is conserved in Granville Country Park, alongside the fragments of an earlier beam engine. The only headstocks remaining in situ are those of Granville Colliery (SJ 721114), which was the last deep mine in Shropshire, working until 1979. They

58   *A drawing from a geological section of the Granville Mine (SJ 725120), made in 1864 by T. Doody. The engine house to the left accommodates a Cornish pumping engine, while that to the right contained a vertical winding engine.*

are the headquarters of a naturists' group. Some surface buildings of the Madeley Wood Mine remain within the Halesfield industrial estate (SJ 713055). Components of collieries discovered during archaeological investigations include a horse gin found in 1987 near Granville Colliery (SJ 711117) of which an oak rope roll nearly 2m. in diameter remained, and a powder house built by the Madeley Wood Company in the 19th century, which measured approximately 10m. x 10m., had a brick vaulted roof, and was built into a hillside.[73]

THE COALBROOKDALE COALFIELD: MANUFACTURES

The range of manufactures dependent on the use of coal was much greater in the Coalbrookdale Coalfield than in any other part of Shropshire. Such manufactures proliferated during the 17th century, and some remained important in the 20th century.

Limeburning was one of the oldest such manufactures. The Silurian limestone on Benthall Edge was quarried on a small scale as early as the 13th century. Kate Clark has used a Harris Matrix to show that the first stage of large scale exploitation was concerned with the beds of stone which were best suited for use in blast furnaces, and that subsequently the lower quality beds were quarried for lime burning. Documentary evidence shows that limestone from Benthall Edge was used at the blast furnaces in Coalbrookdale in the first half of the 18th century. Few kilns are associated with the first stage of exploitation, but the tramway which formed part of the second stage, running away from the river towards the agricultural areas to the south, served no fewer than twenty kilns. Another railway, constructed by 1801, descended by a steep inclined plane (SJ 666034) to the banks of the Severn, where a bank of lime kilns remains.[74]

On the opposite bank of the river the workings on Lincoln Hill were even more extensive. Many visitors in the late 18th century went to the Rotunda (SJ 668038), constructed by Richard Reynolds at the southern end of the ridge, and looked down on a chasm, 400 m. long and 48 m. wide in 1758, on the bottom of which were ranks of lime kilns, and from which large-scale adits penetrated the sides of the cliff faces. The tithe map of 1847 marks 32 kilns in the area. The hill has been distorted by collapses and the tipping of waste, and the shafts which gave access to the underground workings in the limestone have been grouted with concrete. Exploration in the 1970s revealed pillars up to 10m. high and 7m. square supporting a working area approximately 100m. x 48m. Two small limekilns are preserved on the Wharfage in Ironbridge (SJ 668036), close to a third, a substantial structure, cylindrical in plan, which is probably the one painted by J.M.W. Turner and Paul Sandby Munn.[75]

By 1800 ironmasters were looking further afield for supplies of limestone. In the near vicinity supplies were obtained from the southern end of Wenlock Edge by tramways which ran to the Severn from Tickwood to the Stoneport at the western end of the Gorge (SJ 660038) and from Gleedon Hill to a wharf by Buildwas Bridge (632041).[76] Archaeological evidence shows that limeburning on a considerable scale took place in the Ironbridge Gorge until the mid-19th century. The kilns were not well-located for the distribution by land of agricultural lime, nor was the pace of building such as to account for the local use of all that was produced. It would appear that there must have been a substantial river-borne trade in lime. Small-scale workings on both Lincoln Hill and Benthall Edge continued into the 20th century.

The mines and quarries of the carboniferous limestone outcrop at Lilleshall and Church Aston have been exhaustively chronicled by Adams and Hazeley.[77] Archaeological evidence for early working is provided by squatter cottages like that whose preservation was secured by the Shropshire Mining Club (SJ 739177) constructed by 1681. Large-scale exploitation began with the construction in the 1760s of the Donnington Wood Canal, whose branches ran right up to the quarries. Stone from some beds was burned to make hydraulic cement. Underground workings reached a depth of 75m., and beds up to 20m. thick were exploited. By the 1840s stone suitable for blast furnaces was running out in the Lilleshall workings although some remained in Church Aston. The underground workings flooded in 1860 and the principal site (SJ 735165) is now a lake, surrounded by vegetation, bounded on one side by a steep cliff of pink limestone. In the early 1880s over 7,000 tons p.a. were being produced by a labour force of just over thirty. Traces of tramways, the canal system and shafts remain in the landscape, together with several substantial kilns. The longest of the terraces of 'barracks' which accommodated the miners and quarrymen has been demolished, although a shorter row survives under cosmetic timber-framing (SJ 733165).

The sites of the workings in the Carboniferous limestone at Steeraway (SJ 694095) and The Hatch (SJ 645084) have not been the subject of detailed archaeological survey. The former, which included underground workings, were linked by railway with the Watling Street turnpike road at the Old Hall (SJ 656110) by the 1730s, and despatched limestone in the opposite direction to the Horsehay furnaces in the 1750s. A steam winding engine was employed by the early 19th century, in mines which in the 1840s were 36m. deep. By the 1870s the two sites were in the same ownership and still employed up to 20 men, but numbers declined and operations ceased in 1918.[78]

The manufacture of bricks in the Ironbridge Gorge appears to have commenced in the 17th century. The bricks used in the octagonal tower of 1618 at Willey Hall and in various other gentry houses in the district were almost certainly made in the area. Nevertheless the earliest surviving working-class houses in the Gorge are of coal measure sandstone, and some of those which do not survive were probably of more ephemeral materials. It was only in the 18th century that the one-and-a-half storey cottage with brick walls and a ceramic-tiled roof became commonplace in the area. A cottage on Hodge Bower dated 1714 and Tea Kettle Row in

59 *The Coalbrookdale Company's brickfields at Lightmoor (SJ 676053) in the 1920s. A steam engine to the left is almost concealed by waste tips. Materials are being moved on a narrow gauge Jubilee track railway system, probably military surplus from the First World War.*

Coalbrookdale (SJ 666047) built between 1735 and 1742 show how brick had become the accustomed building material.[79] There are no identifiable remains of the earliest brickworks in the coalfield. From the mid-18th century the Coalbrookdale Company began to exploit the deposits of clay between Lightmoor and Coalbrookdale, where brickmaking continued well into the 20th century and there are many remains, now largely hidden by trees. Brickmaking became part of the activities of most of the principal ironworking concerns in the late 18th century.

Roofing tiles were made on a large scale in Jackfield in the mid-19th century, in substantial manufacturing units, some of which can still be recognised. By the 1840s there were up to half a

60   *Bricks, typical of those made in the Ironbridge Gorge in the 19th century, in the wall of a riverside warehouse in Ironbridge (SJ 667035). The half-chevron pattern on the central brick is formed by the 'kiss-marks' of roofing tiles placed on edge on the surface of the brick during firing.*

dozen substantial works in the riverside parts of Broseley, with sheds for clay preparation, moulding and drying, with round kilns and rectangular drying stoves on the downhill sides of each complex. From the 1870s there was increasing mechanisation. The Milburgh Tileries (SJ 683025) at Jackfield, built by Thomas Prestage in the 1870s, continued in production until the 1940s, but remained scarcely altered until the late 1960s when the steam engines and much of the production machinery were salvaged by the Ironbridge Gorge Museum Trust. The brickworks within the open air museum at Blists Hill (SJ 695034) is well-preserved and exemplified the semi-plastic process for making tiles introduced in the 1890s. Many roofing tile works closed after 1900. Alfrey & Clark have suggested that the huge dumps of waster tiles to be found on the riverside in Jackfield are evidence of problems in production, resulting either from attempts to use inferior clays, or from insufficient drying times. The tile manufacturers formed a trade association in the 1880s, after which their products were stamped with makers' names, and with inscriptions like *Iron Broseley* or *Sovereign Broseley* indicating the type of tile. Some roofing tiles were fired in the same kilns as the characteristic buff-coloured bricks of the Ironbridge Gorge. Chevron-shaped 'kiss-marks' on the sides of bricks, indicating that tiles were laid on them during firing, can be seen on many buildings.[80]

Larger brickworks developed in the late 19th century in the northern part of the coalfield, where Blockleys works still flourishes (SJ 682120). The most spectacular site was the Lilleshall Company's Donnington Wood Brickworks (SJ 712114) of 1875, which had a circular 13-compartment Hoffman kiln. Nothing remains of it, but there are good photographic records.[81]

The making of pottery was well-established in the Ironbridge Gorge in the early 18th century. Investigation of waste tips in the early 1980s revealed evidence of the manufacture of plates, dishes, bowls, storage jars, chamber pots mugs, teapots, coffee pots, posset pots, strainers and ointment pots. The wares were generally similar to contemporary wares in North Staffordshire, although decoration tended to be more less ornate. Some white salt-glazed stoneware was found, as well as red-bodied earthenwares, slip wares and black-glazed wares on red or buff bodies, the latter the pottery known to collectors as *Jackfield ware*. Systematic study of walls made of waste materials revealed many saggars with holes in the sides, which were used for making salt-glazed wares. Some similar wares were discovered in the early 1970s on a site in Little Wenlock (SJ 664069) known to have been used for pottery manufacture in the mid-18th century.[82]

Alfrey & Clark have used cartographic and archaeological evidence to show how the earthenware pottery evolved from a cottage with a kiln on the end, into a semi-courtyard form, evident in Morris Thursfield's works at Jackfield by the 1720s, and repeated in the 1770s at Benthall (SJ 668022), where some stubs of walls remain. While earthenware manufacture continued in the Ironbridge Gorge in the 19th century its scale remained modest, and Thursfield's pottery in Jackfield was displaced by the decorative tile works of Craven Dunnill. William Allen produced Salopian art pottery at Benthall between 1882 and the First World War.[83]

The name 'Broseley' came to be synonymous with tobacco pipes in the 17th century. Of all industrial archaeological artefacts the tobacco pipe, which is usually stamped with its makers' name, and is usually datable by its shape, is perhaps the most useful. The Broseley industry has been studied in depth by David Higgins. The site of Henry Bradley's works at 11 Lodge Lane, Benthall, dating from *c*.1660-1690, was investigated in 1986. Remains of a muffle kiln were found, together with about 100 mould types and different marks, suggesting that this was a substantial workshop, employing several journeymen. By contrast Richard Shaw's workshop of the early 19th century at Benthall Villa Farm seems to have been a modest family-scale operation.[84]

Only 12 men and six women were engaged in pipemaking in Broseley and Benthall in 1841, but the number rose to 36 in 1851, and to 91 in 1861, declining to 74 in 1871 and 49 in 1881. Nevertheless the increase in the scale of manufacture in the 1850s is evident, something which is reflected in the premises used, and in the number employed by the principal manufacturers, the Southorn family. In 1861 Joseph Southorn was employing seven, William Southorn, 28, and Edwin Southorn, 28. The latter had 40 employees in 1871, and William Southorn had 70 in 1881. William Southorn (*c*.1792-1853) who was born at Cardington, probably established a pipemaking business in Broseley in 1823, which by 1838 was located off Legge's Hill (SJ 671023), and remained there until the 1930s. William's son Edwin set up an independent concern, taking over *c*.1850 the building adjacent to the *New Inn* in Benthall (SJ 670027) which had been the pipeworks of Noah Roden. He manufactured some of the best English pipes of the period. After 1876 the works passed into other hands and probably fell out of use in the 1890s. The other substantial works was an older building in King Street, Broseley (SJ 671022), adapted for pipe-making in 1881 by R. Smitheman & Co., who employed five men and two boys. It was sold to the Southorn family

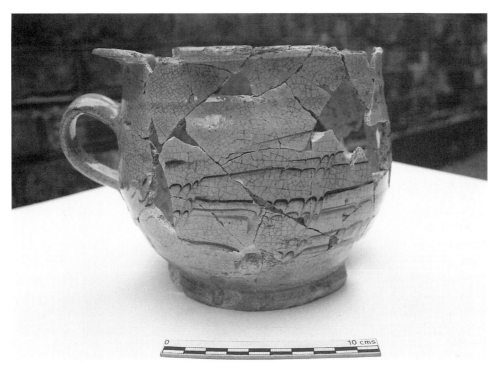

61   *An early 18th-century chamber pot, slip-washed, trailed and marbled, with a flat-topped rim, re-assembled from sherds found on a waste tip in Jackfield in 1982.*

62   *A saggar used for firing salt-glazed wares in the mid-18th century, found in a collapsed wall in Broseley.*

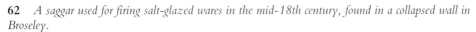

Author's collection

63   *Clay tobacco pipes being manufactured at the Broseley Pipeworks in the 1940s.*

in 1923, although they did not make use of it until the 1930s. Pipes were being manufactured there until 1960, using a kiln which remains a distinctive feature of the Broseley townscape. The equipment has been conserved by the Ironbridge Gorge Museum.[85]

The establishment of the Caughley china works (SJ 697705) marked a revolution in the ceramics industry in the coalfield, both in technology, since the manufacture of porcelain was still new to Britain, and in the organisation of production. The works was comparable to contemporary potbanks in North Staffordshire. The buildings were in the form of a square, and a clock occupied a prominent position on the front elevation. China clay and ball clay were imported from the West of England, and delivered from the Severn by a railway. Coal and refractory clay for saggars were obtained locally. The factory closed in 1814, and all its buildings have disappeared, although excavations revealed sherds which considerably enlarged knowledge of its products.[86]

The china works at Coalport (SJ 696024) was part of an ambitious plan by William Reynolds to create a new town at the eastern terminus of the Shropshire Canal. The first part, the works of John Rose on the northern side of the canal, was in operation by 1795, and the oldest surviving building, a three-storey brick structure of five bays, was built in that year. Essentially it is a building designed to accommodate workers sitting at benches. The adjacent premises occupied by Anstice, Horton & Rose were incorporated into John Rose's factory in 1814, when the Caughley works was also absorbed and closed. The Coalport works remained one of the largest producers of pottery in England for much of the 19th century, but there were few changes to the modes of production until Charles Bruff undertook major alterations from 1902. The works closed in 1926, when production was transferred to Stoke-on-Trent, and passed into various other industrial uses. Part was opened as a museum in 1976. Two bottle ovens remain, with part of a third, and in some of the buildings it is still possible to sense the workshop scale of operations, even in a factory which at its peak employed over 400 people. Excavations have added considerably to our understanding of the range of products at Coalport, showing, for example, that fine earthenwares, marbled wares, mocha wares and cream wares were being produced in the factory's early years.[87]

The Coalport china works was a factory on a considerable scale, but it was dwarfed after 1870 by the construction of even larger ceramics factories producing decorative tiles. George and Arthur Maw of Worcester leased the former Benthall Ironworks in 1852 and began to manufacture encaustic tiles, of the kind then in demand for the decoration and restoration of Gothic churches. In 1867 Henry Powell Dunnill (1821-95), a Yorkshireman, moved to Broseley taking over the former Hargreaves & Craven roofing tile works. A new company was formed in 1870 and in 1871, when he was employing 89 people, Dunnill sought tenders for

64   *The Coalport China Works, c.1900.*

65 *A fireplace at No.52 Belle Vue Road, Shrewsbury (SJ 495115), built c.1850, and incorporating some of the first patterns of encaustic tiles produced by Maw & Co. at their Benthall works.*

the construction of the Jackfield Encaustic Tile Works, opened on 25 February 1874 with a warehouse warming. The factory was designed by Charles Lynam (1829-1921) who was also commissioned by Maw & Co. to build a works at Jackfield, which by 1900 was the largest tileworks in the world. Both factories were designed for logical sequences of production, from clay reception and preparation to decoration and packing. Both companies produced increasingly diverse ranges of tiles and architectural ceramics in the late 19th century and early 20th century. Their products decorate state parliament houses in Australia, and railway stations in India. [88] The Craven Dunnill works was closed in the 1940s and after use as a foundry is now part of the Ironbridge Gorge Museum. Most of the original buildings remain. The kilns have been demolished but evidence of the foundations, together with those of the Ash Tree pottery which previously stood on the site, have been uncovered. The Maws factory closed in 1969 and is now a craft centre. Large collections of samples and moulds are held by the Ironbridge Gorge Museum. The principal known locations of tiles by Maw & Co. and Craven Dunnill are recorded in the Tile Location Index, maintained by the Tiles & Architectural Ceramics Society.

The first Abraham Darby and his partners smelted copper ores and made brass in Coalbrookdale in the first two decades of the 18th century, but brassmaking ceased in 1714, when the equipment was sent down the Severn to Bristol, it is doubtful whether the copper furnaces were used after Darby's death in 1717, and there are no longer visible remains of either operation.[89] Nevertheless non-ferrous metals continued to be smelted in the Ironbridge Gorge. By 1731 Thomas Barker

66 *(Top right) The restored showroom at the former Craven Dunnill decorative tileworks (SJ 686029), now the Jackfield Tile Museum.*

67 *(Bottom right) The* Mountain Daisy *public house at Sunderland, which utilises decorative tiles made by Craven Dunnill at Jackfield.*

had built a smelter in Benthall (SJ 671034) for lead ores mined by the London Lead Company at Llangynog, which from 1739 was used for smelting ore from The Bog in Shropshire. The smelter remained in use at least until 1786, and appears in early views of the Iron Bridge, a single-storey structure, with a clerestory ventilator in the roof, and an iron-banded chimney on the river side. Nothing now remains of the smelter. A second smelter in Benthall was located close to the subsequent site of the Iron Bridge (SJ 673033) and had been converted to a malthouse by 1765. Fragments of a building remain in section on the river bank. A third lead smelter is known only from documentary records. It stood on the boundary of the Coalbrookdale Company's property at Dale End (SJ 668036) and was working in the 1750s and 1770s. A fourth lead smelter, whose name was preserved by the name of the terrace 'Smelthouse Row', stood on the river bank near Coalport (SJ 691028) and was worked by William Reynolds and his successors in the first decade of the 19th century, but probably not for long afterwards. A piece of zinc blende (sphalerite) was found on the site in 1981. Nothing now remains above ground of the structures relating to an industry, described by *The Agreeable Historian* in 1746 as 'vastly poisonous, and destructive to everything near it'.[90]

Glassmaking was of only modest importance in the Coalbrookdale Coalfield. A glasshouse making both windowpanes and bottles, set up at Snedshill between 1673 and 1676, was still working in 1696, but there are no subsequent references to it and its site is unknown. There was a short-lived glassworks in Broseley in the early 18th century. The erection of a glassworks at Wrockwardine Wood (SJ 698126) was proposed by William Reynolds in 1791, and the works continued under different ownership until *c*.1841. Plans and an engraving show that there were two English glass cones. The works used local refractory clays, and for a time crushed furnace slag was employed as a raw material, although sand from Little Dawley was often used. The principal products were green bottles, but some jugs and 'friggers', ornamental pieces, remain in the district, and several are held by the Ironbridge Gorge Museum and the Victoria & Albert Museum. Nothing remains above ground but fragments of wasters and crucibles are occasionally found in the gardens of the dwellings which occupy the site.[91]

The only well-documented saltworks in the coalfield region were at Preston-on-the-Weald Moors (SJ 672148). Two adjacent works, one owned by the Charltons of Apley Castle, the other by the Newport family, pumped up brine which was boiled in iron pans, using coal from Oakengates, with the evaporation process accelerated by the addition of blood delivered in barrels from butchers' shops. The works was derelict in 1799 and probably never worked afterwards. Traditions that salt was produced from the brine found in the Ironbridge Gorge have yet to be confirmed by documentary or archaeological evidence.[92]

The manufacture of tar and other hydrocarbons has a long history in the coalfield. In 1696 Martin Eele set up cauldrons in Jackfield (SJ 686030) for extracting tar, pit and oil. An oily layer, which could have related to this period, was observed during deep excavations on the site in the mid-1980s. In 1786 William Reynolds was driving a tunnel, intended to accommodate a canal, into the hillside on the north bank of the Severn (SJ 693025). His miners struck a spring of natural bitumen which was collected and sold in barrels, initially producing as much as 55 gallons a week, although this had declined to no more than two or three barrels a year when production ceased in 1843. The tunnel was extended for over 1,000m. and served as a ventilation outlet and drainage level for mines in Madeley. It was explored in the 1960s by the Shropshire Mining Club, and a section was subsequently cleared of debris and opened to the public as part of the Ironbridge Gorge Museum.[93]

Much remains to be learned about the use of tar and allied substances in the 18th century. In 1767 British Oil was being made from bituminous rocks alongside the Coalbrookdale—Horsehay railway, and there was a range of 'coal tar buildings' at the Madeley Wood ironworks when it was purchased by Abraham Darby III in 1776. Two ranges of kilns for making coke and utilising the by-products were built in the 1780s by Archibald Cochrane, 9th Earl Dundonald, whose patent for the process was taken out in 1781. A range of 20 kilns, with adjacent plant for refining by-products was built behind the Calcutts ironworks (SJ 685029) and a further range at the Benthall furnaces (SJ 671030). The Benthall works closed by 1799 but that at the Calcutts continued, under different ownership until the closure of the blast furnaces in the 1830s. Coke was also made at kilns built by William Reynolds at Madeley Wood and Ketley in the 1790s, and by John Wilkinson at Willey, but these were short-lived. In the 1840s ironworks were using coke made by traditional open heap methods, which continued at Blists Hill until 1912. The Lilleshall Company set up coke ovens at Lodge Bank (SJ 717121) which continued for 20 years after the closure of the nearby Lodge Furnaces, and Priorslee ironworks, where there were over 40 beehive ovens by 1870. In 1912 the only integrated coke and by-product plant in Shropshire was set on the site. It continued working until 1928.[94]

One of the most significant uses of steam power in the coalfield was in milling grain. At the very birth of the rotative steam engine, William Reynolds sought James Watt's advice on the construction of an engine to power two sets of mill stones. There were steam-powered corn mills which probably dated from the 1780s near to Reynolds's works at Ketley and Madeley, and more were built in the 19th century. The most important survivor is the mill at Wrockwardine Wood (SJ 697126), a four-storey brick structure alongside the canal, constructed in 1818. The mill was the last source of traffic carried up the canal inclined plane at Trench, and continued to grind animal feed until the 1970s.[95]

The principal new use for coal in the 20th century has been in generating electricity. There was no public supply of electricity in the coalfield until 1930, but in 1925 the West Midlands Joint Electricity Authority, a consortium of municipal and private undertakings, decided that Ironbridge was an ideal site for a large power station. Construction began in 1929, most of the plant and building materials arriving by rail, and the station (SJ 653042) was opened on 13 October 1932. The chief engineer was E. F. Hetherington and Ivan Daughtry acted as consultant architect. Initially just one 50MW generating set was used but a second was installed in 1935-36, and two more in 1938-39. Wellington had received its first supply via Bridgnorth in 1930, receiving current at a sub-station at Watling Street, topped with a pylon (SJ 663110). A new station, 'Ironbridge B' (SJ 658039), was constructed on an adjacent site in the 1960s, and the 'A' station of 1929-32 was demolished in 1983, although the steel truss bridge of 1930 which gave access to it still survives. Coal from Halesfield Colliery was regularly worked to the 'A' station and, until it ceased producing coal in 1979, Granville Colliery supplied the 'B' station. [96]

THE COALBROOKDALE COALFIELD: IRON AND ENGINEERING

The most important of the coal-using industries was the manufacture of iron. In the late 17th century the coalfield was a source of iron ore, which was smelted, using charcoal as fuel, at water-powered sites at Coalbrookdale, Kemberton, Leighton, Willey and Wombridge.

The mining of iron ore has profoundly influenced the landscape of the coalfield. The Ballstone, Blackstone and Pennystone iron ores occur in nodules in strata of clay or shale. The whole of a stratum was mined by longwall methods, dumped on the surface, and allowed to weather. Gangs of women and girls were employed to pick out the nodules, and carry them in baskets to the 'ranks', where they were loaded into plateway wagons which took them to the blast furnaces. This was one of the dominant forms of employment for women in the coalfield. The gangs seem to have been largely self-directing, once contracts were agreed with the iron companies. Each summer many young women ore pickers migrated to London to work in market gardens. Middle-class objections to the employment of women as ore pickers seem to have been motivated as much by dislike of the self-reliance which it engendered as by the arduous nature of the tasks involved.[97] Tips of clay and shale, in which small, rejected nodules of iron ore can still be found, survive in many parts of the coalfield, most notably in Telford Town Park and the Granville Country Park.

Alfrey & Clark have shown the importance of early, probably 16th-century investment in water power in Coalbrookdale, and how the concept of re-cycling water was introduced by Abraham Darby II, using horse pumps in 1734, and a steam engine by 1744. The system was extended with the installation of the *Resolution* engine in 1781, after which water from the Boring Mill Pool flowed along a tunnel 800m. long, to be pumped 37m. up a shaft from which it was released into the Upper Furnace Pool.[98]

Abraham Darby's use of coke in the smelting process at Coalbrookdale in 1709 stimulated the growth of iron-making in the Coalfield, although it was not until the 1750s, in the time of the second Abraham Darby, that any degree of 'take-off' was achieved. The reasons for the delay are not wholly evident. The iron which Darby produced was more suited to founding than for forging into wrought iron, which restricted its sales. Moreover there may have been no clear cost advantage in operating a furnace with coke rather than with charcoal. A change in the operation of the furnace, of which the details are unclear, seems to have been achieved about 1753, after which coke-blast iron found a ready market with forgemasters.[99] Darby built a new furnace at Horsehay which came into blast in May 1755, and immediately began to supply the principal forges in the Midlands. In the next 45 years more than 30 blast furnaces were built in the coalfield, which in 1805 produced 50,000 tons of pig iron, a fifth of all the iron smelted in Britain. The proportion could have been much higher in the 1780s.

Coal and coke displaced charcoal in the forging of wrought iron, with the adoption of the 'stamping and potting' process patented by John Wright and Richard Jesson in 1773, and widely used in Shropshire, and the puddling process patented by Henry Cort in 1784, which displaced 'stamping and potting' after 1800. The development of the rotative steam engine by James Watt freed ironworks from dependence on water power, and by 1800 steam engines operated blowing machines, powered hammers and rotated rolling mills.

Some of the ironworks in the coalfield closed during the depression following the Napoleonic Wars, difficulties in finding markets being compounded by the exhaustion of mines. The industry recovered nevertheless. Twelve new blast furnace complexes were constructed between 1800 and 1851, while some older works remained in use. Production continued to rise, reaching a peak of nearly 200,000 tons in 1869, four times as much as in 1805, but now only two per cent of national output. Subsequent decline was rapid. Most blast furnaces in the coalfield had ceased to operate by 1900. The Blists Hill furnaces worked until 1912, and those of the Lilleshall Company at Priorslee until 1959. Only at Priorslee was a steel plant established alongside blast furnaces and that only operated between 1882 and 1922.

Iron was smelted with coke at 31 sites in the Coalbrookdale Coalfield. There are substantial remains of the blast furnaces at seven of them, and landscape evidence at others.

Table 4.1: **Coke-blast furnaces in the Coalbrookdale Coalfield**		
Name	**Parish**	**Grid ref.**
Barnett's Leasow	Broseley	SJ 679032
Benthall	Benthall	SJ 672030
Blists Hill	Madeley	SJ 694033
Broseley Bottom Coal	Broseley	SJ 682013
Calcutts	Broseley	SJ 686030
Coalbrookdale Lower	Madeley	SJ 667045
Coalbrookdale Upper	Madeley	SJ 667048
Coneybury	Broseley	SJ 683017
Dark Lane	Dawley	SJ 703086
Dawley Castle	Dawley	SJ 688061
Donnington Wood	Lilleshall	SJ 704125
Hinkshay	Dawley	SJ 693072
Horsehay	Dawley	SJ 673071
Ketley	Wellington	SJ 670108

Table 4.1 *continued*			
Langley Field	Dawley	SJ	699072
Lawley	Wellington	SJ	666094
Lightmoor	Dawley	SJ	682053
Lodge	Lilleshall	SJ	721123
Madeley Court	Madeley	SJ	698052
Madeley Wood (Bedlam)	Madeley	SJ	678033
Newdale	Wellington	SJ	672097
New Hadley	Wellington	SJ	682115
Old Park	Dawley	SJ	694094
Priorslee	Shifnal	SJ	702099
Queenswood	Wombridge	SJ	696108
Snedshill	Shifnal	SJ	701115
Stirchley	Stirchley	SJ	699074
Willey (New)	Willey	SJ	673006
Willey (Old)	Willey	SO	672978
Wombridge	Wombridge	SJ	691115
Wrockwardine Wood	Wrockwardine	SJ	702115

Much of the upper part of the water-power system at Coalbrookdale remains, including the Upper Furnace Pool, and the New Pool further upstream. The new works constructed between 1755 and 1780 all used recycling systems like that pioneered at Coalbrookdale. The pool at Horsehay, which, as hostile observers remarked, proved difficult to make watertight in 1754, is now all that remains of the ironworks. At Willey the pools constructed by John Wilkinson for the New Furnace in the 1750s can still be traced, but a road of the early 19th century, built after the furnace was blown out, cuts through the bottom pool. The site of the Old Furnace at Willey can readily be recognised, on a hillside supported by stone retaining walls, and surrounded by slag. There are substantial remains of the dams of the Benthall ironworks. A slightly different system was employed at Madeley Wood, where water was lifted from the Severn by a steam engine, whose bob wall remains, flowing into a substantial stone reservoir, also still in situ, and from it through a deep wheel pit.

In 1780 John Wilkinson blew in a new furnace at Snedshill. Nothing has remained on the site for many years but the furnace was important as the first to be built to be blown directly by a steam engine. Subsequent ironworks did not require water-power systems. The best remaining blowing engine houses, one of 1841 and one of the early 1870s, are at Blists Hill, alongside the only remaining steam blowing engines in Britain, the pair of beam engines *David* and *Sampson*, constructed by Murdoch Aitken & Co. of Glasgow for the Priorslee works of the Lilleshall Company in 1851, and a vertical engine once used in the same company's steel plant.

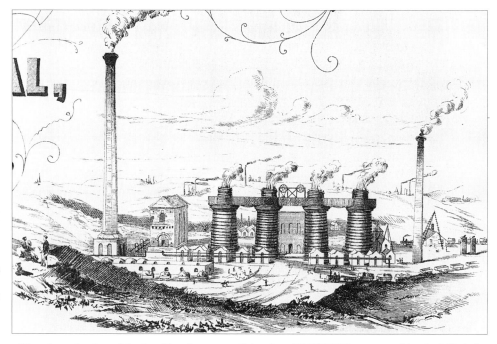

Ironbridge Gorge Museum Trust

68 *An early view of the four blast furnaces at Priors Lee (SJ 702099) constructed by the Lilleshall Company in 1851. The engine house to the left accommodated the beam blowing engines* David *and* Sampson, *now at the Blists Hill Open Air Museum.*

The Old Furnace at Coalbrookdale remains the subject of detailed analysis. The furnace ceased operation *c*.1818, and its present form probably dates from its re-building after an explosion in 1801. The inscriptions on its lower beams were interpreted by a German expert on the rebus to mean Brooke, Basil and Ethelfleda: 1638: Ethelfleda and Basil Brooke. It has since been argued that older pictures of the furnace beam suggest that the date was 1658, and that the interpretation of it to read 1638 dates from the restoration of the structure in 1959. In either case it is difficult to match the date with the evidence that there was probably no blast furnace at Coalbrookdale before the outbreak of the Civil War in 1642, and that the Brooke family did not occupy it in 1658. It was shown in 1981 that in its final years the furnace was blown from three sides. Evidence of a large-scale rebuilding, possibly when the beams inscribed 'Abraham Darby 1777' were inserted, is being revealed as the furnace is closely scrutinised.[100]

At Madeley Wood the stacks of two furnaces survive of three which once operated on the site. Much is still to be learned as the remains of the ironworks are uncovered. The two furnaces at Hinkshay were destroyed by explosives but parts of the bases remain in a nature study area. The bases of the Stirchley furnaces are preserved in the Telford Town Park, alongside the high chimney, built, to no avail, by the Wellington Coal & Iron Company in 1872. The bases of three furnaces at the Lodge, left after the works was demolished in 1905, have been restored as part

69   *The forehearth of the Old Furnace, Coalbrookdale (SJ 667048) in the 19th century.*

of Granville Country Park. The massive retaining wall, in ashlar sandstone, and the adjoining canal make this a particularly impressive site. Parts of the bases of the blast furnaces at Old Park and Dark Lane were briefly revealed during site clearance in the 1970s.

In 1873 there were 11 forges making wrought iron in the coalfield, with a total of 232 puddling furnaces. Nothing remains of any of these works, other than a few fragments of foundations of the Stirchley Ironworks (SJ 700075) observed during civil engineering work in the mid-1980s. Fortunately the process of forging wrought iron by puddling, with structures and machines brought in from elsewhere or built as replicas, continues in the G. R. Morton Ironworks at the Blists Hill Open Air Museum.[101]

Two important forges of earlier date have been studied. The Upper Forge at Coalbrookdale (SJ 669041) stands on a site which was used for ironmaking for at least two centuries, and for other industrial purposes after it ceased to manufacture wrought iron in 1843. The surviving main building was probably built soon after 1753, but has been much altered, and other buildings have long been demolished.[102] The experiments of the Cranage brothers using coal and coke to refine wrought iron were carried out at the Upper Forge in the 1760s, but it is doubtful whether it will ever be possible to identify remains of the structures in use at that time. One of the most important forges in the area was at Wrens Nest, where John Wright and Richard Jesson installed a steam engine in 1779, probably in a forge occupying two ancient mill sites constructed before 1771 by George Matthews of the Calcutts works. The engine initially re-cycled water, but was later put to work hammers. The stamping and potting system was used, but the works had a relatively short life, ceasing operation about 1812. Traces of the water power system remain, together with slag, vitrified bricks and some fragments of the pots used in the process.[103] Two large double-gabled buildings of 1759-60 at Newdale, surveyed before demolition in 1985, provide rare evidence of 18th-century ironworks buildings other than furnaces, although their purpose is uncertain.[104]

Several companies making wire and wire rods were set up in the northern part of the coalfield in the latter part of the 19th century, all with Wesleyan connections. The Trench Ironworks (SJ 685124) and the Shropshire Ironworks (SJ 686122) were both located alongside the canal basin at Trench and were in the same ownership from 1872. The works of the Haybridge Company (SJ 663114) was in the fork of the railways from Wellington to Stafford and Wolverhampton. The former plant closed in 1931, the latter in 1983.[105]

Shropshire's principal 20th-century engineering concern had the same origins, and was served both by the Shrewsbury Canal and the Wellington-Stafford railway. The Castle Iron Works at Hadley (SJ 675124) was established in 1871 to make bar iron and wire. The company went bankrupt in 1888, and between 1900 and 1904 the site was used by G.F. Milnes & Co. Ltd for the production of tramcars, and served the same purpose for different owners between 1905 and 1908. In 1910 it was bought by Joseph Sankey & Co. for the making of motor vehicle wheels and body parts. In the 1920s and '30s it was one of the few prosperous companies in the coalfield, making steel pressings of many kinds, and had about 1,500 employees in 1939, a total which rose to over 6,000 by the 1970s. The company survived the economic crisis of the early 1980s with a much reduced labour force. The archaeology of the site has yet to be analysed. Another engineering concern alongside the Wellington-Stafford railway was C. & W. Walker of Donnington, makers of gas purification plant and gas holders established in 1859. By 1900 the firm had about 800 workers and was supplying world markets. Operations ceased and the site was cleared without being surveyed in the 1980s, but some of its products survive. The No 3 gas holder at the former Banbury Gasworks still bears the inscription 'C. & W. Walker, Donnington, Shropshire, 1933'.[106]

Six of the groups of blast furnaces in the coalfield in 1800 were parts of significant engineering concerns, making

Irontbridge Gorge Museum Trust

70 *Score marks made by the waterwheel of the Old Furnace, Coalbrookdale (SJ 667048), discovered in 1982.*

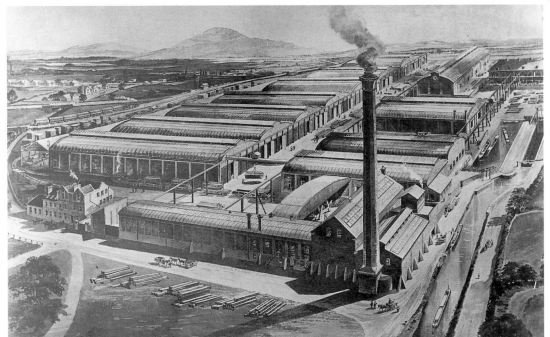

steam engines and bridges, and in some cases, great varieties of smaller castings. No buildings of that period survive, but there are substantial remains of two of the coalfield's late 19th-century engineering works.

The Lilleshall Company dates from 1764 when Earl Gower formed a partnership with John and Thomas Gilbert for developing the minerals on his Shropshire estates. It became a significant ironmaking concern under the direction of John Bishton when the partnership was renewed, and called the Lilleshall Company, in 1802.[107] In 1861 with the construction of the New Yard (sometimes called the Phoenix Foundry) at St George's, it became a leading engineering concern. Within the next decade it supplied eight pairs of blowing engines for blast furnaces and numerous steam hammers and saddle tank locomotives. The works extended over 4.4 ha. In the early 1870s there were more than 70 machine tools in the machine shop, two steam hammers in the forge, and cranes in the foundry capable of lifting the heaviest castings then in demand. At the turn of the century steam engines were supplied for the waterworks in Shanghai, and a large gas engine for a railway in Japan. Further substantial orders were gained in the 1920s but the works clearly suffered a crisis of management, and was closed in 1931. The company re-opened the premises in 1937, letting out portions to other firms. The buildings remain, in a multiplicity of uses, and await full evaluation. The principal surviving product of the works, the pair of beam engines constructed in 1895-1900 which pumped sewage from West Ham into the Northern Outfall Sewer in east London, has been saved from destruction but remains inaccessible to the public. A late product, an inverted vertical triple expansion pumping engine, supplied to the Bristol Water-works Company in 1923, is conserved at the Chelvey Pumping Station, but is also inaccessible.

The Coalbrookdale Company has a long history in engineering. It was supplying parts for Newcomen steam engines in the 1720s, and complete steam engines by the 1790s. Its engineering shops were located in the upper part of the site near the Old Furnace and were water-powered until 1872. The present erecting shop was constructed in 1878-79, and is approximately 77m. long and 12m. wide. Steam engines powered line shafting for machine tools, and for an overhead crane, and standard gauge railway sidings extended through the building.[108]

It is ironic that this great building was constructed after the best-known products of the Coalbrookdale works had been despatched to customers. Like the Lilleshall Company its markets were world-wide. Whaling pots of indeterminate date bearing the inscription 'Coalbrookdale' are found in many parts of the Pacific. In 1838 the company began to manufacture art castings. Their display in the Crystal Palace in

71 *(Top left) The Hadley Castle works (SJ 675124) of G.F. Milnes & Co in the first decade of the 20th century. On the right is the Shrewsbury Canal, with the Castle Lock, and the basin serving the works with a drawbridge carrying the towpath across the entrance. In the centre of the works tramcars await despatch on railway wagons, while the Stafford-Wellington line of the L&NWR is to the left. The works was taken over by Joseph Sankey in 1910.*

72 *(Bottom left) Pumping engines for the waterworks in Shanghai under construction at the New Yard works (SJ 704113) of the Lilleshall Company in 1927.*

Ironbridge Gorge Museum Trust

73 *The engineering shop at Coalbrookdale (SJ 668045), constructed in 1879. The building is 77m. long and 12m. wide.*

1851 brought much attention, and the ceremonial gates which featured in it still stand near the Albert Hall, London. Subsequently displays were mounted at most of the international exhibitions in the second half of the 19th century. The most distant artefact is perhaps the statue of the colonial administrator J. R. Godley, cast at Coalbrookdale in 1865, which stands outside the cathedral in Christ Church, New Zealand.[109]

Nevertheless it is not a work of art but a useful object which is the company's best known product. The Iron Bridge, built in 1777-81, was universally acknowledged at the time as the first in the world, and drew the world's attention to what was happening in the coalfield. It was proposed by the Shrewsbury architect Thomas Farnolls Pritchard (1723-1777) in a letter to the ironmaster, John Wilkinson, in 1773. Pritchard had carried out commissions for Wilkinson, as well as for the Harries family of Benthall, and, probably, for Abraham Darby III at Hay Farm. In February 1774 proposals for an iron bridge across the Severn near Coalbrookdale were announced.

The first subscribers' meeting took place in 1775, when Abraham Darby III agreed to take responsibility for the construction. An Act of Parliament was obtained the following year, and, after some disagreements among the shareholders, work on a small scale began. The iron ribs were placed in position during the summer of 1779, perhaps before the completion of the stone abutments. The bridge was opened to traffic on New Year's Day 1781. In the following decades it attracted many visitors and was depicted in numerous paintings and engravings. It symbolises the scale and the significance of the developments in mining and manufacturing which were taking place in the area at the time. It is also a measure of the difference between the Coalbrookdale Coalfield and the other Shropshire coalfields.[110]

Conclusions

The most evident contrast between the Shropshire coalfields is in their markets. All the coalfields supplied landsale coal for customers within a short distance, for brick-works and for lime kilns. The pits of the Shrewsbury Coalfield had only one other significant type of custom, the lead smelters at Pontesford and Malehurst. The only other use in the Oswestry coalfield was for the manufacture of coke, but substantial quantities were carried by rail to distant markets. Coal from the Wyre Forest was

Ironbridge Gorge Museum Trust

74 *The most celebrated product of the Coalbrookdale Ironworks, the Iron Bridge (SJ 672033).* A View of the Iron Bridge, taken from the Madeley side of the River Severn *(James Fitler, 1787).*

used for ironmaking for a short time and was similarly taken to distant customers along the Severn Valley Railway. Coal from the Clee Hills was put to a surprising variety of uses, ironmaking, pottery manufacture, and the making of clay pipes, and for a time was taken considerable distances into Wales, but exports were destroyed by the standard gauge railway.

The Coalbrookdale Coalfield presents many contrasts. For three centuries coal was supplied along the Severn to customers 90 km. away in Gloucestershire. From the 1720s steam engines were installed throughout England. By the end of the 19th century tiles were being installed in parliament houses in Australia and in Indian railway stations, steam pumping engines in Shanghai and statues and fountains in New Zealand. At least for a time in the 1790s and 1800s the entrepreneurs of the coalfield displayed a remarkable degree of intellectual prowess, playing with ideas like the oil engine and the integrated alkali works which did not come to fruition for many decades, and attracting the attention of leading figures of the time.

Even so, the five very different Shropshire coalfields had much in common. All were affected to some extent by changes during the Industrial Revolution. All except Clee Hill were making use of steam pumping and winding engines by 1800. All made use of plateways. All except the Oswestry coalfield became involved with ironmaking. All were stimulated by turnpike roads. All were affected by canals, although the Clee Hill and Shrewsbury coalfields may have been affected adversely.

The standard gauge railway affected the coalfields in different ways. While the Coalbrookdale Coalfield benefited from the easier despatch of secondary products, it may have lost ground in the market for coal. The Oswestry and Wyre Forest coalfields obviously benefited from their railway links, but the Shrewsbury and more particularly the Clee Hill coalfields demonstrably lost markets when railways opened. The pits which remained open in the second half of the 20th century in the Coalbrookdale Coalfield were modernised, with steel headstocks, compressed air and electrical systems, and pithead baths, as were the single large pits developed in the 1920s in the Oswestry coalfield and in the 1930s in the Wyre Forest. The mines in the Shrewsbury Coalfield and on Clee Hill were never modernised in this way.

There are also similarities in the patterns of settlement in the five coalfields. Squatting did much to shape the Ironbridge Gorge, Ketley Bank and Wrockwardine Wood in the Coalbrookdale Coalfield, and it dominates the whole landscape of Clee Hill. It can also be observed at Trefonen and in parts of St Martin's in the Oswestry Coalfield, at Hookagate and Annscroft in the Shrewsbury Coalfield, and at Chelmarsh Common in the Wyre Forest, where the example of Highley shows how an industrial landscape can be shaped by factors of landownership which date from the middle ages.

Brick terraced housing is a feature of 19th-century settlement in all five coalfields, at Horsebridge, at Lower Chirk Bank, at Dark Lane, Hinkshay and the Aqueduct, at Bedlam on Titterstone Clee, and above all in Highley. The most characteristic 20th-century housing dates from the first quarter of the century, and consists of semi-detached pairs and short terraces in the 'Garden City' style, visible at St Martin's and in Highley but, except for the 12 dwellings forming Castle Houses at Hadley (SJ 679122), absent from the Coalbrookdale Coalfield.

Few structures survive which relate directly to coal mining, although there are rather more constructed by secondary, coal-using industries. A few engine houses are well-known and cared for. There are probably rather more weighbridge offices which tend to survive when other buildings are demolished. The county retains two distinguished pithead baths.

Waste heaps remain in all five coalfields. They have slowly been colonised, by grass, by birch and then by oak trees. In the same way a whole mining landscape is subject to change, the evidence of mining activity slowly supplanted, by agriculture and forestry in the Wyre Forest, by the housing estates and factories of the new town of Telford in the Coalbrookdale coalfield. But mining communities remain. The scattered cottages on Clee Hill would never have been built were it not for the coal beneath the dhustone. There would not be a new town in the Coalbrookdale Coalfield if the area had not undergone an industrial revolution in the 18th century. Highley, Western Rhyn and St Martin's are unmistakably mining villages, whatever the current occupations of their inhabitants.

Mining at any location is a passing phase in human history. Minerals are exhausted or their extraction ceases to be profitable. Many centuries of non-ferrous mining are coming to an end at Falun, Freiburg and in the Harz. The cessation of coal mining in South Wales and in Northumberland and Durham would only recently have been regarded as beyond credulity. Yet even when mining has ceased, it shapes the present and the future, of landscapes and communities.

Just as a pitheap may merge into the landscape, and with a covering of vegetation come to look like any other small hill, so a mining community may superficially come to look like a commuting settlement, whether in the rural isolation of Asterley or the planned landscape of Telford. Just as closer examination of a pitheap will show that its vegetation is determined by past mining activity, so closer examination of a community, of the building materials and of the types of house, shop and chapel, will reveal its origins. The miners' trains stop running. There are no more Sunday School anniversaries at Primitive Methodist chapels. The Co-operative Store no longer pays a dividend. Brass bands do not march through the streets, and the Miners' lodge banners have been laid up. No one now reads the *Colliery Guardian*, and the Mutual Improvement class has ceased to meet. Nevertheless the railway embankment, the chapel, the Co-op supermarket, the banners in museums, the waste tip, remain as evidence of the reasons why communities grew up, and the task of the industrial archaeologist is to subject that evidence to continuing analysis.

❖ ❖ ❖

5

THE TEXTILE INDUSTRIES

◆　◆　◆

The manufacture of textiles is part of every civilisation and changes in the ways in which the production of fabrics was organised are at the heart of those events which historians describe as the Industrial Revolution. Shropshire has never been regarded as one of the principal textile-producing counties, yet one of the most formal early modern textile manufactures focused on Shrewsbury, the county was much influenced by the growth in scale of textile manufacturing around 1800, and 'vernacular' production of fabrics was widespread. Shropshire thus provides an appropriate case study for assessing the impact of industrialisation on the manufacture of textiles.

VERNACULAR PRODUCTION

The most widespread textile activity in the county in the 18th century was 'custom weaving', a form of 'vernacular' or subsistence production. In most parts of the county flax and hemp were grown on small plots, often adjacent to farm-steads. Fields called *hemp butts* are numerous in the county. Arthur Young in 1776 noted when passing through Shropshire that every farmer grew about two acres of hemp, and every cottager all he could spare from potatoes and beans.[1] The hemp was retted; it appears in containers rather than pools, although there are field names linked with flax retting in Ellesmere, West Felton and Eyton-on-the-Weald-Moors. After being scutched, heckled and spun by the families who grew it, the yarn was woven by full-time *custom* weavers, defined in 1840 as 'domestic artisans...employed to weave the yarn spun in private houses'.[2]

In the northern part of Telford some 156 of 846 probate inventories, 18.4 per cent of the total, made between 1660 and 1750, refer to hemp or flax, and almost exactly the same proportion, 18.5 per cent, list spinning wheels. By contrast, ownership of looms was confined to 23 specialist weavers.[3] The same pattern occurs in other parts of the county.

In the 1660s 'Shropshire Canvas' was being shipped down the Severn through Gloucester, but manufacture of fabrics from hemp or flax for national markets seems to have ceased by 1700. Edward Harries in 1795 insisted that Shropshire spinners did not spin 'for manufactures' and Nightingale in 1813 noted that hemp and flax, like cabbages, were grown 'in small quantities'.[4]

Custom weaving continued in Shropshire well after the middle of the 19th century. Thomas Rogers of Pontesbury was making his living as a weaver in 1851 when he was aged 68, while in Minsterley William Hughes, aged 86, was working as a weaver, with a journeyman, aged 80, and also carrying out the duties of parish clerk. At Myddle Wood Charles Manley was still weaving at the age of 70 in 1851. Two weavers, Richard Rogers and Nathan Davies, lived in adjacent but separate households at Ifton Rhyn in 1841. The latter was still working 20 years later at the age of 84. Other aged custom weavers included John Edwards of Craignant in Selattyn parish, still working in 1851 at the age of 85, and Joseph Windsor of Rhosygadfa, Whittington, a hand loom weaver in 1861 at the age of 76.

The best documented Shropshire custom weaver is John Jeffreys of Llanymynech, born in 1825, the last of several generations of linen weavers, who was apprenticed at Welshpool, before succeeding to his father's trade. He operated two looms in a shed adjacent to his cottage, and produced table-cloths, towels, sheeting and striped linsey-woolsey cloth until the end of the 19th century, in the latter years using yarn from Yorkshire. He was reputedly the last weaver in Shropshire to make linen cloth.[5]

The best archaeological evidence of custom weaving is the work shop at Cockshutford (SO 580850), the squatter settlement in Clee St Margaret, occupied in 1861 by Samuel Hall, a 73-year-old woollen weaver, who had used the premises for at least 20 years. The tithe map identifies the building as Hall's loom shop. It

75 *Samuel Hall's loom shop at Cockshutford, SO 580850.*

is located in the grounds of a stone cottage, occupied in the mid-19th century by a blacksmith. Samuel Hall's cottage, now replaced by a 20th-century dwelling, stood on the next plot. The building is of rubble sandstone with some dhustone and brick, is 3.94m. long and 3.52m. wide, with a height to the eaves of 2.5m., and is currently roofed with corrugated iron.

Some custom weavers made woollen as well as linen cloth, and there is plentiful evidence in Shropshire of 'vernacular' production of woollen cloth in small factories. Several rural fulling mills remained in production for much of the 18th century. Strafford's Mill at Wrickton (SO 646853) was still working in 1783. On the slopes of the Long Mynd, the Upper Mill at Smethcott remained in use, at least as a dyehouse, until after 1800, while the fulling mill at Woolstaston ceased working between 1757 and 1777. A fulling mill at Allscott (SJ 613133) was built in 1689, and remained in operation in 1745. Field name evidence suggests that many more fulling mills operated in the county before the 17th century.[6]

This tradition of local production for local markets continued for much of the 19th century, when the preparation and spinning phases, as well as fulling were mechanised, while hand looms remained in use for weaving. In 1814 a woollen factory at Upper Mill, Wentnor (SO 381940) was offered for sale, newly built, with its stock and tenters, and the prospect of 'plenty of good country work'.[7] Broad Street Mill in Ludlow (SO 512742) had included a fulling mill since the 16th century. In the mid-19th century it was a small woollen manufactory, with five hand looms, making flannel, blankets and cloth for horse collars, all sold locally. It operated until the 1870s.[8]

Nineteenth-century woollen cloth manufacture at Morda followed the same tradition. In 1841 Edward Evans, woollen manufacturer, was employing about half a dozen weavers. His fulling mill at Weston (SJ 297275), which in 1817 had two pairs of stocks, and detached buildings used for spinning and weaving, appears to have been destroyed by fire and rebuilt as a corn mill. Morda (Lower) Mill (SJ 289281) used for cotton manufacture in the early 19th century, and subsequently for paper-making, was taken over in the 1880s by D. Rogers and Co, who made blankets, tweeds and flannels until the 1930s. A retired farmer who grew up at Hengoed recalled in 1994 that in 1922 his mother took fleeces to Morda Mill to be made into blankets.[9]

At Church Stretton, Carding Mill Valley takes its name from Brooks Mill (SO 445945), which in the 19th century worked on the same scale and served the same kind of markets. In 1841 it employed 10 males and two females, including two wool pickers and a sorter, two yarn slubbers and a carding engine feeder, two spinners and two flannel weavers. Ten years later the labour force had grown to 19 of whom nine had been born in Newtown, centre of the Welsh flannel industry, and one in Osset in Yorkshire, but there were only seven employees in 1861 and six in 1871. By 1891 the works was operated by two members of the Williams family who had owned it since the 1850s, other members gaining employment in the aerated water works which they had established nearby, and in the operation of the refreshment rooms and tea gardens in the valley. Richard Williams was advertising tweeds and blankets in the 1890s, and offering to provide cloth for farmers in part-exchange for wool.[10] The Silurian Mill on the Shropshire side of the Teme at Knighton (SO 287725) was converted from a corn mill in 1860. It was disused by 1880, but still workable when offered for sale in 1906, when its equipment included a 4.2m.-diameter waterwheel, a steam engine with a 12in. (0.3m.)-diameter cylinder, self-acting mules, and 22 plain flannel looms.[11]

The only part of Shropshire producing fabrics for national markets in 1660 was Bridgnorth, where probate records show that large-scale manufacture of the woollen cloth called frieze continued into the second decade of the 18th century. Entrepreneurs appear to have undertaken the preparation and finishing of cloth themselves, but spinning or weaving were sometimes entrusted to outworkers. George Southall, a clothier who died in 1667, owned equipment for preparing, spinning and finishing cloth, as well as 'on peece att the weaver's'. Samuel Higgins who died in 1681 had stocks of cloth and wool, together with cards for carding, boards and shears for finishing, and dyestuffs. George Bickerton who died in 1718 had possessions worth £870, including quantities of wool, yarn and cloth. Twenty pieces of cloth worth £20 were with weavers, and 357 lbs of wool had been put out for spinning. The best indication of the scale of the trade is provided by the inventory of Moses Law who died in 1712. He had wool of various kinds worth £93, yarn for 48 pieces of cloth worth £104, 141 pieces of completed frieze worth £423, kerseys, plains, druggetts, and other cloth worth £110, tools for carding, eight looms, and dyeing equipment, the whole of his possessions being valued at £1,864. Law lived in Underhill Street, north of the bridge (SO 717931). After Bickerton's death there is no further evidence of large scale woollen cloth manufacture in Bridgnorth, and there appears to be no continuity between frieze manufacture and the carpet weaving introduced in the town in the late 18th century.[12]

THE DRAPERS' TRADE

Shropshire was also involved in one of the most important textile trades of the early modern period, the production of woollen fabrics, 'cottons' or 'webs' in North and mid-Wales, for export through Blackwell Hall, London, to the poorest parts of Europe, and to America where it was used to clothe black slaves. The *de facto* right to trade in such fabrics had been acquired in 1624 by the Shrewsbury Drapers' Company, who controlled it until the 1790s.[13]

Thomas Pennant noted in the 1770s that Shrewsbury still drew profit from the woollen cloth manufactures of Montgomeryshire, about seven hundred thousand yards a year passing through the town's market. Owen and Blakeway recalled how each Thursday Welshmen in country coats of blue cloth and striped linsey waistcoats sold cloth to the Drapers in The Square, the end of the market being marked by the ascent of the members of the Company in order of seniority into the market hall. The formal market came to an end about 1795, the year after the spectacular bankruptcy of Joshua Blakeway, a leading Draper, and in 1803 the Company gave up the lease of the upper room of the market hall. The ancient, and by the 1790s archaic, market ceased to be viable with an increasing concentration in Wales on the production of flannel, involving the mechanisation of preparation and spinning, and consequently the concentration of production, and different patterns of marketing through the markets established in Welshpool, Newtown and Llanidloes.[14]

Welsh cloth was finished by shearmen in Shrewsbury, who were traditionally reckoned to be poor and exploited by the drapers. In the late 17th century the prosperity of finishers and dyers in Wellington suggests that some work may have been contracted out to that town. The scale of the finishing trade diminished in the first half of the 18th century. Probate records survive for 29 clothworkers and shearmen who died in Shrewsbury between 1660 and 1679, but for only seven between 1730 and 1749.[15] The frankpledge list for the town in 1709 includes 47 clothworkers, but there are only 21 on that for 1731. Nevertheless the trade continued, and 14 cloth dressers and nine shearmen claimed votes in the Shrewsbury election of 1796.

Shrewsbury merchants continued to participate in the Welsh cloth trade after the loss of the market. As late as 1865 a property sale included a warehouse in Frankwell which had been used for many years for wool and flannel. An insight into the operation of such warehouses is provided by the sale notice in 1794 for Joshua Blakeway's warehouse on St Chad's Hill, where 12,000 yards of cloth were stored, together with 40 quires of packing paper, and 400 ells of hurden packing cloths.[16]

The demise of Shrewsbury's role in the Welsh cloth trade had two significant effects on textile manufactures in the county. First, it stimulated an element of imitation, as flannel manufactories based on Welsh practice were established in and around the county town. Secondly, it led some entrepreneurs to seek other outlets for their capital.

WELSH-STYLE FLANNEL

Arthur Aikin remarked in 1797 that Shropshire was participating in the manufacture of flannel. The 'greatest undertaking' he considered to be the mill erected by Cook & Mason at the Isle (SJ 457158), on the Severn upstream from Shrewsbury, where a tunnel across the neck of the isthmus conveyed water to a wheel which provided power for spinning and fulling. The mill operated until the 1820s when the stock included two carding engines, nine jennies, 20 looms and two sets of fulling stocks. Nothing now remains on the site.[17]

In Shrewsbury itself flannel manufacture was concentrated in Barker Street, where shearmen had traditionally lived. In 1800 Thomas Child, flannel manufacturer, was using a chestnut mare to power carding machinery on his premises, where he also had looms. By 1813 Rowley's Mansion (SJ 489125) was in use as a woollen manufactory. The principal manufacturer, the demise of whose business was remembered with regret in the 1890s, was a Mr Rowbottom whose stock, when he sold up in 1830, included carding machines, jennies and frames for spinning, and looms. The machinery was powered by a single horse.[18]

A more ambitious enterprise was the integrated woollen factory built in 1790 in Coleham, Shrewsbury (SJ 496122), at the confluence of the Severn and the Rea Brook by Powis and Hodges. With two five-storey ranges, one 33.9m. x 12m. the other 31.3m. x 12m., and a four-storey block, 13.8m. x 12m., it was amongst the largest woollen mills built by that time. Power was derived from a small steam

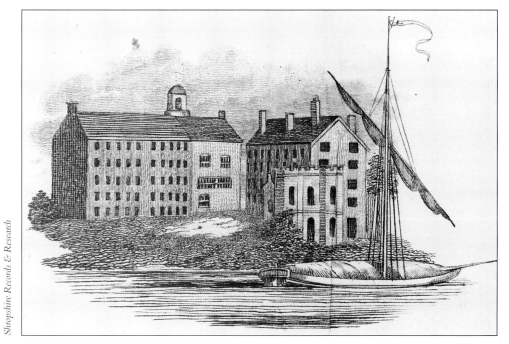

76   *The textile mill in Coleham, Shrewsbury (SJ 496172), constructed for Powis & Hodges in 1790 and leased by Charles Hulbert from 1803. To the right is Hulbert's 'Castle', the home which he built for himself.*

engine, and a 4.57m. diameter water wheel, and equipment included billies for carding, jennies for spinning, looms and fulling stocks. The enterprise quickly went bankrupt and for about a decade the mill stood empty or was used to house prisoners of war. It subsequently became part of an ambitious cotton manufacturing enterprise.[19]

COTTON MANUFACTURE

In 1803 during the period of commercial optimism which followed the Treaty of Amiens the factory was leased by Charles Hulbert, a Mancunian, who was intending to weave yarn spun at Turner's mill at Llangollen, producing calicoes to be printed at the works of Roberts & Warren at Morda.[20] He began operation with 97 workers, which rose to a maximum of 123. Hulbert encountered difficulties in personnel management, losing some trained employees to factories in Stockport and Manchester which offered higher wages. In 1811 Luddite threats prevented him from operating power looms. The hope of a legacy which would have provided him with capital proved unavailing. By 1814 he was turning towards retailing. The property was gradually tenemented as dwellings and workshops, and was sold in 1825. The site is now occupied by the Territorial Army for whom a drill hall was built in place of the four-storey building at the rear in 1881. A photograph taken during the construction of the adjacent pumping station *c.*1900 shows the longer of the five-storey buildings alongside the road, and part of the other five-storey block at right angles to it. The buildings appear to have been demolished in the 1920s. Hulbert meanwhile became an auctioneer and publisher, and a prolific antiquarian.[21]

There was a concentration of textile manufactures on the Morda, south of Oswestry. Hulbert's associates, Henry Warren of Bury and John Roberts of Oswestry, leased two of the mill sites on the Morda Brook, Morda (Lower) Mill (SJ 289281) and Upper Weston Mill (SJ 297275). The printworks was operating in 1804, when it was valued at over £24,000. The partnership was dissolved in 1806 but production continued under Henry Warren's direction until 1818. Upper Weston Mill was later a corn mill and has been demolished. Morda (Lower) Mill after being used for paper making in the mid-19th century, reverted to textile use as Rogers's woollen factory from 1800 until the 1930s. The site remains in industrial use but the only old buildings are some low stone structures which may have been drying sheds for the paper mill.[22]

There were two other cotton mills in Shropshire. Little is known of that in Broseley, other than that in 1792 it was worked by Messrs Jennings, Latham and Jennings, who operated an adjacent wholesale warehouse for textiles. The mill might be the three-storey west range of the Broseley Pipe Works (SJ 671022), which measures 11m. x 5m., and is probably of late 18th-century date, but this can only be surmise. [23] The other mill stood on the River Rea in Stottesdon parish (SO 662804), was built c.1794 at a cost of £4,000, had a 4.26m. diameter, 3.65m. wide waterwheel and machines for carding and spinning. All that is known about the mill comes from attempts to sell it between 1804 and 1827. It appears to have been demolished by 1840, but the water power system remains. Slag on the site suggests that it was constructed on the site of Prescot Forge which ceased to operate in the early 1790s.[24]

MIGHTY FLAX MILLS

Shropshire's most important role in the Industrial Revolution in the textile industry came in the linen sector. Its capital originated in the traditional trade in Welsh woollens. In the 1790s the brothers Thomas (d.1833) and Benjamin (d.1834) Benyon owned warehouses in Shrewsbury and Dolgellau which were used for storing flannel. Both lived in Quarry Place which suggests that they were among Shrewsbury's richest citizens. By 1792 they were acquainted with John Marshall (1765-1845) the pioneer of mechanisation in the Yorkshire linen industry. The following year the brothers invested £9,000 in Marshall's mill in Water Lane, Leeds. A second mill was opened in Leeds in 1795, but it was damaged in a fire on 13 February 1796, recommencing operations in July. By May 1796 the partners had decided to build a new mill in Shrewsbury, and had admitted Charles Bage to their partnership by the following month. On 26 September 1796 they purchased a site at Ditherington (SJ 497136), on the north side of Shrewsbury, and within a year had constructed on it the first iron-framed building in the world.[25]

Charles Bage (1751-1822), who designed the mill, was the son of the novelist-mechanic Robert Bage (1728-1801) and had resided in Shrewsbury since 1776, making his living as wine merchant and surveyor. He had a profound understanding of the structural properties of iron, shown by his comments in 1801 on Thomas Telford's design for a single bridge of one iron arch to replace London Bridge. He was acquainted with William Strutt (1756-1830) of Belper, who first used iron columns in textile mills, and with William Reynolds, who made available to him the results of tests on the structural properties of iron carried out while the Longdon Aqueduct was being designed.

The mill began operation in 1797 and was soon profitable. In 1804 Marshall bought out his partners. For the next 82 years it formed part of the Leeds company which claimed to be Europe's largest flax-spinning concern. Until *c.*1830 some yarn was produced, and cloth was woven on hand looms, but increasingly the mill specialised in making thread. John Marshall's grandsons decided to wind up the company in 1885 and the Ditherington Mill ceased operation the following year. The business was not, as is sometimes suggested, transferred to the United States, although some skilled workers probably migrated to Jersey City, NJ.

The *Shrewsbury Chronicle* in 1797 [26] hailed the Ditherington Mill as a fireproof building. Its importance was acknowledged for a few years afterwards, but it was subsequently neglected by historians of architecture, and it was not until the 1940s that it was 'rediscovered' by Turpin Bannister of the University of Illinois, and by Professor A.W. Skempton who demonstrated that it was indeed the first iron-framed building. The main mill building and most of its subsidiary structures remain, and have provided stimulating evidence about the development of the site and about the evolution of textile mills in general.

The main mill[27] is 53.94m. long and 12.04m. wide, and consists of four floors, with an additional attic storey. The upright columns and the cross beams are of iron, although timber was used in the staircases, and possibly to form trusses and battens for fixing slates. On each floor are three lines of cruciform columns, supporting cross beams from which spring shallow brick arches, the nine northerly bays being 3.04m. in span, the six to the south 3.2m., which form the floors above. Just to the south of the mid-point of the mill is a bay 3.66m. wide which originally contained a cross-wall rising through the first three floors. Wrought iron tie rods 2.54cm square run through the mill to the east of each line of pillars. On the attic floor a central line of columns supports sloping beams from which spring arches of shorter radius. This roof structure, used in no other mill, would have excluded from the factory any fire which might have broken out in timber which may have been used to fix slates. Power from the steam engines was not conveyed to the attic storey. No original doors or windows remain in the mill, but these were certainly of iron. A 20 h.p. Boulton & Watt engine was installed at the south end of the mill in 1797. It was replaced in 1811 by a 60 h.p. engine, which was succeeded by a 30 h.p. Corliss engine by Hick of Bolton in 1874-75. It was probably at this period that the two top storeys of the present engine house were added, as additional storage space. At the north end of the mill a 40 h.p. engine was installed by mid-1800, and was replaced by a 56 h.p. engine in 1819-20, and by another Corliss engine in 1875. Archaeological evidence suggests that the engine at the north end drove machinery on the upper floors of the mill through shafting which ran through

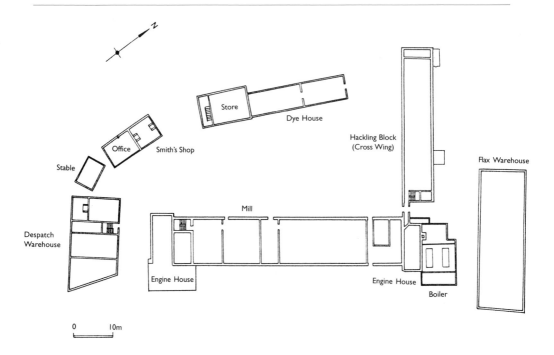

77   *Plan of the Ditherington Flax Mill, re-drawn from an original in the Boulton & Watt Collection of 1811, Birmingham Libraries.*

˙78   *The eastern elevation of the Ditherington Flax Mill, c.1900, after alterations by William Jones & Co. The lean-to alongside the canal and the large pyramidal malt kiln had just been completed.*

Shropshire Records & Research

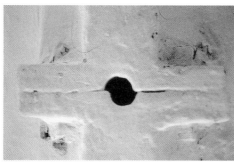

79 *The first floor of the Ditherington Flax Mill showing three lines of cruciform columns, the cross beams abutting to the right of the central columns, and the wrought iron tie rods holding together the brick jack arches.*

80 *A 5cm. hole within the flanges at the joint of a cross beam on the second floor of the Ditherington flax mill, through which drive shafts transmitted power to machines.*

the capitals of the central line of columns on the third floor. The engines at the south end appear to have driven machinery through shafting running through the similar capitals of the central line of capitals on the ground floor. Grooves cast in the flanges of the beams where they meet just off the centre line of the mill create holes, 5cm. in diameter, through which machinery on the first and second floors could be driven by small vertical shafts. Access to the mill was by means of the staircase at the south alongside the 20 h.p. engine. Since the mill was using less than 600 tons of flax a year in the 1820s, materials could have been carried between floors, and the building lacks hoists or taking-in doors. There are no traces of early sanitation, heating or lighting systems, although gas lighting was installed in 1811. The mill is built of bricks made in the vicinity, measuring 10 x 11 x 24cm (approx.), the size which appears to have been employed in all the buildings on the site built before June 1805.

The principal subsidiary buildings are the cross wing or hackling block, and the flax warehouse, both of which are iron-framed. The cross wing, completed by 1803, originally had a timber frame but was destroyed in a fire on 24 October 1811. It was rebuilt with an iron frame, its length shortened from 41.68m. to 36.6m., and its width increased from 6.27m to 10m., the northern wall being on a new alignment. The iron frame consists of two lines of pillars carrying nine sets of beams supporting brick arches like those in the main mill. The cruciform columns have moulded star-shaped capitals, now encrusted with paint. The cross-wing has a pitched roof carried on cast iron queen-post trusses.

The flax warehouse, completed by June 1805, the first building in the complex to be constructed of 'standard', (7.5 x 9 x 21cm.) bricks, is a four-storey structure of nine bays, 26.8m. long and 11.9m. wide. Eight cast iron cross beams are carried on two rows of cruciform columns. The brick-vaulted roof appears to be in suspension, hanging from the iron-framed trusses. The warehouse had the minimum of fenestration, although one small iron-framed window, apparently from the primary phase of construction, remains in the south wall.

Recent comparative work by Giles & Goodall in West Yorkshire, by Falconer and others in Cumberland and North Yorkshire, and by Watson in Scotland,[28] makes it possible to see the Ditherington mill in its context within the linen industry. Iron-framing was certainly adopted because it was believed to be fireproof, but it was particularly closely associated with linen manufacture. By 1816 iron-framed structures formed the principal buildings used for spinning in nine flax-spinning complexes, far more than had been built in the much larger cotton and woollen sectors.

It seems likely that there were standard formulae for flax-spinning complexes and for equipping the buildings used for spinning, probably devised by the Leeds engineer Matthew Murray (1765-1826), who once worked for Marshall, and whose Round Foundry was adjacent to Marshall's mill in Leeds. Bundles of flax were produced seasonally and, once delivered to mills, were stored in warehouses which did not need windows. Flax was then heckled in a building separate from the main mill, the process dividing the short fibres, the *tow,* from the long fibres, *line.* The line was conveyed to the fourth floor where preparation continued on drawing and roving frames, the resultant sliver proceeding to the third floor for spinning. The tow was prepared on heavier machines on the ground floor, and the sliver produced went to the first floor for spinning.

This hypothetical sequence offers a convincing explanation of the original mode of operation of the Ditherington mill. Subsequently the uses of the buildings changed. A new process, wet spinning, was introduced in the early 1830s, when part of the cross wing came to be used for spinning. An engineering shop was established on the ground floor of the main mill, which by the 1860s also housed a woodworking shop making reels from Swedish timber, and a printing department producing labels for the many varieties of thread then being manufactured.[29]

Most of the other buildings which formed the mill complex survive. Near the south entrance, one wall is all that remains of a small warehouse for finished products, subsequently a threadmakers' shop and a packing shop, which was completed by 1801, and constructed from the same 'great bricks' as the main mill. It was demolished in the 1970s. The adjacent blacksmiths' shop and stable also date from before 1805. The next building on the west side of the courtyard is the stove block, substantially altered in 1841-43. The presence of great bricks in the older portions suggests that it dated from before 1805. It was probably designed by Bage who was drawing plans for such a building in October 1802. The first dyehouse was built before 1804 but the present building was constructed in the early 1850s. It has fine quality brickwork and a roof with composite trusses of cast iron and wrought iron members. There were two gasworks, one built in 1811 and later converted to a carpenters' shop, the other of 1842, but nothing remains of either. The iron-framed roof of a small stable block was removed to the Ironbridge Gorge Museum in the 1970s.

The first apprentice house and a smaller house for the factory clerks were constructed before June 1800 by John Simpson (1755-1815). The former was the terrace now nos. 56-59 St Michael's Street (SJ 496137), named Ann's Hill after Simpson's daughter, while the clerks' house was the adjacent No 55 St Michael's Street. Both are constructed from the same 'great bricks' used in the mill. The apprentice house at the north end of the mill complex was built in 1812 at a cost of £3,329.[30]

The flax mill bordered the Shrewsbury Canal north of the Factory Bridge where the turnpike road to Market Drayton crossed the canal. Some of the land between the road and the canal was used for the construction of eight blocks of housing, each measuring 11.04 x 7.38m., and consisting of four dwellings. The

81 *The Apprentice House of the Ditherington Flax Mill in St Michael's Street (SJ 496137), outside the perimeter of the mill complex, built for the proprietors by John Simpson before June 1800.*

landowner John Mytton agreed with the partners early in 1797 that he would construct four blocks and rent them to the millowners for £80 p.a.[31] The other four blocks were doubtless built soon afterwards. Houses of this type, called 'cluster' or 'quadruplex' houses, were built by the Strutts at Belper, and by the Evans family at the textile village of Darley Abbey near Derby, both places with which Bage was familiar. The design was subsequently copied in the *cité ouvrière* at Mulhouse, from where it spread to Spain and the Ruhrgebiet. Only these 32 dwellings were constructed by the millowners. Two terraces at the south end of the complex, one of up to seven dwellings called Davies's Buildings, the other later numbered 1-12 St Michael's Street, were built by others, although the maltsters, William Jones & Co owned both between 1926 and 1936.

The Ditherington Mill was one of the principal employers of labour in Shrewsbury for nearly a century. In 1813 some 433 people were employed there, a total which had risen to 475 by 1819. An estimate that there were 800 employees in the 1840s is probably an exaggeration. After a period of diminishing activity the total was no more than 300 when closure was announced in 1885. Census evidence suggests that the labour force was overwhelming young. In a sample of 377 flax workers in 1851, 207 or 55 per cent were aged under twenty, and 123 or 33 per cent under sixteen. There were 65 females between 18 and 24 employed, compared with only 41 males, suggesting that many boys left for other work in their late teens, while girls continued at the mill until they married. There were many more men than women among the employees over thirty.

In 1811-12 John Marshall established a bleachworks [32] on the site of corn mill on the Rea Brook at Hanwood (SJ 441093). He opened a similar detached bleachworks at Wortley, serving his Leeds mill, in the following year. The main building was an iron-framed, four-storey structure, in which, by the 1880s, power was provided by a waterwheel and a compound horizontal steam engine. By 1851 64 men and boys were employed at Hanwood. Six young skilled men in their early twenties lived in a cottage within the bleachyard complex, while other employees were accommodated in the 23 dwellings in Factory Row, the terrace on the eastern side of the lane which approached the mill from the Shrewsbury - Minsterley road. The mill was converted to grind barytes and has subsequently been demolished, as have the older four-room dwellings in Factory Row, but five cottages at the southern end, built in the mid-19th century remain.

The Benyon brothers and Charles Bage, having terminated their partnership with John Marshall in 1804, established a parallel flax-spinning business, by constructing new iron-framed mills both in Leeds and Shrewsbury. The latter was a five-storey structure in Castlefields (SJ 497131), 63.65m. long and 10.83m. wide, with a 20h.p. engine at the south end and a 75h.p. engine by Fenton & Murray of Leeds at the north end. A cross wing west of the main block provided accommodation in 1811 for the reeling and warping departments, the counting house and the stoves. Detached buildings included a dyehouse, a bleaching works, a woodworking shop, a smiths' shop, a gasworks and a warehouse. Thomas Benyon died in 1833 and Benjamin Benyon in 1834. [33] The mill was put up for sale in full work in October 1833 and again in 1835 and 1836. Charles Hulbert observed a 'spirit

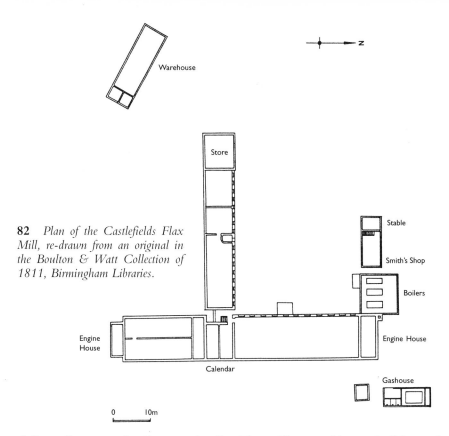

Warehouse

N

Store

Stable

Smith's Shop

Boilers

82 *Plan of the Castlefields Flax Mill, re-drawn from an original in the Boulton & Watt Collection of 1811, Birmingham Libraries.*

Engine House

Engine House

Calendar

Gashouse

0   10m

of discord' among the Benyon family. The mill was sold to a builder and most of the buildings had been demolished by 31 May 1837. The shock to the local economy was severe, and the closure was seen as a reason for the fall in Shrewsbury's population during the 1830s.[34]

The Castlefields mill stood close to the line of the appropriately-named Benyon Street, constructed in the 1850s. The only surviving part, known in 1811 as the 'new building', is the iron-framed 22.3m. x 7.16m. block, now houses numbered 5-8a Severn Street, which stood about 25m. south-west of the corner of the cross wing. A sale plan shows that this was a warehouse. The herring-bone lintels above the windows of 5-8a Severn Street are identical with those of the much later cottages on either side of the block, suggesting that, like other flax warehouses, it was sparsely fenestrated. To the west of the warehouse, the building which had probably served as the apprentice house was converted to Cadran Place a block of back-to-back dwellings, and remained until the 1930s or 1940s, when it was replaced by a block of flats.[35]

The warehouse became one of several linen weaving workshops in Shrewsbury, first, in the 1830s, the property of one Sacheverell Harwood, then, after he had sold it in 1843, of Robert Minn, a native of Sherburn, Yorkshire, born in 1799. The inscription 'Minn & Co, Home Made Linen Warehouse' was legible on the wall of an adjacent cottage until the 1970s. Apart from Minn, seven weavers were living in the Castlefields area in 1851, three of them in adjacent dwellings, which may have been within the block in Severn Street. Hannah Minn, widow of Robert, was still operating a linen weaving business from 13 Severn Street in 1871.

An earlier weaving concern was that of Paddock & Davies which from *c*.1814 to 1818 operated in three of the large rented rooms within Hulbert's cotton factory in Coleham. The Benyons also had a weaving factory in Coleham, probably the 'noggin manufactory' noted by Charles Hulbert as existing in 1802, although its site is unknown, as is that of the Benyons' weaving workshop in Barker Street.[36]

The most significant weaving factory in Shrewsbury was built by Charles Bage in Kingsland (SJ 489119) after he withdrew from his partnership with the Benyons in 1815-16. It was a single-storey structure, 27.43m. long with a brick vaulted roof, spanning 9.14m. and 22cm. thick. Bage employed up to 70 people, operating 30 hand looms and 24 power looms, the latter worked by a 4 h.p. steam engine. Products included linen, huckaback and sailcloth. After Bage died in 1822, the business went bankrupt, his widow closing the factory on 26 October 1826.[37] The buildings were subsequently used by George Burr as a leadworks.

The Shrewsbury linen industry reached its zenith about 1820 when the Ditherington and Castlefields spinning mills together were employing at least a thousand people, 70 weavers were work-

ing for Charles Bage, and others for smaller concerns. The main mill buildings at Ditherington and Castlefields were the biggest built in the flax industry before the late 1830s, substantially larger than any individual buildings in Yorkshire, although the complexes in Leeds of John Marshall and the Benyon brothers were larger than those in Shrewsbury. The Shrewsbury mills were similarly exceptional in the amount of power deployed within them. The engines at Ditherington provided 116 h.p. by 1820, while 95 h.p. was available at Castlefields by 1811. By 1820 Marshall's Mill in Leeds had 234 h.p. available, and Benyons' Mill 136 h.p., but no other Yorkshire mill approached the power output of those in Shrewsbury. Shrewsbury had two mills in the vanguard of flax-spinning technology and structural innovation, but it failed to develop a baggage train of smaller concerns, like the 'old irregular-looking houses seemingly much disfigured with alterations and additions' which comprised

83 *The south west elevation of Nos. 5-8a Severn Street, Shrewsbury, once the flax warehouse of the Castlefields Flax Mill, and later linen weaving workshops, SJ 496131.*

the majority of the flax mills in Leeds in 1821. It was perhaps for this reason that no buyer emerged to take over the Kingsland Mill in the 1820s or the Castlefields Mill in the 1830s. Linen weaving thereafter seems to have been no more than an urbanised version of the vernacular trade which persisted in the Shropshire country-side, while Marshall's mill increasingly specialised in thread manufacture and employed fewer and fewer people. The Shrewsbury mills were an artificial transplant, made possible by the Benyons' capital and their love for their native town. Flax spinning did not make significant use of local raw materials, nor did it draw on local textile traditions. While Marshall's mill operated for 90 years, flax spinning in Shrewsbury has something in common with some of the state-sponsored car plants of the 1960s, like the Hillman Imp factory at Linwood or the Triumph works at Speke, well-capitalised, equipped with up-to-date technology, but ultimately failing to take sufficient root to survive beyond a single generation of products.

RIPPLES FROM AFAR

Shropshire also experienced distant ripples from the Industrial Revolution in silk manufacture. In the 1770s a water-powered silk mill was operated by William Jackson in Mill Street, Ludlow. It was offered for sale in 1777 and 1786 and subsequently converted to a wool warehouse but has now been demolished.[38] In Whitchurch in the 1820s Messrs. Whitfield & Sergeant constructed a silk mill, 44 m. long and 10.6m. wide and in brick, alongside the canal (SJ 535415). Its two storeys provided working space for 200 people, but it was so designed that three further storeys could be added. Power was provided by a 10 h.p. steam engine by Galloway of Manchester for four 104-bobbin doubling frames, a hard silk engine with 100 swifts, and four 100-bobbin drawing frames. It was offered for sale in 1831 and by 1851 had been converted to a warehouse by Thomas Burgess, a cheese factor and corn merchant.[39]

LOCAL SPECIALISMS

Carpet manufacture was established in Bridgnorth by entrepreneurs from nearby Kidderminster in the 1790s and became the town's principal industry. Both the principal factories in Friars Street (SO 718933) and the Pale Meadow Mills in Spital Street (SO 721927), demolished in the 1980s, consisted largely of north-lit sheds of mid- or late 19th-century date. Other buildings in Listley Street and St Mary Street were used by carpet makers in the early 19th century. Various wool spinning enterprises in the town in the late 19th century probably produced yarn for carpet-manufacture. Rural mills in the vicinity were also involved in the industry. The Town Mills at Pendlestone were reconstructed in 1845. The main building is iron-framed and of two storeys. The upper floor is illuminated by cone-shaped lights set into the roof in the same style as those used by Ignatious Bonomi in Marshall's Mill at Leeds about five years earlier. The building is in the Tudor Gothic style and was originally more heavily crenellated. Power was provided by a waterwheel at the northern end, later replaced by a turbine, and supplemented by a steam engine at the opposite end. The three-storey water-powered mill at Burcote (SJ 746954) was built in 1799 by William & Joseph Macmichael to provide yarn for Bridgnorth's carpet weavers. Power was provided by a 6m. diameter water wheel for a devil and three carding engines on the ground floor and six spinning frames, with a total of 256 spindles, and drawing frames on the floors above. The mill was offered for sale in 1815 and subsequently converted to a corn mill. A four-storey mill at Eardington (SO 708899), 18.28m. long and 8.53m. wide, was built in 1794 by William & George Hallen to spin flaxen and woollen yarn, for which there were respectively 96 and 104 spindles. It was sold in 1798 after the Hallens went bankrupt and was subsequently converted to a corn mill.[40]

Market Drayton in the 19th century supplied national markets with horsehair cloth. Cotton, which was usually mixed with horsehair yarn, was spun at the town's workhouse from the 1760s, and the governor appointed in 1783 was sometimes described as a 'cotton manufacturer'. In 1810-11 Samuel & Peter Davies began construction of an iron-framed mill intended for the manufacture of thread, probably cotton thread. Iron castings for the main mill building were supplied by William Hazledine, and machinery was delivered, but when the property was offered for sale in 1811 buyers were asked to remove the buildings.[41] The manufacture of horsehair cloth for use as sieves in malthouses and dairies, and in upholstery, had begun in the town by the late 1790s. The principal building was the Victoria Mill (SJ 671334), rebuilt as a horsehair cloth works in 1855 by H. & W. Sandbrook. It was commonly remarked in the mid-19th century that the three manufacturers employed about 200 people in Market Drayton. The labour force was largely female. In 1861 Joseph Haslam employed three men, six boys, 34 women and 20 girls. At least four weavers in 1861 were unmarried women living in some of the worst accommodation in the town, some of their children working as hair weavers' servers. The industry was in decline by the end of the century. Haslam's works was sold in 1903 to H. W. Woodcock who continued to make horsecloth until 1934. One of Haslam's factories, in Shropshire Street (SJ 674340), is now used by a baker.[42]

Shropshire's textile industry varies from the most 'vernacular' type of production for local markets, through the modest specialisms of towns like Bridgnorth and Market Drayton, and enterprises like flannel factories and silk mills which represented the distant ripples of large scale growth in other counties, to the great Shrewsbury flax mills, in their time larger and more innovative than any others in the world, save their owners' parallel mills in Leeds. The county's textile history highlights two paradoxical themes—the profound impact of the Industrial Revolution in the late 18th century, and the dogged persistence of small-scale local manufactures throughout the 19th century. Study of the industry also brings out the contrast between our understanding of Ditherington Mill, which is constantly increasing because the mill still stands and can be viewed in new contexts as research progresses, and our ignorance of so many mills which have long since been demolished.

◆ ◆ ◆

6

Untold Treasures:
Landscapes of Upland Mining

◆ ◆ ◆

S hropshire was for a time one of the chief sources of lead ore in Britain. At its peak in the early 1870s the ore field around the Stiperstones produced about 10 per cent of the British output of lead. Lead ore was mined on a significant scale in the region for nearly two centuries, and its mining monuments are amongst the most impressive in Britain. Other sources of non-ferrous ores are dispersed across the county. None is of national importance, but their surviving remains illuminate the perpetual optimism of mining speculators.

THE STIPERSTONES REGION: MINERALS AND ECONOMY

The principal minerals which occur in veins in the Stiperstones region are *galena* or lead sulphide (PbS), *sphalerite*, zinc sulphide or zinc blende (ZnS) and *barytes* or barium sulphate (BaSO4). Small quantities of silver and fluorspar have also been produced. The metallic ores are found in three principal setts, one around Snailbeach, another extending from The Bog to Tankerville Mine, and a third along the valley of the Hope Brook, incorporating The Grit and The Gravels mines. Barytes deposits occur more widely and were exploited from Cothercot in the east to Wotherton and Bulthy in the west.[1]

The pig of lead preserved at Linley Hall which bears the inscription of the Emperor Hadrian is evidence of Roman interest in the mineral deposits of the Stiperstones region. Mining of lead on a substantial scale was in progress by 1739 at the Bog mine (SO 356978), ore from which was being smelted in the Ironbridge Gorge.[2] In 1777 Jonathan Scott constructed there the first Watt steam pumping engine in the orefield. The arrival of the engine was symbolic of increasing mining activity. John Lawrence of the White Grit Co leased extensive mineral rights, worked a smelter at Malehurst and coal mines at Pontesford, built Watt pumping engines at Roman Gravels (SO 334998) in 1783, and at the Grit in 1793, and had interests in the Pennerley and Bog mines. His family prospered during the Napoleonic wars but their wealth was destroyed by litigation in the 1820s.[3]

Modern exploitation at Snailbeach began in 1761 when Thomas Powys leased the mineral rights. His operations quickly established that this was a rich mine, indeed the richest in the county. In 1782 it was leased by the Snailbeach Mining Company which worked it for more than a century.[4]

Falling prices and the law suits faced by the Lawrence family led to a decline in the industry after 1815, but prosperity gradually returned. Production figures are available from 1845, when 3,551 tons of lead ore were mined in the county, some 4.54 per cent of national output. Over the next 20 years production varied between 2,729 tons and 4,491 tons, following no particular pattern.[5]

Confidence was reflected in the installation in 1839 by a reconstituted Bog Mine Co of a 370 h.p. steam pumping engine, with a 70-inch cylinder, named the *Queen Victoria* and built by the Coalbrookdale Co. Crowds from as far away as Shrewsbury and Bishop's Castle swarmed over the hill, cannon were fired, and visitors feasted on ale, bread and cheese, while listening to music provided by harpists and fiddlers. The Company's agent delighted in the moral reform, symbolised by the building of a chapel, which had come with the revival of mining. Optimism was not sustained. The mine closed in 1844, and was re-opened in 1856 by a fraudulent company which went into liquidation three years later.[6]

In the mid-1860s the Shropshire mines attracted speculative capital from the City of London and elsewhere, and a tide of new investment raised production year by year from 1867.[7] It reached a peak of 7,932 tons in 1875, and did not fall below 7,000 tons for six years from 1871. There was a slight decline after 1877, although output in 1883, 6,495 tons, was 12.7 per cent of national production. Thereafter decline was rapid. Output had fallen below 2,000 tons by 1889, and exceeded that figure in only three years during the 1890s. It fell below 1,000 tons in 1902 and only 132 tons were mined in 1911. Lead mining in Shropshire had effectively ceased by the outbreak of the First World War. In the two parishes of Westbury and Pontesbury, 178 were employed in lead mining and smelting in 1841, a total which increased to 304 in 1851, but fell back to 201 ten years later. There was a modest increase to 248 by 1871, a slight falling back to 191 by 1881, and a catastrophic fall to 61 in the following decade.

The silver content of Shropshire ores was rarely high enough to make refining profitable but small quantities were produced in 1854 and 1861, and then annually from 1872 until 1883, which was the peak year of production with an output of 11,388 ounces, amounting to 3.31 per cent of UK output. Zinc ore production was recorded in 1858 and annually from 1863 until 1913. Output was 210 tons in 1863, rising to peaks of 837 tons in 1875, 914 tons in 1882, and 880 tons in 1897. Output slumped to 37 tons in 1910, but recovered slightly to 444 tons in 1913. The 759 tons mined in 1872 formed 4.09 per cent of UK output. Some fluorspar production was recorded in 1874–75, and between 1877 and 1879.

Silver, zinc and fluorspar were marginal to the mining economy of south Shropshire, but barytes sustained the industry on a modest scale for more than three decades after lead mining ceased. Barytes production was first recorded in 1857 when a thousand tons mined in Shropshire contributed 7.99 per cent of national output. No production was recorded in 1859, 1863 and 1866, but annual output figures subsequently appeared regularly, reaching peaks of 4,870 tons in 1875, 4,939 in 1884, 7,170 tons in 1890, 8,771 tons in 1901, 9,597 tons in 1906 and 13,772 tons in 1913. Between 1890 and 1893 and between 1901 and 1906 over a quarter of the national output of barytes came from Shropshire, and production continued until after the Second World War.

THE STIPERSTONES REGION: THE ARCHAEOLOGY OF LEAD-MINING

The archaeology of the region is dominated by the remains of Snailbeach Mine, one of the richest sources of lead in Europe which produced 131,900 tons of lead ore between 1845 and 1913 with a maximum output of 3,852 tons in 1846. Modest quantities of zinc ore were produced between 1858 and 1912, with a maximum output of 378 tons in 1902. Some fluorspar was produced in the 1870s, and some silver in the early 1880s. Barytes production was first recorded in 1860, but remained at a low level until after 1900, reaching a peak of 3,734 tons in 1913, and continuing until after the Second World War. Numbers of workers at Snailbeach are recorded from 1877, when 176 were employed underground and 180 on the surface, a total of 356. The number fell during the recession of the early 1880s, no more than 86 being employed in 1885, but revived to 150 in the following year and remained around that level until the end of the century. It had fallen below a hundred by 1910. The pumping engine was halted in 1911 and the sections of the mine below the drainage adit were allowed to flood.[8]

Conservation and evaluation of the surviving components of the Snailbeach Mine only began in the early 1990s. Much that remained in the 1960s has been destroyed or allowed to decay, including two headstocks, an engine house, a dressing plant with a line of wrought iron kibbles filled with ore, and a jig with a spiral classifier. Most surviving buildings date from the 1870s when the Cornishman Henry Dennis reorganised the mine. The site of a dressing shed, once occupied

Barbara Ridgway

84   *One of the wooden headstocks which remained at Snailbeach (SJ 375021) in the 1960s.*

by eight jigging machines and four buddles, awaits excavation. The reservoir, from which the machines were supplied with water, remains at the head of the valley. There is a winding engine house of 1872, a compressor house of 1881 and a blacksmiths' shop. On Lordshill above the main concentration of buildings, stands a Cornish engine house of 1856. The white tips of spoil from the dressing processes were one of Shropshire's most prominent industrial landmarks, and their removal at great expense in 1994 is much regretted.

Snailbeach ore was smelted at Pontesford from the early 1780s until 1862-63 when a new reverberatory smelter was constructed on the hillside about 800m. north of the mine (SJ 373030). Fumes were conveyed through a flue which cut across the site to a chimney high on Lordshill, which also served the boilers of the nearby Cornish engine. The chimney, used until the closure of the smelter in 1895, remains intact, and some sections of the flue can be traced.[9]

Henry Dennis was largely responsible for the construction of the 2ft. 4in. (0.71m.) gauge Snailbeach District Railways the Act of Parliament for which (36 & 37 Vic c 207) was obtained in 1873. The line opened in 1877 and linked standard gauge sidings at Pontesbury (SJ 393063) with Crows Nest (SJ 371018), where there were sidings for ore delivered by road from mines to the south. A reverse siding ran up to the shafts and dressing floors of the Snailbeach Mine, and a further branch served the smelter. Between 1878 and 1883 the railway carried on average 14,000 tons of minerals per year.[10]

The best-preserved remains of the Snailbeach District Railways are within the mine complex, where the locomotive depot has been restored by Shropshire County Council, and some lengths of track remain in situ. The depot was memorably photographed with 4-6-0T locomotives built by the Baldwin company in the United States for military service in the First World War, and used at Snailbeach from 1923.

The railway outlasted the mine. In 1905 a branch was opened serving the quarry of the Ceiriog Granite Co on the north side of Eastridge Wood near Habberley. Carriage of roadstone increased the railway's receipts and, in 1909, 38,000 tons were carried. The branch was closed in 1922. In 1923 the railway was taken over by Colonel Stephens and receipts from the carriage of barytes and of roadstone from a quarry on Callow Hill remained buoyant during the 1930s. Loads of stone were worked by steam locomotives until 1946, when Salop County Council, which leased the line the following year, began to use a farm tractor. The track was abandoned in 1959 when the quarry was made accessible to lorries.[11]

The Roman Gravels Mine ranked second after Snailbeach in terms of size and output. Its site remains a mining landscape of unusual interest. Output declined substantially after the demise of the Lawrences and in 1859 totalled no more than 61 tons. It had risen to 1,550 tons by 1873 and remained at over 2,000 throughout the 1870s, peaking at 3,109 in 1883. By 1892 it had fallen to 993 tons and never again reached significant levels. In 1877 there were 252 employees, 156 of them working underground, but only four men were employed by 1894. East Roman Gravels employed 89 miners in 1881, suffered severely in the recession during the years which followed, but subsequently recovered. Ten miners were employed in

85 *The engine house of the Ladywell mine (SO 328994) erected by Arthur Waters in 1875.*

1884. The number rose in the late 1890s to a peak of 111 in 1898, but was reduced to four by 1909. The workings were developed in the 1870s by Arthur Waters (1834-1887), a Cornish mining engineer, who was also concerned with the Tankerville and Ladywell mines. Extensive spoil tips line the A488 road which was crossed by a three-level wooden bridge (SO 334998), photographed about 1890 with the top deck occupied by miners, perhaps queuing for their wages. An engine house for a 60-inch Cornish engine by Harveys of Hayle erected in 1878 stands on the hillside, with some pump rods remaining in the shaft. Below it in the valley stands an older pumping engine house constructed about 1865, and the ruins of engines which drove winding gear and compressors. Another Cornish engine house of *c.*1850 remains at the adjacent East Roman Gravels mine, together with the ruins of a winding engine house.[12]

Most surviving structures reflect the period of investment with speculators' funds from the City of London in the third quarter of the 19th century, or even later workings for barytes. The most prominent features of the landscape are the 19 engine houses of which there are significant remains.

Table 6.1: **Steam engine houses in the Stiperstones lead-mining region**			
Central Snailbeach	Pumping	1860s	SJ 347022
East Grit	Pumping	1870s	SO 326981
East Roman Gravels	Pumping	1850s	SJ 336003
(West Tankerville)	Winding (California)	1870s	SJ 336002
Ladywell	Pumping & winding	1875	SO 328994
Old Grit	Pumping	1783	SO 326981
Roman Gravels	Pumping	1878	
	Pumping	1860s	SJ 334000
	Winding Compressor	1870s	
Ritton Castle	Pumping	1853	SO 349980
Snailbeach	Winding	1872	SJ 373021
	Compressor	1881	SJ 373021
	Pumping (Lordshill)	1857-58	SJ 374020
	Halvans	1899	SJ 373023
Tankerville Watson's Shaft	Pumping	1876	SO 355995
Oven Pipe	Pumping & Winding	1870s	
White Grit	Pumping	1860s	SO 319979
Wotherton	Pumping	1865	SJ 279004

The Tankerville or Ovenpipe Mine (SO 355995) is characteristic of the speculative boom of the 1860s and '70s. It was worked on a small scale in the early 19th century, then came under the management of Arthur Waters, who discovered a new vein of ore in 1862. A new shaft was sunk and an underground engine installed. For a time in the mid-1870s the mine was prosperous. Output in 1875 peaked at 1,700 tons of ore, but by 1877 costs were increasing as prices were falling. A new company was formed, and the labour force rose to 171 in 1880, but mining stopped in 1884 and was never resumed. Two substantial pumping engine houses built by Waters remain, together with the ruins of a winding engine house.[13]

At the Bog (SO 356979) the monuments of lead mining have mostly been destroyed, with the exception of a small powder magazine and a blind adit. Two reservoirs used for dressing ore remain; one of them, dating from 1872, is bisected by a tramway built to carry barytes by Sir James Ramsden in the early 20th century.[14]

An outstanding monument to local mining skills is the Boat Level, a 2.8km.-adit which drains water from The Bog and other mines into the valley of the Minsterley Brook (SJ 358002). Its excavation was directed by John Lawrence, and was probably completed in 1797, the year in which the Boulton & Watt engine draining the Bog Mine was sold. Explorers of the level have surmised that it is too narrow to have been used for transport, but it was described as a navigable level when the Bog Mine was sold in 1830, when the stock of the mine included two wooden boats and an iron one.[15] It thus seems likely that the Boat Level was used for carrying out ore, although the vessels must have been small. The outlets remain of two drainage levels in the Hope Valley, the Wood (or Hope) Level (SJ 339008) driven in the 1790s by John Lawrence, and the Leigh Tunnel (SJ 331034), the venture which brought his son to bankruptcy. Water from Snailbeach is drained into the Hope Brook along a 1.3km.-adit driven in the late 1790s. For a time it carried a rod drive system from a waterwheel on the brook to pumps raising water up the mine shaft to the adit level.

Archaeological evidence of the growing sophistication of ore-dressing techniques in the 19th century is not plentiful in the Stiperstones region, although the accumulations of fine waste materials at Snailbeach, Roman Gravels, Pennerley and elsewhere show that Shropshire mine owners were concerned to increase the quality of the concentrates they sent to smelters. The change is reflected in the occupations of people working at the mines. In 1851 four lead ore washers were living on Pontesbury Hill. Ten years later two lead ore washers and two lead buddlers were living on the hill, and there were 13 ore washers in Westbury parish, some of them women.

The first lead smelter in the region was established at Malehurst (SJ 384060) in 1778, and acquired by John Lawrence in the 1790s, when he also built a smelter adjacent to the *Nag's Head* inn at Pontesford. Both were adjacent to mines in the Shrewsbury coalfield. The Malehurst smelter was no longer in use by 1831. The Snailbeach Company built a smelter at Pontesford (SJ 409061) in 1784, in which water power was employed to blow ore hearths. The smelter building measures 55m. x 7.3m.,

86 *The pumping engine house at the White Grit lead mine (SO 319979), dating from the 1860s.*

and from it a 110m. flue lead to a pair of chimneys, one 48m. and the other 55m. high, constructed in 1832. It closed in 1863 when the new reverberatory smelter on the hillside below Snailbeach Mine came into operation. Some parts of the building incorporated within an agricultural warehouse, together with vitrified refractory bricks re-used in farmyard walls, are the only significant remains, the chimneys having been demolished early in the 20th century. Lawrence's smelter was worked by the White Grit Co in the 1830s, and by George Burr of the lead works in Shrewsbury in the years immediately before its closure c.1880. In 1851 Thomas Bennett, lead and coal mine agent, who appears to have been responsible for one of the smelters, employed 40 men and 15 boys, while Robert Rogers, superintendent of the other lead works, employed 50 men and 20 boys. Lead was also smelted in the Ironbridge Gorge.[16]

Most lead miners lived in the parishes of Pontesbury, Westbury (including Minsterley) and Worthen. In 1851, 50 lead mine workers were recorded living on Pontesbury Hill where John Lawrence had encouraged squatting in the early 19th century. Some lead miners lived in the coal mining settlement of Horsebridge (SJ 368061), some 4 km. from the nearest lead mine. Squatter cottages on the margins of cultivation still line the road southwards from Snailbeach, which runs past the Tankerville and Pennerley Mines towards The Bog, and a similar pattern of settlement can be observed in the Hope Valley around the Roman Gravels mine. Investment in the extraction of lead always carried risks, and companies were clearly reluctant to put their capital into housing. In the depression of the 1880s many mining families were sustained by the modest holdings which surrounded their cottages.

BARYTES MINING

While lead mining in Shropshire had effectively ceased by 1914, the mining of barytes continued until the late 1940s. Some came from the unflooded workings of the major mines like Snailbeach and The Bog, which yielded respectively 3,734 and 2,904 tons in 1913, and the remainder from smaller mines which only produced barytes. Amongst these was the Wotherton No 2 Mine (SJ 279004), which worked between 1865 and 1911. The sandstone engine house has been adapted as a dwelling. Barytes was loaded on to trailers to be hauled away by traction engines in a lay-by which still remains off the B4386. Production reached a peak of 6,100 tons in 1901. The Huglith Mine (SJ 405015) began production in 1910, employed up to 65 miners, and produced up to 20,000 tons a year in the 1930s. More than a dozen other mines were worked for barytes in the late 19th century and early 20th century, but only two, Bulthy (SJ 309133) and Gatten (SO 387992), produced more than a thousand tons in any one year.[17]

The marketing of barytes depended on the availability of mills where the mineral could be ground into a form in which it could be used in paint manufacture or cosmetics. At least five water-powered mills served the Stiperstones region. A barytes miller is mentioned in the census for Minsterley in 1871. The Cliffdale Barytes Co operated at Waterwheel (SJ 365024) in the Hope Valley from 1863 until c.1926. Taylor, Gilbertson & Co worked a mill on the brook south of

87 *The engine house of the barytes mine at Wotherton (SJ 279004), which operated from the 1860s until shortly before the First World War.*

Minsterley (SJ 374045) between 1893 and *c.*1909, when it was converted to a milk depot. Barytes was crushed at Sutton Mill (SJ 504107) on the edge of Shrewsbury and at Hanwood (SJ 441093) where the mill, established on the site of the flax bleachyard after its closure in 1886, worked until 1922, and was supplied with barytes from Wotherton. The mill at Malehurst (SJ 384060) opened in 1922 and worked until *c.*1948. Huglith Mine was its main source of barytes which was conveyed by an aerial ropeway 5.6km. long, built in 1911. Barytes from The Bog was carried to Minsterley by a similar 8.8km. ropeway.[18]

There was also a barytes mill at Maesbury (SJ 304259) which supplied materials to paintmakers, set up before 1861 by Edward Peate. Supplies of barytes were delivered by rail to Oswestry and the products sent to Liverpool. Just one paint grinder, William Williams aged 60 born in Cropredy, Oxfordshire, was living in Maesbury in 1861, but subsequently the mill employed three or four people. It closed soon after 1900. Nothing remains of its buildings, but a pair of mid-Victorian dwellings, 'Paint Mill Cottages', marks its site.

COPPER MINING

Shropshire's copper mines are scattered widely, but none was of national significance. Mineral statistics available after 1845 record production in only four years, 1866-68, when the maximum output was 98 tons of ore in 1867, and 1878 when 325 tons were produced.[19]

Modest quantities of copper ore were found in the Stiperstones mining region. The Pulverbatch census for 1861 records two copper miners living at Lawn Hill (SJ 416030). The workings at Westcott (SJ 402012), of which some ruined structures remain, were usually regarded as a copper mine, and were responsible for Shropshire's appearance as a source of copper in the Mineral Statistics for 1866-68, but never produced significant quantities of ore.

A small copper mine on Hayton's Bent Common (SO 517801) in Stanton Lacy parish was established in 1754 by John Lawrence. It appears still to have been working in the 1770s, but Roderick Murchison, noting abandoned adits in the 1830s, remarked that it had never produced any profits. Some spoil tips remain.[20]

There are several deposits of copper ores in the sandstones of north Shropshire. Historically the most significant is Pim Hill mine (SJ 487214) which was leased to Abraham Darby I and partners in 1710. Doubtless ore from the mine formed part of the charge of the smelting furnace which Darby had established at Coalbrookdale, alongside his iron and brass works, but it is doubtful whether Darby worked the mine for the full 14 year period of his lease. The mine was operated again in the 1860s and 1870s but proved unproductive. Three shafts remain about 100m. apart, two of them infilled, together with a small open cast. Malachite has been recorded in an adjacent quarry. Darby's lease of 1710 may have included the nearby Yorton Bank Mine (SJ 498238), which was the subject of prospecting in the 19th century. The shaft is no longer visible.[21]

The Clive or Grinshill Mine (SJ 515142, 513263) was probably the most productive in the region. There were at least six shafts, one of which (SJ 513238), sunk in the 1860s retains some pumping apparatus. The mine was worked in the 18th century, and in the 1860s provided employment for over thirty men. 'Mine Cottage' in Clive was one of the surface buildings. Ore was leached in 24 stone tanks which were sold in 1869 to the Bryntail Mine near Llanidloes (SN 915869), where eight remain.[22]

Copper was also found near Hawkstone and Weston-under-Redcastle, where local gentry agreed to mine copper in 1697. There were further attempts to work copper in the 1860s at Wixhill Mine (SJ 559287), but only some earthworks which might be the remnants of adits remain.[23]

The only significant monument of copper mining in North Shropshire is the ruin of the engine house at Eardiston (SJ 365246), remnant of a mine which was worked spasmodically for more than 40 years, and supposedly had ten shallow shafts. It was leased in 1827 to David William Jones, a limeman from Crick-

88   *A remnant of the engine house at the 19th-century copper mine at Eardiston (SJ 366246).*

heath, who quickly abandoned it. From 1836 it was worked by the Eardiston Copper Company, under the direction of William Allsopp from Liverpool who drove a 160m.-drainage adit. In 1839 the company sought 'good steady workmen', offering 'constant employment on tribute, by bargain or by day'. Two years later the labour force seems to have consisted of four miners, all lodging with a farm labourer. In 1840 operations were taken over by a London company who erected the engine house, but ceased work in September 1844 and removed the engine. In 1859 the mine was leased by the Ruabon Spelter Works, who handed over in 1863 to the British Copper Co, a Scottish concern, which became insolvent two years later. The mine was never worked again. Its output over four decades was probably less than 500 tons of ore, which was apparently carted to Queen's Head, whence it was dispatched by canal to Liverpool, St Helen's or Cheadle.[24]

MINING AT LLANYMYNECH

Deposits of malachite, galena and calamine on Llanymynech Hill have been worked since prehistoric times, and Roman coins have been found in the principal remaining feature of the mine, the 'ogof' or cave, which is on the Welsh portion of the hill. Some ore was being worked in the early 18th century but 19th-century operations were on a modest scale. Only one or two workers were employed before the 1870s, but by 1881 there were seven lead miners and two copper miners living at the northern end of the hill. The Crickheath Mine at Pant (SJ 273233) recorded an output of 85 tons of lead ore and 60 tons of zinc ore in 1884, when it provided employment for eight underground and four surface workers. The mine was abandoned in 1886, but one miner was apparently still finding some lead ore on the hill in 1891. Spoil tips containing malachite remain on the summit and there are traces of adits.[25]

Lead ore from Llanymynech Hill was being smelted in the 1840s and 1850s at Maesbury, although the output from the Hill alone would not have required a sizeable smelter. Three lead furnacemen, all born in Pontesbury, were living in the area in 1861. The smelter closed during the 1860s. It was located on a canalside site (SJ 315250) called the 'Smelting House' on the tithe map, which was subsequently occupied by an artificial manure works. The 46m.-high chimney destroyed in 1892 may have been built as part of the smelter rather than the manure works.[26]

LEAD-PROCESSING IN SHREWSBURY

Burrs' works in Shrewsbury was the principal lead processing plant in the county. Thomas Burr, the founder of the company, was a London plumber who moved to Shrewsbury between 1811 and 1813. The family retained contacts with the lead trade in the capital, leasing in 1853 a works in Commercial Road, Lambeth, managed by John Burr, younger son of Thomas.[27]

The company's first premises were on the south side of Beeches Lane, although referred to as Wyle Cop. The property was amalgamated with that on the corner of St Julian Friars when the Century Cinema, the building now occupied by an antiques showroom, was built. Early in the 19th century the site had been occupied

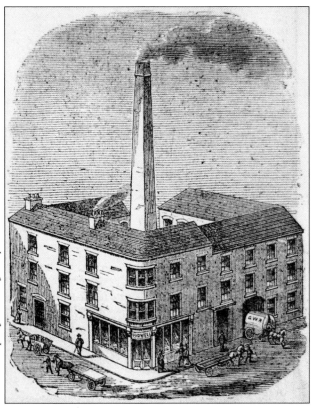

Eddowes Salopian Journal 14 January 1880

89   *The premises of G.W. Dodwell, plumber, at the corner of Wyle Cop and Beeches Lane in Shrewsbury (SJ 494123), which from 1814 until 1854 was the lead works of Burr & Co. While Dodwell may, as the picture suggests, have used the tall structure in the centre of the complex as a chimney, and it was so regarded by Salopians, it had been built as a shot tower.*

by Wicksteed's Starch Works, and was used until 1814 by John Haycock & Co as a soap factory. Thomas Burr appears first to have set up a workshop to make lead pipes by extrusion, and then to have constructed a shot tower. The Burrs left Beeches Lane in 1854, and the site was subsequently occupied by another plumber, G.W. Dodwell. The shot tower was demolished in 1904.[28]

In 1829 Burr purchased Charles Bage's linen weaving factory in Kingsland, which had been offered for sale two years earlier. The Kingsland site was probably not developed until the business had been taken over by Thomas Burr's sons, Thomas and William, in 1836. The Burrs purchased the Cann Office estate to the west of the Bage factory in 1849, and the property, between the factory and Trouncer's brewery, in 1852, acquisitions which enabled them to relinquish the Beeches Lane premises.[29]

The 1:500 map of 1882 shows that the core of the Kingsland works was Bage's vaulted weaving shed, 27.43m. long and 9.14m. wide. Other buildings were erected around it, and components of the complex in 1847 included a lead rolling mill, a melting furnace and casting bed, a hydraulic pipemaking machine, two steam engines, furnaces and ovens for the production of red lead, machinery for grinding and dressing red lead, and a mill and smelting furnace for manufacturing white lead, the value of which totalled £3,240. In 1853 a 46m. high shot tower was constructed, and a vehicle ferry installed to convey waggons across the Severn en route to the railway freight depot. The products were sheet lead, piping, shot, and oxides in the form of white and red lead. The labour force in 1861 consisted of 35 men, five boys and a woman. George Burr operated one of the smelters at Pontesford in the 1870s, which may have led to the erroneous belief that there was a smelter at Kingsland. Pollution caused by the works was the subject of many complaints in the 1850s, and as late as 1883.[30]

The lead works closed early in 1894, and was demolished soon afterwards, the shot tower collapsing as it was being taken down at 11.45 a.m. on 3 May 1894. The site became a recreation ground. One building remained, the cottage No 5

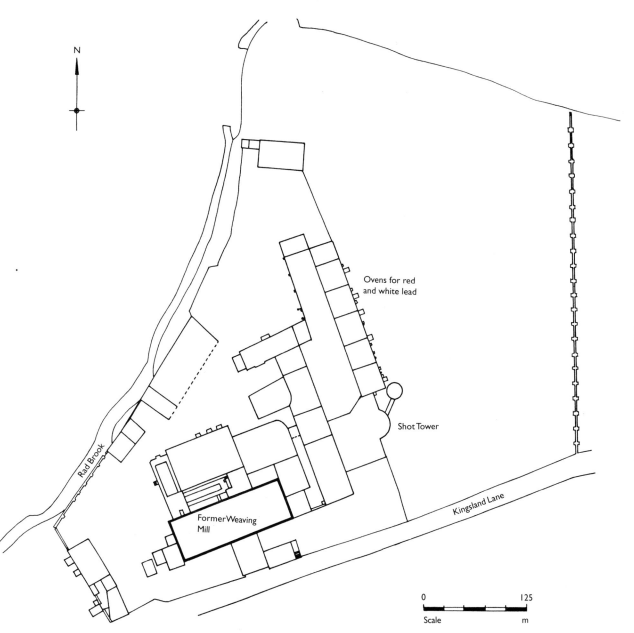

90 *Plan of Burrs Lead Works, Shrewsbury, re-drawn from the First Edition of the Ordnance Survey 1:500 plan of 1882.*

Kingsland Lane, the home in 1890 of William Owen, foreman at the works, but by 1899 of Samuel Morgan, a gardener. It was standing in 1970 but has subsequently been demolished.[31]

CONCLUSIONS

The dank playing field alongside the Severn in Kingsland Lane is an inadequate reminder of an industry which was innovative, but covered Shrewsbury with toxic fall-out. By contrast the lead mining region around the Stiperstones is one of the most evocative industrial landscapes in Britain. Its epic qualities appear the more remarkable in contrast with the modest scale of non-ferrous mining elsewhere in the county. Spoil heaps, the ruins of engine houses, the tracks of railways and tramways, the remaining miners' cottages, stimulate respect for past achievements at Snailbeach or Roman Gravels, whereas The Bog, denuded of its principal structures, and Tankerville, where much was expended for little reward, are reminders of the vanity of so many human endeavours.

◆   ◆   ◆

7

LINEAR LANDSCAPES:
THE ARCHAEOLOGY OF TRANSPORT

◆ ◆ ◆

A long-distance transport system has a unity which transcends particular topographical contexts. A canal's locks and lock-keepers' cottages reflect its history as a transport undertaking, as well as that of the communities in which particular locks or cottages happen to be located. Decisions about milestones and tollhouses on a turnpike road, signals and goods sheds on a railway, the towpath on a river will have been taken by the central bodies of those organisations. Such transport systems are most rewardingly studied as linear landscapes rather than technological phenomena. A main line railway has more in common with a navigable river or a turnpike road than with the plateways from which its technology derives or the mineral lines which feed it with freight.

AIR TRANSPORT

The only linear landscapes which link Shropshire with the air transport industry are the vapour trails of transatlantic airliners from Montreal or Los Angeles heading for Heathrow across the chill dawn skies. The county has no significant connections with aircraft manufacturing. It is ironic therefore that Shropshire is one of the best places in Britain for studying the history of civil aviation. The Aerospace Museum at Cosford began on a small scale in the 1970s, and is now one of the Royal Air Force Museums, under the control of a board of trustees. Apart from numerous military and experimental aircraft it houses the British Airways collection which illustrates as well as any in the world the development of airliners since the late 1930s. Aircraft which can be seen, not all of them versions for civilian passenger use, include a Junkers 52, a Douglas DC3 Dakota, an Avro York, a Vickers Viking, a De Havilland Comet 1a, a Vickers Viscount 701, a Bristol Britannia, a De Havilland Trident 1c, a Boeing 707 and a Vickers VC10. The collection is supplemented by displays, and by some fine models of pre-Second World War passenger aircraft.

PIPELINES

Scarcely more visible than vapour trails are the pipelines which cross the Shropshire landscape supplying water to great cities. The earliest was established by Wolverhampton Corporation under parliamentary powers obtained in 1855 from Cosford

Brook pumping station (SJ 781046) to Tettenhall, through which the first water flowed on 8 October 1858. Between that time and 1914 a further six pumping engines were added, two of them supplied by the Lilleshall Company in 1879-82. In 1906 a 1.2km. aerial ropeway was constructed to supply the pumping station with coal from a siding on the Shrewsbury-Wolverhampton railway. The pumping station was converted from steam to electric operation in 1948, and the chimney demolished in 1948.[1]

The dams in the Elan Valley designed by James Mansergh (1834-1905) created reservoirs from which water was conveyed to Birmingham by a pipeline 118km. long, about one third of it passing through Shropshire, which was built in the opening years of the 20th century. It cuts across Bringewood Chase south of Ludlow, entering Shropshire (SO 495742) before bridging the Teme (SO 522737) and the Ledwych Brook (SO 537738). The water is led over a concrete aqueduct at Bennetts End (SO 582744) before entering Studley Tunnel through the lime-stone between Gorstley Rough and the Novers, and emerging on to another aqueduct. It crosses the Corn Brook (SO 606747) and passes beneath the Ludlow-Cleobury Mortimer road at Hollywaste (SO 649757) before reaching a pumping station and depot (SO 657763) where four 2ft.-gauge diesel locomotives were once employed. It crosses the Rea (SO 675767) north of Cleobury Mortimer and then takes an east-north-easterly course through the Wyre Forest to cross the county boundary at Button Oak (SO 753780) before bridging the Severn (SO 775783).[2]

91 *The Cosford Brook pumping station (SJ 781046) from which water has been pumped to Wolverhampton since 1858.*

92 *The viaduct which carries the pipeline from the Elan Valley reservoirs to Birmingham across the valley of the Corn Brook on the southern side of the Clee Hills (SO 606747).*

93 *The pumping station and depot on the Elan Valley-Birmingham pipeline at Hollywaste (SO 657763), bearing the date 1902, and the crest of the City of Birmingham.*

The dam at Lake Vyrnwy, the work of George Deacon (1843-1909), Borough and Water Engineer of the City of Liverpool, was the first high masonry dam in Great Britain, and when completed in 1891, impounded the largest artificial reservoir in Europe. The 109km. pipeline between the lake and Liverpool enters Shropshire west of Oswestry. The filter beds at Llanforda (SJ 277295) form one of the largest installations on the system. A 2ft.-gauge railway system was worked by diesel-mechanical locomotives until the 1980s. The aqueduct skirts the northern edge of Oswestry, the appropriately-named Liverpool Road having been built along its line c.1900. It takes a course north of and almost parallel to the Cambrian Railway to Hindeford, where it crosses the Ellesmere Canal (SJ 335330), before taking a north-easterly direction, crossing the county boundary west of Brookhill (SJ 412390).[3]

A more recent pipeline runs into the Black Country from Chelmarsh Reservoir (SO 737847) built for the South Staffordshire Water company in the late 1960s, from which an aqueduct over the Severn supplies a waterworks on the opposite bank (SO 750870).

THE SEVERN NAVIGATION

The River Severn was already the source of much wealth in Shropshire in 1660. Francis Ap Owen of Dowles who died in 1669 had a trow, a barge and a boat worth £100, and wood to the same value awaiting despatch on the Severn. Richard Brooke of Madeley who died in 1670 owned a vessel called the *Jonathan* worth £40. Abel Jones of Shrewsbury who died in the same year had a pair of barges worth £42. Edward Jefferies of Bridgnorth who died in 1673 operated on a lower scale. He owned a barge and a cockell boat, which with their equipment were worth only £8, and his movable possessions were valued at only £24.[4] The contrast between the bargemen highlights the two main traffics on the Severn. The wealthier owners were concerned with the carriage to ports below Gloucester, particularly Bristol, of Shropshire's more valuable manufactures, iron, leather, grain, cheese and paper, and with the return freight of groceries, tobacco, wine, spirits, Baltic timber, and most goods which could not be produced in the county. At least some of their vessels needed to be capable of surviving the dangerous tidal waters below Gloucester. Many bargemen, perhaps the majority, never sailed so far but made their living by carrying bulk cargoes over short distances, particularly taking coal from the Ironbridge Gorge downstream to Bridgnorth, Bewdley, Worcester, Tewkesbury and Gloucester.

The Severn Navigation developed when coal from Broseley and Madeley was first mined on a large scale in the late 16th century. The Wolverhampton University Port Books project has shown that it was part of a thriving commercial economy by 1700.[5] It made possible the growth of the Shropshire iron industry in the 18th century. In conjunction with the Staffordshire & Worcestershire Canal it carried the produce of Shropshire ironworks to numerous customers in the Black Country and Birmingham. In conjunction with the Shropshire Canal it was able to carry increasing quantities of coal down river, about 50,000 tons a year being exported from Coalport alone by c.1802, and as much as 80,000 tons by 1830. The navigation declined with increasing competition from railways after 1840 and particularly after the opening of the Severn Valley Railway in 1862. The last commercial vessel on the Shropshire portion of the river sank after it hit one of the piers of Bridgnorth bridge on 25 January 1895.[6]

The Shropshire portion of the Severn was never improved. In 1786 a bill to permit the construction of 16 locks between Diglis (Worcester) and Coalbrookdale, which had been surveyed by William Jessop, the most able canal engineer of the time, was rejected by the House of Commons, after much pressure from Shropshire bargemen. John Randall remarked some 80 years later that 'As a class bargeowners are opposed to innovation' and that the oldest men remember how when George III was king they shouted themselves hoarse and tossed their caps in honour of victory over attempts to improve the channel. When the river below Stourport was improved by the construction of locks in the 1840s, the Shropshire bargeowners were given exemptions from tolls, but there was no serious proposal to construct locks further upstream.[7]

The Shropshire Severn thus remained a river which could be used without payment, and which was free from the kind of bureaucratic control which generates documentary records. Archaeology is thus of particular importance in gaining an understanding of how the river was operated.

Artefacts contribute but little to increasing understanding of the river. A few small items survive, like an anchor displayed in the Museum of the River at Ironbridge, but not enough to justify serious analysis. No boats used on the Upper Severn survive, so that images provide the most valuable evidence.

George Perry in describing vessels on the Severn in 1758 drew a distinction between trows, of between 40 and 80 tons, with main, top- and sometimes mizzen masts, and single-masted barges and frigates, of between 20 and 40 tons. Both types were up to 60ft. long.[8] Such a simple classification can cause confusion, although Perry was trying to distinguish between the larger vessels which could safely navigate the estuary and those which usually went no further downstream than Gloucester. Analysis of pictorial and documentary evidence shows that Severn bargeowners used a wide range of vessels. Whatever their size Severn vessels were of similar construction, clinker-built, with D-shaped sterns, with masts which could be lowered to pass bridges. Inventories provide evidence of the equipment carried on barges, which included chains, ropes, tarpaulins, hooks, planks, poles, shafts, oars, sails, stays, blocks, windlasses, anchors, beams and scales, pitch, tar, oakum, barrels, chests, shovels and scoops. Some had awnings which could be erected over the stern sections to provide accommodation for the crew in the want of a cabin. The most valuable vessels recorded before 1660 include the 'great trow at Gloucester', the property of Francis Owen of Madeley in 1732, valued at £70, his 'middle trow' valued at £60, a trow belonging to Richard Lacon of Bridgnorth valued at £67 10s.0d. in 1735, the trow *Loving Brother* belonging to Thomas Andrews of Bridgnorth in 1723 which was also worth £60. These vessels were, like a half-completed 70-ton vessel on the stocks at the Rovings in 1796, intended for trade in the Bristol Channel, to the ports of South Wales and on the Stroudwater Navigation. Some of the larger trows seem to have carried 'oars vessels' or 'tow boats' which could be used to help get free from sandbanks in the estuary.[9]

Most vessels trading in Shropshire were smaller and less valuable. While vessels from the county traded to Bristol well into the 19th century, an increasing amount of traffic after 1700 appears to have been trans-shipped to Lower Severn trows at Gloucester. Many bargeowners had ranges of vessels, like the Shrewsbury owner whose fleet in 1812 comprised the *Defiance* of 40 tons, the *Mary* of 35 tons and the *William* of 14 tons. John Rees, also of Shrewsbury, was working until 1835 with the *Cambrian* a 55-ton barge, the *Hannah* a 42-ton barge, and a capital boat of seven tons. The 20 boats working from Shrewsbury in 1837 comprised two of 50 tons, one of 45 tons, five of 40 tons, two of 35 tons, two of 30 tons, one of 12 tons, one of 10 tons, three of eight tons and three of six tons. One of the 50-ton barges, the *Eliza*, property of Thomas Bratton, was sketched by William Vandyck Brown, while moored at Frankwell Quay.[10] An engraving shows a large vessel moored at Cound Lane End, probably a trow owned by one of the Dodson family. One of the last depictions of a trow is in a photograph of the Severn Warehouse, Ironbridge, probably taken in the 1880s. An earlier photograph of the boatyard on the other side of the river, probably taken in the 1860s, is a rare view of some of the medium-sized vessels used in the coal trade.[11] The smallest vessels, shown in numerous illustrations of Bridgnorth and Shrewsbury, were probably used to move goods between barges and wharves in the principal river ports. The larger vessels worked with crews of up to four men. Two vessels were moored overnight at Madeley on census day in 1861, the *Hannah*, on which three watermen were sleeping, and the *Industry* where slept the captain, Thomas Doughty, and three watermen.

Iron vessels were not uncommon on the Shropshire portion of the Severn in the 19th century. John Wilkinson's celebrated *Trial* was launched at Willey Wharf in 1787. While it proved no cheaper than boats of conventional construction, it was imitated. The Onions family of ironmasters in 1820 were working four iron barges, one worth as much as £150, while the wrought iron frigate *Salop* was offered for sale at the Meadow Wharf, Coalbrookdale, in 1837.[12]

The nature of the river meant that much of a bargeman's time was spent waiting. The principal trade, in coal from the Ironbridge Gorge, was dependent on 'flushes', sudden increases in the water level. In 1784 it was remarked that when the river level rose, it was commonplace for between 60 and 80 vessels to leave the vicinity of Coalbrookdale, carrying as much as 4,000 tons of coal downstream. In consequence quite remarkable numbers of barges could sometimes be seen in the Gorge. In May 1836 Charles Hulbert counted no less than 72 from Coalport Bridge. Most vessels had a draught of between three and four feet. A journey to Gloucester from Ironbridge took about 24 hours, but few vessels were able to accomplish more than 20 voyages a year.[13]

John Randall wrote in the 1850s that Shropshire barges 'go down with the stream and are drawn back by horses'.[14] Bargemen also made use of sails, when and where this was possible. Before the construction of towpaths, vessels were dragged upstream by gangs of 'bow haulers', who were the subject of much moral disapproval from the propertied classes. The small vessels portrayed in some views of the river may have been used by bow haulers to return home after they had dragged up a vessel over the section they were accustomed to work. The towpath between Bewdley and Coalbrookdale was authorised in 1772 but was not completed until 1800. That between Coalbrookdale and Frankwell Quay, Shrewsbury, received parliamentary assent in May 1809, and was completed the following November. No towpath was constructed upstream from Frankwell, although some traffic continued to used this stretch of the river until the 1850s. Observation of the circuitous course of the Severn between low sandstone cliffs shows that bowhaulers must have spent much of their time wading through the water. No records of the towpath companies survive, but there is some archaeological evidence of their activities. The towpath acts designated one side or other of the river as the right of way, the left bank through Shrewsbury, the right bank from the horse ferry provided by the company at Underdale to Cressage Bridge, the right bank to Coalport, and thence the left bank past the county boundary to Bewdley. Bridges were provided across most of the tributaries at their points of confluence. An iron bridge cast by the

Ironbridge Gorge Museum Trust

94 *Severn barges moored at the premises of Edward Gother, boat builder, in the Bower Yard, Benthall (SJ 667035) in the late 1850s. This is an unusual picture of some of the smaller Severn barges which were used principally for carrying coal.*

Coalbrookdale Company in 1828 crosses the mouth of the Borle Brook (SO 753817), while that of the Mor Brook (SO 733885) is spanned by a bridge cast by Onions of Broseley in 1824. A small stone arch crosses the mouth of the Leighton Brook. There is no trace of any means of crossing the delta at the mouth of the Cound Brook. Between Eardington and Arley evidence can be observed of excavation to create a more level course for the towpath, and erosion has revealed that it was re-surfaced from time to time, on some occasions with waste materials from the Coalport Chinaworks. The towpaths were financed by tolls charged on horses—not on boats—and the companies were responsible for clearing fords for the passage of vessels at low water. The Bewdley-Coalbrookdale company relinquished its powers on Lady Day 1885, while those of the Coalbrookdale-Frankwell trust were taken over by Shrewsbury Borough Corporation.

Perry showed that in 1756 there were 313 barges owned by 182 owners at work on the Severn at Bewdley and places upstream. Of these, 6% of both owners and barges were to be found in Shrewsbury, 46% of owners and 44% of barges in the Severn Gorge, 30% of owners and 28% of barges in Bridgnorth, and 10% of owners

95 *The east elevation of the Severn Warehouse, Ironbridge (SJ 666034), designed by Samuel Cookson and erected c.1840. The building was first used by the Coalbrookdale Company as a warehouse, then as a lemonade factory, then for the making of bicycle parts, and as a garage, before it was opened as a visitor centre by the Ironbridge Gorge Museum Trust in 1977.*

and 15% of barges in Bewdley. There remained 15 owners and 21 barges in the smaller settlements, four of each at Pool Quay, three owners and seven barges at Cound, and eight owners and 10 barges between Bridgnorth and Bewdley. Evidence from later periods suggests that the relationship between the ports stayed much the same.

At Shrewsbury most warehouses were grouped around Mardol Quay and Frankwell Quay, constructed in 1607 by Rowland Jenks. The area was considerably altered by the construction of the Welsh Bridge on a new alignment in 1796, and by the demolition of the buildings on Mardol Quay after the Second World War. There were yards on the two quays specialising in handling timber, and warehouses suitable for hops, cider, spirits, grain and lead. Some cargoes were handled on the upstream side of the English Bridge, where Marine Terrace now stands. The Union Wharf, near the Castle at the bottom of St Mary's Water Lane, was constructed by Thomas Groves in 1823.

In the Ironbridge Gorge, Stephen Duckworth has identified from documentary, cartographic, pictorial and archaeological sources 16 principal wharves upstream from Coalport Bridge: Meadow, Ludcroft, Wharfage, Bower Yard, Benthall Rails, Ladywood, Barnetts Leasow, Bedlam Furnaces, Coalford, Lloyds Head, Calcutts, Lloyds, Jackfield Rails, Werps, Coalport Chinaworks, and the Shropshire Canal terminus.[15] To these could be added Swinney Wharf and Willey Wharf further downstream. Some, like the Coalbrookdale Co.'s Ludcroft Wharf, or the terminus of the Shropshire Canal at Coalport, were the result of large-scale investment in the late 18th century or early 19th century. Others, with relatively simple facilities, remained in use with little change from the 16th century until the end of the navigation. Duckworth's meticulous examination of the Calcutts wharf, identifying wooden posts, remnants of wharf walls, and towpath levels, shows that much archaeological evidence remains even on a site covered by waste tips and eroded by flooding.

Commercial warehouses were concentrated along The Wharfage, a quay built during the first half of the 18th century. Three remain, with pulleys and taking-in doors making them instantly recognisable as warehouses, together with the Coalbrookdale Company's single-storey transit warehouse (now the Museum of the River), an extraordinary Gothic structure of c.1840, designed by Samuel Cookson, which must have been subject to severe flooding from the time it was built. It was served by plateways which ran down Coalbrookdale. From Dale End they extended in an upstream direction to the Meadow Wharf, which in 1816 was handling all the iron despatched by the Lightmoor Co., and much of the coal from the Coalbrookdale Co.'s collieries. The deep water, enabling vessels to moor in summer without injury was seen as one of the advantages of the wharf.

The interchange at Coalport where the Shropshire Canal came to the riverside is worthy of study in its present condition, and has enormous archaeological potential. The north bank of the river is lined by a massive stone wall, topped in places by bricks held together in cast iron frames. The 20m. slope between the canal and the river was crossed by seven diamond-shaped railways, which ran on to drawbridge-like constructions which could be extended above the holds of waiting barges.

These devices were probably the 'suspended trams' mentioned by John Randall in his description of Coalport in the 1850s.[16] They were probably used for moving coal, since pigs or bars of iron were traditionally carried by strong men in the pockets of leather aprons. A large warehouse where small consignments were handled spanned the canal and projected over the river. Dominant features of the landscape were the huge piles of coal awaiting transit. It is astonishing that when the Coalport branch railway opened in 1861, it was anticipated that it would deliver large quantities of freight to be despatched by barge. The L.N.W.R. laid rail connections into the interchange area, but they do not seem to have been extensively used, mineowners and ironmasters preferring to despatch their freight direct to customers by rail. The main topographical features of the interchange were restored in the early 1970s, and the stonework at the end of some of the diamond-shaped railways can be seen, together with the base of a pillar crane.

In Bridgnorth, iron rings to which barges were moored, as depicted on several illustrations, remain on the piers of the bridge. The river frontage on Underhill Street is dominated by a mid-19th century development in the Italianate style, consisting of two three-bay, three-storey blocks, with blind arcading in their front elevations, flanking a two storey, nine-bay range. Between this building and St Mary's Steps stands the 'Old Malthouse' a two-storey structure, with lucams above the former taking-in doors in the gables. Adjacent to the bridge stands the four-storey Ridley's Warehouse, once used for the storage of grain, on the upstream side of which is Riverside, where the level of the roadway was raised in 1887. The hanging nets of river fishermen were noticeable in the area in the 1850s. The river frontage in Bridgnorth is backed by soft sandstone cliffs in which are many traces of cave workshops and dwellings, some of which were still occupied in the mid-19th century.

There are few traces of wharves and warehouses in the smaller riverside settlements. There was a 'common landing place for timber' near the mouth of the Perry in 1728, and a quay with a warehouse where iron was landed at Pimley in the 1660s. Cound Lane End was a wharf of some importance, and a base for a small fleet of barges. There was a mooring at Cressage from which a barge broke loose and crashed into the temporary bridge at Buildwas in 1791, and a wharfage at Sheinton where a man was drowned in 1862. At the Rovings in Barrow parish were a boat-building yard, a wharf where Caughley porcelain was loaded, and a public house, traditionally kept by a bargeowner, which closed during the 1860s. Bargate Wharf (SO 753809) in Kinlet parish, on the border with Arley in Staffordshire, was probably a loading point for timber from the Wyre Forest as was a 'load' used in the 18th century further downstream at Dowles.

In course of the 18th century barges were constructed in Shrewsbury, on the site now occupied by the Sixth Form College, at the Bower Yard, Benthall, at several sites in Jackfield, at the Rovings, and in three yards in Bridgnorth. By 1851 only two barge builders remained, Edward Gother at Benthall, and William Oakes at Bridgnorth. The sale of Oakes's yard in 1856 makes it possible to identify the principal components of a boatbuilder's establishment. He had oak, ash and elm timbers in the round and in planked form, together with deal planking. Long lengths would be leant against each other to form the kind of tent-like structure depicted in several illustrations of the river. Oakes's yard also included a black-smith's shop, three sawpit sheds and an almost completed 40-ton barge.

One of the curious features of the Severn in Shropshire is the succession of islands in the river. David Pannett showed in the 1970s that all the islands were on the sites of fish weirs, that there are substantial archaeological remains of many of the 28 weirs in the county listed in 1575, and that archaeological and field name evidence records the sites of six weirs not on that list. Weirs were fences of stakes in which were set basketwork fish traps. A weir impeded traffic and was usually by-passed by an artificial channel dug within the parish or manor to which it belonged, thus creating an island, usually called a bylet. Most fish weirs were medieval in origin, and many listed in 1575 probably went out of use soon afterwards. Some remained as significant sources of food. That at Little Shrawardine was still being operated in 1661 when the 'Materialls for the Weare or fishinge garth' were valued at five shillings in an inventory of Edgar Dyos. Little Shrawardine (SJ 391152) was still a fishery in the 19th century. Fitz Weir (SJ 453162) was the subject of a water colour in 1878, while that at Montford (SJ 422145) was similarly portrayed in 1897, and the Preston Boats weir (SJ 510117), was still intact in the 1920s. The channels around many weirs have filled with silt, but well-defined islands remained at Holywell (SJ 504134), Pimley (SJ 520142) and Sutton Maddock (SJ 707017), and the stubs of stakes are visible at low water at Montford, Bromley's Forge (SJ 439165) and Preston Boats. A bowling green occupies the bylet at Bridgnorth (SO 719929), whose by-pass channel carries little water except in times of flood. The barge gutter at Coton Hill (SJ 490134) is similarly silted up.[17] The bylet, called Poplars Island, was the scene of a fête in 1857 which resulted in disaster when the bridge of boats linking the island to Coton Hill collapsed.

Some of the Severn's tributaries were navigable. The lower reaches of the Vyrnwy were certainly used by barges carrying iron and lead ore in the early 18th century, and in 1824 one Thomas Jones stole a cow's hide from a barge on the river at Melverley. The Tern also carried barges. A vessel sunk in the river near Attingham Park in 1757 had once been used by Joshua Gee the ironmaster to convey iron to Upton Forge, and the Coalbrookdale Co. accounts in 1737-38 record the despatch of small quantities of pig iron to Tern Forge. The best evidence for the navigation is archaeological. In 1969 Dr Michael Lewis excavated the remains of a lock at the mouth of the river, which had walls of ashlar blocks joined by iron cramps set in lead, and a floor of transverse timbers with brick paving. The lock could have passed a boat 23ft. long and 7ft. 8in. in beam (7m. x 2.33m.). The lock was probably built c.1710 when Tern Forge was being constructed. About 1797 Humphry Repton, the landscape gardener, cut away one side, and incorpo-rated it in a weir, designed to create a lake visible from Attingham Park. The weir collapsed in a flood in the 1830s.[18] It is even possible that the Teme was navigated. It would seem sensible to move iron from the furnace and forge at Bringewood (Herefordshire) to Ludlow by river, and at least one print of Ludlow castle shows five sailing vessels on the Teme. It is doubtful whether there was ever through navigation from Ludlow to the Severn.

CANALS

Shropshire's first canals, some of the earliest in Britain, were an integral part of the economy of the Coalbrookdale Coalfield. The first long-distance waterways in the county were the products of the 'canal mania' of the 1790s, the Act of Parliament for the Leominster Canal being passed in 1791, and those for the Ellesmere and Shrewsbury companies in 1793. The two latter waterways were linked in 1835 when the Birmingham & Liverpool Junction Canal was opened between Autherley and Nantwich with a branch from Norbury Junction to Wappenshall.

THE SHREWSBURY CANAL

The Shrewsbury Canal linked the tub boat canals of the Coalbrookdale Coalfield with the county town. The company purchased 1.6 km. of the private Wombridge Canal which gave it access to the hub of the tub boat system at Donnington Wood.

At Trench (SJ 688121) an inclined plane conveyed vessels into a 6.5km. stretch along which 11 locks lowered boats to a 19.3km. pound extending to the terminus at Shrewsbury, with aqueducts crossing the Tern at Longdon, the Roden at Rodington and the Uffington Brook at Pimley, and a tunnel beneath Haughmond Hill at Berwick. The canal's principal source of water was a reservoir at Trench supplied chiefly from mine workings. The canal was opened to Long Lane in 1794, to Berwick Wharf in 1796 and to its terminus in Shrewsbury in 1797. Two sections in Shrewsbury were closed respectively in 1922 and 1939, and the whole waterway was closed by the LMSR Act of 1944. Hopes of reopening it in the 1960s were finally frustrated by the breaking of its line by drainage authorities. The section between the Comet Bridge in Shrewsbury and Uffington is now a public footpath.[19]

The Trench inclined plane, which raised boats 22.9m. over a distance of 204 m. was of the type which had become standard on the Shropshire Canal. Its working life extended for 127 years, and when its last traffic ceased in 1921 it was the last surviving canal inclined plane in Britain. The stonework of the docks

96 *The guillotine frame which lifted the gate of Hadley Park lock on the Shrewsbury Canal (SJ 671133).*

at the head of the incline remained until the 1970s when a road obscured all traces of the previous landscape, except for the public house, once the *Shropshire Arms* now the *Blue Pig* which can be seen in many pictures of the plane.

The 11 locks were built 6ft. 7in. wide for the passage of tub boats. After 1835 locks 10 and 11 were widened to 7ft. 4in., permitting standard narrow boats to pass to Shrewsbury. Boats of 6ft. 2in. beam, called 'Shroppies' or 'narrer-narrer boats' were constructed to operate to and from Trench. Several years after the canal opened Telford said that the locks were 81ft. (24.68m.) long, thus capable of admitting trains of four 20ft. tub boats, but that they had intermediate gates which enabled the economic passage of one, three or four boats. Tony Clayton in the late 1970s discovered traces of grooves, probably the locations of intermediate gates, in the chamber walls of locks 4 and 6, and infilling in the walls of locks 10 and 11. From the beginning the locks had vertical lower gates lifted within 'guillotine' frames, with suspended counterbalances. From 1840 cast iron counterbalances rising and falling in wells at the side were substituted at locks 1, 2, 3, 5, 7, 8, 9 and 10, thus simplifying the construction and operation of the gates.[20]

Table 7.1: **Locks on the Shrewsbury Canal**		
1	Trench	SJ 683125
2	Bakers/Castle	SJ 677125
3	Turnip	SJ 673131
4	Hadley Park	SJ 671133
5	Peaty	SJ 670135
6	Shucks	SJ 669136
7	Wheat Leasows	SJ 668137
8	Britton	SJ 666141
9	Wappenshall	SJ 652150
10	Eyton/Drawbridge	SJ 652150
11	Eyton Lower	SJ 643153

Aqueducts carried the Shrewsbury Canal over the Pimley Brook, the River Roden and the River Tern. The abutments, the last traces of the first modest structure, were removed in the early 1990s. The Roden Aqueduct at Rodington (SJ 589242) was characteristic of the first generation of canals, a stone structure of three arches, the crowns of which were a considerable distance below the parapet, in order to accommodate the great thickness of puddled clay needed to seal the waterway.

The principal engineering work and the most significant surviving monument on the Shrewsbury Canal is the 57m. long, 4.9m. high aqueduct over the River Tern at Longdon. Josiah Clowes died early in 1795, and on 10-12 February of that year floods severely damaged the preparatory works for the aqueduct. Thomas

Telford was appointed engineer to the company on 28 February and instructed to report on what might be done at Longdon. On 14 March the canal proprietors approved the construction of an iron aqueduct, supplied by William Reynolds & Co., to be completed by 14 September 1795, although it was not until 14 March 1796 that it was opened for traffic.

The aqueduct consists of a trough whose sections are bolted together through flanges, with a towpath alongside it. Trough and towpath are supported at each end by masonry abutments, and at intermediate points by cruciform cast iron columns, with diagonal bracing struts of similar section. John Healey has pointed out that the hand-made bricks and sandstone used in the eastern abutment at Longdon resemble the materials used at Rodington, suggesting that it was the work of Clowes, and that it formed part of a planned symmetrical structure consisting of three central arches, flanked on each side by a cutwater and two arches linked to the abutments. The west abutment, which is of sandstone rather than brick, appears to have been built by Telford, on foundations provided by Clowes, and appears to be misaligned with the present iron structure. Telford used only one of the original pier footings as a base for the trough columns. The other two sets of supporting columns were constructed on new foundations. Charles Hadfield has shown that Longdon was not a test of the practicability of constructing the Pontcysyllte Aqueduct, for little progress could have been made with the project before the proprietors of the Ellesmere Canal determined to build an iron trough at Pontcysyllte on 14 July 1795.[21]

The other principal engineering work canal is the 887m.-long Berwick Tunnel, part of the final section of the waterway opened to traffic in January 1797. It had a 3 ft. wide cantilevered towpath, beneath which water could circulate, like that on the Pontcysyllte Aqueduct. The ends are bricked up and much of the western abutment has collapsed due to earth-moving in an adjacent field.

The Shrewsbury Canal had distinctive accommodation bridges, lifting structures, whose decks were raised by chains attached to beams pivoted on upright wooden square-section columns, sustained by diagonal braces at the bases. The last to survive, at Wappenshall (SJ 661146) and Rodington (SJ 592142), were demolished in the 1970s. Flat, broad channel-section cast iron bridges were also used on the canal. The largest was Teague's Bridge in Wombridge (SJ 693124), now in the custody of the Ironbridge Gorge Museum. Another, which spanned the entrance to the basin at Long Lane (SJ 635155), has been re-used at the Coalport China Museum, while a third remains in situ east of Pimley (SJ 523143), at a point where canal water appears to have been diverted to supplement the flow to Uffington Mill.

In Shrewsbury an extensive coal wharf was created, now bounded by Castle Foregate, New Park Road, Beacalls Lane and Howard Street, in which space was taken by the principal coal suppliers including William Hazledine and the Lilleshall Company. Expectations that the canal would substantially reduce the cost of coal in the county town were speedily disappointed. After the canal was linked to the national system the Butter Market was constructed on its southern edge, and the canal extended up to its doors. After its functions were assumed by the general market in 1869, the Butter Market was adapted as a railway warehouse, serving that

97   *The lifting bridge across the Shrewsbury Canal at Wappenshall (SJ 661146), photographed in the late 1960s, and since demolished.*

function for about a century. After a period of disuse, it was adapted as a night club in the 1980s. In 1840 a boat builder, Edward Evans, occupied a site fronting the Castle Foregate. By 1859 the canal was in the ownership of the London & North Western Railway which constructed a line through a short tunnel under Howard Street, which fanned out into sidings linked by wagon turntables which occupied most of the eastern side of the yard. A travelling crane was constructed alongside the Beacalls Lane boundary, together with a brick goods shed, which still remains, to the north western corner of which abutted a small corn mill. By the 1880s the canal was cut back, extending only half way across the wharf, its route to the former Butter Market being occupied by a railway siding. Traffic at the coal wharf ceased in 1922.

The course of the canal remains between New Park Road and Factory Bridge. The town gasworks and the brickyards in the area received coal by canal. At the northern extremity adjacent to the Golden Ball public house was a basin where, in 1840, coal from the mines at Uffington was being unloaded. It was filled in between 1880 and 1900. The principal canal users on this stretch were the occupiers of the plot which extended back from the frontage now occupied by Nos. 106-10 St Michael's Street, which appears to have been in canal company ownership by the 1830s. Between 1835 and 1838 warehouses were constructed on the canal bank for three carrying companies, Pickford & Co., Henshall & Co., and Joseph Jobson. The site was subsequently used for milling and malting, and was served by a branch canal. The only user on the section which looped west of the turnpike road between Factory Bridge and Comet Bridge was the Ditherington Flax Mill whose boiler house was on the canal bank. The canal was officially closed south of Comet Bridge in 1939.

THE ELLESMERE CANAL

The Ellesmere Canal took its name from the north Shropshire town where its inaugural meeting was held on 31 August 1791. When the promoters obtained their Act of Parliament in 1793 they intended to construct a strategic waterway linking the Mersey, the Dee and the Severn. The rivalries and disputes of the years which followed have been elucidated by Charles Hadfield and Edward Wilson and need not be repeated. The company's network was completed in 1813 when it merged with the earlier Chester Canal. It had been constructed under the supervision of Thomas Telford, but in accord with strategic engineering decisions taken by William Jessop, and in the face of financial constraints. It was essentially a route from the Mersey at the new town of Ellesmere Port to Chester, thence along the old Chester Canal to Hurleston near Nantwich, from which another section of the Ellesmere Canal proper ran westward to Grindley Brook, where it entered Shropshire, across the mosses on the border with Maelor to Frankton, where it forked, one line going south-west to join the Montgomeryshire Canal at Carreghofa, the other north west, extending through the Oswestry Coalfield to Chirk, whence it continued across the Pontcysyllte Aqueduct to Trevor Basin, which served the heavy industries of Ruabon, and along the Vale of Llangollen. Short branches extended into Whitchurch and Ellesmere, while another failed to reach Prees, but served a wharf at Edstaston and lime kilns at Quina Brook. The intended route to the Severn at Shrewsbury left the Montgomery line below the locks at Frankton but was abandoned in a field south of Weston Lullingfields. The Ellesmere & Chester Canal was linked with the national network in 1835. It was a modestly profitable regional network, but, faced with the threat of railway competition, it became one of the constituents of the Shropshire Union Railway & Canal Co. in 1845, and with that company was taken over by the L.N.W.R. in the following year. Loss of traffic led to threats of closure as early as the 1870s. By the 1920s the canal was in competition with road transport as well as railways. The whole of the Shropshire section of the former Ellesmere company had effectively fallen out of use by 1939. L. T. C. Rolt failed to force a way through the weeds to Pontcysyllte in 1947 but succeeded in 1949, and in 1952 Edward Wilson and others followed suit. In 1954 it was decided to retain the waterway as a means of supplying reservoirs near Hurleston. It became a popular route for pleasure craft, and is now called the Llangollen Canal.[22]

The current main line enters Shropshire (SJ 532444) north of Grindley Brook locks (SJ 523429) where it is crossed by the turnpike road from Whitchurch to Chester. A canalside settlement developed around the bridge, of which the most prominent remaining feature is the lock-keeper's cottage. The buildings of a steam corn mill also remain, but limekilns and a boat-building yard have disappeared. A short section of the Whitchurch branch has been restored, from its junction with the main line (SJ 527415), where there is a fabricated steel lifting bridge, to the over

Table 7.2: **Shropshire sections of the Ellesmere Canal**

Section	Opened	Disused	Current state
Grindley Brook-Frankton	1805	1939	Reopened
Grindley Brook-Sherryman's Bridge	1808	1936-8	Part reopened
Sherryman's Bridge- Castle Well Wharf	1811	1936-38	Dry bed
The Cottage-Quina Brook	1806?	1939	Part marina, Part nature reserve, part dry bed
Brook House-Ellesmere	1904	1939	Reopened
Frankton-Perry Aqueduct	1796	1936	Reopened
Perry Aqueduct-Carreghofa	1796	1936	Under restoration
Frankton-Horderley	1795	1937	Abandoned
Horderley-Weston Lullingfields	1797?	1917	Abandoned
Frankton-Chirk	1795	1937	Reopened

bridge at Chemistry (SJ 531415). Further along the line of the branch at Sherrymill Hill (SJ 537416) the onetime silk mill, the corn mill and the gasworks have disappeared but a British Gas depot remains on the site of the latter. The corn mill of 1828 remains at the terminus of the branch at New Wharf (SJ 541414).

From Whitchurch the canal pursues a southerly course across the mosses on the borders of Shropshire and Maelor. The limekilns at Brickwalls (SJ 513377) form part of a garden. The canal is crossed by a steel lifting bridge, replacing an earlier wooden structure. Morris Bridge (SJ 493354) is also of this type. At the Cottage, junction with the Prees branch (SJ 489351), the main line is spanned by a roving bridge. The canal passes into Maelor for a sort distance (SJ 481354—SJ 454349) before reaching the remains of the wharf at Hampton Bank (SJ 451344), where L.T.C. Rolt spent the summer of 1947. The circuitous course to Ellesmere, north of Colemere and round the southern edge of Blakemere reveals some of the most delightful of all canal scenery. The canal passes through an 80m. tunnel before the junction with the town branch opposite the elegant Beech House (SJ 401342) of 1806, once the company headquarters. A sundries warehouse remains on the Town Wharf (SJ 398348), but the creamery, which replaced a Victorian foundry, was demolished in 1991, and the gasworks has long since disappeared. The maintenance depot (SJ 400342) on the main line is still used, but is much less busy than when Edward Wilson memorably recorded its operations in the late 1940s.

The section of the Prees Branch from The Cottage to Whixall Marina (SJ 496341) is crossed by the only two remaining wooden lifting bridges on the Ellesmere Canal, Allman's Bridge (SJ 492349) and Starks Bridge (SJ 492347). Beyond the Marina a nature reserve extends to Waterloo (SJ 497332), once a busy wharf. The only buildings which remain of the canal settlement are cottages, but

98 *Lifting bridges on the Prees branch of the Ellesmere Canal: Starks Bridge (SJ 492347) in the foreground, the Allmans Bridge in the distance.*

the site of the former lime kilns, worked by Jebb & Co. in 1828, can easily be identified. The remainder of the canal bed is dry. The warehouse overlooking the basin at Edstaston (SJ 517321) is now part of a residence. By 1810 it was a busy centre for sundries traffic with direct services to Chester connecting to Liverpool and Manchester. In 1816 pig and bar iron, and iron castings from the Coalbrookdale Coalfield were being despatched, as well as locally-produced grain and malt, and there was a heavy inward traffic in shop goods for the Coalfield. The wharf, where coal and lime were handled, was on the opposite side of the road. Two ranks of lime kilns remain at the branch terminus at Quina Brook (SJ 523328).

The main line pursues a circuitous but southerly course from Ellesmere to Welsh Frankton, one of the most vital communities along the canal. The settlement was ranged along the short flight of locks which descended from the main line (SJ 371318) to the junction of the lines to Carreghofa and Weston Lullingfields (SJ 368311). Boats were frequently moored for the night at Frankton, where stables provided accommodation for their motive power and the Old Canal Tavern re-freshment for their crews. The company employed a toll collector who lived alongside the locks. A boat building business, owned in 1861 by John Evans, who employed six men and two boys, and lived in an adjoining cottage, occupied a dry dock by the second lock pound. Only two boatbuilders were working at Frankton in 1891. Restoration of the locks is gradually bringing life back to the community.

Few traces remain of the line of the Ellesmere which was intended to reach the Severn at Shrewsbury. There was a wharf at Horderley (SJ 381311), terminus of a building contract in 1796, and again the terminus of the branch after the bank was breached in 1917. The principal centre of traffic was at Weston Lullingfields (SJ 420265) where there was a bank of four lime kilns, together with coal handling facilities, stables, a crane, a weighing machine and a warehouse from which much cheese was despatched, which was used for dances between the two world wars. In the 1960s the wharf retained much of its atmosphere. Its various structures were recognisable and an old delivery wagon remained on the site. Much has now changed but the Regency-style buildings which fringed the wharf remain, together with some traces of the lime kilns.

The line towards the Montgomery Canal pursues a south-westerly course from Frankton to Pant. It crossed the River Perry on a low brick aqueduct of three arches (SJ 363298). At Rednal are traces of a diversion from the intended line requested by the Revd. John Lloyd which took the canal close to his house at Woodhouse. Subsequently the intended line was constructed and used. At Rednal the canal is crossed by the Shrewsbury & Chester Railway. A basin and sidings, the site of which was later used by the artificial manure works of Messrs Richards, provided exchange facilities for freight in the 1860s. The two-storey canalside building (SJ 351276) opposite the lane to Rednal and West Felton station must have been the landing point for passengers joining trains from a canal passenger service from Newtown established in 1853. At Queen's Head (SJ 340268), where the canal is crossed by the Holyhead Road, a small donkey-powered railway built by 1880 and still in use in the 20th century brought to the canal sand from a quarry to the south. There were limekilns on the north bank, and a warehouse remains on the south bank. A three- and four-storey range to the south of the canal accommodated a steam flour mill.

West of the Holyhead Road are Aston Locks (SJ 328256) and another wharf at Maesbury Marsh, alongside the Navigation Inn (SJ 314250). Sundries were handled at a warehouse on the wharf, destroyed by fire in 1968, while canalside industries included a lead smelter and an artificial manure works. Further west is the junction of a branch (SJ 303248) which led to Maesbury Hall Mill.

The canal then enters the Oswestry Coalfield. An early 19th-century railway from pits around Sweeney ran to Gronwen Wharf (SJ 304246). The course of the railway was traced in the 1940s by Edward Wilson who discovered about a hundred stone sleeper blocks, and concluded that it was laid with rails approx. 1.37m. long.[23] Redwith or Morton Wharf (SJ 3012410) where the canal is crossed by the road from Knockin to Llynclys is still recognisable as a canal installation but no traces remain of its limekilns. At Crickheath Wharf (SJ 292234) the canal was joined by another early 19th-century railway which brought lime-stone from quarries near Porthywaen. At Pant and Llanymynech other railways brought limestone to kilns and wharves on the canal, which passes into Wales as it goes under the bridge carrying the road from Oswestry to Welshpool (SJ 266210).

The current main line of the Ellesmere Canal pursues a north-westerly course from Frankton locks to Chirk. After passing New Marton locks (SJ 332342, SJ 328347) for over 1km. it forms the boundary between St Martin's and Whittington.

St Martin's Moor, home of many boatmen in the 19th century is a canal community which has turned its back on the waterway (SJ 324356). Cottages from the canal era are interspersed with modern dwellings, and a coal merchant remains in business. Warehouses remain on either side of the main road on the eastern bank. The canal became a vital element in the economy of the Oswestry Coalfield between Moreton Hall (SJ 300357) and Upper Chirk Bank (SJ 294370).

The Ellesmere Canal crosses the River Ceiriog on the 254m. long, 25.5m. high Chirk Aqueduct (SJ 286373). The county boundary follows an old line of the Ceiriog, and six of the aqueduct's 10 arches are in Shropshire. Charles Hadfield has shown that the design was changed many times after William Jessop had recommended to the company in July 1795 that an iron trough should be erected. It was probably Thomas Telford who decided soon afterwards to construct a masonry aqueduct, in which, perhaps as late as 1799, it was resolved to insert a cast iron bottom, rather than many feet of puddled clay. Iron side plates were added in 1870. The aqueduct was opened to traffic at the end of 1801 and remains the most spectacular way of crossing the frontier between England and Wales.

THE SHROPSHIRE UNION

The Ellesmere Canal was joined to the Shrewsbury Canal by Telford's Birmingham & Liverpool Junction Canal, a 63.5km.-long waterway linking the Staffordshire & Worcestershire Canal at Autherley outside Wolverhampton with the Ellesmere & Chester Canal at Nantwich which was authorised in 1826 after much political turmoil, and opened on 2 February 1835. Its principal source of water is the Knighton Reservoir, the feeder stream from which enters the canal just inside Shropshire (SJ 733274). In 1846, along with the Shropshire Canal, the Shrewsbury Canal and the Ellesmere & Chester Canal, it formed the Shropshire Union Railway & Canal Company, and its main line is often, in consequence, called the 'Shrop-shire Union'.[24]

The Birmingham & Liverpool Junction Canal carried some commercial traffic until the 1970s, and is traversed by many touring boats. Its archaeology has been elucidated by Jonathan Morris.[25]

The canal enters Shropshire south east of Cheswardine village (SJ 736274), and continues northwards for about three miles to the Staffordshire border (SJ 694314). At Park Heath Wharf (SJ 731275) the former weighbridge office remains. The wharf was used from 1891 by the Whitehouse family for the distribution of coal from Littleton Colliery near Cannock. At Goldstone Wharf (SJ 704294) the ware-house has been converted to a dwelling, while the adjacent public house is a popular eating house. The Cheswardine Road bridge (SJ 700301) frames the entry to the deep Woodseaves Cutting, on the rims of which spoil from the excavations, up to 10m. high was deposited on specially purchased land, thus increasing the apparent depth of the cutting. A small cave high on the western side of the cutting, 350m. north of the bridge, appears to have housed a blacksmith's hearth during an early stage of construction. The most celebrated feature of the cutting, thanks to Eric de Maré's photograph, is a 13.4ft. high, stone arched accommodation bridge (SJ 697307). de Maré called it the 'Rocket' bridge, but this name is not

99 *The town wharf at Market Drayton (SJ 684346) on the Birmingham & Liverpool Junction Canal. The tall building to the right of the bridge was a corn mill.*

used locally, and possibly the photographer misheard the colloquial name of the cutting, 'the Rockin'.

The canal re-enters Shropshire as it crosses the culverted River Tern (SJ 685343), and remains in the county for about 8km. The basin at Market Drayton (SJ 684346) was in water by 1829 when it was used by boats carrying spoil for embankments. It was subsequently used by the principal carrying companies, by William Hazledine who sold there coal from the Coalbrookdale Coalfield, and by William Tomkinson, who dealt in guano, corn and salt. At the north end of the basin the mid-19th-century Shropshire Union Carrying Co. warehouse was incorporated in 1914 into a newly-built corn mill which operated until the early 1970s. The adjacent *Bleak House* was the home of the canal agent. At the point where the canal is crossed by the road to Norton in Hales, is Victoria Wharf (SJ 678353), which is still occupied by coal merchants. At Adderley Wharf (SJ 671391) is a cottage once occupied by the lime burner who worked the kilns which formerly stood on the side of the winding hole. The five locks at Adderley lower the canal by 9.4m., and after passing through them the canal enters Cheshire (SJ 660410).

The 16.9km. 'Newport Arm' of the Birmingham & Liverpool Junction canal, sanctioned in 1827 and opened on 2 February 1835, leaves the main line at Norbury Junction, Staffordshire (SJ 793227) and enters Shropshire south of Forton (SJ 752200) at the foot of the flight of 17 locks which descends from the junction with the main line at Norbury.[26] Six further locks complete the descent to the level of the Shrewsbury Canal. The section through Newport is still in water, and one canalside warehouse remains (SJ 743194), although a larger example now serves as the sawmill at the Blists Hill Open Air Museum. After passing through Ticket House lock (SJ 738194) and Polly's Lock (SJ 733191) the canal turns south-west across the Weald Moors, and crossed Kynnersley Drive on an aqueduct (SJ 686165), more commonly called the Duke's Drive Aqueduct, which bore the arms of the Duke of Sutherland, and was demolished as part of a drainage scheme in the late 1960s. South of the aqueduct was the junction with the 1.3 km. branch to a wharf at Lubstree (SJ 692152), opened in 1844 and closed in 1922. A warehouse with a canopy over the canal and pedimented end elevations remains at the terminus.

Wappenshall, where the Newport Arm of the B.& L.J.C. joins the Shrewsbury Canal was one of the most interesting canal communities in Shropshire. The junction occupied land owned by the Dukes of Sutherland who constructed a wharf where shop goods for the whole of the coalfield were received, together with limestone for ironmaking from Llanymynech and Trevor Rocks, while the principal outward cargoes were coal and iron. The lock at Wappenshall is now a weir, the accommodation drawbridge has been replaced by a concrete structure and the road bridge has been flattened. The elegant skew bridge across the junction appears to have been personally designed by Telford and remains intact. Two warehouses remain. The smaller, 13m. x 9m., which retains a cast iron pillar crane, was built in 1835, the larger, 22m. x 8m., constructed on arches springing from piles and spanning an arm of the canal, was begun in 1838. There are remains of a winch in the gable of the south elevation, and a hoist remains on the first floor. Other surviving buildings include the toll clerk's residence, a two-storey three bay, brick house with semi-octagonal bow front and overhanging eaves, the weighing machine house, a single-storey brick hut, and a public house, now Bridge House, construction of which was in progress in December 1836. The wharf opened on the same day as the canal. Full accounts remain of every item handled until 1850, when the sundries traffic may have ceased.[27]

THE LEOMINSTER CANAL

The Leominster Canal was one of the least successful of the waterways of the Industrial Revolution, and was literally marginal to the Shropshire economy, but its archaeological remains are of unusual interest.[28] The canal was intended to link the Severn at Stourport with Leominster. It received parliamentary assent in 1791 and construction was directed by Thomas Dadford junior. The section from the Mamble collieries to Woofferton was opened in 1794 and extended to Leominster in 1796, making a total length of 30km., along which boats 70ft.-long and 6ft. 10in. in beam could be navigated. The canal was never linked with the Severn and its chief, perhaps its only economic function was to carry westwards the produce of Sir Walter Blount's mines around Mamble. For Shropshire it was chiefly important as a contributor, with the Clee Hill pits, to the coal supply of Ludlow, from the wharf at Woofferton. The canal was sold in 1858 to the Shrewsbury & Hereford Railway who formally closed it, drained it the following year, and sold some of the land which was used for the railway between Tenbury and Woofferton.

100 *One of the outer arches of the aqueduct carrying the Leominster Canal over the River Teme (SO 537687). The central arch was destroyed in a military exercise during the Second World War.*

The most easterly section of the Leominster Canal in Shropshire is in the parish of Neen Sollars which it enters near Southnett Wharf House (SO 673705) and leaves by the aqueduct over the Rea (SO 651703), a single brick arch. The section between the crossings of the Corn Brook (SO 627686) and the Ledwych Brook (SO 573684) is in Shropshire, and it re-enters the county as it crosses the Teme Aqueduct (SO 537687), a three-arch structure of brick and stone the central span of which was blown up during a military exercise in the Second World War. The earthworks of the section between the aqueduct and the old railway (SO 533685) are well-preserved and the site of the wharf at Woofferton (SO 519684) can still be recognised. The canal leaves Shropshire south of the wharf (SO 514680).[29]

TURNPIKE ROADS

Shropshire's roads, particularly the routes running into Wales were notoriously bad in the early 18th century. In some areas roads had been raised above flood levels. Celia Fiennes in 1698 noted that the last two or three miles of the approach to Shrewsbury from Whitchurch followed a causeway, which can still be recognised in parts of St Michael's Street and Ditherington. John Loveday in 1732 wrote that

> A causey wide enough for one horse runs from Shrewsbury with some Interruption for about 8 miles on the way to Welshpool.

At that time, it seems, wheeled vehicles could scarcely penetrate west of Shrewsbury, but in 1813 an observer could remark that the county's public roads were tolerably good and in a general state of improvement. In Shropshire as in other counties, transport possibilities were transformed in the 18th century by the activities of turnpike trusts.

As in other counties, routes towards London were the first to be made the responsibility of turnpike trusts. In 1725 (12 Geo I, c.9) a trust was created for the routes from Shrewsbury to Ivetsey Bank, on Watling Street, the Roman route from Wroxeter to London, with a branch from Oakengates to Shifnal, forming part of what was to become the most frequently used route to the capital.

Most of Shropshire's main roads and a few minor ones came under the control of turnpike trusts during the 18th century.[30] Thirty-eight Acts of Parliament designated new turnpike trusts in Shropshire (excluding those in the Halesowen/Oldbury area) of which two were passed before 1750, twenty-four between 1750 and 1769, four between 1770 and 1799, and eight after 1800. While the period between 1750 and 1769 was the peak of legislative activity relating to Shropshire's roads, the extent of change brought by the Acts which renewed the powers of trusts (which normally had a term of 21 years) is less easily measured. Some renewal acts enabled existing trusts to take over substantial new stretches of road. Paradoxically some acts which set up new trusts, like that for the Atcham-Dorrington road in 1797 (37 Geo III c.172) were for routes of little importance, and the trusts were effectively run by existing, larger trusts. Some trusts set up to run long stretches of road, like that for Watling Street, and that for the Chester Road established in 1760 (33 Geo II c.51) which extended from Chester through Shropshire to Stonebridge in Warwickshire, were quickly broken up into administrative districts, which were in effect separate trusts. Equally some large trusts worked closely together. Tenders for collecting tolls on the Shrewsbury Division of Watling Street, the Welsh Bridge Roads and the Coleham Bridge roads were all sought in the same advertisement in 1825.

The turnpike road system in Shropshire was wound up in the second half of the 19th century.[31] After many amalgamations and splits amongst turnpike trusts, roads in the county fell under the control of 46 separate turnpike authorities by 1850. Some sections of road which had fallen out of use, like the Norton Crossroads-Wroxeter-Acton Burnell route which forded the Severn, were given up by the relevant trusts early in the 19th century. The first substantial section of main road to be disturnpiked was the portion of the Chester Road between Whitchurch and Tern Hill where tolls ceased to be collected in 1854. Six trusts ceased operation during the 1860s, but the majority, a total of 35, were disbanded in the following decade, leaving three to follow in the 1880s, with just one, the Wem-Bron-y-garth trust, continuing to collect tolls until 1893, when only one other turnpike road remained in Britain.

Shropshire has relatively few ancient signposts. A sandstone pillar outside the *Bell* at Tong marks distances to Newport, Chester, Brewood, Lichfield, Shifnal, Salop and to a town whose name is indecipherable. At Craven Arms an obelisk at the crossroads (SO 433827) gives distances to many towns, the inclusion of Holyhead suggesting that it dates from after 1780. A stone at the junction of the London and Wenlock roads in Shrewsbury lists Shifnal, Birmingham and Oxford as staging posts en route to London, and gives distances to Bath and Bristol, and is probably also of late 18th-century date. Of the three, it is likely that only the pillar at Tong pre-dates the turnpike era.

The most visible remains of turnpike trusts are mileposts and tollhouses. The county's mileposts vary considerably. Those on the Bishop's Castle Trust are of local stone, with crudely carved inscriptions. Some around Shrewsbury, like that on the Welsh Bridge-Minsterley road at Radbrook, were of soft sandstone, which has weathered beyond recognition. Those on the Leighton Trust were of roughly-shaped stone with iron plates attached, carrying the inscriptions. The posts on the Wem-Bron-y-Garth road were of neatly shaped stone with iron plates on which the inscriptions were painted. Carved milestones were installed along the wholly new Minsterley—Churchstoke turnpike in the mid-1830s. The majority of the mileposts which survive are of cast iron, are triangular in plan, with the inscriptions on thicker and chamfered sections at the top, and on plinths at the bottom. The Coalbrookdale Company was offering several variations of this design in the 1840s.

101 *The 18th-century obelisk recording distances by road from the* Earl of Craven's *inn in the parish of Stokesay (SO 433827) which in the 19th century gave its name to the railway town of Craven Arms.*

Nearly 300 tollhouses were used by turnpike trusts in Shropshire. Some were adaptations of existing cottages, like that which still survives at Nobold (SJ 474101) on the Coleham—Longden road, but most were probably purpose-built. The majority have disappeared as a result of road-widening, or because the standard of accommodation provided was inadequate for 20th-century requirements. The tollhouse at Prescot (SJ 426120) on the approach to Baschurch from Shrewsbury, a single-storey building of dressed sandstone blocks, with a hipped roof, and probably of only two rooms, was damaged beyond repair when it was hit by a car in January 1939. Similarities between tollhouses built by the First and Second Ludlow turnpike trusts, semi-octagonal towers, whether of brick or stone, triangular-headed windows with pairs of stone lintels, suggest that the two organisations worked closely together.

SHROPSHIRE MILEPOSTS

102 *(Above from left to right) A milestone on the Bridgnorth and Cleobury Mortimer turnpike trust north of Horseford Bridge (SO 699864) • A milestone near Hope (SJ 339010) on the new turnpike road from Minsterley to Churchstoke constructed in the 1830s. It is curious that at this late date the trust decided to use stones rather than cast iron mileposts. • A cast iron milepost erected by the Welsh Bridge trust on the Shrewsbury-Baschurch road near Leaton (SJ 473180), indicating that this is an outlying portion of the parish of St. Mary, Shrewsbury.*

(Below from left to right) A cast iron milepost on the Shrewsbury-Bridgnorth turnpike road north of Cross Houses (SJ 530081). The moulder has inserted the letter 'n' into the mould the wrong way round. • A cast iron milepost on the A442 north of Norton (SJ 727005) usually regarded as the road from Telford (or Wellington) to Bridgnorth, but the distance from Shifnal indicates that this section was part of a Staffordshire turnpike, running through Newport and Shifnal to Bridgnorth. • A cast iron milepost east of Aston Eyre (SO 656939) on the turnpike road from Morville to Shipton opened in 1843. It is unusual for distances to London to be shown on Shropshire mileposts. The inscription on the right-hand side of the plinth shows the name of the township, Aston Eyre. The left-hand side is blank.

Some tollhouses can readily be recognised by their form. Several trusts favoured octagonal or semi-octagonal towers, like that built by the Oswestry trust at Porthywaen (SJ 258235). Some tollhouses are undistinguished in appearance but can be recognised by their situations near road junctions or river crossings, like that at Harpswood (SO 691915) which controls a crossing of the Mor Brook and the junction of the Bridgnorth—Ludlow road with the route from Brown Clee to Bridgnorth. Some were idiosyncratic in design, but without functional features, like the double-fronted cottage with ogee windows on the ground floor which controls the Brockton road at Minsterley (SJ 372051). Others, like that built at Burcote (SJ 618105) c.1805, which became redundant after 30 years when the Overley Hill diversion on the Holyhead Road was constructed, are little different from any other contemporary working-class cottages.

The best-preserved turnpike records in Shropshire are those of the two Ludlow trusts, which enable improvements to be recognised.[32] At Henley (SO 532761) on the road to Bridgnorth, the old line of road by-passed by a scheme authorised on 27 November 1828 is clearly visible.

There is relatively little evidence in Shropshire of the construction of wholly new routes in the 18th century. Most turnpike trusts either took over existing main routes, like Watling Street, or adapted rambling lanes into passable through routes, like the road from Tern Bridge through Leighton to Buildwas Bridge, turnpiked in anticipation of the construction of the Iron Bridge in 1778. One of the few wholly new routes was that from Ludlow to Cleobury Mortimer, constructed amidst the mines on Clee Hill in the 1750s.

After 1800 it appears that the trusts sought more radical improvements, of which there is plentiful archaeological evidence, sometimes making up for a dearth of documentation. Around Shrews-bury, the gradient through New Street was eased in 1824, and some time before 1832 the old road to Baschurch, now familiar to visitors to the West Midland Showground as the access route to the car parks, was abandoned in favour of the present road. A bend was taken out

103 *The stone tollhouse erected by the Second Ludlow Turnpike Trust at Temeside (SO 517742). Elements of the octagonal plan, and the triangular-headed windows topped by pairs of stone lintels were used by the trust on other tollhouses. This tollhouse controlled the road to Steventon, probably in order to deter long-distance travellers from using it to avoid paying toll rather than because there was potential for significant revenue.*

104   *The tollhouse built by the Bishop's Castle trust on the road to Brockton at Minsterley (SJ 372051).*

of the route from Coleham Bridge towards Church Stretton when the route through Old Coleham was replaced by the present line along Moreton Crescent, probably in 1815-16. The trustees of the Ellesmere road decided to ease the gradient on Cross Hill by the excavation of a cutting in 1828, following an accident to a coach.[33]

One of the first major schemes was undertaken on the Welshpool road on either side of the Welsh border. West of Halfway House the turnpike road ran past the Rose and Crown (SJ 319112), through Lower Winnington towards Buttington, crossing the Welsh frontier at SJ 295102. In 1801 a new line was authorised (41 Geo III c.88) diverging to the north between mileposts 10 and 11 (SJ 323117), beginning with a straight stretch of 2 km. running in a north-westerly direction to Plas-y-Court. The road crosses the frontier about 0.5 km. further on at Gate Farm. There were gates on the new section at Middleton and Trewern, both in Wales, and at the Rose and Crown on the old section which was disturnpiked on 1 May 1837.

The Kidderminster Trust completely re-routed the Kidderminster-Bridgnorth road through the parish of Alveley, probably in 1809-10.[34] The Wolverhampton Trust moved their road towards Newport some 100m. to the east, probably as a means of enlarging the park at Kilsall Hall. The landscape in the vicinity has been completely changed by the construction of R.A.F. Cosford and the M54 motorway. The Burlton and Llanymynech trust constructed the straight stretch of road eastwards from Ruyton-XI-Towns towards Baschurch in 1837.[35] Greenwood's map of 1826-27 shows the present road from Shrewsbury to Prees Heath north of the crossroads with the Shawbury-Wem turnpike (SJ 540253) as an 'Intended Road'. The old line remains, lined with a scatter of squatter-like cottages. Greenwood shows the old line of the Shrewsbury-Montgomery road, west of the Westbury boundary (SJ 351072) as far as Little Worth (SJ 332051), part of the Bishop's Castle trust, going through Aston Pigott and Aston Rogers. By the mid-1840s the present route, marked as 'new road' on the Worthen Tithe Map, had been constructed.

Some schemes were even more ambitious. The roads south from Ludford Bridge (SO 512741) towards Richards Castle and Woofferton, the roads to Hereford and Worcester, were re-routed by the Ludlow First Turnpike in the 1830s, and a new tollhouse built where the roads diverge (SJ 499725). The old line of the Hereford route was preserved as a footpath, but public rights on the former Worcester road were extinguished, and in Ludford village a timber-framed inn was left isolated by the diversion (SO 513742).[36]

Three roads were built by newly constituted turnpike trusts. A new trust (57 Geo III c.12) was responsible for the road between Coalbrookdale and Wellington, built as a means of relieving unemployment in 1816-7, although in practice the new route was administered as part of the Madeley trust. In 1834 an act was obtained (4 & 5 Wm IV c.11) for a road from Minsterley to Churchstoke, up the Hope Valley and through the mining area at Roman Gravels, creating a new route between Shrewsbury and Bishop's Castle. The route remains as a testament of the skills of the last generation of engineers to work for the turnpike trusts, with its two spacious tollhouses at Plox Green (SJ 367048) and Pultheley (SO 324947). Five

105 *John Gwynn's bridge at Atcham (SJ 540093) of 1768-76, preserved after it was by-passed by a concrete bridge in 1929.*

106   *Thomas Telford's bridge of 1800 over the River Roden at Lee Brockhurst (SJ 548267), known as Lee Bridge. It forms part of the road from Shrewsbury to Whitchurch and was by-passed in 1962.*

years later the last new turnpike act affecting Shropshire was passed, authorising a road from Morville to Shipton, creating a low-level route from Bridgnorth to Ludlow, avoiding the 1,100ft. summit at the *Three Horseshoes* on the existing turnpike through Burwarton. It was opened in 1843.

Many new bridges were constructed in Shropshire during the turnpike era, although the larger examples were the responsibility of Quarter Sessions rather than the trusts. The county's bridges have been expertly described by the late A.H.Blackwall.[37] The first significant bridge of the 18th century was constructed by the borough of Oswestry across the Tanat at Llanyblodwell (SJ 241229) in 1811, a three-arch structure, with a central span of 12m. The most important stone bridge in the county is at Atcham (SJ 540093), where John Gwynn's structure of seven Grinshill stone arches, built in 1768-76, remains in unaltered condition, having been by-passed by a concrete bridge in 1929. Telford's Montford Bridge (SJ 432153), completed in 1794, a similar structure in red sandstone, has a cantilevered footpath, but otherwise remains in its original condition, as does the Welsh Bridge in Shrewsbury, built by John Carline and John Tilley in 1796. The English Bridge was much altered in 1927. One of the best of Telford's smaller bridges is Lee Bridge (SJ 558268), now by-passed, a sandstone arch with a span of 11m. Anthony Blackwall's research showed that considerable investment was made in bridges through the latter parts of the 19th century when long-distance traffic had been reduced by railway competition.

Shropshire's iron bridges comprise a unique feature of its Industrial Archaeology. The first iron bridge is discussed in Chapter Four. The second in Shropshire,

Telford's structure at Buildwas (SJ 645045), was replaced in 1905, but an inscribed portion of one of its ribs is displayed alongside the replacement's replacement, completed in 1992. The Cound Arbour bridge (SJ 555053), cast by the Coalbrookdale Company in 1797, is probably the oldest iron bridge still open to traffic. By c.1811 Thomas Telford had developed a standard design for iron bridges, used at Stokesay, Meole Brace, Cound and elsewhere, but the only example remaining is at Cantlop (SJ 517063), now happily by-passed and preserved as part of a picnic site. A rib from Stokesay Bridge (SO 438818) is preserved at the Ironbridge Gorge Museum, while ribs from the Cound Bridge of 1818 (SJ 558057) have been re-used in the centre of Telford. The bridge at Coalport has the most complex history of any iron bridge. It originated as a wooden bridge in 1780. The superstructure was rebuilt on three sets of iron ribs after 1795. One half-rib was replaced and two complete ribs added, and an iron superstructure was erected in place of the wooden one in 1818.[38]

The development of stage coach services in Shropshire was memorably described, doubtless from their own memories, by Owen and Blakeway. They noted that in the late 18th century there was 'a vast increase of posting and stage-coaches' in Shrewsbury. Stage coach services can be analysed, since they were advertised, their fares and timings are known, and estimates can be made of how many horses they employed. Posting, private hire operation, is scarcely documented at all, yet clearly it accounted for a large part of long-distance passenger transport. According to Owen and Blakeway a coach from London took four days to reach Shrewsbury

107 *Thomas Telford's bridge of 1813 at Aston Cantlop (SJ 517063) on the Shrewsbury-Acton Burnell road, the only example of one of Telford's cast iron arches which remains in situ in Shropshire.*

in 1753, and two days in 1764. By the early 1770s coaches were running without overnight stops, and in 1774 one service with a small fast vehicle, the *Modern Machine*, claimed to do the journey in 24 hours, while a larger coach, the *New Fly*, took 36 hours. The same contrast in times can be observed until the demise of stage coaching in the late 1830s, and especially after the introduction of light, fast Mail coaches in 1785. In 1788 the *Royal Mail* took 22 hours to London and the *Fly* 30 hours. The larger coaches were doing the journey in 26 or 27 hours in the mid-1820s, and by the early 1830s the *Wonder* and the *Nimrod*, both large coaches, were getting to the capital in about 15 hours.[39]

From the late 1770s Shrewsbury became a hub for stage coach services. The principal network was centred at the *Lion* which had been built by the lawyer John Ashby in 1777. The inn was taken over in January 1781 by Robert Lawrence, previously landlord of the *Raven and Bell* next door, who had begun a service to Holyhead in 1779. The road through Shrewsbury superseded that through Chester as the principal route for travellers between London and Dublin. Coaches from Holyhead to London connected at Shrewsbury with services to Bristol and Bath, which began to run in 1779. Direct services to Manchester and Liverpool which began in 1807 also connected at Shrewsbury for the south west. From the 1790s services began to the Welsh coast resorts of Aberystwyth and Barmouth 'for the bathing season'. Some coaches ran the Potteries and Macclesfield but no regular pattern of service developed in that direction. On the main routes, to London by various routes, to Bath and Bristol, to Aberystwyth and Barmouth, to Holyhead and to Liverpool and Manchester there was competition between the principal Shrewsbury inns. Foremost was the *Lion*, followed by the neighbour, the *Raven and Bell*, and by the *Talbot*, built in Market Street in 1775 by the Oteley family of Pitchford Hall. A few services also operated from the *Elephant and Castle* and from the *Britannia*, but these inns did not act as hubs as did the larger establishments.

Shrewsbury's coaching was quickly affected by the opening of railways. The Liverpool & Manchester Railway, acknowledged as the first main line railway, opened in 1830. By 1834 the *Hawk* coach from Shrewsbury ran to Liverpool, connecting by rail to Warrington and Manchester. In 1837, following the opening of the Grand Junction Railway from Birmingham into Lancashire, services for Liverpool and Manchester began to run to Whitmore, where they connected with trains. The following year most of Shrewsbury's London services became feeder coaches, running into the terminus of the London & Birmingham Railway at Curzon Street, Birmingham. Services to the south-west were re-routed to Birmingham to connect with trains in the early 1840s. Shrewsbury's coach operators accommodated the railways for more than two decades, increasing services which supplemented those offered by the railway companies. By 1861 the *Royal Mail* to Aberystwyth was the only coach operating out of Shrewsbury, and in July of that year the end of the coaching era was marked by the sale of the 30 horses which had worked the service.

Shrewsbury's principal inn was the *Lion*, built by John Ashby 'to promote the general good of this town and country'. Its great glory was and is its ballroom, which was designed as an assembly room for county society. Most of its stabling and coachhouses lined the inn yard, but some were situated on the other side of Belmont back at the rear of the yard. The Talbot also had extensive stabling off Swan Hill and Cross Hill, while as late as 1903 the *Britannia's* stables were reckoned to accommodate 20 horses.[40]

Outside Shrewsbury the only other significant hub for coaching traffic was Ludlow, but in 1811 services amounted to only 10 departures a week from the *Crown* and nine from the *Angel*, many fewer than the daily total from Shrewsbury.[41]

THE HOLYHEAD ROAD

The most spectacular road improvement of the Industrial Revolution period was not the achievement of private turnpike trusts but of a public authority.[42] The Act of Union between England and Ireland of 1800 led to many complaints by MPs for Irish constituencies about the routes between London and Dublin. A series of inquiries culminated in the appointment of the Holyhead Road Commission (55 Geo. III c. 151) in 1815, charged with the duty of improving the route from London to Dublin through Coventry, Birmingham, Wolverhampton, Shifnal, Shrewsbury, Oswestry, Llangollen and across Snowdonia to Bangor, the Menai Straits and over Anglesey to Holyhead. Thomas Telford, county surveyor in Shropshire since 1788, who had recommended the route to an inquiry in 1810, became surveyor to the Commission. A new Act of Parliament in 1819 (59 Geo III c 30) vested in the Commission all the powers of the existing turnpike trusts on the route west of Shrewsbury, so that the sections previously the responsibility of the Welsh Bridge and Oswestry trusts passed to the new body.

The first priority was improvement of the road in Wales, and little work was done on Shropshire sections in the early years of the Commission's life. During the 1820s the road through Shifnal was re-aligned, a new route was built avoiding Priorslee village and the centre of Oakengates, and a high embankment was built across the valley of the Ketley Brook (SJ 669110). West of Wellington improvements were delayed since Telford hoped to build an entirely new route

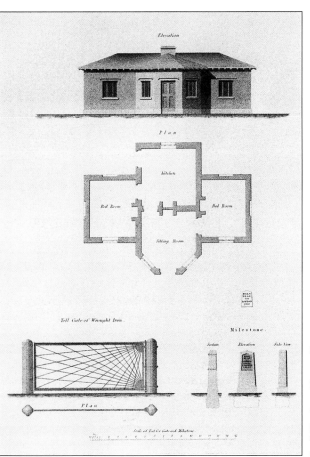

108   *Thomas Telford's designs for tollhouses, gates and mileposts on the Holyhead Road. From the atlas accompanying Telford's Autobiography.*

Ironbridge Gorge Museum Trust

109   *The Gallowstree Bank tollhouse on the Holyhead Road at the approach to Oswestry (SJ 296288), built to the design of Thomas Telford, and similar to but not identical with the plan in the* Autobiography.

direct to Chirk, avoiding the county town. This proposal was eventually dropped, and schemes in the vicinity of Shrewsbury were implemented. The cutting up to The Mount (SJ 484130) was completed in 1829, and most of the road from the Frankwell to Shelton was re-aligned. A direct approach to the English Bridge cutting through the precincts of the Abbey was completed to Telford's design in 1837. More drastic schemes to create boulevards taking traffic quickly through the centre of Shrewsbury were dropped. Two major schemes at Overley Hill west of Wellington and Montford Bank west of Shrewsbury were completed respectively in 1835 and 1838, after Telford's death in 1834. West of Shrewsbury the road is lined with elegant mileposts, of Telford's design, made in the masons' yard where the stone for the Menai Bridge was worked, and installed in 1828. Most of the Shropshire examples remain in situ. For the most part existing tollhouses in Shropshire continued in use, but two new ones were built at Gallowstree Bank, Oswestry (SJ 296288) which remains in situ, and at Shelton (SJ 465132), which was removed to the Blists Hill Museum in 1973. Much of Telford's road in the county is now by-passed, but the scale of projects like the Ketley embankment and Montford Bank can still be appreciated. It is only since the 1960s that modern improvements have led to significant changes in the routing of Telford's road.

The stages in Shropshire for the principal Holyhead coaches were the *Jerningham Arms* at Shifnal, to which horses hauled coaches from Wolverhampton, the *Falcon* at Haygate, Wellington (actually in Wrockwardine parish), the *Lion* in Shrewsbury and the *Wynnstay Arms* in Oswestry, from which the next stage concluded at Llangollen.

20TH-CENTURY ROAD TRANSPORT

As the turnpike trusts gave up their powers in the 1860s and 1870s, Highway Districts, set up by Quarter Sessions, cared for main roads, while Quarter Sessions took responsibility for bridges, the number in the care of the county increasing from 169 to 269 between 1878 and 1886. From 1888 main roads became the responsibility of the newly-established county council, which bought its first steam roller in 1890.[43]

Within 15 years the new body faced problems of managing change. By 1903 125 motor cars had been registered in Shropshire. In the spring many took to the roads, some driven by *cads* and *foreigners* according to some complaints, blowing their horns and covering cyclists

110 *A milepost south of West Felton (SJ 348250)*

in white dust.[44] From 1911 the 'white roads of Shropshire' were steadily blackened as tarred surfaces were applied. Garages were established, some developing from coaching making businesses, and Britain's first roadside filling station was opened at F.A. Legge's garage in Abbey Foregate, Shrewsbury in the early months of 1914.

After the First World War Shropshire attracted many motoring tourists and charabanc parties. As many as 30 coaches might arrive in the Carding Mill Valley on a Sunday in summer, and in the mid-1930s the sides of the Mere at Ellesmere would be heavily congested with cars. The County Surveyor, W.H. Butler, was responsible for an enlightened programme of road improvements. The county's first by-pass, at Gobowen (SJ 306333-SJ 303336), avoiding bends which were notorious as 'the worst death trap in the county', was opened in 1926. A new concrete bridge and by-pass for Lower Corve Street in Ludlow were completed in 1931, and the St George's by-pass, taking Watling Street traffic away from the shopping centres of St George's and Oakengates, was built in 1931-32 under a government unemployment relief scheme. Construction of the Shrewsbury by-pass, most of which made use of existing lanes to the east and south of the town, began in 1931 and it was opened in 1933. The Church Stretton by-pass was almost complete at the start of the Second World War in 1939.[45]

Many buildings were adapted to cater for motoring. Benbow House on Coton Hill in Shrewsbury was converted to a garage by the coachbuilder, Mark Davies, in 1911. The cruck house at No 18 Abbey Foregate in Shrewsbury became Strefford's

111   *The Midway Truckstop at Prees Heath (SJ 555380).*

(later Cureton's) garage in the mid-1920s. The *George Hotel* in Market Street, Shrewsbury, by the mid-1930s had a garage accommodating 20 cars and fitted with a turntable.

Motoring created new landscapes. Prees Heath (SJ 556381), where the A49 from South Wales to Lancashire crosses the A41 from London to Merseyside, is Shropshire's archetypal 20th-century roadside settlement. The *Raven* is an imposing mock-timbered wayside inn. Next to it, along what appears to be the original line of the road, stand the rustically-inspired Breckland Café and the cheerfully Modernist Midway Truckstop. Ye Olde Raven Garage of the 1930s is now a car auction showroom. On the opposite side of the main road is the *Cherry Tree Inn*, eccentrically timber-framed, and another garage, and the landscape is completed by a scatter of semi-detached houses and bungalows. Prees Heath awaits analysis.

Perhaps the county's most imposing roadhouse was the *Nautical William* at Fenn Green, Alveley (SO 771833) opened in 1937 and designed for Derick Burcher, a 'live wire' in the motor industry, by an architect called F. Webb 'to give the impression of a liner's superstructure'. The building has been post-modernised and is now a nursing home.[46]

THE MAIN LINE RAILWAY

Shropshire's intricate railway politics in the 1840s have been described by several previous writers.[47] Two local companies, the Shrewsbury & Birmingham and Shrewsbury & Chester, became involved in bitter conflict in the late 1840s and early 1850s with the London & North Western Railway which had taken over the Shropshire Union Railway & Canal Company in 1846. Ultimately the two Shrewsbury companies made an alliance with the Great Western Railway, which reached Wolverhampton in 1854. The lines from Chester to Shrewsbury and thence to Wolverhampton, which had opened in 1848 and 1849, eventually became part of the Great Western's route from Paddington to Merseyside. From Shrewsbury to Wellington the route was shared with the L.N.W.R., as were the lines to Hereford and Welshpool. The administration of the county's largest station at Shrewsbury was similarly a joint responsibility. The L.N.W.R. had its own route to Crewe, while the G.W.R. approached Crewe from Wellington via Market Drayton, and by the 1870s a networks of other branch lines crossed the county. North Shropshire was served by the Oswestry, Ellesmere & Whitchurch and Oswestry & Newtown sections of the Cambrian Railways, and Oswestry itself became the headquarters of the company. The North Staffordshire Railway ran to Market Drayton from Silverdale. The Potteries, Shrewsbury & North Wales Railway, an ambitious concern in the 1860s, became a sleepy by-way from Shrewsbury to Llanymynech and Criggion, which was closed in 1880, and re-opened as the Shropshire & Montgomeryshire Light Railway in 1909. The Bishop's Castle Railway, opened in 1866, was a gloriously anarchic private line. The Cleobury Mortimer & Ditton Priors Light Railway, opened in 1908, did much to stimulate the economy of the Clee Hills region.

For many years the G.W.R. and L.N.W.R. competed for London traffic but after the shortening of the Great Western route by the opening of the 'Bicester cut-off' in 1910 that company gained an advantage. Nevertheless in the 1920s and 1930s the 10.35 a.m. from Euston to Shrewsbury was a large train, which carried through portions for Swansea, and for Aberystwyth. Some of the most important passenger services to pass through the county were those on which the two major companies co-operated, the through services from Lancashire and Scotland to the West of England through the Severn Tunnel which began in 1888 and continued until 1969.

Shropshire's main lines bear many traces of their origins. Richard Morriss has analysed the county's passenger stations and identified 157, of which less than 20 remain open. Much archaeological evidence remains of the first decades of Shrewsbury's railway history when each of the companies whose trains ran into the town was nominally independent, and had its own locomotive shed, carriage sidings and freight depot.[48]

Shrewsbury station, which extended over the bridge spanning the Severn, was shared by the two companies. The building, in Tudor Revival style, was designed, like other stations on the Shrewsbury & Chester Railway, by Thomas Penson. The complex was radically altered between 1899 and 1903. The forecourt was lowered by excavation, and the present ground floor of the station added beneath Penson's original building. The bridge over the Severn was widened with fabricated steel girders carried on thick cast iron columns. The track layout was extended to the north, and the junction with the line to Crewe re-aligned, necessitating the widening of the bridge crossing the Castle Foregate, and the re-alignment of Howard Street. The enlargement of the station made possible the abandonment of ticket platforms which had been erected on the lines from Wellington, by the Underdale Road

112 *Shrewsbury Station (SJ 493129), designed by Thomas Penson, and opened in 1848. The ground floor was added after excavation of the original forecourt in 1899-1903.*

113 *Thomas Penson could work in the Italianate style as well as in Elizabethan Gothic. His station at Gobowen (SJ 303334), junction for Oswestry, opened in 1848.*

bridge, and Hereford, at the end of the Abbey Foregate triangle, in 1886. Part of the all-over roof remained on the station until 1964.

Elsewhere in Shrewsbury there are traces of the locomotive depots, carriage sidings, freight depots and marshalling yards of the small companies which were taken over by the L.N.W.R. and the G.W.R. The Shrewsbury & Chester Railway established a freight depot off Castle Foregate, which from 1858 was bounded by the L.N.W.R.'s line from Crewe. From 1862 it was shared by the West Midland Railway (the Severn Valley) and the volume of traffic became too great to be handled with ease. The G.W.R. subsequently built another depot north of the Ellesmere Road bridge. The L.N.W.R.'s freight depot was the 'New Yard', the road access for which was also from Castle Foregate, which was separated from the G.W.R. depot by the Bagley Brook. The L.N.W.R., of which the Shropshire Union Canal & Railway Company was part, also used the canal basin as a freight depot, gaining access to it by a siding under Howard Street in 1859.

114 *The original locomotive depot of the Shrewsbury & Chester Railway (SJ 492132), north of Shrewsbury Station.*

The Shrewsbury & Birmingham locomotive depot was on the south side of its tracks near to the Underdale Road bridge, with the SUR & CC depot on the opposite side of the line. By 1864 both had become freight depots and were worked jointly, but the reservoir which provided water for Shropshire Union locomotives remained well into the 20th century. The Shrewsbury & Chester company built a depot on the south side of their line, behind the *London Apprentice*

Russell Mulford Collection

115 *Coleham sheds (SJ 499119) at Shrewsbury in 1953, showing one of the depot's most celebrated express locomotives, G.W.R. 'Castle' class No.5097* Sarum Castle.

116 *The 'Shelf' sidings alongside the Shrewsbury & Hereford Railway (SJ 497116), south of Shrewsbury, which accommodated numerous redundant steam locomotives in 1967-69, giving rise to rumours that they were being assembled for a strategic reserve of motive power. On the right is a Stanier 8F locomotive. A Cross Country diesel unit, then the usual rolling stock for local trains between Shrewsbury and Hereford, passes on the main line.*

public house, which was used for its original function for little more than two decades. It was put to other railway purposes for a century, and is now part of Furrows Garage. The locomotive sheds at Coleham, well-remembered in Shrewsbury, originated in 1856, were much enlarged in the 1880s, and have now completely disappeared.

The Shrewsbury & Hereford company carriage sheds on the eastern side of its tracks, just outside the station, were enclosed within the Abbey Foregate triangle when the direct connection between the Hereford and Wellington lines was completed in 1867. The Shropshire Union kept its carriages north of its line between the Underdale Road and Monkmoor Road bridges and the Severn Valley Railway alongside its tracks south of Sutton Bridge Junction. The 'shelf' sidings alongside the lines to Hereford probably originated as the Shrewsbury & Hereford company's marshalling yard, but were celebrated in the late 1960s as a dump for redundant steam locomotives from Lancashire and Cheshire en route for scrap yards in South Wales. Rumours persisted that the locomotives assembled there were destined for a secret strategic reserve in a military base in the Welsh Marches.

Nine signal boxes once controlled Shrewsbury's rail traffic. Two, the L.N.W.R. buildings at Severn Bridge Junction and Crewe Bank, have recently been listed, the former as the largest manually operated signal box remaining in Britain. Along the Shrewsbury & Hereford line four early signal boxes, with low-pitched slate roofs,

Collection of Dr. Paul Collins

117 *A picture of the 1930s which epitomises the 'joint' character of Shrewsbury Station. A Great Western 'Dean Goods' 0-6-0 locomotive brings in a train, probably from the Welshpool direction since it includes ex-Cambrian Railways carriages, past the magnificent Severn Bridge Junction signal box (SJ 496126), built by the L.& N.W.R.*

118 *The characteristic Shrewsbury & Hereford Railway signal box at Marshbrook (SO 441898), with the former station buildings in the background.*

remain in use at Dorrington (SJ 489033), Church Stretton (SO 456936), Bromfield (SO 496775) and Woofferton (SO 515685).

Shropshire's outstanding railway bridges are the Belvidere Bridge by which the Wellington line from Shrewsbury crosses the Severn (SJ 520125), an iron arch, cast by the Coalbrookdale Company, the Albert Edward Bridge (SJ 660037) of 1862 by which the lines from Wellington and Madeley Junction crossed the Severn to Buildwas Junction, another iron arch cast by the Coalbrookdale Company, and the viaduct across the Ceiriog at Chirk (SJ 287371). This was originally a masonry structure of 10 arches, with spans of timber construction at either end, but the wooden arches were replaced by stone ones in 1858. The only significant tunnel is at Oakengates on the Shrewsbury & Birmingham, which is 430m. long. There are shorter tunnels at Ludlow and Bridgnorth. The locomotive depot at Ludlow (SO 513753), operating from 1857 until 1951, has been adapted for other uses.

Many goods warehouses have been adapted for other uses, like that at Hodnet (SJ 622278), a polychrome brick structure, six bays deep and three across, now used as a store by the National Rivers Authority, while the nearby goods yard remains a road-served coal depot, and the once-rail-served cattle market (SJ 621282) is a County Council road depot.

119 *The Shrewsbury & Hereford Railway signal box, freight depot and passenger station buildings on Shropshire's southern border, at Woofferton (SO 513682). In the background is the distinctive outline of Titterstone Clee.*

120 *The ex-G.W.R. goods warehouse at Hodnet (SJ 621278), used as a store by the National Rivers Authority.*

121   *The goods shed of the North Staffordshire Railway at Pipe Gate (SJ 737408). The rear part of the premises is used for the fabrication of steel boats for canal cruising.*

Craven Arms is a railway junction town.[49] Before 1850 the town consisted of little more than the wayside inn, built by the Earl of Craven and taking his name. The opening of the Shrewsbury & Hereford line in 1852, and of the lines to Knighton, Bishop's Castle and Much Wenlock, stimulated the growth of the town. A locomotive depot, carriage sidings and marshalling facilities were built, and there were extensive freight facilities, including cattle docks, a crane for loading timber, and sidings to the gasworks, to an oil depot, a farmers' co-operative yard, and a large woodworking concern. Its north Shropshire equivalent is Gobowen, junction for the Shrewsbury & Birmingham's Oswestry branch, where similar facilities were built around Thomas Penson's elegant Italianate passenger station, and where a small settlement was stimulated to grow into a substantial village by the trade brought by the railway.

Little remains of the Cambrian Railways routes in Shropshire, apart from the track between Oswestry and Blodwell Junction, nominally still open for stone trains, but in practice disused. The company's outstanding monuments are the vast passenger station buildings at Oswestry (SJ 295298) and Ellesmere (SJ 396351), together with the locomotive and carriage works at Oswestry.

The Severn Valley Railway between Hartlebury through Bewdley, Bridgnorth and the Ironbridge Gorge to Shrewsbury was opened in 1862, rather too late to invigorate the economy of the region which 70 years previously had been amongst the most dynamic in Britain. Its history was undistinguished, a little more than a by-way but never a main line, until after its formal closure when, from 1966, it was

122 *The former Cambrian Railways station at Ellesmère (SJ 396350), opened in 1863, and closed in 1964.*

developed into Britain's premier preserved railway. In some respects it bears few resemblances to its own history. At Bridgnorth is a substantial depot housing many more steam engines than would ever have operated there in the past. Trains are sometimes hauled by locomotives which would never normally have worked the line, a 'King' class 4-6-0, *Flying Scotsman*, 3,300 h.p. 'Deltic' diesels. Nevertheless at places like Highley Station (SO 749830) the landscape of early 20th-century railways has been sensitively re-created and, when a train of Great Western stock hauled by a small Great Western locomotive calls at the station, there is a powerful evocation of the past.

◆　◆　◆

8

PERSPECTIVES

◆ ◆ ◆

The study of Shropshire's industrial heritage had begun long before 1955 when Michael Rix, who, as deputy warden of the Shropshire Adult College, had grown to appreciate the monuments of the Ironbridge Gorge, published his article in *The Amateur Historian* in which the term *Industrial Archaeology* was first used in print.[1] Several elements of the industrial conservation movement, which was to blossom in Shropshire, as elsewhere, in the 1960s, can be observed before the Second World War. The Iron Bridge was scheduled as an ancient monument in 1934. In 1938 Dr. D. H. Robinson gave to a field society a paper on the county's canals which had a sound archaeological base, and, given the lack of secondary literature, a remarkable degree of accurate historical detail.[2] When thanking him, the antiquarian W.J. Slack argued that Shropshire had a proud industrial history, and that its industrial monuments merited study and protection. Canal cruising was established on a commercial basis on the Ellesmere and Shropshire Union canals during the 1930s.[3] The Darby family of Coalbrookdale were among the subjects of a study of Quaker industrialists published by Paul Emden, some 14 years before Arthur Raistrick's *Dynasty of Ironfounders*, which appeared in 1953, and helped to influence Allied Ironfounders Ltd to establish Coalbrookdale Works Museum.[4] During the Second World War L.T.C. Rolt visited Ironbridge as an inspector with the Ministry of Supply, and was impressed with the Bedlam furnaces, the use of plateway wagons at Horsehay in the fabrication of landing barges for the D-day invasions, in a coal pit wound by a horse gin, and above all with 'the great black semi-circle of Darby's iron bridge springing over the Severn'.[5]

It has been argued that the growth of the industrial conservation movement was due to particular features of English society in the years after the Second World War.[6] The 'successes' of the movement in Shropshire have been well-chronicled. In 1954 the future of main line of the Ellesmere Canal was assured, and its success as a cruising waterway, together with sustained pressure of public opinion have made possible the restoration of the Montgomeryshire arm of the canal, which is now in progress. On 6 July 1966 a meeting in Kidderminster established the Severn Valley Railway. The first train ran along the restored railway into Bridgnorth on 25 March 1967, and the project subsequently became one of the best in Britain.[7] Shropshire has also featured in another aspect of railway preservation, in the main line running of preserved steam locomotives. The routes through Shrewsbury from

Chester and Crewe to Hereford have been among the most popular for such runs, and Dorrington station bridge has become a regular watering point for locomotives. Other conservation issues are unresolved. The evaluation and conservation of the Snailbeach lead mine only began in the late 1980s. The future of the major surviving structures is assured but what kind of interpretive system will evolve is uncertain. The Ditherington flax mill ceased to be used for malting in 1987, and awaits imaginative new uses. Its status as a Grade I listed building should ensure its survival.

There are currently many smaller indications of appreciation of the industrial past. Private initiatives have saved some of the county's best water mills. Local authorities have paid due attention to industrial monuments in landscape conservation schemes—Wrekin District Council in the Granville Country Park, Shrewsbury & Atcham District in the Old Shrewsbury Canal Park, and Shropshire County Council in the Severn Valley Country Park at Highley and Alveley. English Heritage

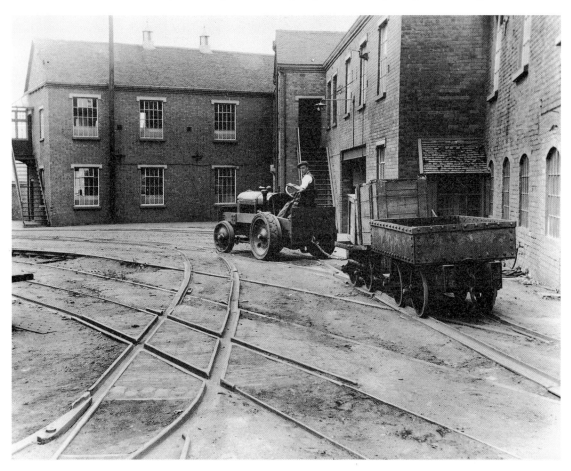

123   *The Coalbrookdale Coalfield as seen by L.T.C. Rolt in the 1940s: a tractor hauling wagons on the plateway system at Horsehay (SJ 672071). Track of this type has been re-laid in the Blists Hill Open Air Museum.*

have listed such structures as the Shrewsbury signal boxes. Private collectors of china, decorative tiles, and Sentinel steam wagons also contribute to the base upon which understanding of the industrial past is founded.

The Ironbridge Gorge Museum is in an international context the most significant industrial conservation project in Shropshire, although it evolved from the same kind of popular initiatives as the Severn Valley Railway and the Shropshire Union Canal Society. In 1959 Allied Ironfounders uncovered the Old Furnace at Coalbrookdale and established a small museum alongside it. Although open only during the summer months and for only four hours a day the museum attracted many visitors, and its success was the justification for the establishment of the Ironbridge Gorge Museum Trust in 1967. The trust was founded at the initiative of Telford Development Corporation, as the result of much pressure from local and national organisations to accord protection to the industrial monuments of the Gorge. During the 1970s many of its prime objectives were achieved and it set the standards by which the conservation and interpretation of industrial monuments came to be judged in an international context.[8] The Museum in turn gave birth to the Ironbridge Institute, whose purpose, *inter alia*, was to raise standards of practice and awareness of theory in Industrial Archaeology in Britain and further afield. This study is therefore one of many outcomes of a broad movement for industrial conservation.

124   *A steam engine being removed from the Milburgh Tileries, Broseley (SJ 683026), for the Ironbridge Gorge Museum Trust during the autumn of 1970. This volunteer project did much to establish the credibility of the museum.*

There is a symbiotic relationship between effective conservation policies and the growth of understanding. Monuments will only be conserved and interpreted if they are understood, and the justification for conserving buildings must be based on arguments derived from knowledge and not on the mindless assertion of questionable superlatives. It can be argued that the 'successes' in industrial conservation in Shropshire have depended on sound historical understanding of why buildings and structures are important, and on eloquent advocacy of that importance. Once monuments are preserved, they can continue to be studied, and their significance can continually be re-assessed as thinking progresses.

This book is based on the premise that Industrial Archaeology is the study of recent centuries through physical evidence of all kinds. Nevertheless there are three major areas of study which are not explored here, nor, by convention, in most works on Industrial Archaeology, which justifies some explanation.

It is philosophically indefensible to omit agriculture from archaeological studies of recent centuries. Its exclusion can be partly justified on pragmatic grounds, shortage of space, the author's ignorance and the lack of coherent published works. A more cogent reason might be that agricultural buildings evolve over a long period, and that barns, dairies, ploughs and wagons of recent centuries are better seen in an extended agricultural context than in a broader chronological setting. Nevertheless the model farm buildings constructed between 1760 and 1860, like those on the Duke of Sutherland's estate, or the extraordinary Italianate farmstead at Trewern (SJ 293328) near Oswestry, have much in common with contemporary industrial buildings, their sources of power, their transmission systems, and the iron machines which they housed. The integration of such buildings into the broader pattern of industrial archaeological understanding is one of the tasks of coming years.

Similarly there can be no philosophical grounds for neglecting the polite architecture of the county, although there are other studies in preparation.[9] Even a county-based study shows that the industrial archaeologist must be concerned with the activities of architects. Thomas Farnolls Pritchard, reinvigorator of old country houses, was also the designer of the Iron Bridge. Charles Bage, surveyor and wine merchant, was not a professional architect but he designed three textile mills of international consequence. Thomas Telford was an architect who designed churches and villas before he applied his sense of proportion to bridges and tollhouses. Samuel Cookson (d.1853), of the Coalbrookdale ironworks, toyed with the Gothic style in his warehouse in Ironbridge and in a school at Dawley. Thomas Penson (1790-1859) provided the Shrewsbury & Chester Railway with its varied stations. Of the later Victorian architects, Samuel Pountney Smith (1812-83), student with his uncle John Smallman of Quatford, designer of the ill-fated Bridgnorth market, worked mainly on church architecture and private houses, and came no nearer to industrial buildings than the corn exchange and the market hall in Much Wenlock. Perhaps the most prolific designer of industrial buildings was A.B. Deakin (1853-1940), who was responsible for the wool warehouse on the Welsh Bridge in Shrewsbury, the maltings in Mardol and the Perseverance Ironworks, as well as large houses in Belle Vue and Kingsland. Other 20th-century architects designed buildings when commissions were available. Arthur Edward Oswell (1849-1931) who did much work on churches and schools, designed many branch banks for Lloyds Bank, the Alliance Insurance office in The Square in Shrewsbury, and the Sentinel Wagon Works. Frank Shaylor (1867-1956) was responsible for the offices and printing works of the *Shrewsbury Chronicle*, as well as a bank in Oswestry, public buildings in mid-Wales, numerous suburban houses in Shrewsbury in the Arts and Crafts style, and also No.31 Shelton Road, which in 1934 marked the appearance of German-style Modernism in the county. There is an essential common concern between the industrial archaeologist and the historian of architecture.

This study shows similarly that military structures are an essential element in the development of 20th-century industry. Industrial archaeologists, interested in the adaptive re-use of airfield control towers or the sergeants' messes of army bases share many concerns with military historians and archaeologists investigating the original purposes and uses of such buildings.

To study manufactures in the Shropshire countryside is to examine a continuing element in human history. To examine the manufactures of market towns is to appreciate that radical change can occur, over decades, to patterns established for many centuries. To study coalfields or upland mining regions leads to an appreciation of the passing nature of so much human ambition. Yet everywhere manufactures leave legacies, water mills used for stripping pine furniture, huge maltings which shelter racing eights, and settlements like St Martin's in the Oswestry coalfield, which, although its mine has been closed for a quarter of a century, remains as Rolt saw it 'unashamedly a colliery village'.[10]

Examination of a county with varied landscapes puts the 'industrial revolution' in its context. If any part of England experienced 'revolution' in the 18th century it was the Coalbrookdale Coalfield. The consequences of the innovations made there in ironworking technology, in mechanical and structural engineering, in the organisation of production, in the application of science to manufactures and mining, were momentous, and affected other parts of Britain, and, ultimately, many other countries. Yet those changes were paralleled in other, lesser coalfields, which also adopted steam engines and plateways, used turnpike roads, and attempted to become involved in ironmaking. The insignificance of such enterprises throws into focus the profound changes which occurred in and around the Ironbridge Gorge. The small scale of 'vernacular' textile manufactures similarly emphasises the significance of Shrewsbury's colossal flax-spinning mills. The 'industrial revolution' is also reflected in ambitious projects whose prospects of success now seem forlorn, the cotton mill at Stottesdon, the Leominster Canal, James George's ironworks at Knowbury.

Study of Shropshire reveals something of the evolution of the 'factory', the complex where varied processes are applied to manufacture a product capable of use either as a capital item, like a steam engine supplied to a mine, as material for a secondary manufacturing process, like thread supplied to a tailor or a shoemaker, or as consumer goods, like a tea service or a cheese. The Coalbrookdale Ironworks, producing pots and pans for customers in the Borderland and overseas in the mid-18th century was perhaps the county's first 'factory' in this sense, but while it made castings for steam engines and other machines it did not evolve into an 'engineering factory' making complete machines until the 1790s, at the same time that the

125 *Puddled wrought iron being rolled in the G.R. Morton Ironworks within the Blists Hill Open Air Museum, which takes its name from the Ironbridge Gorge Museum Trusts's first Honorary Curator.*

brothers Hazledine were setting up their own 'factories' in Shrewsbury and Bridgnorth. The Caughley chinaworks of the 1770s was clearly a 'factory' in every sense of the word, and a line of development can be traced through the larger factory at Coalport of the 1790s, the large, well-organised brick and roofing tile works of the 1850s and '60s, to Charles Lynam's two vast decorative tile factories in Jackfield of the 1870s and '80s. The textile factory came to Shropshire from elsewhere, the mill in Coleham of 1790, and the Ditherington flax mill of 1796-97 represented something wholly new in the county. There was a flurry of textile mill construction in the following years which was not sustained. Engineering factories developed in most towns in the mid-19th century. Establishments like the Oswestry locomotive and carriage works and the Perseverance Ironworks in Shrewsbury had parallels elsewhere, but the most substantial engineering works in the county of the 19th century were the New Yard at St George's of the late 1850s, and the rebuilt Coalbrookdale Works of the 1870s. By the time of the First World War it was accepted that the Sentinel works making such complex engineering products as steam wagons could be moved from Glasgow to the edge of Shrewsbury and go quickly into production. More recently Bavarian dairying technology has been transferred to a similar site on the edge of Market Drayton.

Archaeological study of industrial monuments and landscapes reveals the evolution of the purpose-built 'factory', designed to accommodate particular technological processes, as a consistent theme. It also shows that the persistence of manufactures is a consequence of a tradition of adaptive re-use of buildings and structures which began long before the subject became fashionable as a philosophical concept in the 1970s. Iron forges were changed to corn mills or paper mills in the early 19th century, when the Whitchurch silk mill was used as a cheese warehouse, and Charles Bage's weaving mill at Kingsland became the nucleus of a lead works. Around 1900 William Jones converted a flax mill and a steam corn mill into malthouses. A corn mill at Hanwood was converted to a bleach works which in turn became a barytes mill. A sawmill at Minsterley passed through a spell as a military forage depot before being adapted as a creamery. In the 1930s hangars and concrete sheds built during the First World War for the Royal Flying Corps were serving as factories and workshops. By the late-1960s many buildings built for the forces during the Second World War had been similarly adapted. In the 1940s and '50s premises in the Ironbridge Gorge left derelict by ironworking and ceramics concerns became nurseries for new manufactures.

Archaeological study persistently raises new questions about the industrial past as well as stimulating respect for past achievements. Understanding of Ditherington Flax Mill has increased because it has been possible continually to re-examine the structure, and because it has been re-interpreted in a succession of different contexts, not just as a landmark in the history of structures, but as a building designed to accommodate particular technologies, as a workplace, as the focus of a suburb. Our understanding of any aspect of the past increases from qualitative not just from quantitative gains, from better-directed research rather than merely from the accumulation of more data. It is hoped that this book provides not only a context for future investigations but that it also poses questions which will stimulate an understanding of the industrial past in its widest contexts.

REFERENCES

◆ ◆ ◆

ABBREVIATIONS:

E.S.J.	Eddowes Salopian Journal
S.C.	Shrewsbury Chronicle
S.R.O.	Shropshire Record Office
S.R.R.	Shropshire Records & Research
T.S.A.S.	Transactions of the Shropshire Archaeological Society
V.C.H.	Victoria County History

CHAPTER TWO

1. Report of the School called Industry Hall in the Parish of Prees, Shropshire (1804); Bishton, J., Salop: Report to the Board of Agriculture (1794).

2. Gough, R., *The History of Myddle*, edited by David Hey (Harmondsworth: Penguin, 1981), pp.108, 126-7; Hey, D., *An English Rural Community: Myddle under the Tudors and Stuarts* (Leicester: Leicester University Press, 1974), pp.153-67.

3. *V.C.H.* vol.8, pp.76, 103, 121, 137, 144, 166; Booth, D.T.W., *Watermills on the River Rea in South Shropshire (1990); Tucker, G., Some Watermills of South-West Shropshire (1991).*

4. Booth, *op.cit.*, pp.7-8, 12, 17; Boucher, C.T.G., ''Broadstone Mill', *Transactions of the Newcomen Society,* vol. 36 (1963-4), pp.159-63.

5. George, J., *Daniel's Mill: its history, millers and restoration* (n.d.).

6. Booth, *op.cit.*, pp.7-8.

7. Watts, S., *All's Grist to the Mill: a Survey of Rindleford Mill in the Parish of Worfield* (1986-7).

8. Robinson, D.H., *The Sleepy Meese* (1980), pp.22-5.

9. Tucker, *op.cit.*, p.38.

10. Goodman, K.W.G., 'Tilsop Furnace', *West Midlands Studies*, vol.13 (1980), pp.40-6.

11. Mutton, N., 'Charlcotte Furnace', *T.S.A.S.*, vol.58 (1965-8), pp.84-8; Mutton, N., 'Charlcotte Furnace 1733-79', *Bulletin of the Historical Metallurgy Group*, vol.6 (1966), pp.18-49.

12. Eaves, M., & Hall, S., *Water Power System and Blast Furnace at Leighton, Shropshire* (1993-4).

13. I am indebted to Mr James Lawson for much of the information contained in this table.

14. *S.C.* 11 January 1793; 18 April 1794; 2 August 1811.

15. *S.C.* 18 April 1794; 2 August 1811.

16. Cox, N., 'Imagination and Innovation of an Industrial Pioneer: the First Abraham Darby', *Industrial Archaeology Review*, vol.12 (1990), pp.130-4.

17. Mutton, N., 'Eardington Forges and Canal Tunnel', *Industrial Archaeology,* vol.7 (1970), pp. 53-9; Mutton, N., 'The Forges at Eardington and Hampton Loade', *T.S.A.S.,* vol.58 (1965-8), pp.235-43.

18. S.R.O. 625/1.

19. Pape, T., 'The Early Glass Industry in North Staffordshire', *Transactions of the North Staffordshire Field Club*, vol.67 (1933), pp. 116-20.

20. Lloyd, L.C., 'Paper Making in Shropshire', *T.S.A.S.*, vol. 44 (1937-8), pp.121-87; Lloyd, L.C., 'Paper Making in Shropshire: Supplementary Notes', *T.S.A.S.*, vol. 53 (1949-50), pp. 152-63.

21. *S.C.* 6 September 1816.

22. Inventories of Richard Fosbrook of Alveley, 1730, and William Fosbrook of Claverley, 1731, from Hereford Record Office, transcribed by members of Shropshire County Council/University of Birmingham classes at Bridgnorth.

23. *S.C.* 26 January 1788; 25 February 1825.

24. Lloyd, L.C., 'Paper Making in Shropshire', *T.S.A.S.*, vol. 44 (1937-8), pp.179-81; Robinson, *op.cit.*, p. 92.

25. Booth, *op.cit.*, p.25.

26. Robinson, *op.cit.*, pp.90-1; *E.S.J.* 3 December 1829.

27. Robinson, D.H., *The Wandering Worfe* (1980), pp.116-8.

28. Trinder, B., *The Industrial Revolution in Shropshire* (1981), pp.130-1; S.C. 1 April 1836.

29. Inventory of Thomas Sandford of Prees, 1726, from Lichfield Joint Record Office, transcribed by Shropshire County Council/University of Birmingham class at Shrewsbury.

30. Seaby, W.A. & Smith, A.C., *Windmills in Shropshire, Hereford and Worcester* (1984), pp.5-6, 9-12, 18-20.

31. *V.C.H.*, vol. 8, p.210; Toghill, P., *Geology in Shropshire* (1990), p.92.

32. Scard, M. A., 'The Development and Changing Organisation of Shropshire's Quarrying Industry 1750-1900', *Industrial Archaeology Review*, vol. 11 (1988), p.173; see also Scard, M.A., *The Building Stones of Shropshire* (1990).

33. Scard, M. A., 'The Development and Changing Organisation of Shropshire's Quarrying Industry 1750-1900', *Industrial Archaeology Review*, vol. 11 (1988), pp.177-83.

34. *V.C.H.* vol.8, p.281.

35. *ex.inf.* Mr Donald Harris.

36. Whitehead, T.H., Robertson, T., Pocock, R.W., and Dixon, E.E., *Memoirs of the Geological Survey of England and Wales: the Country between Wolverhampton and Oakengates* (1928); Robinson, D.H., *The Wandering Worfe* (1980), p.29; S.F.W.I., *Shropshire Within Living Memory* (1992), pp. 187-8; Wilson, E., *The Ellesmere and Llangollen Canal* (1975), pp.96-7.

37. Prees Parish Records, *ex inf.* Meriel Blower; *Historic Buildings in Telford No.18, Apley Castle.*

38. Morris, J., *The Brick and Pipeworks, Woodhouse Fields, Bourton, Much Wenlock, Shropshire* (1990-1).

39. Smith, W. & Beddoes, K., *The Cleobury Mortimer and Ditton Priors Light Railway* (1980), pp. 39, 53.

40. Williams, G., *The Wenlock Limestone Industry: an historical note* (1990); Holmes, D., *The Working of the Silurian Wenlock Limestone in South-East Shropshire* (1986-7).

41. Trinder, B., 'The Wooden Bridge at Cressage', *Shropshire Newsletter* No.35 (1968), pp.1-6.

42. Brown, I.J., *A History of Limestone Mining in Shropshire* (1977), pp 20, 23.

43. *V.C.H.*, vol.8, p.210.

44. MacLeod, M., Stratton, M., & Trinder, B., *Llanymynech Hill: an Archaeological and Historical Evaluation* (1987); Aikin, A., *Journal of a Tour through North Wales* (1797), pp.5-7; Pennant, T., *Tours in North Wales* (1883), vol. 3, pp.168, 204.

45. *E.S.J.* 6 January 1841.

46. Kent, J., *The Barrow Farm Maltings, Barrow* (1991-2).

47. Rowley, R.T., *The History of the South Shropshire Landscape 1086-1800* (1967)

48. Nightingale, J., *The Beauties of England and Wales, vol.13, part 1, Shropshire* (1813), p.36.

49. I am grateful to Dr Peter Hobson, formerly of the University of Wolverhampton, for his guidance in the study of the Wyre Forest.

50. *E.S.J.* 15 April 1868.

51. *Ironbridge Weekly Journal* 22 February 1871.

52. *V.C.H.* vol.11, p.316.

53. Wilson, *op.cit.*, pp.97-8; *S.C.* 29 January 1892.

54. Ellis, R., *The Industries of the Dudmaston Estate* (1984-5).

55. Inventories from Adderley parish in Lichfield Joint Record Office, transcribed by Shropshire County Council/University of Birmingham class in Shrewsbury.

56. University of Wolverhampton, Port Books Data Base.
57. Trinder, B., 'The Archaeology of the British Food Industry 1660-1960: a preliminary survey', *Industrial Archaeology Review*, vol.15 (1993), pp.129-30.
58. Kelly & Co., *Directory of Shropshire* (1879), p.479.
59. Trinder, *op.cit.*, p.134.
60. Trinder, *op.cit.*, pp.133-4.
61. *Ex inf.* Mr J. Wilde of Oswestry, 1993. I am grateful to Mrs Jessie Hanson for this information.
62. *V.C.H.* vol.11, p.232.
63. *Ex inf.* Mr R.M.J. Freeman of Pimley Manor, Shrewsbury.

CHAPTER THREE

1. Eliot, G., *The Mill on the Floss* (Nelson edition, n.d.), p.129.
2. Marsh, P., 'Shrewsbury Markets in the Nineteenth Century', in, Trinder, B., ed., *Victorian Shrewsbury,* pp.19-23.
3. *E.S.J.* 9, 16, 23 January, 7, 21 February 1861.
4. Marsh, *op.cit.*, pp.24-8.
5. Marsh, *op.cit.*, pp.23-4.
6. *E.S.J.* 25 April 1888.
7. Earnshaw, D. *et al, Whitchurch Remembered* (1980), p.14.
8. Earnshaw, D. *et al, Whitchurch Remembered* (1980), p.19.
9. Seaby, W.A. & Smith, A.C., *Windmills in Shropshire, Hereford and Worcester* (1984), pp.5-6.
10. *E.S.J.* 14 November 1877.
11. Woodward, I., *The Story of Wem and its Neighbourhood* (1951), p.61.
12. Trinder, B. & Cox, J., *Yeomen & Colliers in Telford* (1980), pp.69, 111-2; inventory of William Podmore of Newport, 1744, in Lichfield Joint Record Office, copied by members of Shropshire County Council class in Newport.
13. Nankivell, J.W., *Chapters from the History of Ellesmere* (1983), pp.37-8.
14. Watkin, I., *Oswestry with an account of its old houses, shops &c.* (1920), pp.150-2.
15. *E.S.J.* 9 May 1888.
16. *E.S.J.* 27 February 1856.
17. MacDonald, W., *An Illustrated Guide to Shrewsbury* (1897), pp.36-7; *S.C.* 4 May 1923.
18. *S.C.* 18 January 1820; 15 September 1830; Hulbert, C., *Memoirs of Seventy Years of an Eventful Life* (1852), p.263; *E.S.J.* 4 March 1868.
19. *E.S.J.* 1 July 1868; Review Publishing, *Industry of Shropshire: Business Review* (1891), p.26.
20. *E.S.J.* 2 January 1828; Macdonald, *op.cit.*, pp.38-9; Hulbert, *op.cit.* p.263; Jones, I.C., *The Industrial Archaeology of Coleham Riverside* (1992-3).
21. *Ex inf.* Dr David Jenkins.
22. Smith, N., *An investigation into the commercial life, trades and craft industries of 19th century Much Wenlock* (1988-9), p.26.
23. Jones, *op.cit.*; Hulbert, *op.cit.*, p.263; Hulbert, C., *History and Description of the County of Salop* (1837), p. 308.
24. Watkin, *op.cit.*, pp.31, 160.
25. *S.C.* 4 February 1831.
26. Wright, T., *The History and Antiquities of the town of Ludlow* (1826), pp. 198-200; British Parliamentary Papers, 1840, XXXIV, *Report of the Assistant Commissioners... for Hand Loom Weavers,* p.543.
27. Wilding & Son, *Shropshire: a Beautiful English County* (1935), pp. 73-4; Macdonald, *op.cit.*, p.47.
28. *V.C.H.*, vol.11, p.230.
29. Macdonald, *op.cit.*, p.45.

30. *Ludlow & Church Stretton Chronicle* 14 January 1911; Review Publishing Co., *op.cit.,* p.23; *E.S.J.* 24 February 1864; *S.C.* 11 April 1890, 27 April 1894.

31. *S.C.* 3 March 1854; 4 January 1867; 26 January 1892; 18 March 1892.

32. *V.C.H.* vol.11, p.230; the late Mr. T.W. Pollard kindly arranged for me to see the Tan Bank carriage works.

33. Goff, A., *A Study of the former Coachbuilding Workshops, No.1 Church Street, Bishop's Castle, Shropshire* (1992-3).

34. Trinder, B., *The Making of the Industrial Landscape* (1982), pp.209-12.

35. I am grateful to Professor Jennifer Tann of the Univesity of Birmingham and Ron Fitzgerald of the Leeds Industrial Museum for observations on the Soho Foundry and the Round Foundry, Leeds.

36. Tonkin, S.M., 'Trevithick, Rastrick and the Hazledine Foundry, Bridgnorth', *Transactions of the Newcomen Society,* vol. 26 (1947-49), pp.171-84; Dickinson, H.W., & Lee, A.,'The Rastricks: Civil Engineers', *Transactions of the Newcomen Society,* vol. 4 (1923-4), pp.48-63; *S.C.* 9 November 1810; 18 February 1812; 16 April 1830; *Report of the Commissioners appointed to enquire into the application of iron to railway structures,* p.186.

37. Smith, E.C., 'Joshua Field's Diary of a tour through the Provinces, 1821, part 2', *Transactions of the Newcomen Society,* vol. 13 (1932-3), pp.18-9; *Dictionary of National Biography,* sub Hazledine; S.R.R., Phillips MSS, vol.5, 267; Jones, *op.cit.*; Macdonald, *op.cit.,* p.44; *S.C.* 30 October 1840; *E.S.J.* 6 September 1876; 10 April 1878; 15 January 1879; see also Figure 41.

38. *E.S.J.* 2 May 1838; 28 April 1847; 12 May 1865; 22 January 1879.

39. *Shropshire Conservative* 18 June 1842; *E.S.J.* 1 May 1878.

40. Macdonald, *op.cit.,* pp.40-1; Review Publishing Co., *op.cit.,* pp.12-3; *E.S.J.* 8 January 1868; 3 June 1868; 5 August 1868; 3 March 1869; 29 December 1876; 25 February 1885; *S.C.* 17 November 1893; 13 July 1917; *Wellington Journal* 13 May 1905; 25 November 1905; the winnower at Long Beach was observed by Henry Quinn.

41. I am grateful to Dr David Jenkins for information about the Market Drayton foundries.

42. Earnshaw, *op.cit.,* p.62.

43. *Friends of the Ironbridge Gorge Museum Newsletter,* No.30 (1978).

44. I am grateful to Ken Jones for information on the Shropshire Works.

45. Christiansen, R. & Miller, R.W., *The Cambrian Railways* (1967), vol. 1, p.138; vol. 2, pp. 20, 110, 156-8, 176; Watkin, *op.cit.,* p.333.

46. *E.S.J.* 30 October 1878.

47. Hughes, W.J. & Thomas, J.L., *The Sentinel: A History of Alley & MacLellan and the Sentinel Waggon Works, vol.1* (1975); Thomas, A.R. & Thomas, J.L., *The Sentinel: A history of Alley & MacLellan and the Sentinel Waggon Works, vol.2* (1987); *Steaming,* no.33 (1990).

48. Baldwin, M., Elliott, W., & Davis, J., *Cleobury Chronicles, vol.1* (1991), pp.40-7.

49. Macdonald, *op.cit.,* p.42; *E.S.J.* 30 January 1867; 3 March 1880; 21 July l880; 18 January 1882; 12 January 1887; 9 July 1887; 13 November 1887; *S.C.* 15 December 1893; 13 March 1894; 19 June 1903; 26 January 1940.

50. *S.C.* 24 October 1975.

51. *E.S.J.* 14 May 1879; 31 December 1884; I am grateful to Mrs. Stella Straughen for information on Kingsland.

52. *E.S.J.* 13 October 1880; 18 May 1881; *S.C.* 7 April 1933.

53. *S.C.* 16 December 1831; 6 December 1865.

54. Macdonald, *op.cit.,* p.47.

55. Wilding & Co., *Shropshire: a beautiful English county* (1914), p.121.

56. *Daily News,* 2 November 1912.

57. Lee, J.M., 'Cherry Orchard: the growth of a Victorian Suburb', in Trinder, B., ed., *Victorian Shrewsbury* (1984), pp.115-6.

58. *E.S.J.* 6 November 1865; 18 April 1866.

59. Lee, *op.cit.*, p.119.

60. *S.C.* 31 October 1851; *E.S.J.* 23 February 1853; 2 March 1853; 16 August 1853; 9 May 1866; 6 June 1866; 16 January 1867.

61. Lee, *op.cit.*, pp.119-22.

62. *E.S.J.* 26 January 1853.

63. Hughes and Thomas, *op.cit.*, pp.120-8.

64. Wilding & Co., *Shropshire: a beautiful English county* (1935), pp.76-8; Chatwood Security Co., leaflet, copy in Ironbridge Gorge Museum; *S.C.* 15 January 1926.

65. *S.C.* 6 June 1919.

66. *Ex inf.* the late Mr. G.R.Fletcher; *S.C.* 13 April 1934.

67. Temple, J.T., *Industrial Archaeology of Aviation in Shropshire* (1984).

68. Hardy, T., *The Life and Death of the Mayor of Casterbridge* (1886 - Pan edition 1978), pp. 260-1.

69. I am grateful to Dr. David Jenkins for information about Little Drayton.

70. Partridge, C.A., *Handbook to Ludlow* (1878), p.129.

71. The engines are recorded on a 45 r.p.m. record, *The Music of Machinery: Vol.1, Shrewsbury Pumping Station*, Big Ben Records, MOM1.

72. Tucker, D.G., 'Electricity Generating Stations for Public Supply in the West Midlands, 1888-1977', *West Midland Studies*, vol.10 (1977), pp.8-28.

73. *Shropshire Magazine*, October 1976, p.15; *Ironbridge Quarterly*, 1993.4.

CHAPTER FOUR

1. Toghill, P., *Geology in Shropshire* (1990), pp.130-1.

2. Ward, T.O., *The Medical Topography of Shrewsbury* (1841), p.63.

3. Murchison, Sir R., *The Silurian System* (1839), pp.92-94; *Shropshire Conservative* 24 April 1841.

4. *V.C.H.* vol.8, pp.279-80; *S.C.* 8 May 1812, 29 January 1831; S.F.W.I., *Shropshire within Living Memory* (1992), p.52.; *E.S.J.* 15 April 1868.

5. *V.C.H.* vol.8, p.322.

6. Brook, F., & Allbutt, M., *The Shropshire Lead Mines* (1973), pp.65-6.

7. *E.S.J.* 22 March 1843; *Shropshire Magazine* January 1870, pp.28-9.

8. *V.C.H.* vol.8, p. 83; for Lower Long Wood see also Chapter 2.

9. Murchison, *op.cit.,* p.83; *V.C.H.* vol.8, p.211; *E.S.J.* 3 June 1835.

10. *V.C.H.* vol.8, p.103; *S.C.* 26 January 1810.

11. *V.C.H.* vol.8, p.280; Brown, I.J., *The Mines of Shropshire* (1976), pp.80-1.

12. *V.C.H.* vol.8, pp.257, 279-80.

13. Poyner, D. & Evans, R., 'The Wyre Forest Coalfield', *Cleobury Chronicle* vol.3 (1994), pp.7-17.

14. Nair, G. & Poyner, D., 'The Coming of Coal: Industrial Development in a South Shropshire Parish', *Midland History*, vol.18 (1993), pp.87-103.

15. Nair & Poyner, *op.cit.;* *S.C.* 16 April 1804, 23 December 1813, 4 January 1815, 1 March 1815, 8 August 1817, 15 August 1817.

16. Smith, W. & Beddoes, K., *The Cleobury Mortimer & Ditton Priors Light Railway* (1980), pp. 23, 80.

17. Poyner & Evans, *op.cit.* pp.11-6; Brown, *op.cit.*, pp.68-77.

18. S.S.W.I., *op.cit.*, pp.29, 45.

19. *S.C.* 19 September 1919.

20. Toghill, *op.cit.*, pp. 129-30.

21. Thomas, R.D., *Industries of the Morda Valley* (1939), pp.12-18.

22. *Ibid,* pp.18-9.

23. *Ibid,* p.11.

24. Stratton, M.J., *The Terracotta Revival* (1993), p.51.

25. Bridges, A.J., *Industrial Locomotives of Cheshire, Shropshire and Herefordshire* (1977), pp. 78-9; Brown, *op.cit.,* p.82.

26. *E.S.J.* 8 July 1857.

27. Toghill, *op.cit.,* pp.132-4.

28. Smith & Beddoes, *op.cit.,* pp.73-84.

29. Murchison, *op.cit.,* p.122.

30. *Ibid* p.123.

31. Goodman, K.W.G., *Hammerman's Hill: the Land, People and Industry of the Titterstone Clee Hill Area of Shropshire from the 16th to the 18th centuries,* University of Keele, Ph.D. thesis, 1978.

32. Anon., *The History of Isaac Jenkins* (n.d.), p.12.

33. Hewitt, P.B., *The Mining, Quarrying and allied industries of the Cleehill Regions from the 1800s to 1930,* C.N.A.A. (Wolverhampton Polytechnic), M.Phil., 1991.

34. Hereford Record Office, inventory of Richard Plummer of Ludlow, 1692.

35. Hewitt, *op.cit.,* pp.26-58; *S.C.* 18 June 1778; 30 December 1780.

36. Commonplace Book *penes* A.M.W.Smith of Ivy Hatch, Kent.

37. *E.S.J.* 11 June 1845, 20 April 1853; *S.C.* 18 April 1851.

38. *E.S.J.* 18 May 1887.

39. Hewitt, *op.cit.,* pp.75, 83, 108, 173-4.

40. Hewitt, *op.cit.,* p.187.

41. *E.S.J.* 16 October 1861.

42. Hewitt, *op.cit.,* 165, 187, 169; Jenkins, A.E., *Titterstone Clee Hills: Everyday Life, Industrial History and Dialect* (1988), pp.29-32, *E.S.J.* 12 January 1876.

43. S.R.R., *G.W.R. Regulations for the Clee Hill Branch* (1933).

44. *E.S.J.* 11 May, 13 July 1881.

45. Jenkins, *op.cit.,* p.35.

46. Hewitt, *op.cit.,* p.169.

47. Toghill, *op.cit.,* pp.125-9.

48. Wanklyn, M., 'Industrial Development in the Ironbridge Gorge before Abraham Darby', *West Midlands Studies,* vol.15 (1982), pp.3-7; Trinder, B., *The Industrial Revolution in Shrophsire* (1981), pp.3-12.

49. Alfrey, J. & Clark, K., *The Landscape of Industry: patterns of change in the Ironbridge Gorge* (1993), pp.115, 149-50; Trinder, *op.cit.,* pp.187-88.

50. Alfrey & Clark. *op.cit.,* p.180.

51. Trinder, *op.cit.,* pp.190-5; Alfrey & Clark, *op.cit.,* pp.184-5.

52. Trinder, *op.cit.,* pp.188-90; Jones, K., Hunt, M.W., Malam, J., & Trinder, B., 'Holywell Lane: a Squatter Settlement in the Shropshire Coalfield', *Industrial Archaeology Review,* vol. 6 (1982), pp.163-85.

53. Trinder, *op.cit.,* pp.195-6; *E.S.J.* 4 January 1860.

54. Alfrey & Clark, *op.cit.,* pp.136-9; Cossons, N. & Trinder, B., *The Iron Bridge* (1979), pp. 37-47.

55. Edwards, H., *The Commercial Centres of Madeley and Dawley 1790-1940,* Ironbridge Institute, Master's dissertation, 1988-89; Trinder, B., *New Industrial Towns in the long Eighteenth Century: the Shropshire Coalfield,* presented to E.S.R.C. Colloqium, University of Leicester, 1994.

56. Trinder, B., *The Industrial Revolution in Shropshire* (1981), p.72.

57. Alfrey & Clark, *op.cit.,* pp.70-74; Lewis, M., *Early Wooden Railways* (1970), pp.95-102.

58. Jones, N.W., 'A Wooden Wagon Way at Bedlam Furnace', *Post-Medieval Archaeology,* vol. 21 (1987), pp.259-66.

59. Trinder, *op.cit.,* pp.71-75; Alfrey & Clark, *op.cit.,* pp.70-4; Lewis, *op.cit.,* pp.157-79, 193-4.

60. Trinder, *op.cit.,* p.98.

61. Gale, W.K.V. & Nicholls, C.R., *The Lilleshall Company: a history 1764-1964* (1979), p.76.

62. Bridges, *op.cit.,* pp.83-4.

63. Trinder, *op.cit.*, pp.75-6.

64. Trinder, *op.cit.,* 77-83.

65. Williams, W.H., 'The Canal Inclined Planes of East Shropshire', *Journal of Industrial Archaeology*, vol.2, pp. 37-56; Tonkinson, R.Ll., *Inclined Planes on the Shropshire Canals*, Birmingham School of Architecture, thesis, 1964.

66. Alfrey & Clark, op.cit., pp.74-76; Beale, R., *The Old Wind, a Preliminary Report* (1988); Trinder, *op.cit.*, pp.75-85.

67. *E.S.J.* 26 June 1861, 17 July 1861.

68. Wanklyn, M., 'Industrial Development in the Ironbridge Gorge before Abraham Darby', *West Midlands Studies*, vol.15 (1982), pp.3-7.

69. Alfrey & Clark, op.cit., pp.40-6.

70. Brown, I.J., 'Underground in the Ironbridge Gorge', *Industrial Archaeology Review*, vol.III (1979), pp.158-69.

71. Trinder, *op.cit.*, pp. 94-5; *V.C.H.* vol.11, p.46.

72. Leese, J.S., 'Old English Power Plants', *Power* (New York), vol.36 (1912), quoted in Trinder, B., *The Most Extraordinary District in the World* (1988), pp.125-6.

73. Isaac, S., *Granville Colliery Horse Gin* (1988).

74. Holmes, D., *The Working of the Silurian Wenlock Limestone in South-East Shropshire*, Ironbridge Institute, Diploma dissertation, 1986-87; Williams, G., *The Wenlock Limestone Industry: an historical note* (1990); Alfrey & Clark, *op.cit.*, pp 34-7.

75. Alfrey & Clark, *op.cit.*, pp.34-7; Smith, S.B., *A View from the Iron Bridge* (1979), pp.40-2, 50-1; Brown, I.J., *The Mines of Shropshire* (1976), p.50.

76. Trinder, B., *The Industrial Revolution in Shropshire* (1981), p.59.

77. Adams, D. & Hazeley, J., *Survey of the Church Aston/Lilleshall Mining Area* (1970).

78. Trinder, *op.cit.*, pp.58-9; Brown, *op.cit.*, pp.13-7.

79. Alfrey & Clark, *op.cit.*, pp.172-3.

80. *Ibid*, pp.49-55, 101-4.

81. Gale & Nicholls, *op.cit.*, pp.40-1.

82. Jones, A., *Finds Typologies: Pottery I: the coarse earthenwares* (1988).

83. Alfrey & Clark, *op.cit.*, pp.95-8.

84. Jones, A., Higgins, D. & Trueman, M., *11 Benthall Lane* (1987).

85. Higgins, D., Morriss, R. & Trueman, M., *The Broseley Pipeworks: an archaeological and historical evaluation* (1988).

86. Trinder, *op.cit.,* p.126; Alfrey & Clark, *op.cit.*, pp.98-9; Houghton, A.W.J., 'The Caughley Porcelain Works near Broseley, Salop', *Journal of Industrial Archaeology*, vol. 5 (1968), pp.184-92.

87. Trinder, *op.cit.*, pp,127-8; Alfrey & Clark, *op.cit.*, pp.99-100; Edmundson, R., 'Coalport China Works, Shropshire', *Industrial Archaeology Review*, vol. 3 (1979), pp. 122-45; Edmundson, R., 'Bradley and Coalport Pottery 1796-1800', *Transactions of the Northern Ceramic Society*, vol.4 (1981), pp.127-55; Blake Roberts, D. & Blake Roberts, G., 'The results of recent excavations in Coalport, Shropshire', *English Ceramic Circle Transactions*, vol.2 (1981), pp.71-81.

88. Alfrey & Clark, *op.cit.*, pp.106-8; Herbert, A.T., 'Jackfield Decorative Tiles in Use', *Industrial Archaeology Review*, vol.3 (1979), pp.146-52; Strachan, S., 'Henry Powell Dunnill: a Victorian Tilemaster', *Journal of the Tiles & Architectural Ceramics Society*, vol.3 (1990), pp.3-10.

89. Cox, N, 'Imagination and Innovation of an Industrial Pioneer: the first Abraham Darby', *Industrial Archaeology Review*, vol.12 (1990), pp.130-1.

90. Trinder, B., *The Most Extraordinary District in the World* (1988), p.16; Trinder, B., *The Industrial Revolution in Shropshire* (1981), pp. 9-10, 131.

91. Trinder, B., *The Industrial Revolution in Shropshire* (1981), pp. 8, 132-3.

92. *Ibid*, pp. 31-33.

93. *Ibid*, p. 129.

94. *Ibid*, pp. 55-8; Gale & Nicholls, *op.cit.*, pp. 52, 61-2, 65, 82, 90.

95. Trinder, *op.cit.*, pp.102-3, 129; *V.C.H.* vol. 11, p.328.

96. Stratton, M.J., *Ironbridge and the Electric Revolution* (1994).

97. Most of the available sources on pit girls are reproduced in a teaching pack, *Shropshire Pit Girls*, published by the Ironbridge Gorge Museum.

98. Alfrey & Clark, *op.cit.,* pp.61-70.

99. Ince, L., *The Knight Family and the British Iron Industry 1695-1902* (1991), pp.33-45; Cox, *op.cit.*, pp.131-2; Trinder, *op.cit.*, pp.13-24.

100. I am grateful to Michael Vanns of the Ironbridge Gorge Museum for showing me his unpublished paper on the dating of the beams.

101. Smith, S.B., 'The Construction of the Blists Hill Ironworks', *Industrial Archaeology Review*, vol.3 (1979), pp.170-8.

102. I am grateful to Wendy Horton of the Ironbridge Gorge Museum Archaeology Unit for discussions concerning current excavations at the Upper Forge and for opportunities to view the site.

103. Trinder, *op.cit.*, p.40; Terry, R., 'Industrial History and Industrial Archaeology of the Linley Valley', Ironbridge Institute, Master's assignment, 1988-9.

104. Alfrey & Clark, *op.cit.*, pp.89-91.

105. *V.C.H.* vol.11, pp.260-1.

106. *Ibid*, p. 164.

107. Trinder, *op.cit.,* p.45.

108. Norris, G., *A Survey of the Heavy Erection Shop, Coalbrookdale*, Ironbridge Institute, Master's course assignment, 1989-90.

109. *E.S.J.* 17 January 1866. I am grateful to Myfanwy Eaves and David Reynolds of the New Zealand Historic Places Trust for confirming that the statue is still in situ.

110. Cossons & Trinder, *op.cit.*, pp.11-51; Trinder, B., 'The First Iron Bridge', *Industrial Archaeology Review*, vol.3 (1979), pp.112-21.

Chapter Five

1. Young, A., *Tours in England and Wales* (1934), p.162.

2. British Parliamentary Papers, 1840, XXIII, *Hand Loom Weavers' Report*, p.352.

3. Trinder, B. & Cox, J., *Yeomen and Colliers in Telford* (1980), pp.61-64.

4. Green, H., 'The Linen Industry of Shropshire', *Industrial Archaeology Review*, vol. 5 (1981), p. 115; Nightingale, J., *The Beauties of England and Wales, vol.13, pt.1, Shropshire* (1813), p.35.

5. Williams, A.B., 'The Rural Industries of Llanymynech', *Montgomeryshire Collections*, vol.47 (1947), pp.67-74.

6. Booth, D.T.W., *Watermills on the River Rea in South Shropshire* (1990), p.9; V.C.H., vol.8, pp.156, 175; vol.11, p.316, Trinder & Cox, *op.cit.*, p.64.

7. *S.C.* 25 November 1814.

8. Lloyd, D., *Broad Street* (1979), p.57; British Parliamentary Papers, 1840, XXXIV, *Hand Loom Weavers' Report*, p.543.

9. Thomas, R.D., *Industries of the Morda Valley* (1978), p.29.

10. Bagshaw, S., *History, Gazetteer and Directory of Shropshire* (1851), p.529; I am also grateful to Ann Pritchett for information concerning Carding Mill.

11. Tucker, G., *Some Watermills of South-west Shropshire* (1991), pp.11-2.

12. Probate inventories from Lichfield Joint Record Office, transcribed by Shropshire County Council adult education research class at Bridgnorth; ex inf. Dr Malcolm Wanklyn.

13. The standard account of the Drapers Company in the 16th and 17th centuries is Mendenhall, T.C., *The Shrewsbury Drapers and the Welsh Woollen Trade in the XVI and XVII Centuries* (1953).

14. Pennant, T., *Tours in Wales* (1883), vol.3, p.224; Owen, H. and Blakeway, J.B., *The History of Shrewsbury* (1826), p.551, *E.S.J.* 3 December 1794.

15. Probate inventories from Lichfield Joint Record Office, transcribed by Shropshire County Council/ University of Birmingham research class in Shrewsbury.

16. *E.S.J.* 3 December 1794.

17. Aikin, A., *Journal of a Tour through North Wales* (1797), p.77; *E.S.J.* 18 February 1824, 3 March 1824, 23 June 1824, 28 July 1824.

18. *E.S.J.* 18 June 1800; *S.C.* 15 June 1830; Nightingale, *op.cit.*, p.164.

19. *S.C.* 9 October 1795; Hulbert, C., *Memoirs of Seventy Years of an Eventful Life* (1852), pp.194-95, 222-3; Hulbert, C., *History and Description of the County of Salop* (1837), pp.307-8.

20. Hulbert, C., *Memoirs of Seventy Years of an Eventful Life* (1852), pp.194-95, 222-3; Hulbert, C., *History and Description of the County of Salop* (1837), pp.307-8.

21. Jones, I.C., *The Industrial Archaeology of Coleham Riverside* (1992-93); Shropshire Records & Research holds a photocopy of the photograph. The location of the print from which it was taken is unknown.

22. Thomas, *op.cit.*, pp.25-8.

23. Higgins, D., Morriss, R. and Trueman, M., *The Broseley Pipeworks: An Archaeological and Historical Evaluation* (1988), p.11.

24. *S.C.* 24 August 1804, 8 July 1808, 17 January 1902.

25. The account which follows is drawn principally from Trinder, B., 'Ditherington Flax Mill—a Re-evaluation', *Textile History*, vol.23 (1992), pp.189-224, which summarises previous work, and is fully referenced. A more detailed description of the buildings is provided in Macleod, M., Trinder, B. and Worthington, M., *The Ditherington Flax Mills, Shrewsbury: a Survey and Historical Evaluation* (1988). See also Skempton, A.W. and Johnson, H.R., 'The First Iron Frames', *Architectural Review*, no.131 (1962), pp.175-86; Bannister, T., 'The First Iron-framed Buildings', *Architectural Review*, no. 107 (1950), pp.231-46; Tann, J., *The Development of the Factory* (1970), pp.135-7; Rimmer, W.G., *Marshalls of Leeds: Flax Spinners 1788-1886* (1960).

26. *S.C.* 1 September 1797.

27. Macleod, Trinder & Worthington, *op.cit.*, pp.21-32.

28. Giles, C. & Goodall, I., *Yorkshire Textile Mills 1770-1930* (1992); Watson, M., 'Broadford Works, Aberdeen: Evidence for the Earliest Iron-Framed Flax Mills', *Textile History*, vol.23 (1992), pp.225-242; Falconer, K.A., 'Fireproof Mills—the widening perspectives', *Industrial Archaeology Review,* vol.16 (1993), pp.11-26.

29. Macleod, Trinder & Worthington, *op.cit.*, p.13.

30. Shropshire Records & Research, Salop Fire Office Registers, 4791/1/4, p.81, policy no.2061; 4791/1/5, p.404, policy no.3819; 4791/1/9, p.381, policy no.10833; J.B.Lawson, 'Thomas Telford in Shrewsbury', in Penfold, A., *Thomas Telford: Engineer* (1980), pp.17-8; Hobbs, J.L., *Shrewsbury Street Names* (1954), p.106; Wakelin, P., *Historical Applications of British Fire Insurance Records* (1984).

31. SRR (Shrewsbury Borough Library), D13322.

32. Macleod, Trinder & Worthington, *op.cit.,* p.14.

33. Tann, *op.cit.,* pp.42-43.

34. Hulbert, *op.cit.* (1837), p.312; *E.S.J.* 9 August 1837, 14 March 1838.

35. Green, H., 'The Linen Industry of Shropshire', *Industrial Archaeology Review,* vol. 5 (1981), pp.114-21.

36. Green, *op.cit.*, pp.114-21; Hulbert, *op.cit.* (1852), pp.195, 234, 255.

37. Hulbert, *op.cit.* (1837), p.308; SRR, Pidgeon MS 3056, 15, 55; *S.C.* 5 October 1827.

38. Wright, T., *The History and Antiquities of Ludlow* (1826), pp.81-2; *S.C.* 26 July 1777, 25 March 1786.

39. Bagshaw, S., *A History, Gazetteer and Directory of Shropshire* (1851), p.342; *S.C.* 14 October 1831.

40. British Parliamentary Papers, 1840, XXXIV, *Hand Loom Weavers' Report*, p.541; *S.C.* 13 July 1798, 5 May 1815.

41. *E.S.J.* 17 April 1811, 17 July 1811.

42. Rowley, N. & S., *Market Drayton: a study in social history* (1966), pp.55-6; I am grateful to Dr David Jenkins for his advice on industry in Market Drayton.

CHAPTER SIX

1. Toghill, P., *Geology in Shropshire* (1990), pp.65-7.
2. Trinder, B., *The Industrial Revolution in Shropshire*, 2nd edn. (1981), p.10.
3. Brook, F., & Allbut, M., *The Shropshire Lead Mines*, pp.23-6; Burt, R., Waite, P. & Burnley, R., *The Mines of Shropshire & Montgomeryshire* (1990), p. 40
4. Brook & Allbut, *op.cit.,* pp.64-73.
5. Burt, Waite & Burnley, *op.cit.*, pp.xi-xv.
6. Shropshire Records & Research, Watton Collection, vol.II, p.332.
7. The production figures which follow are drawn from Burt, Waite & Burnley, *op.cit.*, pp.xxv-xxix.
8. Burt, Waite & Burnley, *op.cit.*, pp. 27-32; *V.C.H.*, vol.8, p.322.
9. Brook & Allbut, *op.cit.*, pp.65-6.
10. Tonks, E.S., *The Snailbeach District Railway* (1974), p. 11.
11. Tonks, *op.cit.*, pp. 23-4, 33, 36, 42.
12. Burt, Waite & Burnley, *op.cit.*, pp.20-22; Brook & Allbut, *op.cit.*, pp. 32-43.
13. Burt, Waite & Burnley, *op.cit.*, pp.14, 34.
14. Brook & Allbut, *op.cit.*, pp.44-50.
15. *S.C.* 15 January 1830.
16. *V.C.H.*, vol.8, pp. 155, 179-80; *S.C.* 18 November 1831; *E.S.J.* 1 February 1843; *Shropshire Magazine*, April 1959, pp.21-2; Allbut, M. & Brook, F., 'The South Shropshire Lead Mines', *Journal of Industrial Archaeology*, vol.10 (1973), pp. 50-54. For smelters in the Ironbridge Coalfield, see chapter IV above.
17. Brown, I.J., *The Mines of Shropshire* (1976), p.102; *V.C.H.*, vol.8, p.137; Reminiscences of Mr. J. Wylde of Oswestry, copy in Ironbridge Gorge Museum.
18. Brown, *op.cit.*, p.105; *V.C.H.*, vol.8, pp.124, 181.
19. Burt, Waite & Burnley, *op.cit.*, p.xxvi.
20. Murchison, Sir R., *The Silurian System* (1839), p.188; Rowley, R.T., *The History of the South Shropshire Landscape 1086-1800* (1967), p.186.
21. Carlon, C.J., *The Gallantry Bank Copper Mine* (1981), pp.10-3; Cox, N., 'Imagination and Innovation of an Industrial Pioneer: the first Abraham Darby', *Industrial Archaeology Review*, vol.12 (1990), pp.130-1.
22. Carlon, *op.cit.*, pp.13-4; Burt, Waite & Burnley, *op.cit.*, p.7.
23. S.R.O. 322/62. I am grateful to Dr. Peter Edwards for this reference.
24. Carlon, *op.cit.*, pp.8-9; Carlon, C.J., *The Eardiston Copper Mine, Shropshire* (1981); Burt, Waite & Burnley, *op.cit.*, p. 18; *E.S.J.* 28 August 1839.
25. McLeod, M., Stratton, M. & Trinder, B., *Llanymynech Hill: An Archaeological and Historical Evaluation* (1987), pp.17-8; Burt, Waite & Burnley, *op.cit.*, p.8.
26. *E.S.J.* 15 November 1854.
27. S.R.R. (formerly Shrewsbury Borough Library), MS 6387.
28. S.R.O. QR/390/196, January 1844; Ward. (1841), p.65; *E.S.J.* 12 June 1878; *S.C.* 19 June 1914.
29. S.R.R. (formerly Shrewsbury Borough Library), Deed 18673.
30. Ranger, W., *Report to the General Board of Health on a preliminary inquiry into ... Shrewsbury (1854)*, pp.68-71; *E.S.J.* 18 May 1853; *S.C.* 31 March 1854; 30 November 1883; S.R.R., Local Pamphlets (1854), p.10.
31. *S.C.* 27 April 1894; 4 May 1894; 25 May 1894. I am grateful to Mrs. Janet Hordley for these references.

CHAPTER SEVEN

1. Robinson, D.H., *The Wandering Worfe* (1980), pp.73-4; MacMillan, B.L., *History of a water supply to Wolverhampton 1847-1947* (1947), pp.33, 38-9, 45, 53.

2. Bridges, A.M., *Industrial Locomotives of Cheshire, Shropshire and Herefordshire* (1977), p.73.

3. Davidson, I., 'George Deacon and the Vyrnwy Works', *T.N.S.* vol.59 (1987-88), pp.81-96.

4. Probate inventories transcribed by members of Shropshire County Council and University of Birmingham adult education classes in Bridgnorth, Shrewsbury and Telford.

5. University of Wolverhampton, Gloucester Port Books data base.

6. Trinder, B., *The Industrial Revolution in Shropshire* (1981), pp.61-71; *S.C.* 1 February 1895.

7. S.R.R., Watton Collection, vol.10, p.280; Trinder, *op.cit.*, pp.69-70.

8. *Gentleman's Magazine*, vol.28 (1758), p.277; reproduced in Trinder, B., *The Most Extraordinary District in the World* (1988), pp.25-6.

9. For pictorial evidence, see Smith, S.B., *A View from the Iron Bridge* (1979), *passim*; evidence from probate inventories is drawn from transcripts by members of Shropshire County Council and University of Birmingham adult education classes in Bridgnorth, Shrewsbury and Telford.

10. *S.C.* 25 September 1812; Hulbert, C., *History and Antiquities of the County of Salop* (1837), pp.5-6; Preston, R.A., 'The Eliza: a Nineteenth century Trow at Shrewsbury', *T.S.A.S.*, vol. 68 (1993), pp.116-7.

11. Harral, T., *Picturesque Views of the Severn* (1824), facing p. 206; Trinder, B., *The Industrial Revolution in Shropshire* (1981), figure 8; see figure 140.

12. Trinder, B., *op.cit.*, p.71.

13. *S.C.* 4 December 1784; Hulbert, C., *op.cit.*, pp.343-8, reproduced in Trinder, B., *The Most Extraordinary District in the World* (1988), pp.104-5.

14. Quoted in Trinder, B., *The Most Extraordinary District in the World* (1988), p.108.

15. Duckworth, S., *The Severn Navigation and River Wharf sites in the Ironbridge Gorge with particular reference to the site at The Calcutts* (1987-8).

16. Quoted in Trinder, B., *The Most Extraordinary District in the World* (1988), p.109.

17. Pannett, D.J., 'Fish Weirs of the River Severn', *Folk Life*, vol. 26 (1987-8), pp.54-61.

18. Denton, J.H. & Lewis, M.J.T., 'The River Tern Navigation', *Journal of the Railway and Canal Historical Society*, vol.23 (1977), pp.56-63.

19. Hadfield, C., *The Canals of the West Midlands* (1966), pp.159-65.

20. Clayton, A.R.K., 'The Shrewsbury and Newport canals: construction and remains', in Penfold, A., *Thomas Telford: Engineer* (1980), pp.23-40.

21. Hadfield, C., *Thomas Telford's Temptation* (1993), pp.81-7; Healey, J., *Longdon upon Tern Aqueduct: a Building Survey and Study of the Masonry Abutments* (1989-90).

22. Hadfield, C., *The Canals of the West Midlands* (1966), pp.166-96, 231-51; Wilson, E., *The Ellesmere and Llangollen Canal* (1975).

23. Wilson, *op.cit.*, pp.71-73.

24. Hadfield, *op.cit.*, pp.231-5.

25. Morris, J., *The Birmingham and Liverpool Junction Canal* (1984-5); Hadfield, *op.cit.*, plate XIII.

26. Hadfield, *op.cit.*, pp. 185-6.

27. Butterfield, R., *The Records of the Canal Wharf at Wappenshall* (1989-90); Guthrie, J. & Pudney, C., *Wappenshall Junction, Shropshire: A Survey of the Canal Developments and the Industrial Buildings* (1988-9); Trinder, B., *The Industrial Revolution in Shropshire* (1981), pp.150-2.

28. Hadfield, C., *The Canals of South Wales and the Border* (1960), pp.191-8; Barnes, H., *A New Map of the Kington-Leominster-Stourport Canal* (1977); Dean, R.J., *Map of the Kington, Leominster and Stourport Canal* (1968).

29. Markham, S., *John Loveday of Caversham* (1984), p.121; Fiennes, C., *The Journeys of Celia Fiennes* (1947), p.226; Nightingale, J., *The Beauties of England and Wales, vol.13, pt.1, Shropshire* (1813), p.38.

30. For the background to the turnpike road system see Albert, W., *The Turnpike Road System in England 1663-1840* (1972); Pawson, E., *Transport and Economy: the Turnpike Roads of Eighteenth Century Britain* (1977).

31. See Appendix Two.

32. S.R.O. 356/23/307-9; S.R.O. 356/23/312-3.

33. *S.C.* 7 April 1824; *E.S.J.* 30 November 1815; 4 June 1818; 2 July 1828; 17 September 1828.

34. *S.C.* 20 September 1809; 15 December 1809.

35. Brown, Y., *Ruyton-XI-Towns: Unusual Name: Unusual History* (1988), pp.63-6.

36. Trinder, B., *The Making of the Industrial Landscape* (1982), pp.137-8.

37. Blackwall, A.H., *Historic Bridges of Shropshire* (1985).

38. Blackwell, *op.cit.*, pp.16-22, 47-53; Cossons, N., & Trinder, B., *The Iron Bridge* (1979), pp. 37-47, 78-89.

39. Evason, C., 'Downhill Journey: Stage Coaching in Shrewsbury 1833-61', in Trinder, B., *Victorian Shrewsbury* (1984), pp.78-95.

40. *E.S.J.* 12 August 1857; *Pugh's Hereford Journal* 7 October 1779; S.R.R. Watton Collection Vol.8, p.102; Ironbridge Gorge Museum, Sale Catalogue, Britannia Hotel, Shrewsbury, 1903.

41. Lloyd, D., *Broad Street* (1979), pp.31-2.

42. Trinder, B., 'The Holyhead Road: an engineering project in its social context', in Penfold, *op.cit.*, pp.41-61; Hughes, M., 'Telford, Parnell and the Great Irish Road', *Journal of Transport History,* vol.6 (1964), pp.199-209.

43. *V.C.H.* vol.3, pp.173, 193.

44. *Wellington Journal* 30 May 1903.

45. *S.C.* 16 April 1926; 26 May 1933.

46. *S.C.* 19 March 1937.

47. MacDermott, E.T., *A History of the Great Western Railway* (1964), vol.1, pp.177-204; Christiansen, R., *A Regional History of the Railways of Great Britain, volume 7, The West Midlands* (1973), pp.80-92, 154-61.

48. Morriss, R., *Rail Centres: Shrewsbury* (1966); Morriss, R., *Railways of Shropshire: a brief history* (1983); Morriss, R., 'A Gazetteer of Passenger Railway Stations in Shropshire', *T.S.A.S.,* vol. 64 (1983-4), pp.89-106; Burke, J.P., 'Railway Cross-roads of the North-west: Shrewsbury', *Modern Railways,* vol.17 (1963), pp.47-56.

49. Smith, W.H., 'Craven Arms & Stokesay Station', *British Railway Journal,* No.32 (1990), pp.90-107.

CHAPTER EIGHT

1. Rix, M., 'Industrial Archaeology', *The Amateur Historian*, vol.2 (1955), pp.225-9.

2. Robinson, D.H., 'An Account of the Shropshire Canals', *Transactions of the Caradoc and Severn Valley Field Club*, vol.11 (1939-42), pp.44-52.

3. Trinder, B., *Fifty Years in Ellesmere* (1986).

4. Emden, P.H., *Quakers in Commerce: a record of business achievement* (1939); Raistrick, A., *Dynasty of Ironfounders* (1953).

5. Rolt, L.T.C., *Landscape with Canals* (1977), pp.54-56.

6. Trinder, B., 'The Origins of the Industrial Conservation Movement in Britain', in Stratton, M., *Interpreting the Industrial Past* (1987).

7. Marshall, J., *The Severn Valley Railway* (1989), pp.168-9.

8. Cossons, N., 'Ironbridge - The First Ten Years', *Industrial Archaeology Review*, vol.3 (1979), pp.179-86.

9. *Victoria History of Shropshire*, vol.4 (forthcoming).

10. Rolt, L.T.C., *op.cit.*, p.149.

APPENDIX ONE
WATER-POWER SITES IN SHROPSHIRE

◆   ◆   ◆

Most of Shropshire is drained by the River Severn. The list works **up** the Severn, taking each tributary in turn, then listing the mills on each in **downstream** order. Streams flowing into the tributaries are likewise listed in downstream order. The Teme, which flows in to the Severn outside Shropshire, is treated first, together with its tributaries.

The list includes only those sites which are known to have worked since 1660, or are considered likely to have done so. Mills of which there is only place name or archaeological evidence, or which were out of use by 1660, are not included.

There are no mills on the Shropshire portions of watercourses shown in brackets.

Only major uses of water-power are listed. Many subsidiary applications, to power barn machinery, to pump water or to generate electricity are unavoidably omitted.

Names of streams in inverted commas have been bestowed for the sake of brevity and convenience, and have no historical authenticity.

Rivers and streams are listed in the following order:

TEME
  Cwmhouse Brook
  Crochen Brook
  'Stowe Brook'
  Clun
    Redlake
    'Treverward Brook'
  Kemp
    'Hurst Brook'
    Unk
  Onny
    West Onny
    East Onny
      Darnford Brook
    Quinny Brook
      Byne Brook
        Heath Brook
    'Stokesay Brook'
  Corve
    Easthope Brook
    'Abdon Brook'
    'Diddlebury Brook'
    Siefton Brook
    Clee Brook
  Ledwych Brook
    (Dogditch Brook)
    Bensons Brook
  Colly Brook
  Corn Brook

Rea
  Winterburn Brook
  Cleobury Brook
  Farlow Brook
  Burrell Brook
  Hopton Brook

SEVERN
  Dowles Brook
  Borle Brook
    Crunells Brook
  Bowhills Brook
  Hempton Brook
  Mor Brook
    Beaconhill Brook
  Dudmaston Brook
  Potseething Brook
  Cantern Brook
  Worfe
    'Atwell Park Brook'
    Neachley Brook
      Killsall Brook
      Albrighton Brook
    Wesley Brook
      Nedge Brook
    Badger Brook
    Stratford Brook
      Brantley Brook
        'Gatacre Brook'

Linley Brook
Dean Brook
'Swinney Brook'
Wash Brook
'Calcutts Brook'
Benthall Brook
Calde Brook
  Horsehay Brook
  Lyde Brook
Farley Brook
Sheinton Brook
  'Kenley Brook'
Leighton Brook
Cressage Brook
Cound Brook
  Combley Brook
  Betchcott Brook
  Lynall Brook
  Bullhill Brook
Tern
  Coal Brook
  Bailey Brook
  Rosehill Brook
  Meese
    Lynn Brook
    'Woodcote Stream'
    Wagg's Brook
    Ellerton Brook
  Platt Brook

229

Strine
  Lilleshall Brook
  Humber Brook
  Ketley Brook
    Hadley Brook
Roden
  Lyneal Brook
  Sleap Brook
  Soulton Brook
Uffington Brook
Rea Brook
  Lowerfield Brook
  Worthen Brook
  Brockton Brook
  Aston Brook
  Yockleton Brook
    'Winnington Brook'
  Minsterley Brook
Habberley Brook

Perry
  Meadow Brook
  Weir Brook
  'Kinnerley Stream'
(Vyrnwy)
  (Tanat)
    Cynllaith
  Morda
    'Sweeney Brook'
    'Aston Stream'
  Pwll Trewern
  Camlad
  Pellmell Brook
  Caebitra
  Aylesford Brook

(DEE)
  (Ceiriog)
    Morlas Brook
    Shell Brook
    Emral Brook

(WEAVER)
  Duckow

ABBREVIATIONS

BGM	Boring mill
BKM	Bark mill
BLM	Blade mill
BNM	Bone mill
BRM	Barytes mill
CEM	Cement mill
CDM	Cider mill
CGM	Ceramics grinding mill
CPW	Calico print works
CTM	Cotton mill
CRM	Corn mill ★
ELG	Electric generator
HCM	Horse cloth mill
FLM	Fulling mill
IBF	Iron blast furnace
IFD	Iron foundry
IFG	Iron forge (may comprehend IRM and/or ISM)
IRM	Iron rolling mill
ISM	Iron slitting mill
LNM	Linen mill
LTM	Leather mill (may comprehend BKM)
OLM	Oil mill
PFB	Power for barn machinery
PTM	Paint mill (may comprehend BRM)
PPM	Paper mill
SKM	Silk mill
SWM	Saw mill
WLM	Woollen mill (may comprehend FLM)
WPM	Water pump

★No distinction is made between various types of corn mill, flour mills, grist mills, provender mills, kibbling mills &c.

TEME

The source of the Teme is 6 km. south of Newtown, from which the river flows south east, beyond Felindre forming the border between Shropshire and Wales. It is joined by the River Clun near Leintwardine, before veering north round Bringewood Chase. It is joined by the Onny at Bromfield then flows round Ludlow where it is joined by the Corve, and then in a generally easterly direction, west of Burford forming the boundary between Shropshire and Worcestershire, eventually flowing out of the county at Monks Bridge. Its confluence with the Severn is at Powick, downstream from Worcester.

Vron or Doly Carn	Bettws-y-Crwyn	SO 167818	CRM
Coed-y-Hendre	Llanfair Waterdine	SO 212785	CRM
Silurian Mills	Knighton	SO 287725	WLM
Stowe	Stowe	SO 310728	CRM
Bromfield	Bromfield	SO 482767	CRM
Bromfield Saw Mill	Bromfield	SO 481768	SWM
Castle Mill	Ludlow	SO 507745	CRM IFD
Mill Street Mill	Ludlow	SO 511742	CRM SKM
Broad Street Mill	Ludlow	SO 512742	CRM WLM
Old Street Mill (or Hockey's Mill)	Ludlow	SO 514742	CRM
Ludford Mill	Ludford	SO 514741	CRM
Ludford Paper Mill (or Temeside Mill)	Ludlow	SO 519743	CRM PPM
Barretts Mill	Richard's Castle	SO 523692	CRM
Ashford Carbonel	Ashford Carbonel	SO 511711	CRM ELG SWM WPM

CWMHOUSE BROOK

A tributary of the Teme which rises on the southern slope of the Black Mountain and flows south to join the Teme north west of Beguildy at SO 190802.

Moat Farm Mill	Bettws-y-Crwyn	SO 188806	CRM

CROCHEN BROOK

A tributary of the Teme which springs from two sources in the western part of Llanfair Waterdaine which join at Cwmbrain, SO 231779. The stream flows into the Teme at SO 232768.

Melyn-y-Grog	Llanvair Waterdine	SO 233769	CRM

'STOWE BROOK'

A small stream which rises on Stowe Hill and flows south east to join the Teme at SO 331732.

Weston Farm Mill	Stowe	SO 329734	CRM

CLUN

A tributary of the Teme which rises near the Anchor on the Welsh border, flows east to Clun where it is joined by the Unk, and at Aston on Clun turns south through Clungunford, and joins the Teme at Leintwardine.

Newcastle Mill	Clun	SO 248823	CRM
Hurst Mill	Clun	SO 318811	CRM FLM
Clunton Mill	Clunton	SO 334812	CRM
Purslow Farm Mill	Clunbury	SO 358807	CRM PFB
Beckjay Mill	Clungunford	SO 396779	CRM

Redlake

A tributary of the Clun which has several sources in the hills south of Clun. It flows south east to Bucknell, and then in an east-north-easterly direction to join to Clun at SO 394738.

Quern Mill	Clun	SO 324760	CRM
Bucknell Upper (or Walk Mill)	Bucknell	SO 344743	CRM
Bucknell Lower	Bucknell	SO 346741	CRM

'Treverward Brook'

A small stream joining the River Redlake from the east.

Treverward Farm	Clun	SO 282782	CRM

Kemp

A tributary of the Clun which springs from various sources in the hills south of Bishop's Castle, provides water for the ornamental pools at Walcot and then flows south to join the River Clun at Aston on Clun.

Brockton Mill	Lydbury North	SO 325859	CRM
Oaker Mill (or Aston Mill)	Hopesay	SO 384816	CRM ELG

'Hurst Brook'

A stream which flows north to join the River Clun immediately upstream from Clun Castle.

Hurst Saw Mill	Clun	SO 317806	SWM

Unk

A tributary of the Clun, which originates in the hills west of Mainstone and joins the River Clun at Clun.

Mainstone Mill	Mainstone	SO 179879	CRM
Birches Mill	Clun	SO 286845	CRM
Bicton Farm Mill	Clun	SO 289827	PFB
Clun Mill	Clun	SO 304813	CRM

Onny

A tributary of the Teme, with two branches joining at Eaton, SO 377896. Both branches rise at the south end of the Stiperstones range, the West Onny below Shelve Hill and the East Onny to the west of Ratlinghope Hill. After the confluence, the river flows in a south-easterly direction past Horderley, Stokesay and Onibury to join the Teme at Bromfield, SO 484766.

Plowden Mill (or Cock's or Cox Mill)	Lydbury North	SO 384872	CRM
Halford Mill	Halford	SO 436833	CRM
Stokesay Mill	Stokesay	SO 437815	CRM
Wootton Mill	Onibury	SO 459783	CRM

West Onny

Lydham Mill	Lydham	SO 334911	CRM

East Onny

Upper Mill	Wentnor	SO 381940	CRM WLM
Whitcot Mill	Norbury	SO 378918	CRM

DARNFORD BROOK

A tributary of the East Onny which rises east of Ratlinghope Hill round which it flows to join the East Onny at Bridges, SO 393964.

Ratlinghope Mill	Ratlinghope	SO 403970	CRM

QUINNY BROOK

A tributary of the Onny which flows south from the Stretton Gap where it is known as the Marsh Brook, to join the Byne Brook at Strefford, SO 449858. It joins the Onny north of Craven Arms, SO 435843.

Queenbatch Mill	Church Stretton	SO 449903	CRM
Marsh Mill	Wistanstow	SO 448880	CRM
Berry Mill	Wistanstow	SO 438845	CRM

BYNE BROOK/EATON BROOK/LAKEHOUSE BROOK

A stream which rises south-west of Cardington flows SW through Rushbury and Eaton under Heywood where it is known as the Eaton Brook. It is subsequently known as the Byne Brook in its lower reaches before joining the Quinny Brook at Strefford SO 449858.

Newhall Mill	Eaton	SO 489890	CRM
Affcot Mill	Wistanstow	SO 450858	CRM

HEATH BROOK

A tributary of the Byne Brook which rises on the southern slopes of Willstone Hill west of Cardington, flows east through Cardington, then south to join the Byne Brook near Rushbury at SO 517909.

Cardington Mill	Cardington	SO 511949	CRM
Cardington Lower (or Gretton Mill)	Cardington/Rushbury	SO 513945	CRM

'STOKESAY BROOK'

A stream flowing less than 2 km. in an easterly direction, joining the Onny near Stokesay Castle.

Stokesay Castle	Stokesay	SO 435817	PFB

CORVE

A tributary of the River Teme which rises in Spoonhill Wood south of Much Wenlock and flows south east to join the Teme at Ludlow.

Broadstone Mill	Munslow	SO 547901	CRM
Hungerford Mill	Munslow	SO 537893	CRM LTM
Stanton Lacy Mill	Stanton Lacy	SO 493790	CRM
Corve Mill	Ludlow	SO 511753	BKM

EASTHOPE BROOK

A tributary of the Corve which originates with springs at the northern end of Wenlock Edge and flows south east to join the Corve south of Brockton at SO 588932.

Easthope Mill (or Greenpool Mill)	Easthope	SO 568946	CRM

'ABDON BROOK'

A tributary of the Corve which flows from the Five Springs between Abdon Burf and Clee Burf, through Cockshutford, north west to Tugford and south west to join the Corve south of Munslow at SO 526863.

Abdon Furnace	Abdon	SO 567867	IBF
Tugford Mill	Tugford	SO 558870	CRM
Broncroft Mill	Diddlebury	SO 547867	CRM

'DIDDLEBURY BROOK'

A tributary of the Corve which has several sources south of Middlehope. It flows south through Diddlebury to join the Corve south of the village at SO 504838.

Turnhalls Mill	Diddlebury	SO 498867	CRM
(or Fernhall Mill)			
Bache Mill	Munslow	SO 501861	CRM

SIEFTON BROOK

A tributary of the Corve which rises near Westhope and flows south to join the Corve at Culmington, SO 484819.

Siefton Mill	Culmington	SO 483833	CRM

CLEE BROOK/PYE BROOK

A tributary of the Corve which originates on the southern slopes of Nordy Bank and flows west then south west to join the Corve near Culmington at SO 498817. Known as the Pye Brook on its lower stretches.

Clee St Margaret	Clee St Margaret	SO 561844	CRM
Bouldon Mill	Holgate	SO 547850	CRM IBF PPM

LEDWYCHE BROOK

A tributary of the Teme which rises near Scirmage in the parish of Cold Weston, flows south east towards Stoke St Milburgh, then south and south west. Is joined by Dogditch Brook at Henley, SO 528766, then takes a south-westerly direction to join the Teme at Burford, SO 581671.

Stoke St Milburgh	Stoke St Milburgh	SO 568821	CRM
Henley Mill	Bitterley	SO 541763	CRM
Caynham Mill	Caynham	SO 544729	CRM
Burford Mill	Burford	SO 575684	CRM
(or Ledwych Mill)			

DOGDITCH BROOK/BENSONS BROOK

A tributary of Ledwyche Brook which rises north of Titterstone Clee near Wheathill and flows south west to be joined west of Bitterley at SO 551777 by Bensons Brook, and joins the Ledwyche Brook at Henley, SO 528766. No mills have been identified on the Dogditch Brook. Bensons Brook rises on the southern slopes of Titterstone Clee Hill and flows west through Bitterley to join the Dogditch Brook west of Bitterley at SO 551777.

Bitterley Mill	Bitterley	SO 559773	CRM

COLLY BROOK/STOKE BROOK

A tributary of the Ledwyche Brook which flows south from Hope Bagot and joins the Ledwyche Brook west of Greete at SO 564704.

Rockhill Mill	Burford	SO 517722	CRM

CORN BROOK

A tributary of the Teme which rises on the southern slopes of Titterstone Clee Hill, and flows south to join the Teme at Monks Bridge, SO 617683.

Cornbrook Furnace	Coreley	SO 604683	IBF
Boraston Mill	Burford	SO 618702	CRM
Coreley Mill	Coreley	SO 615731	CRM
(or Bossell Mill)			
Tilsop Furnace	Burford	SO 616725	IBF
Whatmore Mill	Burford	SO 615715	CRM
(or Wetmore Mill)			

REA

A tributary of the Teme which rises north of Ditton Priors and flows south east through Neenton to be joined by the Cleobury Brook at SO 654848, then takes a southerly course through Stottesdon to Cleobury Mortimer, and flows south west to be joined by the Hopton Brook at SO 657707, crossing the border into Worcestershire and joining the Teme near Newnham Bridge at SO 636686.

Middleton Mill	Ditton Priors	SO 628894	CRM
Duddlewick Mill	Stottesdon	SO 654832	CRM
Hardwick Forge	Stottesdon	SO 660818	IFG
Prescott Mill	Stottesdon	SO 662810	CRM IFG
Stottesdon Factory	Stottesdon	SO 662804	CTM IFG
Detton Mill	Stottesdon	SO 663792	CRM
Walfords Mill	Neen Savage	SO 675767	CRM PPM
Lloyds Mill	Neen Savage	SO 677763	PPM
Cleobury Corn Mill	Cleobury Mortimer	SO 679757	CRM
Upper Forge	Cleobury Mortimer	SO 687757	IFG
Lower Forge	Cleobury Mortimer	SO 688747	IFG
Tetstill Mill	Neen Sollars	SO 661715	CRM

WINTERBURN BROOK

A tributary of the Rea which originates on Neenton Heath and joins the River Rea south east of Neenton.

Faintree Pump	Chetton	SO 656890	WPM
Lower Faintree	Chetton	SO 658885	CRM

CLEOBURY BROOK

A tributary of the River Rea which rises between Cleobury North and Neenton and flows south east to join the Rea at SO 654848.

Cleobury North	Cleobury North	SO 626872	CRM
Charlcott Paper	Aston Botterell	SO 637862	CRM PPM
Charlcott Furnace	Aston Botterell	SO 637861	CRM IBF
Wrickton Mill	Stottesdon	SO 642858	CRM
Strafford's Mill	Stottesdon	SO 646853	FLM

FARLOW BROOK

A tributary of the Rea. The Farlow Brook and its tributaries, the Match Brook, Ingardine Brooke and Wheathill Brook, rise to the east of Wheathill and flow in an easterly direction to join the River Rea at Prescott, SO 662810.

Silverington Mill	Silvington	SO 621799	CRM
Farlow Mill	Farlow	SO 638813	CRM

BURREL BROOK OR PUDDING BROOK

A tributary of the Rea which rises to the west of Cleobury Mortimer, and flows roughly parallel and to the south of the main street of the town, joining the River Rea at SO 679759.

Pinkham Mill	Cleobury Mortimer	SO 678759	CRM
Lower Mill	Cleobury Mortimer	SO 678759	CDM CRM

HOPTON OR MILL BROOK

A tributary of the Rea which rises on the eastern side of Titterstone Clee Hill, flows south through Hopton Wafers, is known as the Mill Brook in its lower reaches, and joins the Rea south of Neen Sollars at SO 657707.

Upper Mill	Hopton Wafers	SO 638769	PPM
Middle Mill	Hopton Wafers	SO 639766	PPM
Lower Mill	Hopton Wafers	SO 638762	BLM PPM
Ditton Mill	Cleobury Mortimer	SO 641736	CRM
Langley Mill	Neen Sollars	SO 653730	PPM
Sturts Mill (or Bradley Mill)	Neen Sollars	SO 654712	CRM PPM

SEVERN

The Severn rises on Plym Llimon and flows through Llanidloes, Newtown and Welshpool, and receives the waters of the Camlad and Pwll Trewern both of which flow partly through Shropshire before entering the county at the confluence with the Vyrnwy south of Melverley at SJ 327158. The river forms the frontier with Wales ford about 2 km. and flows east towards Shrewsbury and then south towards Ironbridge and Bridgnorth. It is joined by the Perry at Bromley's Forge, SJ 440166, the Rea by Coleham Bridge, SJ 496124, the Tern at Atcham SJ 553092, the Cound Brook at Cound, SJ 565063 and the Worfe at Pendlestone, SJ 724944. Downstream from Bridgnorth the Severn is joined by the Mor Brook is at Eardington, SO 733885, and the Borle Brook near Highley, SO 735817, before passing across the county boundary about one mile downstream at SO 753809. Part of the west bank further downstream in Dowles parish was in Shropshire until 1895.

Isle	Bicton	SJ 456158	CRM WLM
Berwick	Shrewsbury	SJ 470148	WPM
Waterworks	Shrewsbury	SJ 496123	WPM
Calcutts Mill	Broseley	SJ 686030	CRM
Waterworks	Bridgnorth	SO 718929	WPM

DOWLES BROOK

A tributary of the Severn which originates as a series of streams east of Cleobury Mortimer, and east of Furnace mill forms the boundary between Shropshire and Worcestershire as far as Dowles, where the ancient boundaries have been changed. It joins the Severn at SO 779763.

Furnace Mill	Cleobury Mortimer	SO 719765	CRM

BAVENEY BROOK

A tributary of the Dowles Brook which has several sources around Baveney Wood and flows south to join the Dowles Brook at SO 709765.

'Baveney Furnace'	Cleobury Mortimer	SO 711764	IBF

BORLE BROOK

A tributary of the Severn which rises near Upton Cresset, and flows south east to its confluence with the Severn downstream from Highley at SO 753817.

The Down Mill	Chetton	SO 681898	CRM
Eudon Mill	Chetton	SO 689897	CRM

Glazeley Mill	Glazeley	SO 706886	CRM
Borle Mill	Highley	SO 793827	CRM
Lockwood Mill	Highley	SO 740820	CRM
(or Logwood Mill)			

CRUNELLS/HORSEFORD BROOK

A tributary of the Borle Brook which rises near Middleton Scriven, and flows parallel to the Horseford Brook which it joins at Horseford Mill, and then flows east to join the Borle Brook at Huntsbottom (SO 715863), the section below Horseford Mill being known as Crunells Brook.

| Horseford Mill | Deuxhill | SO 700864 | CRM |

BOWHILLS/PAPER MILL BROOK

A tributary of the Severn which originates as a series of streams in the south eastern part of Alveley parish and flows north west to join the Severn at Hampton Loade, SO 746864

Bowells Mill	Alveley	SO 771853	CRM
(or Allum Bridge)			
Coton Mill	Alveley	SO 765856	PPM
Gortens Mill	Alveley	SO 763858	CRM
Crows Mill	Alveley	SO 755860	CRM LTM PPM
Hampton Loade	Quatt	SO 748864	IFG

DADDLE BROOK/LYBATCH BROOK

A tributary of the Bowhills brook which rises south of Alveley and flows north to join the Bowhills Brook at SO 757858.

| Checkars Mill | Alveley | SO 676843 | CRM |

HEMPTON BROOK/CHELMARSH BROOK

A tributary of the Severn. The main source rises north of Chelmarsh and flows south east to join the Severn at SO 745876. This stream was dammed in the 1960s to create the Chelmarsh reservoir.

| Hempton Mill | Chelmarsh | SO 742874 | CRM |

MOR BROOK

A tributary of the Severn which originates in a series of streams rising on the slopes of Wenlock Edge south of Much Wenlock, the chief amongst them the Walton Brook or Beggarhill Brook. The brook flows south east to join the Severn at Eardington, SO 733885.

Acton Round Mill	Acton Round	SO 641955	CRM
Callaughton Mill	Much Wenlock	SO 621975	CRM
Aldenham Mill	Morville	SO 651956	CRM
Lye Mill	Morville	SO 676932	CRM
Hubbals Mill	Morville	SO 691915	IFG
Harpsford Mill	Morville	SO 692916	CRM
Eardington Mill	Quatford	SO 717898	CRM LNM
Eardington Upper	Quatford	SO 726897	IFG
Eardington Lower	Quatford	SO 734895	IFG

BEACONHILL BROOK

A tributary of the Mor Brook which rises in the hills west and south of Monkhopton, and flows north and north east to join the Mor Brook at SO 642957, east of Acton Round.

| Monkhopton Mill | Monkhopton | SO 627934 | CRM |

'ALDENHAM BROOK'

A tributary of the Mor Brook which rises south of Shirlet and flows through Aldenham Park to join the Mor Brook at Morville, SO 670937.

Hurst	Morville	SO 672958	IFG

DUDMASTON BROOK

A tributary of the Severn which rises south east of Quatt and flows in a generally south westerly direction through a series of ornamental pools in the grounds of Dudmaston to join the Severn at SO 736888, a short distance below its confluence with a mill race flowing north east from a stream which flows along the southern edge of Dudmaston Park.

Dudmaston Mill	Quatt	SO 737896	BNM
Dudmaston Mill	Quatt	SO 736896	CRM

'POTSEETHING BROOK'

Daniels Mill	Quatford	SO 718917	CRM

CANTERN BROOK

A tributary of the Severn which originates near Astley Abbots and flows in a south-easterly direction to join the Severn at SO 725950.

Cantern Mill	Astley Abbots	SO 716940	CRM

WORFE

A tributary of the Severn which rises at Red Hill near Woodhouse, SJ 712119, north of Watling Street, between the Telford conurbation and Sherrifhales. It turns south at Burlington Pool, the section past Ruckley Grange being known as the Ruckley Brook, and the length further south as the Cosford Brook, then is joined at SJ 782053 by the Neachley Brook, and after forming the south-eastern boundary of the park at Hatton Grange is joined at Ryton (SJ 759028) by the Wesley Brook, and joining the Severn at Pendlestone, SO 724951.

Crackley Bank Mill	Sheriffhales	SJ 766112	CRM		
Burlington House	Sheriffhales	SJ 774113	CRM		
Lizard Mill	Tong	SJ 786098	CRM		
Lizard Forge	Tong	SJ 788088	IFG		
Tong Forge	Tong	SJ 783082	IFG		
Ryton Mill	Ryton	SJ 759028	CRM PPM SLM		
Higford Mill	Stockton	SJ 754006	CRM		
Badger Hall	Badger	SJ 757990	WPM		
Stableford Hall	Worfield	SJ 762988	WPM		
Worfield Mill	Worfield	SJ 758958	CRM		
Davenport House	Worfield	SJ 753951	WPM		
Burcote Mill	Worfield	SJ 746954	CRM LNM WLM		
Rindleford Mill	Worfield	SJ 738955	CRM FLM OLM		
Pendlestone Mill	Worfield	SJ 724944	CRM IFG WLM		

'ATWELL PARK BROOK'

A tributary of the Worfe which rises south of Lilleshall Park and joins the Worfe north of Crackley Bank, SJ 756113.

Atwell Park Farm	Sheriffhales	SJ 756127	CRM PFB WPM

NEACHLEY BROOK

A tributary of the Worfe which begins as the Pickmere Brook originating near Picmoor Wood on the Staffordshire/Shropshire border just north of Watling Street and actually forms the boundary from a point just south of Watling Street to the north end of Norton Mere. It powers Weston Mill in Staffordshire. The brook joins the main stream of the Worfe at SJ 782053.

Tong Castle Mill	Tong	SJ 790067	CRM

KILSALL BROOK/MORNING BROOK

A tributary of the Neachley Brook which originates with several streams rising east of Boscobel which flow in an easterly direction to join the Neachley Brook below Tong Castle at SJ 791067.

Shackerley Mill	Donington	SJ 808063	CRM

ALBRIGHTON BROOK/HUMPHRESTON BROOK

Tributary of the Neachley Brook. Also known as the Humphreston Brook. Its source is one the Staffordshire/Shropshire border W of Chillington Park, from where it flows east to join the Neachley Brook at Cosford, SJ 781047.

Humphryston Mill	Albrighton	SJ 814047	CRM
Clock Mill	Albrighton	SJ 807044	CRM
Cosford Mill	Albrighton	SJ 789041	CRM
Cosford Grange Mill	Albrighton	SJ 786046	CRM

WESLEY BROOK/SAL BROOK

A tributary of the Worfe which rises near Priorslee in a lake formerly a reservoir for the Lilleshall Company ironworks, first created by damming a stream then by subsidence. It was landscaped by Telford Development Corporation in 1977-78. The lake now consists of The Flash (SJ 710104) and The Reservoir (SJ 712102) and the railway embankment separating them, which was once the Lilleshall Company's route to Woodhouse Colliery. The brook flows south east through Shifnal to join the Worfe at Ryton, SJ 759028.

Haughton Mill	Shifnal	SJ 742087	CRM SWM
Shifnal Manor Mill	Shifnal	SJ 741067	CRM IBF
Patcher's Mill	Shifnal	SJ 741056	PPM
(or Paltey's Mill)			
(or Hem Paper Mill)			
(or Shifnal Paper Mill)			
Evelith Mill	Shifnal	SJ 743051	CRM
Kemberton Mill	Kemberton	SJ 744045	CRM IBF
Hinnington Mill	Shifnal	SJ 752036	CRM WPM
Grindle Forge	Ryton	SJ 753034	IFG PPM

NEDGE BROOK/GRANNY'S BROOK

A tributary of the Wesley Brook which rises near Malins Lee and flows east to join the Wesley Brook at the foot of Lodge Hill, SJ 741062.

Hem Mill	Shifnal	SJ 724059	CRM

BADGER BROOK

A tributary of the Worfe which rises north east of Beckbury and flows south then west through Badger to join the Worfe near Stableford, SJ 762988.

Badger Heath Mill	Badger	SJ 783996	CRM
Badger Mill	Badger	SJ 767994	CRM

Stratford Brook

A tributary of the Worfe which originates in streams which rise on the county boundary east of Albrighton, and flows through Patshull Pool, powering Pasford Mill (in Staffordshire) then through Chesterton, and after its confluence with the Brantley Brook at Hilton (SJ 773955), joins the Worfe south of Worfield at SJ 758948.

Chesterton Mill	Worfield	SJ 792978	CRM FLM PPM

Brantley/Claverley/Hilton/Churl/Cut Throat Brook

A tributary of the Stratford Brook which rises near Six Ashes, flows north east skirting Bobbington and forming the county boundary for a stretch, then north through Claverley, where it becomes known as the Claverley Brook, then the Hilton Brook, then the Churl, joining the Stratford Brook at Hilton, SJ 773955.

Ashford Bank Mill (or Robbins Mill)	Claverley	SJ 802933	CRM BNM
Powkhall Mill	Claverley	SJ 791933	CRM
Sutton Mill	Claverley	SJ 789945	CRM PPM
Hopstone Mill	Claverley	SJ 786946	CRM

'Gatacre Brook'

A tributary of Brantley Brook which rises west of Gatacre Park and joins the Brantley Brook at SJ 803922.

Sytch House Farm	Claverley	SJ 782905	CRM
Lower Beobridge Mill	Claverley	SJ 784911	CRM

Linley Brook

A tributary of Severn which rises east of the high ground at Shirlett and flows south through the pools of Willey Park then by a circuitous but generally easterly course to join the Severn at Apley Forge, SO 705983.

Old Willey Furnace	Willey	SO 672979	IBF
Smithies Mill	Willey	SO 674977	CGM CRM SWM
Nordley Mill (or Littlefords)	Astley Abbots	SO 687981	CRM
Frog Mill	Astley Abbots	SO 698976	CRM
Wrens Nest Forge (Upper)	Astley Abbots	SO 701981	IFG
Wrens Nest Forge (Lower)	Astley Abbots	SO 706983	IFG

Dean Brook

A tributary of the Severn which rises south of Broseley and flows east through woodland to join the Severn at SO 705988.

New Willey Furnace	Willey	SJ 673007	IBF
Dean Mill	Willey	SJ 683000	CRM

Swinney Brook

A tributary of Severn, a short stream in the southern part of Sutton Maddock parish flowing south into the Severn at SJ 176017.

Swinney Mill	Sutton Maddock	SJ 706017	CGM CRM OLM

WASH BROOK/HAY BROOK

A tributary of the Severn which rises south of Dawley and flows through Lee Dingle in Madeley parish to join the Severn at SJ 693027.

Madeley Court Mill	Madeley	SJ 695052	CRM
Clock Mill	Madeley	SJ 700041	CRM CEM
Washbrook Mill	Madeley	SJ 699039	CRM

CALCUTTS BROOK

A tributary of the Severn which rises east of Broseley and flows north to join the Severn at The Calcutts, SJ 687030.

Calcutts Upper Mill	Broseley	SJ 684027	CRM
Calcutts Lower Mill	Broseley	SJ 685028	CRM
Calcutts Ironworks	Broseley	SJ 686030	BGM IBF IFG

BENTHALL BROOK

A tributary of the Severn which rises west of Broseley and flows north to join the Severn immediately downstream of the Iron Bridge at SJ 673034.

Benthall Ironworks	Benthall	SJ 672030	BGM IBF
Benthall Mill	Benthall	SJ 672032	CRM

CALDE BROOK

A tributary of the Severn. A natural stream whose course is now almost entirely artifical as a result of its adaptation to provide power for the ironworks in Coalbrookdale. It now originates in the Upper Furnace Pool, Coalbrookdale, which is supplied with water by the Lyde Brook and Horsehay Brook, and extends about a mile southwards to join the Severn at SJ 665036.

Coalbrookdale Mill	Madeley	SJ 669049	CRM
Upper Furnace	Madeley	SJ 667048	IBF
Lower Furnace	Madeley	SJ 667045	IBF
Upper Forge	Madeley	SJ 669042	CRM IFG
Middle Forge	Madeley	SJ 668041	BGM IFG
Lower Forge	Madeley	SJ 667040	IFG

HORSEHAY BROOK

A tributary of the Calde Brooke which rises in the western part of Dawley parish, flows south to Lightmoor and then west to join the Lyde Brook at the head of Coalbrookdale, in the period covered by this survey on the eastern side of the Upper Furnace Pool.

Horsehay Ironworks	Dawley	SJ 673071	CRM IBF
Lightmoor Ironworks	Dawley	SJ 682053	CRM IBF
Park Lane Forge	Madeley	SJ 681048	IFG

LYDE BROOK

A tributary of the Calde Brooke which rises west of Little Wenlock and takes a south-westerly course to join the Horsehay Brook at the head of Coalbrookdale, in the period covered by this survey on the western side of the Upper Furnace Pool.

Little Wenlock Mill	Little Wenlock	SJ 663057	CRM

FARLEY BROOK

A tributary of the Severn which rises south of Much Wenlock and flows in a north-north-easterly direction to join the Severn near Buildwas Abbey at SJ 642045.

Downs Mill	Much Wenlock	SJ 630007	CRM
Farley Upper Mill	Much Wenlock	SJ 631007	CRM

| Farley Lower Mill | Much Wenlock | SJ 633022 | CRM |
| Buildwas Mill | Buildwas | SJ 641039 | CRM |

SHEINTON/HARLEY BROOK

A tributary of the Severn which rises at the foot of Wenlock Edge between Longville and Plaish, and flows north east through Hughley, where it is known as the Hughley Brook, and then to Harley where it takes a more northerly course to its confluence with the Severn at SJ 607049.

Plaish Mill	Cardington	SO 535964	CRM
Holy Mill (or Preen Mill)	Cardington	SO 550955	CRM
Hughley Mill	Hughley	SO 564979	CRM
Harley Forge	Harley	SJ 588001	IFG
Harley Mill	Harley	SJ 600011	CRM
Wigwig Mill	Much Wenlock	SJ 608018	CRM
Sheinwood Mill	Sheinton	SJ 615026	CRM
Sheinton Forge	Sheinton	SJ 607041	IFG

'KENLEY BROOK'

A tributary of Harley Brook which rises south of Kenley and flows south east to join the Harley Brook at SO 570984.

| Kenley Furnace | Kenley | SO 564985 | IBF |

LEIGHTON BROOK

A tributary of the Severn which rises on the southern slopes of the Wrekin and flows south west through Leighton to join the Severn at SJ 608050.

Dingle Mill	Leighton	SJ 617062	CRM
Upper Mill	Leighton	SJ 612058	CRM
Leighton furnace	Leighton	SJ 610055	CRM IBF

CRESSAGE BROOK

A tributary of the Severn which originates in several streams rising to the south and west of the village and flows north to join the Severn at SJ 593043.

| Cressage Mill | Cressage | SJ 592040 | CRM |

COUND BROOK

A tributary of the Severn which rises at the north end of the Stretton Gap and flows north through Leebotwood where it is joined by the Walkmills Brook at SO 477987. Its northerly course continues through Longnor to Condover from where it follows a circuitous and generally easterly route to its confluence with the Severn at SJ 565063.

Carding Mill	Church Stretton	SO 445945	WLM
Dudgeley Mill (or Dagers Mill)	Church Stretton	SO 466960	CRM
Leebotwood Mill	Leebotwood	SO 475986	CRM
Longnor Mill	Longnor	SJ 488006	CRM SWM
Longnor Forge	Longnor	SJ 485013	IFG PPM
Dorrington Forge	Dorrington	SJ 484021	IFG
Condover Mill	Condover	SJ 479046	CRM
Upper Mill	Condover	SJ 493057	CRM
Widnall Mill	Condover	SJ 502060	LTM
Cantlop Mill	Berrington	SJ 523062	CRM
Pitchford Forge (or Eaton Mascott)	Pitchford	SJ 534054	CRM IFG

Upper Cound Mill	Cound	SJ 553050	PPM
Lower Cound Mill	Cound	SJ 555055	CRM

BETCHCOTT BROOK/WALK MILLS BROOK

A tributary of the Cound Brook which originates as a series of streams including the Batchcott Brook on the north slopes of the Long Mynd and flows westwards from Smethcott to Leebotwood where it joins the Cound Brook (or Longnor Brook) at SO 477987.

Upper Mills	Smethcott	SO 448992	FLM
Woolstaston Mill	Woolstaston	SO 457994	CRM ELG
Fulling Mill	Woolstaston	SO 462993	FLM
Fulling Mill	Leebotwood	SO 466993	FLM

LYNALL BROOK

A tributary of the Cound Brook which rises near Ruckley and flows northwards through Acton Burnell, joining the Cound Brook at SJ 545052.

Acton Burnell	Acton Burnell	SJ 530020	CRM

BULLHILL BROOK

A tributary of the Cound Brook which rises near Langley and flows in a northerly direction to join the Cound Brook at SJ 555053.

Langley Mill	Langley	SJ 545005	CRM
Grange Mill	Cound	SJ 551003	CRM

TERN

A tributary of the Severn which originates from springs between Woore and Madeley (Staffordshire), enters Shropshire near Willoughbridge Farm, flows south-west through Market Drayton and turns south after its confluence with the Bailey Brook north east of Hodnet at SJ 629315. It is joined by the Strine at Crudgington SJ 639176, by the Meese at Bolas and the Roden at Walcot, SJ 593124 and flows into the Severn at Atcham, SJ 553091.

Bearstone Mill	Mucklestone	SJ 725390	CRM
Norton Forge	Norton-in-Hales	SJ 704379	IFG
Betton Mill (or Oakley Mill)	Market Drayton	SJ 698366	CRM
Tunstall Hall	Market Drayton	SJ 692352	WMP
Tunstall Mill	Market Drayton	SJ 691352	CRM
Hinsley Mill	Market Drayton	SJ 686345	CRM
Tyrley Mill (or Tern Mill)	Market Drayton	SJ 679337	CRM PPM
Tanyard Mill	Market Drayton	SJ 677338	BKM
Walk Mill (or Drayton Mill) (or Victoria Mill)	Market Drayton	SJ 671334	PPM CRM
Buntingsdale Mill	Market Drayton	SJ 657331	CRM
New Mill	Market Drayton	SJ 636316	CRM
Wollerton Mill	Hodnet	SJ 626298	CRM
Peplow Mill	Hodnet	SJ 643243	CRM
Eaton Mill	Stoke-upon-Tern	SJ 649231	CRM
Longdon Mill	Longdon-on-Tern	SJ 617153	CRM
Allscott Mill	Wrockwardine	SJ 613133	CRM FLM LTM
Walcot Mill	Wellington	SJ 594124	CRM FLM
Tern Works	Atcham	SJ 551098	CRM IFG

COAL BROOK

A tributary of the River Tern which rises in the Bishops Wood area and flows in a north-westerly direction to join the Tern at Market Drayton at SJ 683340. For about 2 km. north of Chipnall it forms the border between Shropshire and Staffordshire.

Chipnall Mill	Cheswardine	SJ 736324	CRM
Shakeford Mill	Hinstock	SJ 677284	CRM
Drayton Old Mill	Market Drayton	SJ 656331	CRM PPM

BAILEY BROOK

A tributary of the Tern which originates in the low-lying land south of Moreton Say and flows south to join the Tern south of Tern Hill at SJ 627314.

Sandford Mill	Prees	SJ 581341	CRM OLM

ROSEHILL BROOK

A tributary of the Tern which rises south of Market Drayton and flows south west to join the Tern at Stoke on Tern, SJ 637280.

Rosehill Mill	Market Drayton	SJ 657306	CRM

MEESE

A tributary of the Tern. The Meese originates with several streams which flow into Aqualate Mere from which the main stream flows north west towards Standford Bridge. It then takes a circuitous but generally south-westerly course to Tibberton from which its takes a westerly direction before joining the Tern at Bolas, SJ 638208.

Chetwynd Mill	Chetwynd	SJ 735215	CRM WPM
New Caynton Mill	Edgmond	SJ 694230	CRM IFG
Old Caynton Mill	Edgmond	SJ 692214	CRM OLM
Tibberton Mill	Edgmond	SJ 681204	PPM SLM
Cherrington Mill	Edgmond	SJ 670207	CRM
Great Bolas Mill	Great Bolas	SJ 648208	CRM PPM

LYNN BROOK/MORETON BROOK/BACK BROOK/MILL BROOK

A tributary of the Meese which originates on the Staffordshire border near Chatwell from which it flows north. It is called the Lynn Brook, then the Moreton Brook, then the Back Brook, then the Mill Brook before it flows into Aqualate Mere at SJ 776200.

Chadwell Mill	Sheriffhales	SJ 786145	CRM PFB
Lynn Mill (or Lindon Mill)	Sheriffhales	SJ 787155	CRM

'WOODCOTE STREAM'

A tributary of the Lynn Brook which rises south of Woodcote Hall and flows north, eventually through underground channels, apparently finding its way into the Lynn Brook.

Woodcote Mill	Sheriffhales	SJ 767154	SWM

WAGG'S BROOK

A tributary of the Meese which rises west of Bishop's Wood and for 8 km. forms the boundary between Shropshire and Staffordshire as far south as Ellerton, before flowing into the Meese below Showell Mill at SJ 716236.

Doley Mill	Cheswardine	SJ 739295	CRM
Ellerton Mill	Cheswardine	SJ 714260	CRM PPM
Sambrook Mill	Cheswardine	SJ 713248	CRM IFG

GOLDSTONE/ELLERTON/SHOWELL BROOK

A tributary of the Meese which rises east of Cheswardine and flows south towards Sambrook forming a confluence with the Meese near Deepdale Farm at SJ 713237.

Westcott Mill	Cheswardine	SJ 709290	CRM
Hinstock Mill	Hinstock	SJ 693262	CRM
Showell Mill	Edgmond	SJ 718242	CRM

PLATT BROOK

A tributary of the Tern which originates from several sources on the eastern side of Sandford Heath and takes a circuitous but generally easterly course to join the Tern near Bolas at SJ 638207.

Wood Mill	Stanton-upon Hine-Heath	SJ 626230	CRM

STRINE

A tributary of the Tern which rises south east of Newport, and flows to the north of the town, then in a generally south-westerly direction and through a variety of channels across the Weald Moors where it is joined by the Lilleshall, Humbers and Hurley Brooks, and by numerous artificial drainage channels, joining the Tern at Crudgington SJ 269176, although drainage authorities during the last two centuries have created other outlets to the Tern.

Longford Mill	Longford	SJ 717181	CRM

LILLESHALL BROOK

A tributary of the Strine which rises in the woods east of Lilleshall Abbey, flows north west past the southern edge of Lilleshall village and is joined by a tributary flowing in from the south at Honnington Grange. The brook continues in a north-westerly direction to join the Strine at SJ 685165.

Abbey Mill	Lilleshall	SJ 734144	CRM
'Middle Mill'	Lilleshall	SJ 733146	CRM
Towns End Mill	Lilleshall	SJ 727149	CRM
Honnington Grange	Lilleshall	SJ 723149	CRM IBF

HUMBER BROOK

A tributary of the Strine which has its origins on the northern fringe of Donnington and flows north-west past the Humbers to join the Strine Brook at SJ 685164.

Lubstree Forge	Lilleshall	SJ 693153	IFG

WOMBRIDGE BROOK/TRENCH BROOK

A stream which flows in a north-westerly direction across Wombridge parish and ultimately joins the Crow Brook which joins the Strine at SJ 668156.

Wombridge Mill	Wombridge	SJ 692116	CRM IBF

HADLEY BROOK

A stream which flows northwards through the township and joins the Crow Brook which flows into the Strine at SJ 668156.

Hadley Mill	Wellington	SJ 676135	CRM

KETLEY/HURLEY BROOK

A tributary of the Strine which rises near Lawley and flows north falling steeply until it is crossed by the Holyhead Road at the settlement of Ketley Brook. Its subsequent course is less steep and from from Leegomery Mill it is known as the Hurley Brook. From Wappenshall to its confluence with the Strine its present course across the Weald Moors is largely in the bed of the Shrewsbury Canal.

New Dale Ironworks	Wellington	SJ 672097	IBF
Ketley Ironworks	Wellington	SJ 688061	IBF
Leegomery Mill	Wellington	SJ 667128	CRM
Eyton Mill	Eyton	SJ 653151	CRM

RODEN

A tributary of the River Tern which rises east of Ellesmere, flows south west towards Wem, after which it follows a circuitous courses through Leebrockhurst, Stanton upon Hine Heath and Shawbury before taking a generally southerly course and joining the Tern at Walcot, SJ 593124.

Wytheford	Shawbury	SJ 569188	IFG
Ercall Mill	High Ercall	SJ 585164	CRM
Harcourt Mill	Stanton-upon-Hine-Heath	SJ 559246	CRM
Stanton Mill	Stanton-upon-Hine-Heath	SJ 566241	CRM
Moreton Mill	Shawbury	SJ 574226	CRM IFG SWM
Wem Mill	Wem	SJ 512285	CRM

LYNEAL BROOK

A tributary of the Roden which flows south of Colemere to join the Roden north of Loppington at SJ 462315.

Lyneal Mill	Ellesmere	SJ 453325	CRM

SLEAP BROOK

A tributary of the River Roden which originates on either side of the A528 between Cockshut and Myddle and flows east to join Roden south of Wem at SJ 505281.

Burlton Mill	Loppington	SJ 459272	CRM

SOULTON BROOK

A tributary of the River Roden which originates south of Whitchurch with several streams flowing in a southerly direction east of Prees then across the Dog Moor eventually coming together to join the Roden downstream from Wem at SJ 545293.

Prees Mill	Prees	SJ 551337	CRM

UFFINGTON BROOK

A tributary of Severn which rises between Astley and Battlefield and flows south through Sundorne where it has been demmed to form ornamental lakes, and flows into the Severn downstream from Pimley at SJ 525141, although a mill stream was diverted to flow towards Uffington and reached the Severn at SJ 527139.

Pimley Mill	Uffington	SJ 523144	CRM
Uffington	Uffington	SJ 527138	CRM IRM

REA BROOK

A tributary of the Severn which originates in Marton Pool. It pursues a north-easterly course and now joins the Severn immediately upstream of the English Bridge in Shrewsbury, SJ 496124, although formerly its confluence was more complex.

New Mills	Pontesbury	SJ 407075	CRM
Cruckmeole Mill	Pontesbury	SJ 429094	CRM
Cruckton Mill	Pontesbury	SJ 431095	CRM
Hanwood Upper Mill	Hanwood	SJ 441093	BRM CRM FLM
Hanwood Mill	Hanwood	SJ 449100	CRM
Redhill Mill	Meole Brace	SJ 468095	CRM
(or Hanley Mill)			
Pulley Mill	Meole Brace	SJ 484102	CRM
Meole Brace Mill	Meole Brace	SJ 487106	CRM
Sutton Old Mill	Sutton	SJ 497108	CRM
Sutton New Mill	Sutton	SJ 504107	BRM CRM IFG
Burnt Mills	Shrewsbury	SJ 503113	CRM
Monks Mill	Shrewsbury	SJ 502121	CRM
(or Prince's Mill)			
Abbey Mill	Shrewsbury	SJ 497124	CRM
Coleham Factory	Shrewsbury	SJ 496123	CRM

LOWERFIELD BROOK

A tributary of the Rea Brook which rises east of Trylystan and flows in a south-easterly direction into Marton Pool.

Marton Mill	Chirbury	SJ 285033	CRM

WORTHEN/BROCKTON BROOK

A tributary of the Rea Brook which originates as the Rowley Brook and Tantree Brook draining the eastern side of the Long Mountain. The brook joins the Rea Brook at SJ 344043.

Walton Mill	Worthen	SJ 298055	CRM
Brockton Mill	Worthen	SJ 318046	CRM
Worthen Mill	Worthen	SJ 327045	CRM

ASTON BROOK

A tributary of the Rea Brook which rises south of Caus Castle and joins the Rea Brook at SJ 347048.

Aston Rogers Mill	Worthen	SJ 343064	CRM

YOCKLETON BROOK

A tributary of the Rea Brook which drains the eastern slopes of the Long Mountain north of Caus Castle and joins the Rea west of Hanwood at SJ 433097.

Vennington Mill	Westbury	SJ 338095	CRM
Upper Mill	Yockleton	SJ 396103	CRM
Lower Mill	Yockleton	SJ 404103	CRM

'WINNINGTON BROOK'

A tributary of the Yockleton Brook which rises in the Winnington area and flows south east to join the Yockleton Brook at SJ 375095.

Hayford Mill	Alberbury	SJ 359107	CRM

MINSTERLEY BROOK

A tributary of the Rea Brook which flows north through the Hope Valley where it is joined by several streams from the east, and joins the Rea Brook at Malehurst SJ 384064.

Hope Mill	Worthen	SJ 353019	CRM
The Waterwheel	Westbury	SJ 365024	BRM CRM
Hogstow Mill	Westbury	SJ 366032	CRM FLM
Minsterley Mill	Westbury	SJ 374045	BRM CRM FLM

HABBERLEY/PONTESFORD BROOK

A tributary of the Rea Brook which rises east of the Stiperstones range, and flows north to join Rea Brook at SJ 407075 north of Pontesford.

Habberley Mill	Pontesbury	SJ 403036	CRM
Skin Mill	Pontesbury	SJ 415051	CRM LTM
Pontesford Upper	Pontesbury	SJ 412065	CRM
Pontesford Lower	Pontesbury	SJ 408065	CRM SWM
Hinton Mill	Pontesbury	SJ 406075	CRM

PERRY

A tributary of the Severn which originates in the hills south of Selattyn and flows in an easterly direction, north of Gobowen, then turns south past Halston, and continues in a generally southerly direction across the Baggy Moors through Ruyton-XI-Towns, turning east towards Baschurch then south east to join the Severn at Bromley's Forge, SJ 440166.

Park Mill	Selattyn	SJ 294325	CRM
Fernhill Forge	Whittington	SJ 318333?	IFG
Rednall Mill	West Felton	SJ 373294	CRM
Ruyton Mill	Ruyton-XI-Towns	SJ 391225	CRM
Platt Mill	Baschurch	SJ 403224	CRM
New Mills	Ruyton-XI-Towns	SJ 405215	CRM
Milford Mill	Baschurch	SJ 419211	CRM
Bent Mill	Baschurch	SJ 422203	CRM FLM
Adcote Mill	Baschurch	SJ 422196	CRM
Yeaton Upper Mill	Baschurch	SJ 433193	CRM
Yeaton Lower Mill	Baschurch	SJ 435193	CRM
Fitz Mill	Fitz	SJ 443181	CRM
Mytton Mill	Fitz	SJ 441176	CRM
Bromley's Forge	Montford	SJ 441166	IFG

MEADOW BROOK

A tributary of the Perry which rises north of Oswestry and flows east to join the Perry at SJ 329325.

Oak Mill	Whittington	SJ 312327	CRM
(or Derwen Mill)			
(or Fernhill Mill)			

WEIR BROOK

A tributary of the River Perry which rises south of West Felton and flows east through Wykey to join the River Perry at SJ 396250.

| Sandford Mill | West Felton | SJ 338236· | CRM |
| Heath Mills | West Felton | SJ 323244 | CRM |

'KINNERLEY STREAM'

A tributary of the Severn which rises of West Felton and joins the Severn at SJ 345170.

| Kinnerley Mill | Kinnerley | SJ 348200 | CRM |

VYRNWY

A tributary of the Severn which enters Shropshire downstream of Llanymynech Bridge, interweaves with the county boundary for a mile or so, probably reflecting a former course in this flat country. It continues south east, forming the county boundary as far as the confluence with the Severn at SJ 337158. It is joined by the Morda (qv) at Mill House, Pentheylin, SJ 304194 but otherwise there are no mills on the Shropshire portions of the river.

TANAT

A tributary of the Vyrnwy which enters Shropshire at its confluence with the Cynllaith, SJ 215238, in Llanyblodwell. For 0.5 km. it forms the county boundary through Llanyblodwell village, re-entering Wales for 0.5 km. before its confluence with the Vyrnwy at SJ 244206.

CYNLLAITH

A tributary of the Tanat which rises in the hills west of Offa's Dyke in the parish of Llansilin, enters Shropshire at SJ 225318 whence it forms the county's boundary as far south as Pont Pentregwyn SJ 217284, then flows south for 5 km. through Llangedwyn, before re-entering Shropshire for 0.5 km. and joining the River Tanat.

Penybont Mill	Llanyblodwell	SJ 215238	CRM

MORDA BROOK

A tributary of the Tanat which rises in the hills west of Offa's Dyke in the parish of Llansylin, and enters Shropshire at Llawnt, SJ 249308, whence it flows south to Llanforda Mill (SJ 255283) thence east past Morda and Maesbury, turning south towards Llanymynech and its confluence with the Vyrnwy at near Pentreheylin Hall, SJ 304194.

Llanforda Mill	Oswestry	SJ 255283	CRM
Penyllan Mill	Oswestry	SJ 278281	CRM
Morda Upper Mill	Oswestry	SJ 287280	CRM WLM
Morda Corn Mill	Oswestry	SJ 287281	CRM
Morda Lower Mill	Oswestry	SJ 289281	CPW PPM WLM
Weston Upper Mill	Oswestry	SJ 293277	CRM CTM
Weston Lower Mill	Oswestry	SJ 297275	CRM WLM
Ball Mill	Oswestry	SJ 304265	CRM
Maesbury Mill	Oswestry	SJ 304259	CRM PTM
Maesbury Hall Mill	Oswestry	SJ 303250	CRM
Llantidmon Mill (or Redwith Mill)	Llanymynech	SJ 290210	CRM
Pentreheylin Mill	Kinnerley	SJ 304194	CRM

'SWEENEY BROOK'

A tributary of the Morda originating in streams rising on Sweeney Mountain which, once united, flow eastwards to join the Morda at SJ 305247, south of Maesbury.

Sweeney Mill	Oswestry	SJ 285253	CRM

'ASTON STREAM'

A tributary of the Morda which rises south of Aston and joins the Morda at SJ 316237.

Aston Mill	Oswestry	SJ 321269	CRM
Park Mill	Oswestry	SJ 320250	CRM

PWLL TREWERN

A tributary of the Severn which rises on the north slopes of Heldre Hill at the north east end of the Long Mountain, where it forms the border between Shropshire and Wales, and then flows west through Montgomeryshire to join the Severn at 266118.

Dingle Mill	Alberbury	SJ 294108	CRM
Old Dingle Mill	Alberbury	SJ 196104	CRM
Hall Mill	Alberbury	SJ 317107	CRM

CAMLAD

A tributary of the Severn which rises on Corndon Marsh near Hyssington, flows south to the Roveries Bridge, then west to Churchstoke, forming for *c*.4 km. the southern border of a salient of Shropshire. From Churchstoke it turns north through Shropshire, flowing through the Marrington Gorge east of Chirbury, is joined by the Aylesford Brook, flowing west out of Marton Pool at SJ 266008, thence follows a circuitous but basically westerly course, in which for two sections of *c*.1 km. each it forms Shropshire's boundary with Wales. It joins the Severn near Forden at SO 209005.

Bromley's Mill	More	SO 333917	CRM
Marrington Mill	Chirbury	SO 272975	CRM
Walk Mill, Marrington	Chirbury	SO 272979	FLM
Walk Mill, Heightley	Chirbury	SO 276998	FLM
Heightley Mill	Chirbury	SO 273988	CRM
Stockton Mill	Chirbury	SJ 265007	CRM

PELLMELL BROOK

A tributary of the Camlad which originates in several springs to the west of Lydham and joins the Camlad at SO 320918.

White Mills (or Wheat Mills)	Lydham	SO 320918	CRM

CAEBITRA

A tributary of the Camlad which rises to the south of Montgomery and flows north east to join the Camlad at Churchstoke (SO 270940). Between Melin-y-wern (SO 234966) and its confluence with the Lack Brook near Churchstoke (SO 167940) the Caebitra forms the border between Shropshire and Wales.

Brompton Mill	Churchstoke	SO 251931	CRM
Mellington Mill	Chirbury	SO 259908	CRM

AYLESFORD BROOK

A tributary of the River Camlad which flows in a south-westerly direction out of Marton Pool to join the Camlad near Stockton at SJ 266007. A tributary rises north of Middleton and flows north then west to join the brook at SJ 284017.

Rorrington Mill	Chirbury	SJ 266007	CRM

CEIRIOG

A tributary of the River Dee which enters Shropshire at Pen-y-bryn (SJ 264375) whence it and the Dee which it joins at SJ 318395 form the county's western and northern boundary for 12 km., to the Dee's confluence with the Shell Brook at SJ 350413. In modern times all mills on the Ceiriog and Dee have been on the Denbighshire bank, but those sections where the boundary and the river do not coincide are probably those of ancient mill sites.

MORLAS BROOK

A tributary of the Ceiriog which rises 1.5 km. west of Offa's Dyke and enters Shropshire at Craignant, SJ 253349. It is the only tributary of the Ceiriog with mills in Shropshire.

Old Paper Mill	St Martin's	SJ 273344	PPM
Wern Mill	St Martin's	SJ 275345	CRM PPM
New Mills	St Martin's	SJ 277345	CRM
Weston Rhyn Paper Mill	St Martin's	SJ 282347	PPM
Weston Mill	St Martin's	SJ 284350	CRM
Erescob Mill	St Martin's	SJ 408362	CRM
Glynmorlas Mill	St Martin's	SJ 313377	CRM SWM

SHELL BROOK

A tributary of the River Dee which rises at Trench, 2 km. north of Ellesmere. From SJ 377383 to its confluence with the Dee at SJ 350413 it forms the county boundary.

Pant Mill	Ellesmere	SJ 354400	CRM

EMRAL BROOK

A tributary of the Dee whose sources rise north of Ellesmere, and join on the county boundary at SJ 425390, then flow north to Worthenbury, eventually joining the Dee at SJ 423494.

Brook Mill	Ellesmere	SJ 418389	CRM
Wood Mill	Ellesmere	SJ 417381	CRM

'WHITCHURCH STREAM'

A stream which rises south of Whitchurch, flows through the town, joins the Red Brook on the county boundary west of the town, and then flows north west to join the Worthenbury Brook which in due course joins the River Dee.

Whitchurch Mill	Whitchurch	SJ 541414	CRM
'Chemistry Mill'	Whitchurch	SJ 528415	CRM

DUCKOW

A tributary of the River Weaver whose main stream rises on the eastern edge of Cloverley Hall park, Calverhall, flows south and east then turns north passes through Shavington Park before forming the county's western boundary with Cheshire for 3 km. before it passes out of Shropshire, 2 km. south of Audlem. It then flows north to its confluence with the Weaver near Nantwich.

Moreton Mill	Moreton Say	SJ 631354	CRM

APPENDIX TWO
TURNPIKE ROAD DATA

◆ ◆ ◆

This list details, as far as possible in the present state of knowledge, the principal turnpike roads in Shropshire and their tollhouses. Some questions about the county's turnpikes await resolution, particularly those concerning merging and separation of trusts. Some turnpike trusts had roads in more than one county, but only Shropshire sections and the tollhouses on them are listed. The list shows each road system at its maximum extent. The responsibilities of some trusts were reduced as others were established—the section of the Shrewsbury-Owestry road beyond the tenth milestone, part of the Welsh Bridge Trust from 1758, passed to the Oswestry Trust when it was established in 1763, and to the Holyhead Road Commission in 1819. Not all the tollhouses listed were necessarily in operation at any one time. No tollhouse is listed twice, although some appear to have been the responsibility of different trusts at different times. Tollhouses administered by the Holyhead Road Commission are listed under the turnpike trusts which had been responsible for the sections of road concerned. Dates of de-turnpiking are taken from SRO QA/4 (SRO 560/739). Grid references of tollhouses for which there is no cartographic evidence (marked ★) are approximations only.

1. Shrewsbury-Crackley Bank & Shifnal

Original Act of Parliament: 12 Geo I, c.9; 1725

Extent:
Shrewsbury-Crackley Bank
Oakengates-Shifnal
Crudgington-the Swan at Watling Street
Cotwall-Shawbirch-Hadley-Oakengates
The Horseshoes, Uckington-Wroxeter-Longnor Green
Atcham Bridge-Cross Houses

Dates of de-turnpiking: 1866 (Wellington district), 1875 (Shifnal district, 1877 (Shrewsbury district)

Tollhouses:

Acton Burnell/Frodesley	SJ	521020
Bratton Field	SJ	633141
Burcot	SJ	618105
Cock, Wellington	SJ	659110
Cronkhill Lane	SJ	537087
Emstrey Hill	SJ	520107
Hadley	SJ	675120
Leegomery	SJ	662135
Long Lane	SJ	635157
Long Waste/Longdon	SJ	614157
Priorslee	SJ	720092
Red Hill/Limekiln Bank	SJ	731108
Shawbirch	SJ	648132
Tern Bridge	SJ	550093
Watling Street	SJ	663111
Wroxeter	SJ	565088★

2. Wolverhampton Roads

Original Act of Parliament: 21 Geo II, c.25, 1748

Extent:
Shifnal-county boundary on road to Wolverhampton
Hales Heath-Tong, Albrighton-country boundary on road to Wolverhamton

Date of de-turnpiking: 1 November 1880

Tollhouse:

Shifnal	SJ	749073

3. Ludlow First Turnpike

Original Act of Parliament: 24 Geo II, c 29; 1751

Extent:
Ludlow-Woofferton-Monksbridge on the road to Worcester
Ludlow-Maidenhead at Orleton on the road to Hereford

Date of de-turnpiking: 1 January 1873

Tollhouses:

Ashford	SO	515704
Burford	SO	586685
Ledwich Bridge	SO	575684
Little Hereford Bridge	SO	546682
Ludford	SO	513741

Ludford Park	SO 508734
Monksbridge	SO 613687
Overton	SO 509725

4. Shrewsbury-Wrexham

Original Act of Parliament: 25 Geo II, c 22, 1752

Extent:
Shrewsbury-Ellesmere-Wrexham
Ellesmere-West Felton-Moreton Bridge-Oswestry
Harmer Hill-Wem-Cotton Wood
Shawbury-Wem-Sandford

Date of de-turnpiking: 1 November 1871 (Wem division); 31 December 1872 (Overton division)

Tollhouses:

Blackwaters	SJ 393327
Coton	SJ 530340
Coton Hill, Shrewsbury	SJ 492134
Creamore	SJ 516298
Edstaston	SJ 522323
Hardwick	SJ 380339
Harlescott	SJ 497165
Palms Hill	SJ 520276
Rednall	SJ 365281
Soulton/Round Hill	SJ 523292
Stockett	SJ 425315
Stone & Cross	SJ 526340
Tilley	SJ 522283
Whip Lane	SJ 321233

5. Shrewsbury-Much Wenlock-Bridgnorth

Original Act of Parliament: 25 Geo II c 49; 1752

Extent:
Shrewsbury-Much Wenlock-Bridgnorth
Bridgnorth-Smithy Brook
Much Wenlock-Church Stretton
Bridgnorth-Black Brook
Atcham-Condover-Dorrington
Wall-Blackwood Limekilns

Date of de-turnpiking: 31 March 1875

Tollhouses:

Borton	SJ 502065
Chilton	SJ 530091
Cressage	SJ 587042
Harley	SJ 600010
Hazler	SO 468933

King Street	SJ 518075
Morville	SO 671939
North Gate, Bridgnorth	SO 715938
Rushbury	SO 513916
Weeping Cross	SJ 513104
Wenlock	SÓ 624994
Wenlock Bank	SO 613995
Westgate, Bridgnorth	SO 709932
Westwood	SO 595983
Wheel Green	SO 763952★

6. Bewdley Roads

Original Act of Parliament: 26 Geo II c 3; 1753

Extent:
Bewdley-Kinlet

Date of de-turnpiking: 1 November 1878

Tollhouses:

Button Bridge	SO 735791
Dowles	SO 735791

7. Ludlow Second Turnpike

Original Act of Parliament: 29 Geo II c 59; 1756

Extent:
Ludlow-Henley-Clee Hill-Cleobury Mortimer
Ludlow-Sheet-Ledwych Bridge (Cainham)
Ludlow-Steventon-Serpent Inn (Ashford Carbonel)
Ludlow-Elton-Court House (Wigmore)
Ludlow-Leintwardine-Pervine Brook near Knighton
Ludlow-Lowse Gate on road from Bromfields Wood to Mocktree
Ludlow-Bromfield-Wistanstow-Church Stretton
Ludlow-Munslow-Beambridge on road to Much Wenlock
Craven Arms-Bouldon
Ludlow-Fishmore-Hayton-Bouldon
Ludlow-Middleton-Three Horseshoes on road to Bridgnorth
Pedlars' Rest, Culmington-Craven Arms
Whitcliffe-Wigmore
Ashford Bowdler-Ledwych Bridge-turnpike road on Clee Hill

Date of de-turnpiking: 1 January 1873

Tollhouses:

Angel (Bitterley)	SO 573759★
Cainham	SO 564767

Cleobury Mortimer	SO 668757
Corve Gate, Ludlow	SO 508753
Fishmore Brook	SO 514764
Hopton	SO 640760
Little Stretton	SO 443919
Lower Galdeford, Ludlow	SO 517742
Ludford (on Wigmore Road)	SO 504743
Maryknowl	SO 482737★
Middleton	SO 533762★
New Bridge	SO 506743★
Old Street, Ludlow	SO 513742★
Peaton Strand	SO 536847★
Pedlars Rest	SO 486844
Sandpits	SO 515753
Stoke Bridge	SO 438818★
Sutton	SO 516830★
Whettleton	SO 460827★

8. Roads leading into Much Wenlock

Original Act of Parliament: 29 Geo II c.60; 1756

Extent:
Much Wenlock-Buildwas Bridge
Much Wenlock-Broseley-Nordley Common
Much Wenlock-Beambridge
Much Wenlock-Barrow-Willey-Nordley Common
Much Wenlock-Gleedon Hill-Cressage

Date of de-turnpiking: 1 November 1870

Tollhouses:

Beambridge	SO 532882
Bourton	SO 619996
Buildwas	SJ 639038
Linley	SO 683992
Marsh	SO 646997
Much Wenlock	SO 628997
Posenhall	SJ 657016
Sheinton	SJ 618037
Willey	SJ 674006

9. Roads from Coleham Bridge, Shrewsbury, to Longden and Church Stretton

Original Act of Parliament: 29 Geo II, c. 61; 1756

Extent: Coleham Bridge-Church Stretton
Coleham Bridge-Longden
5th milestone near Longden to Castle Pulverbatch
3rd milestone to village of Condover

Date of de-turnpiking: 1 November 1877

Tollhouses:

Condover Turn	SJ 486085
Meole Brace	SJ 491110
Nobold	SJ 474101
Nobold, Stanley Lane	SJ 480107
Sutton Lane End	SJ 491107

10. Roads from Shrewsbury to Preston Brockhurst, Shawbury and Shreyhill

Original Act of Parliament: 29 Geo II c.64; 1756

Extent:
Shrewsbury-Preston Brockhurst-Prees Heath
Shrewsbury-Shawbury
Shrewsbury-Shreyhill-Newport
Waters Upton-Hinstock Heath
Crudgington-Hodnet
Harlescott-Uffington-Atcham
Edstaston-Lacon-Cotton-Prees-Prees Lower Heath

Date of de-turnpiking: 1 January 1873

Tollhouses:

Berwick	SJ 543107
Castle Foregate	SJ 494132
Chetwynd Lane End	SJ 738198
Cotwall	SJ 602174
Crudgington	SJ 631181
Darliston	SJ 579325
Harlescott	SJ 512156
Holloway	SJ 555283
Old Heath	SJ 504145
Prees	SJ 555321
Prees Lower Heath	SJ 576328
Quina Brook	SJ 523329
Roden	SJ 571165

11. Roads leading into Tenbury

Original Act of Parliament: 30 Geo II c.38; 1757

Extent:
Burford-Knowle Gate-Clee Hill

Date of de-turnpiking: 1 November 1870

Tollhouses:

Heath/Titrail	SO 593747
Hope Bank	SO 592690
Knowle Gate	SO 598734

12. Roads leading from Welch Gate and Cotton Hill in Shrewsbury

Original Act of Parliament: 31 Geo II c.67; 1758

Extent:
Welsh Bridge-Yockleton-Westbury
Welsh Bridge-Hanwood-Pontesbury-Minsterley
Welsh Bridge-Wattlesborough Heath-Welshpool
Welsh Bridge-Montford Bridge-Nesscliff-Oswestry
Winnington-Middleton-Trewern-Buttington Hall
Coton Hill-Baschurch

Date of de-turnpiking: 1 November 1877

Tollhouses:
Copthorne	SJ	468123
Coton Hill	SJ	489134
Minsterley	SJ	374050
Hanwood	SJ	470113
Kingsland Lane	SJ	478132★
Middleton	SJ	310127
Montford Bridge	SJ	431153
Mount	SJ	484130
New Street	SJ	485127★
Poulton	SJ	387059
Prescot	SJ	426210
Shelton	SJ	465132
Rose & Crown	SJ	319111
Wolf's Head	SJ	371208

13. Roads leading into Kidderminster

Original Act of Parliament: 33 Geo II c.50: 1760

Extent: Kidderminster-Bridgnorth

Date of de-turnpiking: 1 November 1873

Tollhouse:
Quatt	SO	755881

14. Chester-Stonebridge

Original Act of Parliament: 33 Geo II c.51; 1760

Extent:
Cheshire border-Whitchurch-Prees Heath-Sandford-Bletchley-Newport-Welsh Harp at Stonnall (Staffs)
Whitchurch-Ightfield-Cloverley-Bletchley

Dates of de-turnpiking: 31 July 1854 (Whitchurch-Tern Hill), 1 November 1867 (Newport-Tern Hill), 30 June 1870 (Newport-Stonall), 1 November 1877 (Chester-Whitchurch)

Tollhouses:
Bletchley	SJ	624334
Dodington	SJ	538419★
Grindley Brook	SJ	522431
Hinstock (Four Alls)	SJ	695254
Newport	SJ	744196★
Sandford	SJ	580340★
Sedgeford	SJ	551442
Tern Hill	SJ	522431

15. Roads from Bridgnorth and Cleobury Mortimer

Original Act of Parliament: 2 Geo III c.79; 1762

Extent:
Cleobury Mortimer-Cross Houses-Bridgnorth
Cross Houses-Morville
Cross Houses-Cleobury North-Ditton Priors-Brown Clee
Glazeley-Oldbury-Bridgnorth
Cleobury Mortimer-Abberley Hill
Cleobury Mortimer-Milson-Tenbury
Cleobury Mortimer-Bewdley

Dates of de-turnpiking: 1 November 1878 (Cleobury Mortimer District), 1 November 1879 (Cleobury North and Ditton Priors District)

Tollhouses:
The Barns	SO	622717
Baveney Wood	SO	698787
Billinsley	SO	706853
Branstrey	SO	658747
Cleobury North	SO	627874
Ditton Priors	SO	609892
Halfway House	SO	707909
Harpswood	SO	691915
Lightwood	SO	643908
Oldbury	SO	716924
Overwood	SO	681799
Poulters	SO	696755
Six Ashes	SO	683773
Towns End	SO	687760★
Wall Town	SO	692783★
Weston	SO	694758
Yew Tree	SO	721820

16. Roads around Oswestry

Original Act of Parliament: 3 Geo III c.43; 1763

Extent:
Oswestry-10th milepost from Shrewsbury
Gobowen-Queen's Head
Oswestry-Welshpool
Llanrhaidr-Knockin
Oswestry-Llanfyllin
Oswestry-Pontcysyllte
Oswestry-Wrexham
Mileoak-collieries near Oswestry
Oswestry-Rhydycroesau-Llansilin
Llynynmaen Coalwork-Pentrechannel & Treflach
Limeworks
Aston-Llynclys
New Inn-Glyn Ceiriog-Llantsaintffraid

Dates of de-turnpiking: 1 May 1879 (3rd district), 12 May 1882 (4th district), 1 May 1885 (first district),

Tollhouses:
Bryn-y-groes	SJ 248230★
Church Street, Oswestry	SJ 288292
Coed-y-go	SJ 279277
Craignant	SJ 254350
Croes Wylan	SJ 287287
Fernhill	SJ 308257
Gallowstree Bank	SJ 296288
Glyn	SJ 239218
Lawnt	SJ 249308
Llanforda	SJ 283290
Llynclys & Pwllycrwrw	SJ 282241
Llwyn, Oswestry	SJ 297302
Llwynymaen	SJ 272283★
Lodge	SJ 283354
Maesbury	SJ 308257
Mile End	SJ 333299
Mile Oak	SJ 301277
Penyllan	SJ 267281★
Porthywaen	SJ 258234
Queens Head	SJ 340267
Redwith	SJ 302241
Rhydycroesau	SJ 241307
Selattyn	SJ 267339★
Wern-issa	SJ 233238★
Weston Chain	SJ 296276★
Whittington Chain	SJ 327409★
Willow Street, Oswestry	SJ 287299
Woodhill	SJ 273268
Woolston	SJ 320242★

17. Title: Stafford-Sandon

Original Act of Parliament: 3 Geo III c.59; 1763

Extent:
Newport-Eccleshall
Woodcote-Shifnal-Sutton Maddock-Bridgnorth
Newport-Donnington-Watling Street
Harp-Brockton-Edgmond-Chetwynd End
Eccleshall-Ireland's Cross
Hilton-Honnington

Dates of de-turnpiking: 1 November 1867 (most of system), 1 November 1877 (Bridgnorth-Shifnal)

Tollhouses:
Hem	SJ 727056
Kemberton	SJ 722051
Lilleshall	SJ 731164
Worfe Bridge	SO 732958

18. Madeley Turnpike Roads

Original Act of Parliament: 4 Geo III c.81; 1764

Extent:
Buck's Head, Watling Street-New Inns and Beckbury
Birches Brook-handpost in Kemberton

Date of de-turnpiking: 1 November 1867

Tollhouses:
Cuckoo Oak	SJ 704048
Hills Lane	SJ 700044
Lawley	SJ 672089
Meadow Wharf	SJ 660039
Rudge Heath	SJ 788961

19. Whitchurch-Nantwich and Newcastle

Original Act of Parliament: 7 Geo III c.92; 1767

Extent:
Whitchurch-Burleydam-Audlem-Woore-Madeley (Staffs.)-Madeley Heath
Hinstock-Drayton-Adderley-Nantwich

Date of de-turnpiking: 1 July 1875

Tollhouses:
Adderley	SJ 662397
Gravenhunger	SJ 737423
Hinstock	SJ 693264
Spoonley	SJ 666356
Sydnall	SJ 688306

20. *Marchwiel-Bangor-Dodington (Whitchurch)*

Original Act of Parliament: 7 Geo III c.104; 1767

Extent:
Marchwiel-Bangor-Hanmer-Dodington Redbrook-Welshhampton

Date of de-turnpiking: 29 September 1875

Tollhouses:

Redbrook	SJ 515412

21. *Roads leading into Bishop's Castle*

Original Act of Parliament: 8 Geo III c.51; 1768

Extent:
Bishop's Castle & Montgomery to Westbury
Brockton to Minsterley
Bishop's Castle to Ludlow and Clun
Bishop's Castle-Pentre-Montgomery
Bishop's Castle-Churchstoke-Montgomery
Bishop's Castle to Clun and Knighton
Clun to Newton Green
Bishop's Castle to Pulverbatch and Shrewsbury
Bishop's Castle to Churchstoke and Welshpool
Snead to Lydham

Date of de-turnpiking: 1 November 1876 (Montgomery and Second District), 1 May 1878 (Bishop's Castle and First District)

Tollhouses:

Acton	SO 322850
Aston	SJ 352075
Basford	SO 394854
Bishop's Castle, Church	SO 323884★
Bishop's Moat	SO 289895
Bridges/Overs Brook	SO 393965
Clun	SO 303808
Clun Churchyard	SO 300805
Crow Gate/Stank Lane	SO 331877
Edgton	SO 385855
Eyton	SO 371875
Foul Lane End	SO 330891
Hall Orchard/Little Field	SO 326883
Heblands	SO 323902
Horderley	SO 409868
Kempton	SO 361830
Kerry Lane	SO 320886
Knighton	SO 292723
Lagden Lane	SO 327869
Long Lane	SO 420838
Milebrook	SO 312729
Minsterley	SJ 372051
Park Lane	SO 423826

Pulverbatch	SJ 424023
Ridgeway	SO 395864
Twitchen	SO 367793
Westbury	SJ 355090
Wintle Pool/Welsh Street	SO 321892
Wittingslow	SO 426888

22. *Shawbury-Newcastle under Lyme &c*

Original Act of Parliament: 9 Geo III c.55; 1769

Extent:
Shawbury-Market Drayton-Newcastle under Lyme
Shawbury-High Ercall

Dates of de-turnpiking: 10 August 1866 (Shawbury district), 6 November 1872 (Market Drayton-Newcastle under Lyme)

Tollhouses:

Audley's Cross	SJ 722356
Edgbolton	SJ 752220
Hodnet	SJ 614281
Shawbury	SJ 563213★
Tern Hill	SJ 634323
Walton	SJ 590183
Wollerton	SJ 620297★

23. *Welshpool roads*

Original Act of Parliament: 9 Geo III c.56; 1769

Extent:
Montgomery-Marton
Bishop's Castle-Forden
Four Crosses-Pavement Gate

Date of de-turnpiking: 1 November 1876

Tollhouses:

Alberbury	SJ 363141
Aston	SJ 352075
Aylesford	SJ 274013
Chirbury	SO 263982
Chirbury	SO 262983
Llanymynech	SJ 266211

24. *Wem-Bronygarth*

Original Act of Parliament: 11 Geo III c.95; 1771

Extent:
Wem-Ellesmere-St Martin's-Bronygarth

Date of de-turnpiking: 1893

Tollhouses:

Bronygarth	SJ	267370
Bryng-willa	SJ	303362
Eachley	SJ	451343
Horton	SJ	484302
Loppington	SJ	470293★
Newton	SJ	420342
Northwood	SJ	463333
Palmontmawr	SJ	290359
St Martins	SJ	317362
Trimpley	SJ	396348
Wolverley	SJ	475310

25. Burlton, Knockin and Llanymynech

Original Act of Parliament: 12 Geo III c.96; 1772

Extent:
Burlton-Knockin-Llanymynech
Knockin-the Llanraidr Road
Plas Carrick Lane-Coid Iffa
Wolf's Head-Knockin Lane

Date of de-turnpiking: 1 November 1877

Tollhouses:

Knockin	SJ	334223
Knockin	SJ	329223
Llwyntidman	SJ	286207
Marton	SJ	443239
Plas Garreg	SJ	275213
Platt Bridge	SJ	404223

26. Tern Bridge-Leighton-Birches Brook

Original Act of Parliament: 18 Geo III c.88; 1778

Extent:
Birches Brook-Buildwas Bridge-Leighton-Tern Bridge

Date of de-turnpiking: 1 November 1875

Tollhouses:

Briar Hill	SJ	582071
Leighton	SJ	610056

27. Roads leading into Dudley

Original Act of Parliament: 30 Geo III c.102; 1790

Extent: Dudley-New Inns

Date of de-turnpiking: 1 November 1876

Tollhouses: none in Shropshire

28. Stourbridge-Worfield and Bridgnorth

Original Act of Parliament: 56 Geo III c.16; 1816

Extent: Stourbridge-Bridgnorth

Date of de-turnpiking: 1 May 1877

Tollhouses:

Barnsley/Old Lodge	SO 761915

29. Coalbrookdale-Wellington

Original Act of Parliament: 57 Geo III c.12; 1817

Extent:

Coalbrookdale-Lawley-Wellington
Lawley-Balls Hill

Date of de-turnpiking: 1 November 1875

Tollhouses:

Arleston	SJ	664102
Coalbrookdale	SJ	668049
Lawley	SJ	674082

30. Tarporley-Whitchurch

Original Act of Parliament: 10 Geo IV c.77; 1829

Extent:
Tarporley-Whitchurch

Date of de-turnpiking: 1 November 1876

Tollhouses: none in Shropshire

31. Minsterley-Churchstoke

Original Act of Parliament: 4 & 5 Wm IV c.11; 1834

Extent:
Minsterley-Churchstoke

Date of de-turnpiking: 1 November 1879

Tollhouses:

Plox Green	SJ 367048
Pultheley	SO 324947

32. Shipton-Morville

Original Act of Parliament: 2 Vic c.30; 1839

Extent:
Morville-Shipton
Weston-Brockton-Easthope Cross

Date of de-turnpiking: 1 November 1872

Tollhouses:

Marlbrook	SO 574941★
Weston	SO 597928

APPENDIX THREE

ORGANISATIONS CONCERNED WITH INDUSTRIAL ARCHAEOLOGY

◆ ◆ ◆

Cosford Aerospace Museum, Cosford, Shifnal, Shropshire TF11 8UP.

Daniel's Mill, Eardington, Bridgnorth.

Ironbridge Gorge Museum Trust, Ironbridge, Telford, Shropshire, TF8 7AW.

Ironbridge Institute, Ironbridge Gorge Museum Trust, Ironbridge, Telford, Shropshire, TF8 7AW.

Midland Motor Museum, Stansmore Hall, Stourbridge Road, Bridgnorth, Shropshire.

Sentinel Driver's Club, M Tuxford, 3 Rayments Bungalows, Wimbish Green, Saffron Walden, Essex CB10 2XL.

Severn Valley Railway, The Railway Station, Bewdley, Worcestershire DY12 1BG.

Shrewsbury Borough Museum Service, Rowley's House Museum, Barker Street, Shrewsbury SY1 1QT.

Shropshire Museum Service, The Winston Churchill Building, Radbrook Centre, Radbrook Road, Shrewsbury SY3 9BJ.

Tiles & Architectural Ceramics Society (Tiles Location Index) c/o A. T. Herbert, Esq, 40 Wenlock Road, Shrewsbury.

BIBLIOGRAPHY

◆　◆　◆

BOOKS

Aikin, A., *Journal of a Tour through North Wales* (1797). London: J. Johnson.

Albert, W., *The Turnpike Road System in England 1663-1840* (1972). Cambridge: Cambridge University Press.

Alfrey, J. & Clark, K., *The Landscape of Industry: patterns of change in the Ironbridge Gorge* (1993). London: Routledge.

Bagshaw, S., *History, Gazetteer and Directory of Shropshire* (1851). Sheffield: Bagshaw.

Bailey, W, *Bailey's Western and Midland Directory* (1783). Birmingham: Pearson and Rollason.

Baldwin, M., Elliott, Revd W. and Davis, J., *Cleobury Chronicles, I* (1991), Cleobury Mortimer: Cleobury Mortimer History Society.

Bannister, G.F., *Great Western Steam off the Beaten Track* (1975). Truro: Bradford Barton.

Barnard, A., *The Noted Breweries of Great Britain and Ireland* (1889). London: Sir Joseph Causton.

Baxter, B., *Stone Blocks and Iron Rails* (1966). Newton Abbot: David & Charles.

Beck, K. M., *The Great Western North of Wolverhampton* (1991). London: Ian Allan.

Bick, D.E., *The Old Metal Mines of Mid-Wales: West Montgomeryshire* (1977). Newent: The Pound House.

Blackwall, A., *Historic Bridges of Shropshire* (1985). Shrewsbury: Shropshire Libraries.

Booth, D.T.W., *Watermills on the River Rea in South Shropshire* (1990). Halesowen: privately published.

Bridges, A. J., *Industrial Locomotives of Cheshire, Shropshire and Herefordshire* (1977). London: Industrial Locomotive Society.

Brook, F.,*The Industrial Archaeology of the British Isles: 1. The West Midlands* (1977). London: Batsford.

Brook, F. and Allbutt, M., *The Shropshire Lead Mines* (1973). Leek: Moorland.

Brown, I.J., *A History of Limestone Mining in Shropshire* (1977). Newport: Shropshire Mining Club.

Brown, I. J., *The Coalbrookdale Catalogue: Catalogue of Mines* (1968). Shrewsbury: Salop County Library.

Brown, I. J., *The Mines of Shropshire* (1976). Ashbourne: Moorland.

Brown, Y., *Ruyton-XI-Towns: Unusual Name: Unusual History* (1988). Studley: Brewin.

Burt, R., Waite, Peter & Burnley, R., *The Mines of Shropshire & Montgomeryshire with Cheshire & Staffordshire: Metalliferous and Associated Minerals 1845-1913* (1990). Exeter: University of Exeter Press.

Carlon, C. J., *The Gallantry Bank Copper Mine, Bickerton, Cheshire, with a review of mining in the Triassic rocks of the Cheshire-Shropshire Basin* (1981). Sheffield: Northern Mines Research Society.

Carlon, C. J., *The Eardiston Copper Mine, Shropshire* (1981). Kendal: Peak District Mines Historical Society.

Carpenter, R., *The Criggion Branch of the Shropshire & Montgomeryshire Light Railway* (1990). Didcot: Wild Swan.

Cathrall, W., *The History of Oswestry*. Oswestry: George Lewis (1855). Reprint, n.d., circa 1974, Shrewsbury: Salop County Council.

Chapman, S. D., *The Early Factory Masters: The Transition to the Factory System in the Midlands Textile Industry* (1967). Newton Abbot: David & Charles.

Christiansen, R., *A Regional History of the Railways of Great Britain: Vol. VII: The West Midlands* (1973). Newton Abbot: David & Charles.

Christiansen, R. & Miller, R. W., *The Cambrian Railways* (1967). Newton Abbot: David & Charles.

Christiansen, Rex & Miller, R.W., 1971. *The North Staffordshire Railway*. Newton Abbot: David & Charles.

Clow, A. & N., *The Chemical Revolution* (1952). London: Blatchworth.

Coleman, D. C., *The British Paper Industry 1495-1860: A Study in Industrial Growth* (1958). Oxford: Clarendon Press.

Cossons, N. & Trinder, B., *The Iron Bridge: Symbol of the Industrial Revolution* (1979). Bradford-on-Avon: Moonraker.

Davies, A. S., *The Charcoal Iron Industry of Powysland* (1939). Welshpool: Powysland Club.

Davies, D. L., *The Glyn Valley Tramway* (1962). Lingfield: Oakwood Press.

de Maré, E., *Bridges of Britain*, revised edition (1975). London: Batsford.

Denton, J. H., *Canals and Railways: a list of plans and related documents deposited at the Shirehall, Shrewsbury* (1969). Shrewsbury: Salop County Council.

Donaldson-Hudson, R., *An Historical Survey of the Parish of Cheswardine* (1939). Shrewsbury: Wilding.

Doncaster, E. A., *Limes and Cements* (1916), London: Spon.

Duggan, T. C., *The History of Whitchurch, Shropshire* (1935). Whitchurch: Whitchurch Herald.

Earnshaw, D. et al, *Whitchurch Remembered* (1980). Shrewsbury: Shropshire Libraries.

Eckel, E. C., *Cements and Plasters* (1928). London: John Wiley.

Edwards, I., *Davies Brothers, Gatesmiths: Eighteenth Century Wrought Ironwork in Wales* (1977). Cardiff: Welsh Arts Council.

Emden, P. H., *Quakers in Commerce: a record of business achievement* (1939). London: Sampson Lowe.

Falconer, K., *Guide to England's Industrial Heritage* (1980). London: Batsford.

Fiennes, C., *The Journeys of Celia Fiennes*, edited by Christopher Morris (1947). London: Cresset.

Forrest, H. E., *The Old Houses of Wenlock* (1914). Shrewsbury: Wilding.

Forrest, H. E., *The Old Houses of Shrewsbury: their history and associations,* 5th edition (1935). Shrewsbury: Wilding.

Foulkes, F. W., *Hooked on Cheese* (1985). Shrewsbury: Shropshire Libraries.

Foxall, H. D. G., *A Gazetteer of Streets, Roads and Place Names in Shropshire* (1967). Shrewsbury: Salop County Council.

Foxall, H. D. G., *Shropshire Field Names* (1980). Shrewsbury: Shropshire Archaeological Society.

Gale, W. K. V. & Nicholls, C. R., *The Lilleshall Company Limited: a history 1764-1964* (1979). Ashbourne: Moorland.

Gasquoine, C. P., *The Story of the Cambrian: a Biography of a Railway* (1922). Oswestry: Caxton Press.

George, J., *Daniel's Mill: its history, millers and restoration* (no date). Bridgnorth: privately published.

Gough, R., *The History of Myddle*, edited by David Hey (1981). Harmondsworth: Penguin.

Gregory, T., *The Shropshire Gazetteer* (1824). Wem: Gregory.

Griffith, E., *The Bishop's Castle Railway, Shropshire, 1865-1935* (1969). Farnham: privately published.

Griffiths, S., *Griffiths' Guide to the Iron Trade of Great Britain* (1873). New edition, with introduction by W. K. V. Gale (1967). Newton Abbot, David and Charles.

Griffin, A. R., *Coalmining* (1969). London: Longmans.

Hadfield, C., *The Canals of South Wales and the Border* (1960). Cardiff: University of Wales Press.

Hadfield, C., *The Canals of the West Midlands* (1966). Newton Abbot: David & Charles.

Hadfield, C., *World Canals* (1986). Newton Abbot: David & Charles.

Hadfield, C., *Thomas Telford's Temptation* (1993). Cleobury Mortimer: M. & M. Baldwin.

Harris, J. R., *The British Iron Industry 1700-1850* (1988). Basingstoke: Macmillan Education.

Hart, S., *Shrewsbury: a Portrait in Old Picture Postcards* (1988). Market Drayton: S. B. Publications.

Hey, D. G., *An English Rural Community: Myddle under the Tudors and Stuarts* (1974). Leicester: Leicester University Press.

Holland, J., *The History and Description of Fossil Fuel, the Collieries and the Coal Trade of Great Britain* (1835). Reprint (1968). London: Cass.

Hughes, W. J. & Thomas, J. L., *'The Sentinel': A History of Alley & MacLellan and the Sentinel Waggon Works*, vol I, 1875-1930 (1975). Newton Abbot: David & Charles.

Hulbert, C., *History and Description of the County of Salop* (1837). Hadnall: Hulbert.

Hulbert, C., *Memoirs of Seventy Years of an Eventful Life* (1852). Shrewsbury: Hulbert.

Industry Hall, *Report of the School called Industry Hall in the Parish of Prees, Shropshire* (1804). Shrewsbury: M Wood.

Jenkins, A. E., *Titterstone Clee Hills: Everyday Life, Industrial History and Dialect* (1988). Orleton, privately published.

Jenkinson, A., *Shropshire's Wild Places: a Guide to the County's Protected Wildlife Sites* (1992). Church Stretton: Scenesetters.

Lazarus, B., *Country Reflections around Cheswardine* (1988). Cheswardine: Privately published.

Lee, L. J., *A Full List and Partial Abstract of the Quarter Sessions Rolls, 1696-1800* (no date). Shrewsbury: Salop County Council.

Lee, L. J. and Venables, R. G., *A Full List and Partial Abstract of the Quarter Sessions Rolls, 1801-20* (no date). Shrewsbury: Salop County Council.

Lewis, M. J. T., *Early wooden railways* (1970). London: Routledge & Kegan Paul.

Lewis, W. J., *Lead Mining in Wales* (1967). Cardiff.

Livesey Ltd., *Handbook to the Shropshire and Montgomeryshire Railway* (no date). Shrewsbury: Livesey (Reprint, Shrewsbury: Salop County Council, 1977).

Lloyd, D., *Broad Street: its houses and residents through eight centuries, Ludlow Research paper No 3* (1979). Birmingham: Studio Press.

Local Pamphlets, *Handbook to Shrewsbury* (circa 1856), title page missing, bound in volume of Local Pamphlets, Shropshire Records & Research.

Lyons, E., *A Historical Survey of Great Western Engine Sheds* (1972). Oxford: Oxford Publishing Co.

MacDonald, W., *An Illustrated Guide to Shrewsbury* (1897). London & Edinburgh: William MacDonald.

McMillan, B. L., *History of a water supply to Wolverhampton 1847-1947* (1947). Wolverhampton: Wolverhampton Corporation.

Markham, S., *John Loveday of Caversham 1711-1789: the Life and Times of an Eighteenth Century Onlooker* (1984). Wilton: Michael Russell.

Marshall, J., *The Severn Valley Railway* (1989). Nairn: David St John Thomas.

Merchant, H., *Wem: History and Guide* (1907). Wem: Prince.

Merry, E., *A History of Minsterley* (1976). Minsterley: privately published.

Morgan, J. S., *The Colonel Stephens Railways: a Pictorial History* (1978). Newton Abbot: David & Charles.

Morris, B. & Morris, D., *Market Drayton and Norton in Hales* (1989). Loggerheads: Brampton.

Morriss, R., *Rail Centres: Shrewsbury* (1986). London: Ian Allan.

Morriss, R., *Railways of Shropshire: a brief history* (1983). Shrewsbury: Shropshire Libraries.

Mullins, S. P., *Much Wenlock: a town trail* (1991). Shrewsbury: Shropshire Leisure Services.

Murchison, Sir R., *The Silurian System* (1839). London: John Murray.

Murchison, Sir R., *Siluria*, 5th edition (1872). London: John Murray.

Mutton, N., *An Engineer at Work in the West Midlands: the Diary of John Urpeth Rastrick for 1820* (1969). Wolverhampton: Wolverhampton College of Technology.

Nankivell, J. W., *Chapters from the History of Ellesmere* (1983). Birmingham: Lazanica Press.

Nef, J. U., *The Rise of the British Coal Industry* (1932). London: Routledge.

Nightingale, J., *The Beauties of England and Wales, or Original Delineations of Each County*, Vol XIII pt I, Shropshire (1813). London: J Harris.

Owen, H. & Blakeway, J. B., *A History of Shrewsbury* (1825). London: Harding Lepard.

Palmer, V., *Chirk and the Glyn Valley Tramway: a Portrait in Old Picture Postcards* (1988). Market Drayton: S. B. Publications.

Pannett, D. & Trinder, B., *Old Maps of Shrewsbury* (1972). Shrewsbury: Field Studies Council.

Partridge, C. A., *Handbook to Ludlow* (1878). Ludlow: Partridge.

Pawson, E., *Transport and Economy: the Turnpike Roads of Eighteenth Century Britain* (1977). London: Academic Press.

Pearce, A., *Mining in Shropshire* (1995). Shrewsbury: Shropshire Books.

Penfold, A., *Thomas Telford: Engineer* (1980). London: Thomas Telford.

Pennant, T., *Tours in Wales* (1883). London: Henry Hughes.

Pevsner, N., *The Buildings of England: Shropshire* (1958) London: Penguin.

Pidgeon, H., *Memorials of Shrewsbury* (1837). Shrewsbury: John Eddowes.

Pocock, R., *Travels through England of the Rev Richard Pococke*, ed. J. Cartwright (1889). London: Camden Society.

Pocock, R. W. & Whitehead, T. H., *British Regional Geology: the Welsh Borderland*, second edition, (1948). London: HMSO.

Post Office, *The Post Office Directory of Shropshire* (1856). London: Kelly.

Preshous, J., *Bishop's Castle Well-remembered* (1990). Bishop's Castle: privately published.

Price, M., *The Cleobury Mortimer and Ditton Priors Light Railway* (1964). Lingfield: Oakwood Press.

Price, W., *The History of Oswestry* (1815). Oswestry: Price.

Pybus, M., *Under the Buttercross: Market Drayton, a town of Good Food* (1986). Market Drayton: Market Drayton Civic Society.

Randall, J., *Handbook to the Severn Valley Railway* (1863) Madeley: privately published.

Randall, J., *The Clay Industries including the Fictile & Ceramic Arts on the Banks of the Severn* (1877). Madeley: Salopian and West-Midland Office.

Randall, J., *Broseley and its Surroundings* (1879). Madeley: Randall.

Randall, J., *History of Madeley* (1880). Madeley: *Wrekin Echo*.

Ranger, W., *Report to the General Board of Health on a preliminary inquiry into...Bridgnorth* (1853). London: Eyre & Spottiswoode.

Ranger, W., *Report to the General Board of Health on a preliminary inquiry into...Shrewsbury* (1854). London: Eyre & Spottiswoode.

Rayska, U. *Victorian and Edwardian Shropshire from old photographs* (1977). London: Batsford.

Rayska, U., & Carr, A. M., *Telford Past and Present* (1978). Shrewsbury: Shropshire Libraries.

Rees, W., *Industry before the Industrial Revolution* (1968). Cardiff: University of Wales Press.

Review Publishing, *Industry of Shropshire: Business Review* (1891) Birmingham: Review Publishing Co.

Richards, E., *The Leviathan of Wealth: The Sutherland Fortune in the Industrial Revolution* (1973). London: Routledge & Kegan Paul.

Riden, P., *A Gazetteer of Charcoal-fired Blast Furnaces in Great Britain in use since 1660* (1987). Cardiff: privately published.

Riley, G., *The Water Mills of the Borough of Newcastle* (1991). Newcastle-under-Lyme: Borough of Newcastle-under-Lyme.

Rimmer, W. G., *Marshall's of Leeds, 1788-1886* (1960). Cambridge: Cambridge University Press.

Robinson, D. H., *The Sleepy Meese* (1988). Albrighton: Waine Research Publications.

Robinson, D.H., *The Wandering Worfe* (1980). Albrighton: Waine Research Publications.

Robinson, Son & Pike, *Shrewsbury Illustrated* (1894). Brighton & London: Robinson, Son & Pike.

Rolt, L. T. C., *Thomas Telford* (1958). London: Longmans.

Rolt, L. T. C., *Landscape with Canals* (1977). London: Allen Lane.

Rolt, L. T. C., *Narrow Boat* (1944). London: Eyre Methuen.

Rowley, N. & S. V., *Market Drayton: a Study in Social History* (1966). Market Drayton, privately published.

Rowley, R. T., *The Shropshire Landscape* (1972). London: Hodder & Stoughton.

Sayers, R. S., *Lloyds Bank in the History of English Banking* (1957). Oxford: Clarendon Press.

Scott, W. J., *The Great Great Western 1889-1902* (1972). Newton Abbot: David & Charles.

Seaby, W. A. & Smith, A. C., *Windmills in Shropshire, Hereford and Worcester: a contemporary survey* (1984). Stevenage: Stevenage Museum Publications.

Sentinel Wagon Works Ltd., *Sentinel Patent Locomotives* (1931). Shrewsbury: Sentinel Wagon Works.

Shorter, A. H., *Water Paper Mills in England* (1966). London: Society for the Protection of Ancient Buildings.

Shrewsbury Chronicle and Shropshire Libraries, *The Changing Face of Shrewsbury* (1981). Shrewsbury: Shrewsbury Chronicle and Shropshire Libraries.

Shropshire Federation of Women's Institutes (SFWI), *Shropshire Within Living Memory* (1992). Newbury: Countryside Books.

Shropshire Railway Society, *Shropshire Railways Revisited* (1982). Shrewsbury: Shropshire Libraries.

Shropshire Records & Research Unit, *Shrewsbury Then and Now* (1991). Shrewsbury: Shropshire Books.

Smith, D. J., *The Severn Valley Railway* (1967). Bracknell: Town & Country Press.

Smith, S. B., *A View from the Iron Bridge* (1979). London: Thames & Hudson.

Smith, W. & Beddoes, K., *The Cleobury Mortimer and Ditton Priors Light Railway* (1980). Oxford: Oxford Publishing Co.

Stopes, H., *Malt and Malting* (1885). London: Lyon.

Stratton, M. J., *The Terracotta Revival: Building Innovation and the Image of the Industrial City in Britain and North America* (1993). London: Gollancz.

Tann, J., *The Development of the Factory* (1970). London: Cornmarket Press.

Tann, Jennifer, ed., *The Selected Papers of Boulton & Watt: Volume I: The Engine Partnership 1775-1825* (1981). London: Diploma Press.

Tew, D., *Canal Inclines and Lifts* (1984). Gloucester: Alan Sutton.

Thomas, A. R., & Thomas, J. L., *'The Sentinel': A history of Alley & MacLellen and The Sentinel Waggon Works, vol II, 1930-1980* (1987). Worcester: Woodpecker Publications.

Thomas, R. D., *Industries of the Morda Valley* (1939). Oswestry: Woodall, Minshall, Thomas & Co. Reprint (1978), Shrewsbury: Salop County Council.

Toghill, P., *Geology in Shropshire* (1990). Shrewsbury: Swan Hill Press.

Toghill, P., *Onny Valley, Shropshire, Geology Teaching Trail* (1992). London: Geologists' Association.

Toghill, P. & Chell, K., *Shropshire Geology: Stratigraphic and Tectonic History* (1984). Taunton: Field Studies Council.

Tonks, E. S., 1972. *The Shropshire & Montgomeryshire Railway.* London: Industrial Railway Society.

Tonks, E. S., *The Snailbeach District Railway* (1974). Birmingham: Industrial Railway Society.

Townson, R., *Tracts and Observations in Natural History and Physiology: A Sketch of the Mineralogy of Shropshire* (1799).

Trevenna, Nigel, et al., *Steam for Scrap: the complete story* (1992). Penryn: Atlantic Transport.

Trinder, B., *The Industrial Revolution in Shropshire,* second edition (1981). Chichester: Phillimore.

Trinder, B., *The Making of the Industrial Landscape* (1982). London: Dent.

Trinder, B., ed., *Victorian Shrewsbury: Studies in the History of a County Town* (1984). Shrewsbury: Shropshire Libraries.

Trinder, B. *The Most Extraordinary District in the World: Ironbridge and Coalbrookdale,* second edition (1988). Chichester: Phillimore.

Trinder, B., *The Darbys of Coalbrookdale,* second edition (1992). Chichester: Phillimore.

Trinder, B., & Cox, J., *Yeomen and Colliers: the probate inventories of Dawley, Lilleshall, Wellington and Wrockwardine* (1980). Chichester: Phillimore.

Tucker, G., *Some Watermills of South-West Shropshire* (1991). Birmingham: Midland Wind & Water Mills Group.

Turner, K. & S. *The Shropshire & Montgomeryshire Light Railway* (1982). Newton Abbot: David & Charles.

Victoria History of Shropshire, Volume 8, the Hundreds of Condover and Ford (1968). Oxford: Oxford University Press.

Victoria History of Shropshire, Volume 11, Telford (1985). Oxford: Oxford University Press.

Walker, C., *The Steam Railway: Shrewsbury* (1971). Oxford: Oxford Illustrators Ltd.

Ward, A. W., *The Bridges of Shrewsbury* (1935). Shrewsbury: Wilding.

Ward, T. O., *The Medical Topography of Shrewsbury* (1841). Worcester: Deighton.

Warner, A., *Newport, Shropshire: Past and Present* (1983). Newport: privately published.

Watkin, I., *Oswestry with an account of its old houses, shops, etc.* (1920). Oswestry: Owen.

Watkins, G., *The Stationary Steam Engine* (1968). Newton Abbot: David & Charles.

Watkins–Pitchford, W., *The Port of Bridgnorth* (1935). Bridgnorth: R S Fallows.

Watson, N., *A family business: Morris & Co. 1869-1994 (1995).* Shrewsbury: Morris & Co.

Webb, B., *A Ludlow Album: A collection of old photographs* (1981). Shrewsbury: Shropshire Libraries.

Whitehead, T. H., Robertson, T., Pocock, R. W., and Dixon, E. E. L.,*Memoirs of the Geological Survey of England and Wales: the County between Wolverhampton and Oakengates* (1928)

Wightman, J., *Annals of the Rescued* (1860). London: James Nisbet.

Wilding & Son, *Shropshire: a Beautiful English County* (1935). Shrewsbury: Wilding.

Williams, G., *The Wenlock Limestone Industry: an historical note* (1990). Telford: Williams.

Wilson, E., *The Ellesmere and Llangollen Canal: an historical background* (1975). Chichester: Phillimore.

Woodward, I., *The Story of Wem and its Neighbourhood* (1951). Shrewsbury: Wilding.

Wren, W. J., *The Tanat Valley—its Railways and Industrial Archaeology* (1968). Newton Abbot: David & Charles.

Wright, T., *The History & Antiquities of the town of Ludlow* (1826). Ludlow: Proctor & Jones.

ARTICLES

Allbutt, M. and Brook, F., 'The South Shropshire Lead Mines', *Journal of Industrial Archaeology*, vol.10 (1973), pp.40-63.

Baker, N.J., 'The Talbot Chambers Site, Market Street, Shrewsbury', *Transactions of the Shropshire Archaeological Society*, vol. 66 (1989), pp.63-78.

Baldwin, M., 'Ironworking in Cleobury Mortimer, Part 1', *Cleobury Chronicles,* vol.3 (1994), pp.34-49.

Binnie, G. M., 'Masonry and Concrete Dams 1880-1941', *Industrial Archaeology Review,* vol.10 (1987), pp.41-58.

Blake Roberts, D., & Blake Roberts, G., 'The results of recent excavations in Coalport, Shropshire', *English Ceramic Circle Transactions*, vol.2 (1981), pp.71-81.

Boucher, C. T. G., 'Broadstone Mill', *Transactions of the Newcomen Society*, vol.36 (1963-64), pp.159-63.

Brown, I. J., 'Notes on the Mines of the Madeley Court Co', *Shropshire Newsletter,* no. 38 (1970).

Brown, I.J., 'Underground in the Ironbridge Gorge', *Industrial Archaeology Review,* vol.3 (1979), pp.158-69.

Burke, J. P., 'Railway Crossroads of the North-West: Shrewsbury', *Modern Railways,* vol.17 (1963), pp.47-56.

Burne, E. L., '*On Mills* by Thomas Telford', *Transactions of the Newcomen Society*, vol. 17 (1936-37), pp.205-214.

Carpenter, R., 'Bishop's Castle Station', *British Railway Journal,* no. 38 (1991), pp.355-366.

Chaplin, R., 'A Forgotten Industrial Valley', *Shropshire Newsletter,* no.36 (1969), pp.1-6.

Clarke, N. J., 'The Aqueduct: an east Shropshire industrial settlement', *Shropshire Newsletter*, nos. 39 and 40 (1970-71), pp.1-4, 6-10.

Cossons, N., 'Ironbridge: the First Ten Years', *Industrial Archaeology Review*, vol.III (1979), pp.179-86.

Crossley, D., 'The survival of early blast furnaces: a world survey', *Journal of the Historical Metallurgy Society*, vol.18 (1984), pp.112-121.

Davidson, I, 'George Deacon (1843-1909) and the Vrynwy Works', *Transactions of the Newcomen Society*, vol.59 (1987-88), pp.81-96.

Day, W., 'The Shropshire Portion of the Chester-Cardiff road in 1675', *Transactions of the Shropshire Archaeological Society* vol. 60, (1975-76), pp.113-21.

Denton, J. H. & Lewis, M. J. T., 'The River Tern Navigation', *Journal of the Railway and Canal Historical Society*, vol.23 (1977), pp 56-63.

Dickinson, H. W. & Lee, A. 'The Rastricks: Civil Engineers', *Transactions of the Newcomen Society*, vol.4 (1923-24), pp.48-63.

Edmundson, R. S., 'Coalport China Works, Shropshire: a comparative study of the premises and the background to their study', *Industrial Archaeology Review*, vol.3 (1979), pp.122-145.

Edmundson, R. S., 'Bradley and Co., Coalport Pottery 1796-1800', *Transactions of the Northern Ceramic Society*, vol.4 (1981), pp.127-55.

Edwards, I., 'The early ironworks of north-west Shropshire', *Transactions of the Shropshire Archaeological Society*, vol.56 (1957-60), pp.185-202.

Evans, R. C., 'A Year in the Life of Thomas Telford', *West Midlands Studies*, vol.4 (1970-71), pp. 23-31.

Falconer, K.A., 'Fireproof Mills—the widening perspectives', *Industrial Archaeology Review*, vol.16 (1993), pp.11-26.

Goodman, K. W. G., 'Tilsop Furnace', *West Midlands Studies*, vol.13 (1980), pp.40-46.

Green, H., 'New Factory, Severn Street, Castlefields', *Bulletin of the Association for Industrial Archaeology*, no. 2.5 (1976), p.2.

Green, H., 'The Linen Industry of Shropshire', *Industrial Archaeology Review*, vol.5 (1981), pp.114–25.

Hancox, T. C., 'Two East Shropshire Paper Mills', *Shropshire Newsletter*, no.37 (1969), pp.6-7.

Hancox, T. C., 'Ludford Paper Mill', *Transactions of the Woolhope Naturalists' Field Club*, vol.41 (1973), pp.91-94.

Herbert, A.T., 'Jackfield Decorative Tiles in Use', *Industrial Archaeology Review*, vol.3 (1979), pp.146-52.

Hibbs, J., 'The Shropshire Omnibus Association: a note on a producers' co-operative', *Transport History*, vol.2 (1969), pp.301-05.

Houghton, A. W. J., 'The Caughley Porcelain Works near Broseley, Salop', *Industrial Archaeology*, vol.5 (1968), pp.184-92.

Hulme, E Wyndham, 'The Statistical History of the Iron Trade, 1717-50', *Transactions of the Newcomen Society*, vol.9 (1928-29), pp.12-35.

Hughes, M., 'Telford, Parnell and the Great Irish Road', *Journal of Transport History*, vol.6 (1964), pp.199-209.

Hyde, C. K., 'The Iron Industry of the West Midlands in 1754: Observations from the Travel Account of Charles Wood', *West Midlands Studies*, vol.6 (1973), pp.39-40.

Ince, L., 'The introduction of coke iron at the Stour forges of the Knight family', *Journal of the Historical Metallurgy Society*, vol. 24 (1991), pp.107-112.

Jenkins, R., 'The Industries of Herefordshire', *Transactions of the Newcomen Society*, vol. 17 (1936-37), pp.182-97.

Johnson, B. L. C., 'The Foley Partnerships', *Economic History Review*, second series, vol.4 (1952), pp.52-67.

Jones, K., Hunt, M., Malam, J. & Trinder, B., 'Holywell Land: A Squatter Community in the Shropshire Coalfield', *Industrial Archaeology Review*, vol.6 (1982), pp.163-85.

Jones, N. W., 'A Wooden Waggon Way at Bedlam Furnace, Ironbridge', *Post-Medieval Archaeology*, vol.21 (1987), pp.259-66.

Kanefsky, J. & Robey, J., 'Steam Engines in 18th Century Britain: A Quantitative Assessment', *Technology & Culture*, vol.21 (1980), pp.161-186.

Kay, G., 'Charles Lynam—an Architect of Tile Factories', *Journal of the Tiles and Architectural Ceramics Society*, vol. 4 (1992), pp.21-28.

Lawson, J. B., 'Sir Basil Brooke and Bromley's Forge', *Shropshire Newsletter*, no. 44 (1973), p. 7.

Lloyd, L. C., 'Paper-making in Shropshire', *Transactions of the Shropshire Archaeological Society*, vol.44 (1937-38), pp.121-187.

Lloyd, L. C., 'Paper-making in Shropshire: Supplementary Notes', *Transactions of the Shropshire Archaeological Society*, vol.53 (1949-50), pp.152-63.

Malam, J., 'White Salt-glazed Stoneware Manufacture at Jackfield', *West Midlands Archaeology*, vol.24 (1981), pp.45-50.

Morriss, R., 'A Gazetteer of Passenger Railway Stations in Shropshire', *Transactions of the Shropshire Archaeological Society*, vol. 64 (1983-84), pp.89-106.

Mutton, N., 'Eardington Forges and Canal Tunnel', *Industrial Archaeology*, vol. 7 (1970), pp.53-9.

Mutton, N., 'Investigation of the Sites of Charcoal Blast Furnaces at Shifnal and Kemberton', *Shropshire Newsletter* no.43 (1972), pp.17-21.

Mutton, N., 'Charlcotte Furnace', *Transactions of the Shropshire Archaeological Society*, vol.58 (1965-68), pp.84-88.

Mutton, N., 'The Forges at Eardington and Hampton Loade', *Transactions of the Shropshire Archaeological Society*, vol.58 (1965-68), pp.235-43.

Mutton, N., 'Charlcott Furnace 1733-79', *Bulletin of the Historical Metallurgy Group*, vol.6 (1966), pp.18-49.

Nair, G. & Poyner, D., 'The Coming of Coal: Industrial Development in a South Shropshire Parish', *Midland History*, vol. 18 (1993), pp.87-103.

Nankivell, C. R. T., 'Three dwellings in the Dark Lane Rows', *Shropshire Newsletter*, no.41 (1971), pp.12-16.

Nichol, J. D., 'Social and Political Stability in 18th century Provincial Life: a study of the career of John Ashby (1722-1779) of Shrewsbury', *Transactions of the Shropshire Archaeological Society*, vol.59 (1969-70), pp.53-62.

Pannett, D., 'A note on Bromley's Forge', *Shropshire Newsletter* no.36 (1969), p.3.

Pannett, D., 'Fish Weirs of the River Severn', *Shropshire Newsletter*, no.42. (1971), pp.4-7.

Pannett, D., 'Fish Weirs on the River Severn in Shropshire', *Shropshire Newsletter*, no.44 (1973), pp.24-31.

Pannett, D., 'The River Severn—some historical observations', *Shropshire Conservation Trust Bulletin*, no.29 (1973), pp.2-6.

Pannett, D., 'The River Severn at Wroxeter', *Transactions of the Shropshire Archaeological Society*, vol. 66 (1980), pp.48-55.

Pape, T., 'The Early Glass Industry in North Staffordshire', *Transactions of the North Staffordshire Field Club*, vol.67 (1933), pp.116-20.

Pape, T., 'An Elizabethan Glass Furnace', *The Connoisseur*, vol.92 (1933), pp.172-77.

Poyner, D. & Evans, R., 'The Wyre Forest Coalfield', *Cleobury Chronicles*, vol.3 (1994), pp.7-17.

Preston, R. A., 'The Eliza: a Nineteenth century Trow at Shrewsbury', *Transactions of the Shropshire Archaeological Society*, vol.68 (1993), pp.116-17.

Prestwich, J., 'On the Geology of the Coalfield of Coalbrookdale', *Transactions of the Geological Society*, vol.5 (1840), pp.495-505.

Rhodes, John, 'Lead Smelting in the Severn Gorge', *Shropshire Newsletter* XLI, 1971, pp.16-19.

Riden, P., 'Eighteenth Century Blast Furnaces: a New Checklist', *Journal of the Historical Metallurgy Society*, vol.12. (1978), pp.36-39.

Rimmer, W. G., 'Castle Foregate Flax Mill, 1797-1886', *Transactions of the Shropshire Archaeological Society*, 5th series, vol. 56 (1957-60), pp.49-68.

Roberts, S., 'Hinkshay Rows', *Shropshire Newsletter*, no.44 (1973), pp.23-24.

Robinson, D. H., 'An account of the Shropshire Canals', *Transactions of the Caradoc and Severn Valley Field Club*, vol.11 (1939-42), pp.45-52.

Scard, M. Ann, 'The Development and Changing Organisation of Shropshire's Quarrying Industry: 1750-1900', *Industrial Archaeology Review*, vol.11 (1989), pp.171-186.

Scott, H., 'Colliers' Wages in Shropshire 1830-50'. *Transactions of the Shropshire Archaeological Society*, vol.53 (1949-50), pp.1-22.

Shearing, E. A., 'The Shropshire Union Canal and the Peatswood Estate at Tyrley', *Journal of the Railway & Canal Historical Society*, vol.29 (1987), pp.122-138.

Shorter, A. H., 'The Excise Numbers of Paper Mills in Shropshire', *Transactions of the Shropshire Archaeological Society*, vol.53 (1949-50), pp. 145-52.

Smith, S.B., 'The Construction of the Blists Hill Ironworks', *Industrial Archaeology Review*, vol.3 (1979), pp.170-78.

Smith, E. C., 'Joshua Field's Diary of a tour through the Provinces, 1821, Pt II', *Transactions of the Newcomen Society*, vol.13 (1932-33), pp. 15-50.

Smith, W. H., 'Craven Arms & Stokesay Station', *British Railway Journal*, no.32 (1990), pp.90-107.

Strachan, S., 'Henry Powell Dunnill: a Victorian Tilemaster', *Journal of the Tiles and Architectural Ceramics Society*, vol.3 (1990), pp.3-10.

Tolley, R. S., 'The Changing Industrial Geography of Eastern Shropshire', *West Midlands Studies*, vol.5 (1972), pp.1-10.

Tonkin, J. W., 'Hinkshay Row, Dawley', *Shropshire Newsletter* no.33 (1967), pp.2-6.

Tonkin, S M., 'Trevithick, Rastrick and the Hazledine Foundry, Bridgnorth', *Transactions of the Newcomen Society*, vol. 26 (1947-49), pp.171-184.

Trinder, B., 'The First Iron Bridges', *Industrial Archaeology Review*, vol.3 (1979), pp.112-121.

Trinder, B., 'Coalport Bridge: A Study in Historical Interpretation', *Industrial Archaeology Review*, vol.3 (1979), pp.153-57.

Trinder, B., 'The Wooden Bridge at Cressage', *Shropshire Newsletter*, no.35 (1968), pp.1-6.

Trinder, B., 'The Development of the Integrated Ironworks in the Eighteenth Century', *Institute of Metals Handbook* (1988-89). London: Institute of Metals.

Trinder, B., 'The Severn Navigation at Dowles', *Transactions of the Shropshire Archaeological Society*, vol.64 (1983-84), pp.29-34.

Tucker, D. G., 'Electricity Generating Stations for Public Supply in the West Midlands, 1888-1977', *West Midlands Studies*, vol.10 (1977), pp.8-28.

Wanklyn, M., 'John Weld of Willey, 1585-1665: An enterprising landowner of the early 17th century', *West Midlands Studies*, vol.3 (1969), pp.88-99.

Wanklyn, M., 'Iron and Steelworks in Coalbrookdale in 1645', *Shropshire Newsletter*, no.44 (1973), pp.3-6.

Wanklyn, M., 'John Weld of Willey: Estate Management 1631-1660', *West Midlands Studies*, vol.4 (1970-71), pp.63-71.

Wanklyn, M., 'Industrial Development in the Ironbridge Gorge before Abraham Darby', *West Midlands Studies*, vol.15 (1982), pp.3-7.

Wanklyn, M., 'Urban Revival in Early Modern England: Bridgnorth and the River Trade, 1660-1800', *Midland History*, vol.18 (1993), pp.37-64.

Ward, W. W., 'Richard Groom of Wellington', *Methodist Magazine*, vol.62 (1893), pp.568-72.

Williams, A. B., 'The Rural Industries of Llanymynech', *Montgomeryshire Collections*, vol.47 (1941), pp.67-74.

Williams, W.H., 'The Canal Inclined Planes of East Shropshire', *Journal of Industrial Archaeology*, vol.2 (1965), pp.37-56.

PARLIAMENTARY PAPERS

Report of the Assistant Commissioner...for Hand Loom Weavers (1840), XXXIV
Report to the Admiralty upon the Improvement of the River Severn (1847-48), XXXI
Report of the Inspector of Mines for 1874 (1875) XVI.

THESES AND ACADEMIC ASSIGNMENTS

Andreae, C., *A Historical and Structural History of Sheinwood Mill, Shropshire*, Ironbridge Institute, Master's Course in Industrial Archaeology, 1990-91, Module I assignment.

Butterfield, R., *The Records of the Canal Wharf at Wappenshall*, Ironbridge Institute, Master's Course in Industrial Archaeology,, 1989-90, Module II assignment.

Duckworth, S., *The Severn Navigation and River Wharf sites in the Ironbridge Gorge with particular reference to the site at The Calcutts*, Ironbridge Institute, Master's Course in Industrial Archaeology, 1987-88, dissertation.

Eaves, M. & Hall, S., *Water Power System and Blast Furnace at Leighton, Shropshire*, Ironbridge Institute, Master's Course in Industrial Archaeology, 1993-94, Module II assignment.

Edwards, H., *The Commercial Centres of Madeley and Dawley 1790-1940*, Ironbridge Institute, Master's Course in Industrial Archaeology, 1988-89, dissertation.

Ellis, R., *The Industries of the Dudmaston Estate*, Ironbridge Institute, Diploma Course in Industrial Archaeology, 1984-85, dissertation.

Ensum, J., *Highley - Settlement/Community*, Wolverhampton University, MA in West Midlands Studies, 1993, dissertation.

Fenwick, P., *The Smithies Sawmill*, Ironbridge Institute, Master's Course in Industrial Archaeology, 1989-90, Module I assingment.

Goff, A. D., *A Study of the Former Coachbuilding Workshops, No 1 Church Street, Bishop's Castle, Shropshire*, Ironbridge Institute, Master's Course in Industrial Archaeology, 1992-93, Module I assignment.

Goodman, K. W. G., *Hammerman's Hill: the Land, People and Industry of the Titterstone Clee Hill Area of Shropshire from the 16th to the 18th centuries*, University of Keele, PhD, 1978.

Guthrie, J. & Pudney, C., *Wappenshall Junction, Shropshire: A Survey of the Canal Developments and the Industrial Buildings*, Ironbridge Institute, Master's Course in Industrial Archaeology, 1988-89, Module IV assignments.

Healey, J., *Longdon upon Tern Aqueduct: a Building Survey and Study of the Masonry Abutments*, Ironbridge Institute Master's Course in Industrial Archaeology, 1989-90, dissertation.

Hewitt, P. B., *The Mining, Quarrying and allied industries of the Cleehill Regions from the 1800s to 1930*, CNAA (Wolverhampton Polytechnic), M Phil, 1991.

Holmes, D., *The Working of the Silurian Wenlock Limestone in South-East Shropshire*, Ironbridge Institute, Diploma Course in Industrial Archaeology, dissertation, 1986-87.

Johnson, B.L.C., *The Charcoal Iron Trade in the Midlands 1690-1720*, University of Birmingham, MA thesis, 1950.

Jones, I. C., *A Survey of Longwood Brickworks, Shropshire*, Ironbridge Institute, Master's Course in Industrial Archaeology, Module I assignment, 1991-92.

Jones, I, C., *The Industrial Archaeology of Coleham Riverside*, Ironbridge Institute, Master's Course in Industrial Archaeology, Module II assignment, 1992-93.

Kent, J., *The Barrow Farm Maltings, Barrow*, Ironbridge Institute, Master's Course in Industrial Archaeology, Module I assignment, 1991-92.

McDonald, M.R., *The wash-house: an archaeological and functional evaluation with special reference to the "brew 'us" of the Ironbridge/Coalbrookdale area*, Ironbridge Institute, Master's Course in Industrial Archaeology, dissertation, 1987-88.

Morris, Jonathan, *The Birmingham and Liverpool Junction Canal*, Ironbridge Institute, Diploma Course in Industrial Archaeology, dissertation, 1984-85.

Morris, Julie, *The Brick and Pipeworks, Woodhouse Fields, Bourton, Much Wenlock, Shropshire*, Ironbridge Institute, Diploma Course in Industrial Archaeology, Module I assignment, 1990-91.

Norris, G., *A Survey of the Heavy Erection Shop, Coalbrookdale*, Ironbridge Institute, Master's Course in Industrial Archaeology, 1989-90, Module I assignment.

Rogers, E., *Water Power on the Ketley Brook, Shropshire, an Industrial Archaeological Perspective*, Ironbridge Institute, Diploma Course in Industrial Archaeology, dissertation, 1992-93.

Rowley, R. T., *The History of the South Shropshire Landscape 1086-1800*, University of Oxford B.Litt, 1967.

Smith, N., *An investigation into the commercial life, trades and craft industries of 19th century Much Wenlock, and an evaluation of their physical remains*, Ironbridge Institute, Diploma Course in Industrial Archaeology, dissertation, 1988-89.

Temple, J.C., *Industrial Archaeology of Aviation in Shropshire*, Ironbridge Institute Diploma Course in Industrial Archaeology, dissertation, 1984.

Terry, R., *Industrial History and Archaeology of the Linley Brook*, Ironbridge Institute Master's Course in Industrial Archaeology, 1988-89, Module IV dissertation.

Watts, S., *All's Grist to the Mill: a Survey of Rindleford Mill in the Parish of Worfield*, Ironbridge Institute, Diploma Course in Industrial Archaeology, dissertation, 1986-87.

Whall, J., *An Interpretive Scheme Providing Proposals for Presenting the Water Mills at Ludlow to the Public*, Ironbridge Institute, Master's Course in Industrial Archaeology, Module IV assignment, 1990-91.

RESEARCH PAPERS AND CONSULTANCY REPORTS

Beale, R., *The Old Wind: a Preliminary Report* (1988). Telford: Ironbridge Gorge Museum Archaeology Unit.

Clark, K. & Alfrey, J., *Coalbrookdale: First Interim Report of the Nuffield Survey* (1986). Telford: Ironbridge Institute.

Clark, K. & Alfrey, J. *Coalport and Blists Hill: Second Interim Report of the Nuffield Survey* (1986). Telford: Ironbridge Institute.

Clark, K. & Alfrey, J. *Benthall and Broseley Wood: Third Interim Report of the Nuffield Survey* (1987). Telford: Ironbridge Institute.

Clark, K. & Alfrey, J. *Jackfield and Broseley: Fourth Interim Report of the Nuffield Survey* (1987). Telford: Ironbridge Institute.

Edwards, H. et al, *Madeley Wood Powderhouse: a building survey* (1987). Telford: Ironbridge Gorge Museum Archaeology Unit.

Elsworth, J. & White, K., *Granville Country Park: further archaeological investigations* (1988). Telford: Ironbridge Institute.

Higgins, D., *Lightmoor Blast Furnaces* (1988). Telford: Ironbridge Gorge Museum Archaeology Unit.

Higgins, D., Morriss, R. & Trueman, M., *The Broseley Pipeworks: an archaeological and historical evaluation* (1988). Telford: Ironbridge Institute.

Isaac, S., *Granville Colliery Horse Gin* (1987). Telford: Ironbridge Gorge Museum Archaeology Unit.

Jones, A., *Finds Typologies: Pottery I: The Coarse Earthenwares* (1988). Telford: Ironbridge Gorge Museum Archaeology Unit.

Jones, A., Higgins, D. & Trueman, M., *11 Benthall Lane* (1987). Telford: Ironbridge Gorge Museum Archaeology Unit.

MacLeod, M., Stratton, M. & Trinder, B., *Llanymynech Hill: an Archaeological and Historical Evaluation* (1987). Telford: Ironbridge Institute.

Macleod, M., Trinder, B. & Worthington, M., *The Ditherington Flax Mill, Shrewsbury: a survey and historical evaluation* (1988). Telford: Ironbridge Institute.

MacLeod, M. & Thompson, H., *Excavations at Coalport, 1987: An Interim Report* (1987). Telford: Ironbridge Gorge Museum Archaeology Unit.

Stratton, M., *Interpreting the Industrial Past* (1987). Telford: Ironbridge Institute.

Terry, R., *The Swan Malthouse, Ironbridge* (1988). Telford: Ironbridge Gorge Museum Archaeology Unit.

Trinder, B., *Fifty Years in Ellesmere: a report on an adult education class held in the autumn term, 1986* (1986). Typescript-copies in Shropshire Records & Research and Ironbridge Gorge Museum Library.

Trinder, B., 1994, 'New Industrial Towns in the Long Eighteenth Century: the Shropshire Coalfield', presented to ESRC Colloquium at the University of Leicester, February 1994. Telford: Ironbridge Institute.

Trueman, M., *Archaeology in Ironbridge 1985-86* (1986). Telford: Ironbridge Gorge Museum Archaeology Unit.

Trueman, M., *28 Waterloo Street, Ironbridge* (1987). Telford: Ironbridge Gorge Museum Archaeology Unit.

Trueman, M., MacLeod, M. & Jones, A., *The Upper Works, Coalbrookdale: A Rescue Excavation* (1988). Telford: Ironbridge Gorge Museum Archaeology Unit.

Trueman, M. & Ryan, J., *33 Hodgebower, Ironbridge* (1987). Telford: Ironbridge Gorge Museum Archaeology Unit.

Trueman, M., Ryan, J. & Edwards, H., *Benthall Mill: a building survey* (1987). Telford: Ironbridge Gorge Museum Archaeology Unit.

Whittingslow, M. & Smith, P., *Lightmoor Brickworks* (1988). Telford: Ironbridge Gorge Museum Archaeology Unit.

Winkworth, A. et al, *Willey Round House: a building survey* (1987). Telford: Ironbridge Gorge Museum Archaeology Unit.

NEWSPAPERS

Aris's Birmingham Gazette • Berrow's Worcester Journal • Bridgnorth Journal
Eddowes Salopian Journal • Ironbridge Weekly Journal • Ludlow & Wenlock Express
Shrewsbury Chronicle • Shropshire Star • Wellington Journal • Wenlock Express

PRINTED MAPS

Barnes, H., *A New Map of the Kington-Leominster-Stourport Canal* (1977). Tenbury Wells: G. R. Kendrick.

Baugh, Robert, *Map of Shropshire* (1808), reprinted 1983. Shrewsbury: Shropshire Archaeological Society.

Dean, R. J., *Map of the Kington, Leominster and Stourport Canal* (1968). Caterham: Railway and Canal Historical Society.

Greenwood, Pringle & Co, *A Map of the County of Salop from an actual Survey made in the years 1826 & 1827* (1828). London: Greenwood, Pringle & Co.

Toghill, Peter, & Chell, Keith (1984). *Geological Map of Shropshire*. Taunton: Field Studies Council.

Index of Names

◆ ◆ ◆

INDEX OF PLACES

Places named in this index are in Shropshire unless otherwise indicated. The ancient parishes of all entries which are not themselves ancient parishes are indicated: *e.g.* Adeney, Edgmond; and cross references are provided to all entries which relate to particular ancient parishes: *e.g.* Alberbury, *see also* Bulthey, Bragginton, Little Shrawardine, Loton Park, Rowton, Wattlesborough. No attempt has been made to distinguish between ancient parishes within the towns of Bridgnorth and Shrewsbury.

INDEX OF SUBJECTS

◆   ◆   ◆

This index follows the system of classification used in *The Blackwell Encyclopedia of Industrial Archaeology,* ed. Barrie Trinder (Oxford: Blackwell 1992), pp.861-72.